The
Weaver-God,
He Weaves

The Weaver-God, He Weaves

~

Melville and the Poetics of the Novel

~

Christopher Sten

The Kent State University Press

Kent, Ohio, and London, England

© 1996 by The Kent State University Press, Kent, Ohio 44242
All rights reserved
Library of Congress Catalog Card Number 95-37382
ISBN 0-87338-537-3
Manufactured in the United States of America

03 02 01 00 99 98 97 96   5 4 3 2 1

Library of Congress Cataloging-in-Publication Data

Sten, Christopher, 1944–
The weaver God, he weaves : Melville and the poetics of the novel
/ Christopher Sten.
p.   cm.
Includes bibliographical references (p.   ) and index.
ISBN 0-87338-537-3 (hc : alk. paper) ∞
1. Melville, Herman, 1819–1891—Technique. 2. Popular literature—
Technique. 3. Narration (Rhetoric). 4. Fiction—Technique.
5. Literary form. 6. Poetics. I. Title.
PS2388.T4S74   1996
813´.3—dc20   95-37382

British Library Cataloging-in-Publication data are available.

For Jan, Callie, and Lizzy

The weaver-god, he weaves; and by that weaving is he deafened, that he hears no mortal voice; and by that humming, we, too, who look on the loom are deafened; and only when we escape it shall we hear the thousand voices that speak through it.

—"A Bower in the Arsacides," *Moby-Dick*

Contents

Acknowledgments

When I first started working on Melville as a graduate student at Indiana University, I was lucky to have the help and encouragement of a remarkable group of mentors and friends. Terence Martin, Ronald Gottesman, Eugene Lawlis, the late Wallace Williams, and the late J. Albert Robbins all contributed immeasurably to my understanding of this multifaceted author and to my appreciation of the intricacies of narrative. They also had a profound influence on me personally, serving as models of learning and intelligence and of what the critical imagination can do.

In the years since then, I have been struck with great good fortune many times over in the group of colleagues and friends who have been willing to give of their energy and wisdom in support of my project. John C. Broderick, Jon Quitslund, David McAleavey, Robert Ganz, Judith Plotz, Ann Romines, the late Astere Claeyssens, John P. McWilliams, Martin Bickman, Hennig Cohen, Douglas Robillard, Bryan Short, and Robert K. Wallace all read mindfully and commented astutely on individual chapters or combinations of chapters. And James Maddox, friend beyond measure, read most of them and steered me over many a rough sea. All of them did what they could to improve what needed improving, and all worked overtime to save me from the error of my ways. To be sure, the errors that remain are mine, not theirs. Would that I could say the same for the wisdom. Still, I am deeply appreciative of their counsel and friendship, and I am delighted to be able at long last to thank them publicly.

It gives me pleasure also to have the opportunity to thank the George Washington University Committee on Research for summer financial support that

enabled me to complete the chapters on *Redburn* and *Pierre*. Without that funding, and the timely backing of Henry Solomon, formerly dean of the Graduate School of Arts and Sciences, a project that has taken a good portion of my life would have claimed still more.

Thanks, too, to the dedicated editorial staff at The Kent State University Press, especially Joanna Hildebrand, Linda Cuckovich, Julia Morton, and John Hubbell. Their intelligence, wit, and strength of purpose—like their warmth of heart—will be remembered with appreciation always.

My deepest gratitude, however, is reserved for my wife, Jan, and our daughters, Caroline and Elizabeth, who have by turns anchored me, buoyed me up, or filled my sails, in keeping with the weather.

Introduction

This study began as an investigation of Melville's conception of "identity" in the early novels. I had originally set out to discover the essential Melville, the ineluctable man at the center of his autobiographical fiction. Like my predecessors, I had assumed Melville was an untutored genius who wrote quirky autobiographical narratives, narratives that were loosely fictional but bore little relation to the traditional novel. However, before long I started to see how much Melville's fictive personality in the early autobiographical tales was mixed up with the heroes in various individual genres of the novel. I thus revised my plan and set about to understand how the author appropriated the forms and conventions of the novel, and how he departed from them as well. The more I looked into the question, the more I saw that Melville did know something about the novel, that he had read widely in the form and had thought carefully, if also freely, about it, and that his narratives were woven, like the warp and woof on a loom, of his own experience and the collective experience of his predecessors in the novel.

Needless to say, then, this soon evolved into a more complicated study, not just of Melville's idea of identity and the whole spectrum of epistemological issues centering on the difficulties of knowing the self, but of his ideas about the novel as well. For, in the course of my investigations, I came to see that the later, more impersonal novels, too, from *Pierre* on, and not just the early autobiographical ones were shaped by particular genres of the novel, though in these instances Melville in effect redefined them, so much so as to leave to the novel a legacy of remarkable innovation.

In the chapters that follow, then, I argue that Melville wrote a different kind of novel in each of his major works of prose fiction. At the same time, I have continued to focus on Melville's notions of identity. In each case, that is to say, I argue also that Melville wrote with the goal of learning about himself and about the complex matter of identity generally. More than almost any other writer before him, Melville used the many forms of the novel, with their distinctive typologies of the hero, to explore the rich diversity of his own experience and personality. Among writers of English in the nineteenth century, perhaps only George Moore was to show anything like Melville's appetite for variety in the genres of the novel. But whereas Moore's eclecticism resulted from a desire to be always at the cutting edge in the evolution of the novel, Melville's was, I think, more the product of his fascination with the variousness of the forms themselves and of his eagerness to explore the plenitude of his own personality and of human character. I thus approach Melville's fiction from both the public realm of novelistic conventions and the private realm of the author's personality—the one the shaping form or "vessel," as Willa Cather would say, and the other the vital energy and substance. Together, they are the two components that make all art possible.[1]

While there have been several earlier studies of Melville and identity or of Melville and self-knowledge, this is the first to see the subject in the context of the genres of the novel.[2] Indeed, this is virtually the first to see Melville as a novelist at all. Since the 1920s and the Melville "revival," which emphasized the autobiographical dimension of his narratives, Melville has consistently been viewed as a misfit in the history of the novel. Typically, critics have regarded him as a writer of grasping intellect and great intuitive powers but as only marginally interested in the form and little more than superficially conversant with its conventions, if not resistant or even hostile to them. F. O. Matthiessen, for example, in his seminal *American Renaissance* (1941), portrayed Melville as the "American with the richest natural gifts as a writer" but lacking in "equipment as a theorist" of fiction (371, 387). R. P. Blackmur, in "The Craft of Herman Melville: a Putative Statement" (1955), considered him at best "only a novelist betimes." Blackmur argued that Melville never relied much on "the means of the novelist" or used more than "the overt form of the novel" until he wrote *Pierre,* and then with "pitiful" results (142, 125–26, 137). Similarly, William Charvat, in *The Tradition of Authorship in America, 1800–1870* (1968), portrayed Melville as a "trial-and-error experimental writer who never quite knew what he wanted to do . . . until he had done it." Even Richard H. Brodhead, who took the novel as one of his central subjects, in *Hawthorne, Melville, and the Novel* (1976), emphasized Melville's belief in the "value of instinctive composition" and his great "impatience with the ordinary proce-

dures of the novel" (126, 123). More recently, Nina Baym has pushed this view to its extreme, arguing in "Melville's Quarrel with Fiction" (1979) that from early in his career Melville had a "low estimation" of the novel that turned to open hostility in *Pierre,* when he reached the conclusion that "literature is inherently trivial" (910, 919).[3] These and other critics have greatly underesti- mated Melville's command of the novel and the importance of its forms and conventions in the shaping of his narratives. As a consequence, in their read- ings of individual works and in their judgments of Melville's career, they have often misinterpreted his intentions and the grounds of his achievement.

The reasons Melville has failed to gain a solid reputation as a novelist, such as Hawthorne and James have long enjoyed, are complicated but largely un- derstandable. First of all, Melville began his career not as a novelist but as a travel writer, a writer of nonfiction—or so he claimed—and his early reputa- tion has permeated his whole career. Though today his first two books are understood to contain much that is not biographically true, *Typee* and *Omoo* were originally presented as straightforward chronicles of Melville's own ad- ventures, rather than as fictional narratives, and he defended them as such both to his publisher and to the reading public. Yet, aside from what might be extrapolated from his juvenilia, "Fragments from a Writing Desk," exactly why Melville turned to writing in the first place has always been a mystery, as has the question of what kind of book he thought he was writing when he first sat down to compose *Typee.* Almost everything he is known to have said about it dates from the time *after* John Murray, his British publisher, showed inter- est in Melville's Polynesian adventure for his nonfiction series. And at that point, Melville simply had to do whatever he could to convince Murray he was not writing "romance," as Murray had said he suspected he was. If his career was to have a chance at a rousing start with the famous house of Murray, Melville had to deny there was anything fictional about his first narrative, as indeed he did, though Charles Roberts Anderson and others have demon- strated quite conclusively that *Typee* is a mix of fiction, ethnographic sources, and autobiographical fact.[4] Only after the success of his first two books, while in the midst of writing the imaginary voyage called *Mardi,* was Melville able to admit to Murray not simply that he found himself slipping over to the writing of fiction in his third book but that, in effect, he *was* a "romance" writer at heart—in the loose sense, a novelist.[5]

Of course another reason Melville's critics have had trouble seeing him as a novelist is that his writings *are* unusual; they do not fit comfortably into the standard generic categories. Even when it comes to the primary genres—fic- tion, nonfiction, poetry, and drama—they are hard to pin down. Most subtly combine fiction and fact, like *Typee. Omoo,* for example, weaves together the

picaresque novel and the travelogue. *Redburn* mixes the bildungsroman and the personal memoir. Indeed, Melville's first seven books—*Typee, Omoo, Mardi, Redburn, White-Jacket, Moby-Dick,* and *Pierre*—all contain substantial autobiographical material either from his years at sea or from his youth in upstate New York, and his eighth, *Israel Potter,* is based on the memoir of a little-known Revolutionary War soldier. The historical basis of these several narratives has given a pronounced biographical bent to Melville studies, spawning such influential early examinations of the author's work as Anderson's *Melville in the South Seas* (1939), William H. Gilman's *Melville's Early Life and "Redburn"* (1951), and Merrell R. Davis's *Melville's Mardi: A Chartless Voyage* (1952). Though each of these studies made it clear that Melville's early narratives were more fiction than personal history, the fascination with Melville's four years at sea has continued to color our scholarly conception of the man and his work. It has blinded us to the fact that he worked largely within the tradition of the novel. The notion that he wrote thinly fictionalized, autobiographical tales is a myth, the scholarly equivalent of the view—popular in his own time and much lamented by Melville himself—that his fame rested on his being a "man who lived among the cannibals."[6]

The failure to see Melville as writing within the tradition of the novel can be attributed also to a second trend in Melville scholarship, one concerning the extraordinary emphasis in the middle decades of this century on Melville's extensive use of nonfiction sources in his narratives and on his remarkably eclectic reading interests generally. Aside from his reading of Hawthorne's *Mosses from an Old Manse,* which he reviewed with great excitement in the summer of 1850, Melville is best known for his exceptionally wide-ranging use of various nonfictional writings. Important studies in this period, when Melville's modern reputation was taking shape, have linked Melville and Shakespeare; Melville and Milton; Melville and Spenser; Melville and the Bible; Melville and Carlyle; as well as Melville and the many authors of popular whaling narratives, sea adventures, cultural and anthropological studies, and the like—C. S. Stewart's *A Visit to the South Seas in the U.S. Ship Vincennes* (1831), William Ellis's *Polynesian Researches* (1833), David Porter's *Journal of a Cruise in the U.S. Frigate Essex* (1815), Charles Wilkes's *Narrative of the United States Exploring Expedition* (1845), Michael Russell's *Polynesia* (1843), the anonymous *Picture of Liverpool; or Stranger's Guide* (1808), William McNally's *Evils and Abuses in the Naval and Merchant Service, Exposed* (1839), Nathaniel Ames's *A Mariner's Sketches* (1830), J. Ross Browne's *Etchings of a Whaling Cruise* (1846), Thomas Beale's *The Natural History of the Sperm Whale* (1839), Frederick Debell Bennett's *Narrative of a Whaling Voyage round the Globe* (1840), William Scoresby, Jr.'s *Journal of a Voyage to the Northern Whale Fish-*

ery (1823), Charles Wilkes's *United States Exploring Expedition* (1844–46), Owen Chase's *Narrative of the Most Extraordinary and Distressing Shipwreck of the Whale-Ship Essex* (1821), and Henry T. Cheever's *The Whale and His Captors* (1849), to mention only the most prominent nonfictional sources for his novels. Studies of these and other works by Melville specialists include, in addition to those by Anderson, Gilman, and Davis mentioned above, William Braswell's *Melville's Religious Thought* (1943), Charles Olson's *Call Me Ishmael* (1947), Howard P. Vincent's *The Trying-Out of Moby-Dick* (1948), Nathalia Wright's *Melville's Use of the Bible* (1949), Lawrance Thompson's *Melville's Quarrel with God* (1952), Edward Rosenberry's *Melville and the Comic Spirit* (1955), H. Bruce Franklin's *The Wake of the Gods: Melville's Mythology* (1963), and Vincent's *The Tailoring of Melville's White-Jacket* (1970). Besides these, there are, of course, many others, including scores of journal articles and book chapters on Melville's nonfiction sources, that appeared in these years or since.

By contrast, relatively little work has been done on Melville's borrowings from fiction, on his reading in the novel, or on his contribution to its history. As a rule, Melville scholars have been more interested in the sources of Melville's ideas than in the sources of the forms and conventions he used. Symptomatic of the prevailing view, there is no chapter on Melville and the novel in John Bryant's rich and otherwise remarkably comprehensive *A Companion to Melville Studies* (1986). There is a lengthy chapter by Shirley Dettlaff on "Melville's Aesthetics," which includes a section on Melville's "Theory of Fiction," but even here there is little on genre beyond a review of discussions of the romance by Joel Porte (1969) and Michael Davitt Bell (1980).[7]

Otherwise, there have been isolated attempts to see individual novels of Melville's in the context of a given fictional genre or combination of genres. These range from Paul Witherington's "The Art of Melville's *Typee*," which argues that Melville's first book is an experimental novel, and Paul Lewis's "Melville's *Pierre* and the Psychology of Incongruity," which views *Pierre* as an anti-bildungsroman, to Watson Branch's "The Etiology of Melville's *Mardi*" and "The Quest for *Mardi*" (chap. 5 in Bryant), which together see Melville's third narrative as "a potpourri of whaling life, sea adventure, romantic quest, allegory, satire, and occasional digressions of rhapsodic reflection and philosophizing." But other critics have emphasized the influence of nonfictional genres instead, as Janet Giltrow has examined *Typee*, most particularly, in connection with travel literature, in "Speaking Out: Travel and Structure in Herman Melville's Early Narratives," or as Robert K. Martin has viewed the same book in connection with the captivity narrative, in "Enviable Isles: Melville's South Seas." Even so, the prevailing view is that Melville was largely indifferent to matters of form, or that he was making it up as he went along. There has never

been a thoroughgoing genre study of Melville's major fiction nor a systematic attempt to see his long narratives as examples of particular subgenres or secondary genres of the novel (which I will refer to hereafter simply as "genres"), though some years ago Edward Rosenberry, in *Melville* (1979), took a step in that direction when he grouped *Typee* and *Omoo* together as "travel romances," for example, and *Mardi* and *The Confidence-Man* as "philosophical allegories."

Despite sporadic interest here and there, then, a major reason for the scholarly neglect of this subject, no doubt, is that genre study, which fell out of favor in the fifties and sixties once it rigidified into simple taxonomy, has only recently been making a comeback as a useful methodology and valuable heuristic. While the resurgence is still in its early stages, several important studies of genre theory have appeared in recent years that subtilize the subject and otherwise take it well beyond the deadening taxonomic uses to which it was put in the past. It should also be noted that another reason genre theory has been so undervalued by Melvilleans over the years is that, as a Romantic writer, Melville has invited attention from critics who themselves hold Romantic assumptions about literature. In particular, they tend to believe that creative genius, such as Melville is widely believed to have possessed, is not well served by a reliance on established forms or genres; on the contrary, as Brodhead and others argue, it is "constrained" by them.[8]

In the last few decades, however, critical attitudes toward genre have changed dramatically among literary scholars as able critics have taken up the subject and as critical theory generally has gained unprecedented importance throughout the discipline. Thanks to the work of critics from a variety of schools or persuasions, including Tzvetan Todorov, E. D. Hirsch, Paul Hernadi, Hans Robert Jauss, Jonathan Culler, Robert Scholes, Alistair Fowler, Adena Rosmarin, and others, genres are no longer seen as rule-bound schemes of classification that inhibit the literary artist's originality.[9] Instead they are increasingly recognized as necessary tools for artistic creation and communication, for the writer and the reader.

Genres are now understood to have a constitutive function; they are instruments of creation. They guide and support, indeed make possible, the creative process. But genres are also understood to have a heuristic function; they are instruments of meaning. We must identify the genre of a particular work before we can interpret that work. According to Fowler and others, generic rules are not prohibitions but communicative codes, and the author as well as the reader must develop competence in such codes, just as one must develop competence in a language, if communication is to occur.[10] As Culler has said, genres are the sets of norms and conventions that "make possible the production of meaning."[11] But they do so not in a simple formulaic way. It is

not only the genre that "communicates"; the author's "modulation" (Fowler)
of that genre communicates as well. A literary work conveys meaning by its
departure from a set of genre codes as well as by its resemblance to them. To
see one is to see the other. Indeed, as Adena Rosmarin has persuasively argued
in *The Power of Genre* (1985), the impression of a "distinctly *literary* text, one
that seems infinitely particular and heuristically powerful," is created precisely because of our perception of its difference from a given genre.[12] And of
course we must know the relevant genre before we can see the difference.

More than anything, what has brought about the recent revolution in attitude toward literary genres is the revolution in the way genres are understood
or perceived. No longer are they thought to be prescriptive or normative—a
set of formulas fixed in time or a mold into which the writer pours his or her
own version of a recurring story or experience. That may be what defines the
popular versions of such genres as the detective story and the erotic tale, where
a certain predictability is expected and even prized. But it is not necessarily
what defines any one genre in and of itself. Thanks to Jauss and others, we can
now understand genres as fluid, even open, and historically defined con-
structions; they are not fixed classes or Platonic ideals but "groups of historical families."[13] Wittgenstein's notion of "family resemblances" provided a
key breakthrough in this regard, for by analogy we can see how the concept
of the "exemplary," in this case the exemplary text, mediates, as Jauss says,
"the general and the particular." Less abstractly, Fowler has said that every
genre has multiple identifying traits, but not every examplar of a genre necessarily shares any one or even any particular combination of them.[14]

The idea that genres are diachronic—and not timeless or synchronic, or
only partially synchronic—provided another breakthrough, one that is, in
fact, implied in the hereditary analogy of "family resemblances." In Jauss's
conception, "every work belongs to a genre," meaning that "for each work a
preconstituted horizon of expectations," defined by the history of that genre,
"must be ready at hand" (79). But Jauss also has observed that every genre is
always evolving; each addition, each exemplar, changes the genre's history
and the character of the genre itself. Thus "a masterwork is definable in terms
of an alteration of the horizon of the genre," one that is "as unexpected as it is
enriching" (94). Contrary to the traditional view, then, even in the artist's
appropriation of a genre, there is always room for originality. Indeed, for the
ambitious writer, originality is required.

Though it remains controversial, the study of literary genres has gained credibility in recent years as the most promising approach to the knotty problem of
the author's intention. As Robert Scholes has said, though he speaks for a wide
array of structuralist and poststructuralist critics, genre study is "the most

precise and legitimate way into the vexed question of the intentionality of a work."[15] This is so, as Hirsch and others have argued, because it is the author's genre purpose, her idea of the meaning or type of meaning she wishes to communicate, that guides her through the writing process. "Genre" means type or category; and since Aristotle, as Hirsch has pointed out, it has generally been thought that what distinguishes a particular genre, and unifies its various examples, is the idea of purpose. Every language act or expression, no matter how casual on the one extreme or how elaborately stylized on the other, depends on a preexisting typology—not because the exigencies of communication require it, but because the mind cannot formulate its own types, its own purposes, in a vacuum. Hirsch quotes the eminent art historian E. H. Gombrich, who argues in *Art and Illusion* (1960) that "even the shape of the new vessel will somehow belong to the same family of forms as those the craftsman has seen." As always, the innocent eye sees nothing. Variations from the old forms, the established genres, are always possible. New forms can be built out of the old ones. (Indeed, as Todorov has argued, new genres have their origin in other genres.[16]) But, as Gombrich says, "variations can be controlled and checked only against a set of invariants."[17] The most original writer, therefore, Fowler has asserted, is not the one who has no interest in genre but, paradoxically, the one who "has the keenest interest" in the subject. "Only by knowing the beaten track, after all, can he be sure of leaving it."[18]

Of course an author's intention is likely to be a complex matter, involving unconscious motives and other influences (linguistic, literary, institutional, and cultural) as well as conscious ones. But I have taken the position in the following chapters that there is something we can call the author's intention, and that we can know it most surely, or begin to do so, by studying the particular genre, or genres, the author has employed in a given composition, in so far as it can be determined by careful study, and possibly a bit of inspiration. What haunts all efforts at interpretation, as Northrop Frye long ago reminded us, is the nagging feeling that we ought to appraise a work of art in a way that takes into account its nature, and not treat it as something it is not. Genre study addresses this question, and it does so as a first step, before other questions, such as value or accomplishment, are taken up. It also does so in a self-conscious way, and although self-consciousness in a matter such as this is hardly a guarantee of critical acumen, surely it is better to treat it directly than to permit unstated (or latent) assumptions to have their influence unawares.

Speaking specifically of the critic's task, rather than the writer's, Hirsch argues convincingly in *Validity in Interpretation* (1967) that "All understanding of verbal meaning is necessarily genre-bound" because "an interpreter's

preliminary generic conception of a text is constitutive of everything that he subsequently understands, and . . . this remains the case unless and until that generic conception is altered."[19] So fundamental are decisions about genre to the critic's understanding of a text—indeed, to the critic's whole enterprise— that it is, in Hirsch's view, the primary cause of disagreement on virtually any issue regarding that text, even among specialists.

Certainly this would seem to be the case among critics of Melville, where in the criticism surrounding every one of his novels there is wide disagreement about its genre(s) and often sharp disagreement about its meaning. Is *Mardi* a Rabelaisian satire or a "mess," as Harold Beaver has argued?[20] A good book or a bad one? Did Melville know what he was doing in writing it, or was he making it up as he went along? Is *Pierre* an American version of a Shakespearean trag-edy, a sentimental novel, or a satire of one? A masterpiece, a great but deeply flawed novel, as Brian Higgins and Hershel Parker have repeatedly argued,[21] or simply a disaster, as most earlier critics maintained? Is Melville's protagonist to be condemned for his foolishness or congratulated for his virtue? Is *The Confidence-Man* a failed novel, an unfinished novel, or an experimental one? Is it to be read as an expression of Melville's misanthropy? As a critique of the widespread cynicism in his own culture? Or as a test of the reader's own faith?

My assumption throughout has been that if we can decide on the kinds of novels Melville was writing, or thought he was writing, we can more accu-rately judge his purposes, his intentions. Perhaps then we can begin to reach some agreement as to their meaning and to measure, according to standards almost any critic might appreciate, Melville's achievements as a writer.

Just as genre study can result in a more accurate understanding of an author's individual works, so, too, it can lead to a sharper understanding of an author's whole career. In this case, it can lead to the clear recognition that Melville was a novelist, though an idiosyncratic and uncommonly inventive one to be sure. And it can lead to a surer understanding of the evolution of his objectives as a fiction writer and of the character of his contribution to the novel as a historical form or series of forms. We can see, for example, that even at the start of his career Melville worked within the context of well-established genres of fiction, as he worked within the "romance" and the picaresque novel in *Typee* and *Omoo,* but also that he manipulated those genres and reshaped them in original ways to suit his own purposes. We can see that, beginning with his first book, *Typee* (1846), where he placed a young male version of himself in the situation of the typical *heroine* of a sentimental romance threatened with rape and death, he was always thinking with great freshness and freedom. Or we can see, after recognizing that *Mardi* is an example of a popular eighteenth-century form

called the imaginary voyage, and not a wild, self-indulgent, sui generis work, that Melville's development as a novelist was not so volcanic or unpredictable as is generally thought.

Implicit in the chapters that follow is the argument that Melville's rise to mastery as a writer of fiction was a relatively steady climb through his first six narratives, each an instance of a different form of the novel, and that the period beginning with *Moby-Dick* was one of intense experimentation and risk taking, with *Moby-Dick, Pierre, Israel Potter,* and *The Confidence-Man* all breaking new ground in their respective genres—the epic, the psychological novel, the historical novel, and the experimental novel—or radically redefining them. Together, these last novels, the last three especially, show a magnified ambition and boldness, a heightened creative energy and intellectual strength, that belie the common view of a Melville in decline—physically and psychologically, as well as imaginatively—following the demands of writing *Moby-Dick* and the disappointment of its critical failure. Though none of these last three novels ranks with Melville's epic of the Whale in richness, grandeur, or power— what novel does?!—all are unusually innovative works of fiction, and one of them, *The Confidence-Man,* is arguably the most original novel published in the nineteenth century.

Except in my discussions of these last four novels, I do not, perhaps, emphasize Melville's innovativeness in the following chapters as much as I might. In my effort to correct the prevailing view that Melville had little patience for established forms or that he somehow managed to write without them, I generally concentrate on how Melville used the conventions of a given fictional genre or how he worked out his own version of an established form. I want to show how deeply Melville was indebted to the novel and how varied his interest in its forms. I want to make the case for considering Melville as a novelist first and foremost. And yet it needs to be said also that I never assume that Melville was *only* a novelist. Certainly I do not see him as having written unmixed or pure versions of the various genres of the novel. Often in a single work of fiction it is clear that he borrowed from several genres at once, including genres outside the novel—autobiography, travelogue, the essay, the anatomy, and other forms of nonfiction prose, or even poetry and drama, as we know from the polymorphous *Moby-Dick.* In fact, it is the rare author, at least among major figures, who works in a single genre, particularly when it comes to the "loose and baggy monster" of the novel, and Melville is no exception. To keep my discussions manageable, however, and at the same time to make the larger point concerning the variety of novelistic forms Melville used over the course of his career, I focus on what I take to be the master genre, the predominant genre, in each of his narratives.

In making the case for viewing Melville as a novelist, it has not always been possible to establish, on the basis of external evidence, the connection between Melville's narratives and his knowledge of particular genres of the novel. Authors rarely leave explicit accounts of their literary intentions or instructions on how to read their works, and Melville was more private about such matters than most. Unlike Hawthorne, for example, he kept no writer's journals or commonplace books; and unlike James, he composed no ruminative introductions to his collected works. What we know about such matters in Melville's case we know from a few letters, the books he is known to have owned or borrowed, and internal evidence, including his several brief (sometimes misleading) prefaces. More often than not, like other genre critics, therefore, I have had to rely on internal evidence—the author's choice of subject and his structuring of it; his use of the building blocks or conventions, the genre codes of the novel; and his departures from them. Fortunately, this sort of evidence is more than widespread; it is everywhere.

Where the case for Melville's familiarity with a particular genre can be made on the basis of external evidence, I have done so, as in my discussion of *Omoo* as a picaresque novel. But this is not so much an investigation of Melville's sources as it is a study of his poetics of the novel, of his practice of the novelist's art. In most cases, therefore, as in the chapters on *Typee, Mardi,* and *White-Jacket* especially, I simply try to show how Melville appropriated particular genres—the romance, the imaginary voyage, and the political novel respectively. In these chapters, I present Melville as working rather straightforwardly, if also with considerable freedom, within each form, even when he did not do so with perfect success, as in *White-Jacket.* In the case of *Redburn,* where there has been a longstanding critical controversy about whether the hero matures or regresses in the course of the narrative, I take a more indirect approach, though still focusing on Melville's practice of the novelist's art. Relying chiefly on Erik Erikson's model of psychosocial development, rather than the relatively impressionistic standards or measures of maturity used by critics in the past, I attempt first to establish the basis on which Redburn can be said to mature and then argue for reading the book as a version of the bildungsroman.

Moby-Dick and the three narratives that followed it—*Pierre, Israel Potter,* and *The Confidence-Man*—present a more demanding, and intriguing, set of challenges for students of the novel. Beginning with his epic of the Whale, Melville was no longer simply appropriating previous forms or using them in imaginative ways for his own purposes. He was profoundly redefining them, and in the process redefining the future of the novel. As so often in Melville studies, so here, *Moby-Dick* is seen as a special case—an important turning point in Melville's career as a novelist. Here Melville made a truly bold,

imaginative leap and crossed from one primary genre to another. Finding no precedent in the history of the novel for his epic, he turned to the epic poem for his model, updating it to his own time and positioning it in the context of a vernacular culture, the American whaling industry, that had become thoroughly familiar to him. Yet, as the story of Ishmael's quest for spiritual regeneration, it has much in common with the heroic adventure epics of Homer and the poetic religious epics of Dante and Milton.

From *Moby-Dick* through *The Confidence-Man,* then, Melville wrote with new authority, breaking sharply from established forms and moving into the forefront of contemporary practitioners of the novel in both America and Europe. With *Pierre* he took the novel of emotion, the sentimental novel of Richardson and his successors (sensationalized, to be sure, in line with other popular fiction of the early nineteenth century),[22] and at a stroke turned it toward the novel of psychological analysis as it was then being developed by Flaubert and would later be refined by James. With *Israel Potter* he took the popular historical romance of Cooper and others, particularly the Revolutionary War tale, and abruptly turned it in the direction of the novel of historical realism, which also was being developed at about the same time in France and which blossomed in America later in the century, this time in the fiction of Crane. Finally, with *The Confidence-Man* Melville turned to the experimental novel made famous by Laurence Sterne and, in the boldest move of his career, projected it into our own twentieth century. Indeed, it was not until the 1950s, when the "new novel" of Robbe-Grillet and others appeared in France, that the history of the novel finally caught up with the experimentalism of Melville's most difficult book. Four innovative, virtually unprecedented novels, all written in a six-year period at the height of the author's powers—can any other writer of the nineteenth century, with the possible exception of Flaubert, lay claim to such an ambitious program or such a richly varied achievement?

That *Billy Budd,* the late brief novel of Melville's old age, seems not to evidence the same inventiveness and daring of these major narratives of the 1850s is perhaps hardly surprising, given its place in the author's unusual career. More than thirty years separate its composition from that of the earlier major works, and Melville's career as a novelist was far behind him, or so it seemed until the remarkable winter flowering of this "inside narrative." Melville was simply no longer the young man who had struggled, with such energy and ambition, to weave his dreams into the history of the novel. And yet one of the reasons *Billy Budd* is so powerful is that it is an unusual work of fiction, with ties to the drama as deep as its ties to the novel. Though it is sometimes positioned in the broad category of the philosophical novel, I believe it is more accurate to call it a "problem novel," to emphasize its parallels with and origins in the problem

play. Like all drama, *Billy Budd* was written with an eye to removing the sort
of authorial presence and manipulation of point of view associated with traditional fiction. As we know from the careful work of Hayford and Sealts,
Melville revised the manuscript of *Billy Budd* several times in a deliberate
effort to erase his narrator's views and thus create ambiguities about the meaning of Billy's situation and about the resulting dilemma faced by Captain Vere.[23]

But like the genre of the problem play more particularly, *Billy Budd* brings
into focus a profoundly disturbing human dilemma—in this case one we all
experience when we forsake the natural state of childhood and begin to take
on the civilizing objectives of adults—and it leaves us to answer that dilemma
for ourselves, rather than try to answer it for us. In the death of the innocent
Budd, Melville reminds us of what we have sacrificed in ourselves in order to
become adults, men and women of conscious, civilizing intentions. Through
the pain of Billy's loss, Melville challenges us to make a new commitment to
shape our lives—indeed, the whole of civilization that in turn shapes us—in
accord with our early aspirations and ideals. Not coincidentally, much this
same idea is to be found in the motto that Melville, in his late years, had
pasted inside the desk in his Manhattan study where he composed *Billy Budd:*
"Keep true to the dreams of thy youth."[24]

As a story of Melville's faith in consciousness and in the potential for human progress beyond that of the natural-born man (and woman), *Billy Budd*
is an epitome of all Melville had come to believe about the subject since he
first confronted it at the start of his career in *Typee*. Growth of consciousness,
the self-knowledge that experience can bring, at least to those who know how
to read it, is Melville's central subject. Of course, all narrative art, all fiction,
in so far as it portrays scenes of recognition or peripety, is concerned with the
protagonist's growth in self-understanding. Broadly speaking, it is the principal theme of the novel.

However, because so much of Melville's fiction, from *Typee* through *Pierre*,
is autobiographical, it necessarily emphasizes the awakening consciousness of a
young protagonist as he makes his way in strange lands or unfamiliar social and
psychological territories. In *Typee, Omoo*, and *Mardi*, Melville's young hero
stumbles into exotic South Sea island cultures that threaten to absorb or erase
his original identity without leaving so much as a trace, and he has to struggle
to reassert himself or be utterly lost. In *Redburn, White-Jacket*, and *Moby-Dick*,
he must fight to discover and hold on to his true self in a series of foreign, even
hostile, work environments at sea, including a merchant ship, a military ship,
and a whaler, and he must do so in the face of powerful countervailing personalities—the cynical Jackson, the autocratic Captain Claret, and the indomitable
Ahab. And in *Pierre* he is suddenly forced, by a mysterious young woman's

allegations about a dark family secret, to confront the sharp divisions within himself and within his family and his culture. In each instance the protagonist is subjected to intense social and psychological pressures to accommodate himself to a new set of circumstances—to change his way of living and thinking about himself, to go against his natural character or early training, even to take on a new identity. And invariably he does succumb, if only temporarily, and takes on at least the outward signs of a new personality, as Tommo adopts the ways of the Typees or as Ishmael joins Ahab's crew in the wild oath of vengeance toward Moby Dick.

But in almost every case, Melville's protagonist also bounces back as the result of some sudden insight into the "Other" or a new awareness of his earlier self and embraces the essentials of his old identity, though invariably his identity has also been immutably changed, or extended, by the experience. Only the tragic figures, Taji and Pierre, who develop deeply conflicted personalities, are unable to integrate their new identity and their old one. For them there is only the torment of endless self-division, or suicide.

Self-knowledge remains the central subject in the nonautobiographical novels after *Pierre,* as it is in the autobiographical novels before it, but with a significant difference. *Israel Potter, The Confidence-Man,* and *Billy Budd* are all strikingly reader-oriented texts, rather than character studies in the customary sense. In these narratives, it is Melville's readers, more than his protagonists, who are forced to see themselves anew. In fact, the characters themselves rarely experience self-recognition; as a result, they change very little or not at all. In *Israel Potter,* then, Melville's intention was to call into question the complacency of his readers' sense of national identity, ironizing their sense of themselves as heroic, larger-than-life Americans by rewriting the country's Revolutionary War history from the "blue-jean" point of view of a surprisingly plodding, spiritless common soldier. In *The Confidence-Man* Melville's purpose was to heighten his readers' sense of social conscience in what might be called "the dialogics of the self," to make his readers aware of what is lost and gained, spiritually and materially, in all human transactions having confidence, or trust, as their basis. And in *Billy Budd* his aim was to remind his readers of the sacrifice of the Budd-like youth within us all as we take on the conscious aims of adults and the complex, often conflicting, values that define civilization.

Melville's fiction centers on problems of self-knowledge, then, not only because it is autobiographical, concerned with the experiences of youth and a young autobiographical character's coming of age. It does so also because it is profoundly self-conscious and modern, concerned with life defined increasingly by change and by the death of tradition and of traditional ways of thinking. As suggested by the extraordinary occurrence of the Melville "revival" in

Though he had his predecessors, Melville was the first to seize with such force on the subjects of dislocation and exile, the sudden uprooting or dis-placement of individuals, and of whole groups as well, as he does in *Typee* and *Omoo* and *Redburn,* through powerful familial, cultural, and historical pressures and the consequent crisis in identity that such dislocation and alien-ation necessarily bring. All of Melville's novels take this theme, or a variation of it, as their starting point. Like the great modernist writers of dislocation and disinheritance, Conrad and Joyce, Melville came to his subject as the result of personal experience, in the break from his home and country and the four years of wandering on land and sea that followed his failure, while still in his teens, to find regular work in New York during the economic de-pression of the late 1830s. With this radically uprooting, alienating experi-ence, which had still earlier origins in his father's financial failure and death before the boy was twelve, Melville was shocked into a painful kind of self-consciousness and feeling of uncertainty about his identity that in our own century is almost commonplace.

Certainly other writers, such as Dickens and Defoe, from Melville's own time and before have been preoccupied with problems of identity. The worri-some, often comic business of identity formation is, of course, a universal phe-nomenon—common to all times and cultures—and holds an important, even central, place in the history of the novel. But Melville's interest in the subject amounted almost to an obsession, and this in itself is symptomatic of the mod-ern experience, as Erikson and others have observed.[25] The preoccupation with identity is quintessentially modern because the problems that provoke it, even to the point of generating a now predictable "crisis" in the maturing process— problems of frustration, fear, and disappointment stemming from intense so-cial pressures and equally intense psychological needs—are particularly acute in a culture so profoundly in flux as ours. What in the twentieth century is new, what makes the preoccupation with identity so distinctly modern, is the volatil-ity of the forces shaping the lives and outlooks of young people and the feeling of uncertainty that comes with increased awareness of the multiplicity of iden-tity choices calling to them, like sirens, from beyond the narrow domestic spheres—family, town, native region—of traditional childhood.

Melville was not, I believe, so modern as to have anticipated the decon-structionist view that there is no self or that personal identity is an illusion. I find little evidence, at least in his major protagonists, for the view that the individual is nothing more than a capacity for taking on roles or a loose con-geries of appetites, needs, and learned responses, though Israel Potter, an

unusually passive and malleable protagonist, comes close. Melville does, none-theless, seem to have recognized just how tenuous the achievement of iden-tity can be, and how complex. Most of his narratives include minor charac-ters—the "renegado from Christendom and humanity," Lem Hardy, in *Omoo;* the "mad" little cabin-boy, Pip, in *Moby-Dick;* the "tragic-mopers" filling the madhouses described by the Methodist minister in *The Confidence-Man*—who become unmoored from their essential self and so self-alienated as to be lost forever.[26]

For the most part, however, Melville seems to have thought of identity as something persistent and of early origin, if also malleable, at least through the period he termed the "jelly of youth."[27] Identity was something both given and made, something essential and at the same time socially constructed. As a given, it combined elements of heredity, will, and natural capacity—memory and intelligence, great curiosity and still greater pride, a love of life and of pleasure, a strong penchant for letters, and the physical dexterity required of a sailor, to cite just some of the more prominent recurring characteristics of Melville's autobiographical heroes. As a construction of society, it combined elements of early experience, family training, and class values—the privilege of books and education, exposure to a variety of world travelers (including, most importantly, his own father), the social and professional advantages of membership in America's upper class.

Yet because Melville's stories typically begin in medias res, his characters, even the younger ones, are already reasonably well formed when we first en-counter them. Only in *Redburn* and *Pierre* are we given much description of the protagonist's early development. And yet, despite the relatively well-formed identities of his protagonists, Melville did see identity as something quite pliant or impressionable, capable of taking on new roles or even, under the right circumstances, of changing significantly. New dimensions of the self can be added to old ones, as in *Redburn* the title character becomes a skillful sailor with a natural love for the sea, without giving up the essential elements of his prior identity as "the son of a gentleman," though his father has long been dead and his patrimony had been wiped out by bankruptcy. New atti-tudes can be assumed that extend the self, or add to it, as in *Typee* Tommo learns to feel a wider human sympathy, beyond that of his own family and national or racial group, for the same island natives he once feared would cannibalize him and, indeed, for all Polynesian peoples.

In the course of writing *White-Jacket,* however, or in the course of the per-sonal experience that formed the basis of this narrative, Melville's conception of identity changed dramatically from a social and psychological phenom-enon, such as one would find in the writings of Erikson or even Freud, to a

spiritual one, such as one might find in the work of Dante or Augustine. This
is a remarkable development, to be sure, but perhaps not so remarkable in
light of the discovery several years ago that Melville, who is still widely regarded to be one of the great religious skeptics of the nineteenth century, had
been a long-time member of All Souls' Unitarian Church in Manhattan.[28]
The change, I suspect, can be pinpointed to the moment when Melville describes his young protagonist's identity as being all but stripped from him in
the scene where he is called before the mast for his failure to be at his post and
is subsequently threatened with a public flogging, a moment crucial to our
understanding of the hero's later struggle to free himself from the white jacket
following his fall from the yard-arm. Here what Melville dramatizes in the
young hero's instinctive outrage and resistance to authority is that there is an
"Ur-identity" behind the social and psychological dimensions of identity, an
immense capacity or energizing power that underlies the quotidian capacities and past experiences usually thought to define an individual. This Ur-
identity is spiritual in that it is limitless, or virtually so—all-powerful and
eternal—unlike the Ego, which is finite and, as Melville would soon demonstrate in the example of Ahab, doomed to die. The discovery of this Ur-identity,
in turn, lies at the heart of *Moby-Dick*, which he there calls the "soul," and
which he portrays symbolically in the image of the great White Whale, the
objective correlative of Ishmael's own spiritual being. Ishmael's story, as I see
it, is the story of the would-be suicide's saving experience of the protracted,
yet ever-startling, unfolding of his own soul.

It was the discovery of this Ur-self, or soul, that Melville was describing,
too, I believe, when in the middle of his longest letter to Hawthorne he stopped
to confide that he felt he had hardly begun to know himself, or to grow, until
relatively late in life, after he was all but finished with his wandering:

> My development has been all within a few years past. I am like one of those
> seeds taken out of the Egyptian Pyramids, which, after being three thou-
> sand years a seed and nothing but a seed, being planted in English soil, it
> developed itself, grew to greenness, and then fell to mould. So I. Until I
> was twenty-five, I had no development at all. From my twenty-fifth year I
> date my life. Three weeks have scarcely passed, at any time between then
> and now, that I have not unfolded within myself. But I feel that I am now
> come to the inmost leaf of the bulb, and that shortly the flower must fall to
> the mould.[29]

It is significant that Melville was making his way home on the *United States*,
the experience he would later build upon in writing *White-Jacket*, when he

turned twenty-five. Even more significant is the fact that Melville made the admission concerning his inner evolution while he was in the midst of writing *Moby-Dick*. For in doing so he seems to confirm that the drama of Ishmael's growing consciousness of his own soul was Melville's story, too. More than anything else, I would say, what accounts for the power and greatness, the heady confidence, of Melville's epic is the excitement he himself must have felt at the discovery, and unfolding, of his own spiritual identity as he was composing that extraordinary novel.

What happened to the subject matter of Melville's fiction after *Moby-Dick*, why he shifted from the autobiographical narratives of the sea to the more various and readily identifiable genres of the novel in his last four long narratives, has much to do with that discovery. For in *Moby-Dick* Melville had essentially written himself out of a subject, the subject, namely, of his own development. What does a novelist with a pronounced autobiographical bent write about after he has written about the discovery of the soul? In a letter to Hawthorne written late in 1851, after the publication of his magnum opus, Melville had said, with the confidence of a man who had just completed one very sizable project and was unsure what to do next, "So, now, let us add Moby Dick to our blessing, and step from that. Leviathan is not the biggest fish;—I have heard of Krakens."[30]

But, in fact, he could hardly go on in his fiction to take up later developments in his own interior life. For, strictly speaking, there could hardly be any development beyond this point. Therefore, in his next book Melville had to go back to a period in his life before his whaling days and imagine himself, as he did in *Pierre*, as a naive young man—either that or break out of the autobiographical mode altogether. Not surprisingly, Melville's last three novels are all impersonal narratives rather than autobiographical ones, and as such they all testify to the fact that he had indeed "come to the inmost leaf of the bulb" while writing *Moby-Dick*. He was no longer preoccupied with the evolution of his own identity, no longer riding the tide of his own extraordinary growth. Now it was time for him to write as a wisdom figure, the kind of novelist who dispensed his knowledge indirectly. Having come to as full and complete an understanding of himself as any fiction writer ever did, it was time for him to weave dreams of a common destiny.

∾

The Flesh Made Word,

the Word Made Flesh:

Typee as Romance

Despite its popularity, *Typee: A Peep at Polynesian Life* (1846) has almost never been read the way Melville wanted it to be read—and for good reason. Though presented as a piece of informal travel writing, a factual account of the author's "Four Months' Residence in a Valley of the Marquesas," Melville's first book has seemed to its practiced readers to be more like a work of fiction, such as *Robinson Crusoe*, a work often cited by reviewers and critics as its next of kin. In public and in private, Melville always defended his first book as a work of authenticity; to him, *Typee* and its sequel, *Omoo* (1847), were "books of travel"—or so he claimed.[1] When it first appeared, however, it was widely suspected to be a romance, a fiction, or "piece of Munchausenism," as one reviewer said; others felt that, "if not a sheer romance," it was at least "extremely exaggerated" or that its author was "occasionally romancing."[2] Even Melville's British publisher, the eminent John Murray, who finally agreed to bring out *Typee* in his travel series, the Colonial and Home Library, had serious misgivings about its being "an ingenious fiction," and for two years after it was published he continued to press Melville, always to no effect, for "documentary evidences" of his ever having been at the Marquesas Islands.[3]

Modern scholars have confirmed that early readers were right to be wary about the veracity of the book that launched Melville's career. Most notably, Charles Roberts Anderson, in *Melville in the South Seas* (1939), determined that Melville made extensive use of several books on Polynesia while assembling what he avowed to be his own personal impressions of the inhabitants of Nukuhiva. Anderson established that Melville stretched the truth of some autobiographical facts, such as the length of his stay on the island and the

difficulty of his passage into Typee valley, and that he probably fabricated such memorable scenes as his sailing excursions with the beautiful Fayaway and his violent exit from the beach near the natives' village. While never actually concluding that *Typee* is a romance, Anderson did argue that much of the story was fictionalized. Moreover, without ever saying so, he reduced the autobiographical core of the book to just two verifiable facts, the only facts that support Melville's claim in his preface to be speaking "the unvarnished truth" throughout his narrative—namely, that he jumped ship, from the *Acushnet,* with Toby Greene at Nukuhiva on July 9, 1842, and that he was picked up at the same island, alone, sometime in the first half of the next month by a Sydney whaler in need of crew.[4]

With only this very limited evidence to lean on, the modern reader can better sense the bluster in Melville's claim that his disbelieving readers were "a parcel of blockheads" and "senseless sceptics—men who go straight from their cradles to their graves & never dream of the queer things going on at the antipodes."[5] The main reason so many readers have suspected *Typee* to be something other than straight travel writing, however, is not that they are naive about the wonders of the world, and neither is it that the book's incidents themselves are inherently unbelievable. The major reason, I would argue, is that in fashioning the narrative of his Polynesian adventure, Melville borrowed freely from the conventions of the fictional romance, and those conventions, though we may hardly be conscious of them as such, show through the narrative's surface. The details of Melville's South Sea Island story are certainly fresh and exotic for most readers, even today, but the forms in which he cast them, to heighten interest and generate suspense, are so familiar as to make the whole affair seem artificial or unbelievable.

Although he was not in fact the "practiced writer" John Murray suspected him to be, Melville was, at the not-so-tender age of twenty-five, perhaps the next best thing—a smart, eclectic reader with an eye for the popular market and a gifted prose stylist with a talent for mining the works of others to serve his own ambitious purposes.[6] Modern scholars have long known that Melville was an extraordinarily "bookish" author who borrowed eagerly from a wide variety of sources right from the start of his career. What they have all but overlooked is the fact that he borrowed not simply from individual works of nonfiction—travel books, anthropological studies, and the like—but from the tradition of prose fiction as well, freely adopting its forms and conventions and at the same time putting his own distinctive stamp on them.[7]

Before looking at those elements in *Typee* that ally it with the romance, however, a few words of explanation are in order as to why Melville repeatedly denied that his first book was a work of fiction. Most importantly, it should

be recognized that what Melville said about *Typee* after John Murray had agreed to publish it, and what he said or thought about it while he was writing it—its form, its audience, the claims to authenticity he would have to make for it— are not necessarily the same thing. Yet almost everything in the record about Melville's own view of his first book dates from the time *after* the house of Murray began to loom as a possible publisher. We do not know whose idea it was for Melville's brother, Gansevoort, to offer the incomplete manuscript to a publisher who was by nature strongly averse to fictionalizing in any form. It might have been Melville's, but then again it might have been Gansevoort's, for he was the one who had recently become situated in London and labored hard there promoting the manuscript and seeing it through the press. It might even have been the idea of an experienced third party, such as Thomas Low Nichols, an author-friend of Gansevoort's and a man of many parts who is known to have thought Melville's book would be a success if it were pub- lished first in England.[8] We know that, while working on *Typee* before he made the late, largely anthropological, additions in an effort to appease Murray, Melville tried to place the manuscript with the American firm of Harper and Brothers and that it was rejected there on the grounds that "it was impossible that it could be true."[9] However, it cannot be known from this how much authenticity Melville was prepared to claim for it at this point, or whether he was even very concerned about the issue at all.

If the legend of how Melville became a writer is true, he may simply have thought he was setting down the personal anecdotes with which he had been regaling his family circle and silently interposing the published reports of other travelers as a way to fill out his story.[10] If he thought no one during his lifetime would ever detect how much he had borrowed from the Polynesian writings of Charles S. Stewart, Captain David Porter, and William Ellis to pad out his narrative, he must have supposed, too, that he could get away with telling a few stretchers along the way about what he alleged to be his personal experiences in Typee valley. Who would contradict him? The only English- speaking eyewitness to his activities there, after all, was Toby Greene, and he had "long been given up for lost."[11]

Because "the taint of fiction" was the "forbidden thing" in the Colonial and Home Library, Melville had to defend every word of this first book as gospel truth once Murray began to show interest in publishing it.[12] If he retreated even a little and admitted he had taken the romancer's liberty with even the smallest detail, the entire effort would have been lost. The whole elaborate, stitched-together, "ingenious fiction" that Gansevoort was working mightily to assure Murray the book was not, and that Anderson later conclusively dem- onstrated it to be, would come tumbling down on its author's head.[13] John

Murray would have refused publication, or, if the truth came out after the book appeared in print, he would have withdrawn his imprimatur, and any chance of additional printings or future sales would have been lost or seriously jeopardized. Moreover, if word got out after it was published that Melville's book was a kind of fraud, his reviewers would have laughed him to scorn or risen in indignation at the effrontery of his attempt to gull the public. Thus, to assure his budding aspirations as a writer as best he could; to get the book into print, and keep it there, both abroad and at home; and finally, and possibly most importantly, to secure a hearing for what he had to say about the Typee way of life and the devastation that Western colonialism was wreaking on the lives of the South Sea Islanders, he had to pretend that his book was something it was not—a straightforward account of the author's first-hand experience in Polynesia. From the moment John Murray entered the picture, he had to hold the line against what he later called the "reiterated imputation" that he was a "romancer in disguise," though, ironically, that is precisely what he was.[14]

In arguing that *Typee* fits the romance genre—in plot and character, in incident and theme, in structure, setting, and style—I do not, however, mean to say that *Typee* is a romance, a work of straight fiction, or that Melville thought of himself as writing such a work, as he surely did in *Mardi* (1848). My aims are not so extreme. What I do want to argue is that, in shaping the story of his Polynesian adventure, Melville borrowed liberally from the romance form. *Typee* is new wine in an old bottle; it is travel writing—part fact, part fiction—molded to fit various tried-and-true conventions of romance. As an old and popular genre, the romance was all but guaranteed to generate immediate interest and have broad appeal. More than any other, it was the one form he could count on to help his first book to sell.

In the course of my discussion, I will try to add something to the now-longstanding effort among Melville scholars to sort out fact from fiction in *Typee*. But my chief aim is not to be able to claim that a sizable portion—say, one-half or even three-quarters—of the narrative, exclusive of anthropological matters, is either highly embellished or counterfeit and only a relatively small portion is straight factual reporting, though I would say that is a fair estimate. Instead, my principal aims are to point out the extent to which Melville's first book depends for its effects on the conventions of the romance; to indicate on what basis Melville should be considered, at the start of his career, to have been a writer of fiction; and finally, to suggest where, in this first book, his creative powers were most vital and imaginative. *Typee* reveals that, in the beginning, Melville's literary sensibilities were traditional, amateurish, and in tune with popular tastes in the novel, as one might expect of a young, self-tutored writer. But it reveals also that his imagination was quick

and esemplastic, capable of altering, in original ways, the conventions of romance to fit the circumstances of his own experience in Polynesia. If his imagination was not yet possessed of a "heroic passion," as Emerson said the inspired writer's must be, then it was at least capable of impressing his spirited
personality on forms that he took to be "fluid."[15]

The problematic term here, of course, is "romance." As applied to narrative, the term was originally used to describe Old French stories in verse that
portrayed the deeds of chivalric heroes, as in *Roman de la Rose*. However, by
the seventeenth century it had come to mean also what Melville's reviewers
meant when they used the term to dismiss *Typee*: "an extravagant fiction,
invention, or story," in the words of the *OED*; "a wild or wanton exaggeration;
a picturesque falsehood." Clearly they did not have in mind the now-well-
known distinction between romance and novel that Hawthorne was to make,
according to which romance is thought to permit a degree of imaginative "latitude, as to its fashion and material," that the novel, with its concern for verisi-
militude, could not accommodate.[16] For Melville's reviewers the point of con-
tention did not concern the differences between types of fiction but the
differences between fact and fiction. But even so, what they objected to as
fiction-making in Melville's story can be regarded as evidence of "romancing"
in the narrower sense, for the narrative line that Melville followed in *Typee* has
the symptomatic shape of "romance" in the modern, critical sense of the term.

In the discussion that follows, then, I will be relying on modern conceptions of the form, particularly as defined by Northrop Frye, in *Anatomy of
Criticism* (1957) and *The Secular Scripture: A Study in the Structure of Romance* (1976). To be sure, Frye's formulation, extensive and precise though it
is, is not so exact, or so subtle, that one can employ it to tell fact from fiction,
fool's gold from the real thing. But it is sufficiently commodious, systematic,
and penetrating as to make me believe it can help to determine what has the
look of fiction in *Typee* and what does not, what appears to be based on the
writer's effort to build suspense or hold the reader's interest and what appears
to be based on a first-hand experience of events at Nukuhiva.

In his study of this most common of the nonreligious forms of writing in
Western culture, Frye observes that the conventions of prose romance have
remained surprisingly stable since the form first appeared in the late classical
period of Greece. In both ancient romances and modern ones—he cites Scott's
Guy Mannering as a late prototype—Frye observes that the stories tell of mysterious birth, shipwreck, capture by pirates, enchanted islands, narrow escapes
from death, oracular prophecies and magi, foster parents, the hero's loss and
regaining of identity, and his eventual marriage with the heroine.[17] Not all of
these motifs will be found in all romances, to be sure, and not every motif will

appear in just the form described here. *Typee* contains no tales of the hero's mysterious birth, for example, though his birth is a mystery; and the novel begins not with a shipwreck and capture by pirates, but with the hero and his companion jumping ship at Nukuhiva and then being imprisoned by cannibals. But the basic captivity structure is the same, and, what is just as important, so is the effect of suspense for the reader. In the one case, shipwreck forces the hero to make a break with his past, a detour in his life's plan; then outlaws come into the picture to test his courage and honor, sometimes threatening him with death and sometimes trying to make him join their nefarious cause. In *Typee* the hero initiates his own detour rather than having it forced on him, but he finds it still comes to much the same end. For when the Typees are not threatening him with cannibalism (or so he thinks), they are trying to make his stay so blissful that he will want to become one of them. Whether inflamed by the prospect of pleasure or menaced by the threat of pain, Melville's hero, like the hero of a standard romance, runs the risk of losing his identity, from the start of his ordeal to the end. This is, I would say, the book's central theme.

In their starkest, most insidious forms, such threats to the hero's selfhood typically appear in the menacing, if familiar, forms of sex and violence. Romance has always depended for its success on the free and easy play of these sensational themes, or on their more respectable cousins, love and adventure. While Melville treats these subversive matters with some restraint, offering hardly more than the tantalizing "peep" promised by the book's subtitle, the narrator's adventures repeatedly threaten to break out into extremes of violent aggression or sexual fury. And on occasion they do so, as one might expect in a young man's book that is preoccupied, even obsessed, with the pleasures and pains of the flesh.

Strategically placed in the second chapter, for example, as an early promise of still more exciting things to come, there is an orgy scene on the *Dolly* (entirely fictional so far as Melville's own experience is concerned, though based on a well-known historical incident), which occurs when a bevy of naked young girls swims out to welcome the crew. "Our ship," says Melville's narrator, in tones of apparent disapproval (though he had just moments earlier described with keen interest how these same mermaids had performed their toilettes), "was now wholly given up to every species of riot and debauchery. Not the feeblest barrier was interposed between the unholy passions of the crew and their unlimited gratification. The grossest licentiousness and the most shameful inebriety prevailed, with occasional and but short-lived interruptions, through the whole period of her stay" (15). It should be emphasized that in G. H. von Langsdorff's account of this incident, which Melville almost certainly used in shaping this scene, there were native men and boys as well as

women and girls who boarded the ship at Nukuhiva, but Melville makes no mention of any males in the group he supposedly witnessed.

Further comparison with Langsdorff's description shows Melville's account to be much the more provocative of the two; where the early naturalist's is amused yet innocent of rhetorical manipulation, Melville's is alternately voyeuristic and moralizing.[18] The big orgy scene that concludes Melville's book, the infamous "Polynesian saturnalia" that followed the British ouster of the French at Honolulu, is presented in a more condemning tone, but even this is not free of a certain prurient interest. In this instance, the crews of two frigates are said to come together with hundreds of natives from the surrounding islands to celebrate—during a period of ten days when the Hawaiian king suspended all laws—by performing in the open street what Melville refers to, ominously, as "deeds too atrocious to be mentioned" (258).

As eye-opening as the first of these two scenes may be, particularly for a book written in America in the middle of the nineteenth century, I think it is true that, for male readers particularly, the most lasting memories of *Typee* are of the nubile Fayaway, the native nymphet whose very name seems calculated to conjure up libidinous tropical fantasies, and of the hero's repeated efforts to quiet his fears of the Typees' reputed cannibalism. We remember so vividly Tommo's fear of the natives' celebrated flesh-eating practices because Melville makes it the chief source of suspense throughout his hero's stay with the islanders, overriding even his anxiety about the question of whether he will ever find a way to escape the valley and return home.

Why we, or male readers in particular, should recall Fayaway so fondly is not quite so easy to explain, attributable as it is to that mysterious force, the male sex drive. Perhaps it is enough to say that, even if she did have an earthly model, Fayaway is one of the earliest in a long line of pubescent heroines, culminating in Nabokov's Lolita, who have been celebrated by their male creators for their budding beauty and sexual precocity. To be sure, Melville's narrator, the young Tommo, is hardly a middle-aged Humbert Humbert. But as a man in his early twenties, he was several years older than the adolescent Fayaway and a perfect stand-in for those adult male readers everywhere who constituted Melville's principal audience, like the one who punctuated his review of the book with a sigh of profound jealousy: "Enviable Herman! A happier dog it is impossible to imagine than Herman in Typee Valley."[19]

To consider most readers' most lasting memories of Melville's first book is to recognize just how much its popular success, and its author's early reputation, depended on his readiness to exploit the subjects of sex and violence. And exploit them he did, with energy and shrewdness. Important as Fayaway is to the erotic interest of *Typee*, she is hardly the only female in the book to

cavort through its pages while openly exhibiting her charms. In fact, their numbers are legion. Besides the Island queen who lifts her skirts to show off her tattoos in a contest with an old sailor at the end of the first chapter, there are large groups of naked "whihenies" (14) who periodically burst on the scene. There is, for one, a "shoal," or school ("a great quantity," says *Webster's* vaguely), of young mermaids who capture the *Dolly* and force the crew to watch as they perform their Marquesan dances with "abandoned voluptuousness" (15).

There is also an equally amorphous "crowd" of natives that accompanies Tommo every time he goes to bathe in a nearby stream. In this last instance the picture is clouded by the fact that it was a mixed group, "composed chiefly of young girls and boys," who escorted him, but by the time they get into the water Melville mentions only "the young girls" who were to be seen "springing buoyantly into the air, and revealing their naked forms to the waist" (89–90). Then there are "the girls" at the Feast of the Calabashes who "exhibited themselves in gala costume; the most conspicuous feature of which was a necklace of beautiful white flowers." While Melville is careful to say that all of them also wore a short tappa tunic around the waist, this detail becomes all the more significant when it is learned that only "some" of them chose to add to it a simple mantle of the same material (160–61).

At other times, in other ways, and at intervals so regular as to seem a bit obsessive, Melville comments on the beauty of the islanders' naked forms— the female forms especially. He explains how the natives dress or carry themselves or anoint their bodies with "aker"; how they appear walking in the woods, conversing in the village, or "romping" in the privacy of the boudoir; and he repeats what earlier observers have had to say about their physical attractiveness. In no other work of literature in the nineteenth century—possibly in no other work of art in any century, not even excepting the bursting canvases of Peter Paul Rubens—can one find so many barebreasted female forms as Melville managed to bring onto the stage of *Typee*. The only book Melville wrote before his engagement to the respectable Elizabeth Shaw, *Typee* is truly a bachelor's fantasy, a book written by a bachelor for other bachelors, with a playfully erotic message as one of its most insistent themes.

The degree to which Melville exploited the subject of violence in *Typee* is a bit more problematic because we cannot know whether the author's life was ever in any real danger from the islanders. Leaving aside the question of whether Melville ever spent any time with the Typees, we do not know whether they were in fact the cannibals he claimed them to be or at what point in their history they may have stopped the practice of flesh-eating. While Melville can be said to have romanced the subjects of female nudity and sexual precocity among the Typees to some degree, we at least know from earlier eyewitness

accounts and later anthropological studies that the female form was much in
evidence at Nukuhiva during Melville's time there and that the islanders were
sexually active at an unusually early age by Western standards.

However, by contrast, there is no way of knowing whether the threat of
cannibalism was real or imaginary or whether, as now seems most likely,
Melville had decided to make the most of their ferocious reputation in order
to create suspense for his narrative. What can be shown is, first, that the validity of the Typees' reputation for cannibalism is questionable, particularly
among modern anthropologists and, second, that Melville presented the subject in such a way as to maximize the suspense of what he himself referred to
later, in *Omoo*, as his "indulgent captivity" among the natives of Nukuhiva.[20]

As Anderson assessed the matter, there is no available way to verify or
disconfirm the Typees' reputation for flesh-eating. In his view, the testimony
of the earliest observers, particularly Langsdorff, Porter, and Stewart, whose
writings Melville used or knew, as well as John M. Coulter, whose work he
apparently did not know, "is meager, unreliable, and conflicting." This being
the case, Anderson summarized his findings as follows, and his conclusions
have stood for half a century:

> Making allowances for contradiction, distortion, and mistranslation, it
> would seem that the Marquesans, along with most of the other Polynesian
> nations, had practiced cannibalism as a religious ceremony on the bodies
> of slain enemies . . . with the purpose of wreaking vengeance and of ac-
> quiring the virtues of the deceased. But the occasions of these ceremonies
> were certainly infrequent. . . . In historic times, in fact, the ceremony may
> even have subsided into a mere "ritual cannibalism." . . . [But] there is no
> authenticated instance on record of human flesh being eaten as a delicacy,
> according to my discoveries, nor any reliable record of a white man being
> eaten by Polynesians for any reason whatever; finally, I have not been able
> to find a single unequivocal eyewitness account of a Marquesan eating the
> flesh of even a native enemy slain in battle, though in all likelihood this
> custom did exist at one time.[21]

Paradoxically confirming this view, Melville himself later in his story—
after the suspense about his fate had played itself out and he could take on the
more disinterested role of the anthropologist—tried to discount exaggerated
rumors of the natives' cannibalism as presented in "the popular fictions." According to such accounts, he observed scornfully, apparently oblivious to the
fact that he was undermining his own use of the same cliches during the central action of *Typee*, "the crews of vessels, shipwrecked on some barbarous

coast, are eaten alive like so many dainty joints by the uncivil inhabitants; and unfortunate voyagers are lured into smiling and treacherous bays; knocked on the head with outlandish war clubs; and served up without any preliminary dressing." At this point taking the position that the truth of the matter is hardly so extreme, Melville explained that "cannibalism to a certain moderate extent is practised among several of the primitive tribes in the Pacific, but it is upon the bodies of slain enemies alone" (205). Whether these tribes included the Typees, Melville does not say, though his failure to do so would seem to have been calculated, as it permits the reader vaguely to think that fugitive sailors might have their flesh, so to speak, and that the inhabitants of Nukuhiva might eat it, too.

Such equivocation aside, Melville here all but admits that his own life was never in danger from the Typees. As Freud would later confirm in *Totem and Taboo* (1913), the crucial factor among virtually all cannibals is whether the potential victim is an enemy, particularly an enemy slain in battle.[22] Clearly Melville himself did not qualify. Even if he came to be informed about the flesh-eating practices of Pacific islanders only after he had returned home, he had no business stirring up bogus suspense about the fate of his hero by claiming that he felt his life was always in danger, if it is true that he was simply writing a "book of travel." Yet *Typee* depends for its success on the threat that its hero might, at any moment during his stay, be promptly cannibalized. Indeed, so convincingly did the young author handle this feature of his story that, as he would later come to lament to Hawthorne, there was a danger that the only reputation he would ever have was the sensational one of a "man who lived among the cannibals."[23]

The contradiction between Melville's late disclaimer and his repeated suggestion that his life amid the islanders was constantly threatened is an important clue to *Typee*'s status as a romance. For human sacrifice is not simply a standard feature of romance; it is, as Frye has observed, the "crucial episode" in virtually all examples of the form.[24] To be sure, the intended victim is usually a virginal female and not a strapping young male; but aside from the matter of gender, Melville's youthful hero is strikingly similar. As a young American of the educated classes, he is similarly virtuous and refined; like the standard heroine, he is a figure of worth and is possessed of the strength of character to try to preserve his moral standing in the face of life-threatening circumstances and assorted lures of the flesh. Of course young Tommo is not precisely in the situation of the typical damsel in distress, who is constantly made to fear the proverbial fate worse than death. But Melville was able to make very creative adjustments to the romance paradigm to generate much the same kind of suspense.

Seizing on those elements in the Polynesian scene that would most closely approximate the stock circumstances of a captivity romance, Melville shaped his hero's situation in such a way as to achieve the standard effects of the form without straining his readers' credulousness. Death by cannibalism was an exciting, even sensational, new form of the usual threat of human sacrifice, and under the circumstances it could readily be made to seem believable. But the threat of rape was a little harder to manage, since the central character was a male. Moreover, given the narrator-hero's obvious pleasure at the company of the female natives, it would have been inconsistent, even hypocritical, if he were suddenly seen trying to defend his sexual purity against their advances. Any readers not put off by the lack of realism in such scenes surely would have been repelled by the male egocentrism of such a setup. However, the threat of tattooing would accomplish much the same effect as the threat of rape—it was, it might even be said, a form of rape—and it had the added advantage of being an exotic Polynesian custom. Though not so titillating as the threat of sexual violation, it did hold much the same potential for threatening the central character's identity, and it did so while still providing vicarious thrills for the reader.[25]

The threat of rape is a standard feature of romance because the subject holds the predictable voyeuristic fascination of all forbidden matters. But in romance there is often also a serious side to the subject that concerns the development of character and the need for fiction to affirm those values that define the supporting culture's ideals of rectitude and happiness. When the heroine of a romance is put under the pressure of a "fate worse than death," she is being given an opportunity to display those qualities of character—honor, fortitude, probity, highmindedness, and patience, if not genuine stoicism—that the romance is designed to inculcate in the reader. Such a heroine must be shown maintaining her virginity, despite powerfully menacing odds, so that she will be known to be worthy, in the end, of marrying a hero who is her equal. If, that is to say, she is to have any chance of living happily ever after, and in a way the reader can approve, she must be made to struggle to maintain her true identity. For the threatened loss of a young woman's virginity, whether in a romance or in the world it attempts to mirror, is a narrowly localized instance of the more fundamental threat of losing one's sense of self, one's autonomy or independence. At least in Frye's account of the genre, it is this fundamental threat that constitutes the central subject of romance. And it is central because the annihilation of one's identity, as Frye says, is "the one fate which really is worse than death."[26]

While the threat to Tommo of being tattooed against his will is not quite a central feature of the book, it does play a crucial role in his struggle to maintain

his distinctive identity among the natives and in his decision, finally, to try to escape from them. For until Karky the artist suddenly threatens to tattoo his face one day near the end of his stay, Melville's hero is pictured as slipping slowly and with little resistance into the Typee way of life. As he gradually gives in to the pleasure principle that rules the valley, where "day follows day in one unvarying round of summer and sunshine" (213), and begins to lose track even of the passage of time, he notices that the strange wound on his leg has "suddenly healed" (123). Without this reminder of his alienation from the "healthful physical existence" enjoyed by the natives of Nukuhiva, he forgets about his home, his early ties with family and friends, and his cultural past (127). He seems to become, for a time, one of them. However, the threat of tattooing puts an end to his amnesia, forcing him to recognize that his physical appearance would be permanently altered—that he would "never more have the *face*," as he says nervously, "to return to my countrymen, should an opportunity offer" itself (219).

As with the loss of a young woman's virginity, so too with the tattooing of a young man's skin, particularly his face, it is the permanence of the change, and the expectation that one will lose the regard of one's friends and loved ones, that is the source of anxiety. What shocks the pleasure-seeking Tommo back to his true self in the end is the prospect of being ostracized once he returns home, the fear that his family and friends will reject or repudiate him as a slave to the flesh.

Though a preoccupation with violence and a pervasive interest in sex are important signs of *Typee*'s status as a romance, other clues abound. The opening of the book, for example, contains several important motifs and images that are characteristic of the form. There is the common theme of the break in consciousness, what Frye calls the amnesia motif. This is brought into play when Tommo and his friend Toby are still on ship, longing for a change in scenery, for some respite from the "privations and hardships" of six months at sea in a profitless search for whales (3). When the captain finally orders the *Dolly* to head for the nearest islands in search of fresh meat (just one of many signs that the hunger of the flesh for the flesh in this book is universal), the mood of the whole crew relaxes and everyone suddenly seems cast under a "spell" (10). The ship becomes enchanted and acts as though it knows its own way, so the man at the wheel "would doze away by the hour." For nearly three weeks, a "delightful, lazy, languid time," when light trade winds silently swept them toward the Marquesas Islands, "every one seemed to be under the influence of some narcotic." Even the ship's officers were unable to keep on their feet. For the narrator-hero, "reading was out of the question; take a book in your hand, and you were asleep in an instant" (9–10).

Surely this is not the language of straightforward travel writing. Instead, it is the kind of language used in romance to mark the customary shift from the waking world to the world of the unconscious, where pleasurable fantasies, and forbidding nightmares, run free. In this world, the hero's present circumstances, no matter how dull, can be forgotten and his buried self can come to life. However, in romance, more is at stake than a simple escape from the commonplace. What is at issue, finally, is the possible loss of identity, as the hero, fearing the consequences of his present lot, tries to become something he is not. In Tommo's case, what he fears is that he will become a white-haired old sailor whose whole youth will have been eaten up in a luckless search for whale oil. For him, jumping ship is the only way to save his youth.

Like other romances, then, *Typee* begins with what I would call the eternal fountain motif, the hero's search for eternal youth—for the pleasure and daring of ripe flesh and for the knowledge that would destroy the destroying power of age. Certainly boredom with his life at sea is a factor in Tommo's decision to desert ship at Nukuhiva, and so too is what he calls the "unmitigated tyranny" of the *Dolly*'s captain. But such things, Melville's narrator asserts, "could have been endured awhile, had we entertained the hope of being speedily delivered from them by the due completion of the term of our servitude" (21).

The decisive factor, largely ignored in other readings of the book, though Melville devoted more than a page and a half to the matter, is his dismay at the proverbial longevity of Pacific-bound whaling voyages, which commonly extended "over a period of four or five years." What the young narrator most fears is that he will become one of those youths of local legend "whose anxious mothers provide them with bottled milk" on their departure from Nantucket, only to have them return "very respectable middle-aged gentlemen." One story in particular concerning an ill-starred whaler so sticks in his mind that it "always haunted me," he says. Though after many years' absence this ship, aptly named *The Perseverance*, "was given up for lost," from time to time reports of its decaying condition filtered back to the States until finally it was seen "somewhere in the vicinity of the ends of the earth," its sails "all bepatched and bequilted with rope-yarns," its crew made up of "some twenty venerable Greenwich-pensioner-looking old salts, who just managed to hobble about deck" (21–23). It is not a matter of coincidence that, in seeking to conquer the forces of death by jumping ship at Nukuhiva and know the pleasures the flesh is heir to, Melville should have happened on the experience that made him a writer, a master of the word that can live forever.

The amnesia and eternal fountain motifs make a potent combination in romance, for together they ensure the unleashing of powerful unconscious urges and persistent conscious desires that propel the hero out of his commonplace

life on a quest for an enchanted island, some Edenic world of wish-fulfillment fantasy.[27] Yet as Frye points out, in romance this usually means that the hero almost immediately finds himself "falling" into a demonic world of anxiety, nightmare, and other forms of psychic disturbance that begin to undermine his identity. The imaginative universe of romance, Frye explains, has two poles: one "an idyllic world where human desires and ideals can find more scope"; the other "a night world symbolized by human sacrifice, a world which is more an object of moral abhorrence than strictly a tragic one."[28] Thus in *Typee*, Melville's hero jumps off at an island that seems to offer an answer to all his prayers at the same time as it poses an insidious threat to his emotional well-being and even his very existence. Romance is constructed in this dual way not merely because, being a popular form, it must simplify the complex forces at work in the world, but because, being a didactic form as well, it must show that the vision of paradise is finally an illusion. It must demonstrate that what life in Happy Valley offers, in the end, is the certainty of self-destruction. In seeking even a temporary break from his past, Tommo is, in effect, attempting to become something he is not, and this is equivalent to his seeking his own destruction, so important is it for the hero to remain who he is.

To be sure, Melville's hero does not initially set out on a probing inward journey to discover an alternate self; his journey is metaphoric, constructed as an exploration of the falsely idyllic and increasingly nightmarish world of the Typees. As is commonly the case in romance, the quest seems, at the outset, to be little more than a simple adventure—a diversion from the everyday world for the hero, the storyteller, and the reader. But there is a fundamental seriousness, too, that is typical of romance. For in seeking to capture and preserve his youthful vitality, Melville's hero opens himself to the risks that attend all change—to the destruction of his already well-formed identity; to a knowledge of himself, and of the world, that is beyond his capacity to manage; and to a wisdom about life that will weigh him down before his time and perhaps break his spirit. The journey of Melville's hero into the valley of the Typees is, then, in certain essential respects a symbolic one, as in the writings of Conrad, according to which he is shown moving back into his own primitive, ancestral past, where lie the well-springs of humanity's deepest nature and most fundamental urges—sexual omnipotence; the fear of annihilation; greed, bloodlust, and tribal aggression; Oedipal desires and paternal hostilities—all the yearnings and hatreds that flesh is heir to.

When the hero of romance "falls" asleep or otherwise slips into a world of dreams and nightmares, he begins a series of adventures that make up what Frye has called a "descent." This stage, which in drama would be termed the complication or rising action, constitutes the better part of a romance. Usually

in romance, as in *Typee* when Tommo and his companion struggle to make their way down into the valley, there is a dense forest at the start that serves as a threshold marking the hero's crossing into the highly charged underworld of sleep, where erotic interests and other repressed urges run free. That Melville was working symbolically, and not reporting his own experience in the early scenes on the island, can be concluded from the fact that the trek into the Typees' village, which in the book Melville stretched into five days and spread over thirty pages, could have been made in just three or four hours.[29]

Once past the threshold, the hero encounters increasingly difficult and painful trials—restricted freedom of action, loneliness and alienation, identity confusion, physical cruelty, and terror. As he loses more and more freedom of action during his descent, he may suffer imprisonment or an inexplicable paralysis, and he is likely to come face to face with some particularly forbidding image of death. No ordinary hero, Melville's Tommo experiences all of these, as first he is taken captive by the Typees, then suffers an incapacitating leg wound, and at last comes to believe he is being fattened for a cannibal feast. This last event, the cannibal feast, is one which typically signals that the romance hero has reached the nadir of his fall into the night world. The theme of cannibalism is significant, Frye explains, "not for its horrific frisson, but as the image which causes that frisson, the identifying of human and animal natures in a world where animals are food for man. Such a theme merges readily with the theme of human sacrifice in its most undisplaced form, which is the swallowing of a youth or maiden by a subterranean or submarine monster."[30]

As the linking of these images suggests, Melville's preoccupation with the experience of being eaten alive did not begin with his rewriting of the Jonah story in *Moby-Dick*. It began at the very start of his career with *Typee*. Indeed, it might even be said to lie behind his decision to become a writer. Like Poe's preoccupation with premature burial, Melville's phobic fascination with being eaten alive is symptomatic of longings deep in the young author's psyche. For the experience of being swallowed by a monster—as Joseph Campbell has shown in *The Hero with a Thousand Faces* (1949, 1968) and elsewhere—is a universal symbol of the excruciating trial that any hero must go through to be worthy of the name. Melville's interest in the subject is a sign of his fascination with the kind of experience that is so intensely revolutionizing as to make one feel he is being eaten alive. For the writer of lasting merit, that is the only kind of experience worth writing about—the experience of the flesh that is so powerfully transforming it demands to be put into words.

As Tommo goes through his descent, not just into Typee valley but into the whole native way of life, he in effect becomes swallowed into the belly of the whale of Polynesian culture. And as can be expected of a romance hero in

such circumstances, he finds himself being transformed by his experience. To be sure, the alterations in his personality are not so profound as to make him a new man; he never joins the Typees, nor does he become so sophisticated and resilient a personality as Marnoo, the "taboo" figure who moves in and out of Typee culture, indeed throughout the Marquesas Islands, at will. But he does undergo several important changes, particularly in the new attitude of respect he comes to feel for the islanders and their culture, and he is so constantly under pressure to cast off his old ways and join the Typees that the struggle to settle the question of his identity becomes the central theme of the narrative. That his identity will remain at least somewhat in flux, as he is alternately tempted and coerced to become a full-fledged member of the host tribe, is signaled from the moment he enters the village and introduces himself as "Tom," a name he invents on the spot, thinking his own might be too hard for the natives to pronounce, and the chief who welcomes him tries immediately to appropriate it by calling him "Tommo," the name that sticks throughout his captivity (72).[31]

Some of the funniest moments in *Typee* occur when Melville borrows common romance conventions, such as those centering on the adoption of native dress, eating practices, and other daily rituals, to show how hard it is to change one's identity and become assimilated into another culture. In the early days of his captivity, for example, Tommo is treated like a baby. And, in a sense, he is one, for he could hardly be any more ignorant of the behavior patterns that constitute his new cultural surroundings. If he is to survive in his new environment and take on the identity of a Typee, he must first be nurtured by the culture, as an infant would be, and instructed in all its mysterious ways. He thus finds himself in a society that is a kind of "second womb."[32] Further infantilized by his unaccountable leg wound, Tommo is initially assigned a surrogate mother or body servant, the faithful Kory-Kory, who brings him assorted foods and, "as if I were an infant, insisted upon feeding me with his own hands." Everywhere he goes he is transported, like a baby, on Kory-Kory's back, and he is always closely supervised and otherwise treated as "a froward, inexperienced child" (88–89).

Tommo does gain some independence after a while, as he grows accustomed to the ways of the island culture; and his leg wound does mysteriously heal when he temporarily forgets about his past. But, by the logic of Melville's story, because Tommo continues to refuse to be tattooed, he never makes the all-important psychological transition to becoming a true member of the island culture. He never becomes emotionally assimilated, and his original identity as an outsider remains, in the end, intact.

Other changes in the hero's identity are more apparent than real and, more often than not, are again the products of the author's reaching for comic effects. For example, "Tom" is initially portrayed as an incredibly straight-laced, even prudish young man, a proper American boy who is shocked by the forwardness of the island girls and the open display of their physical charms. Waking from a terrible dream on his first morning in the valley to find the house "nearly filled with young females" eager to comfort their distraught visitor, Tommo confesses that "my feelings of propriety were exceedingly shocked, for I could not but consider them as having overstepped the due limits of female decorum" (77). What they may have done to offend the hero's sensibilities is never very clear, beyond the suggestion that they came close enough to fan away a few insects and were quick to offer their two visitors a little food with their own hands. But whatever it was, it hardly seems material. For by the end of the same chapter, Tommo is all but declaring his love for his "peculiar favorite," the beautiful Fayaway, and exclaiming about her "lovely bosom" and her entrancing "summer garb of Eden" (85–87).

Three chapters later, in detailing the various consolations available to the wayward hero such as himself, he mentions that "every evening the girls of the house gathered about me on the mats, and . . . would anoint my whole body with a fragrant oil." "I used to hail with delight," he fondly recalls, "the daily recurrence of this luxurious operation, in which I forgot all my troubles, and buried for the time every feeling of sorrow" (110). So much for the strict Puritan upbringing and highminded purity of America's youth. Surely such an abrupt change is to be predicted, under the circumstances; but just as surely, it is hardly meant to be taken very seriously.

The change in attitude that Tommo undergoes regarding the Typees' cannibalism, however, is quite a different matter. Here the turnabout is meant to be instructive rather than entertaining. In the beginning, he is properly horrified and repulsed by the Typees' reputation for flesh-eating; he reacts as any Western traveler might be expected to. But well before the end, in chapter 27, he is offering an apologia for the practice and its practitioners that is reminiscent of Montaigne's famous defense of the custom in the essay "On Cannibals."[33] Admitting that he had entered the valley of the Typees "under the most erroneous impressions of their character," Melville's hero offers the view that, despite any cannibalism they might practice on the bodies of enemies slain in battle, the people of this tribe are "in other respects humane and virtuous" (203–5). He is not yet so taken with the practice that he is willing to settle in with the Typees; he never experiences the full-scale revolution of identity that the world of romance typically threatens. But it is clear from his newfound

acceptance of the Typees' cannibalism, and his new appreciation for their pacific nature in other respects, that an expansion or deepening of his own identity has occurred. Tommo's increased sympathy for the Typees' way of life, not excluding their (alleged) cannibalism, suggests that an important and lasting version of the life-changing romance experience did occur for him. He came away from his Marquesan encounter a changed man.

This change of heart in Melville's hero, in turn, suggests that a similar transformation had occurred at some point in Melville himself. While it does not necessarily follow that such a change could have occurred only if Melville himself had had an extensive first-hand encounter with the Typees, it does point in that direction. And ultimately, until something like the evidence Melville had promised John Murray turns up, it will be on the basis of the reader's felt conviction of the authenticity of the author's change in attitude toward the Typees that he or she will have to rest the case for Melville's actually having spent part of his summer in 1842 with the natives of Nukuhiva.

Any such conviction will depend, of course, on the reader's sense of the strength of Melville's own conviction regarding his views of the natives and on the faith that Melville would not have changed his mind about the Typees if he himself had not spent at least a little time getting to know them. It will depend, that is to say, on Melville's ability to make us feel the word reconstitute itself, as we read his book, into the literary equivalent of the living flesh. Such a measure is a modest version of what Emily Dickinson asserted to be her test of poetic power—namely, the feeling, in the flesh, that one is in the presence of a profound truth—when she said, "If I read a book [and] it makes my whole body so cold no fire ever can warm me, I know *that* is poetry."[34] The subjective test does not, of course, constitute proof of authenticity; but in the case of Melville's *Typee,* it is all we are likely ever to have.

As Tommo approaches the end of his plunge into the Marquesan world, it becomes evident he will always be of two minds about staying with the Typees. Like the standard hero of romance, he has a double identity, and only one side is involved in the "descent." Part of him yearns to live in the Polynesian paradise as though he were a native, but the other part holds back, knowing that, as a man of another family, another nation, another history, he is not a Typee and never can be. His original self knows that even if the islanders could somehow accept him as one of their own, he would never be willing to pay the price; he could never bring himself to give up all he had become—his identity—before he stepped into their world. Though he admits to having formed a higher estimate of human nature while living among the Typees "than I had ever entertained before," Tommo comes to recognize that in trying to adopt the ways of the natives he was not just putting on a false identity;

he was destroying his true self (203). He may love the image of himself that he sees in the reflecting pool of the South Seas, but he does not become so enamored of it that he falls in and drowns. Like his later incarnation, Ishmael, Tommo has a remarkable alertness, an uncanny capacity for pulling back from the destructive element at the crucial moment.

There is nothing mysterious, or mystical, about this capacity, however. What saves Melville's narrator in the end is what saves every other hero of romance— the restoration of memory. At a critical moment, when he finds himself threatened with the tattooing that would permanently alter his relationship to his own history, Tommo suddenly recalls his home and loved ones (239, 243). It is this quickened memory of his past, of who he is, that makes him see, with a force he cannot deny, how little he desires to become a Typee and how deeply he needs to return to his true self. In *Typee*, and subsequent works, Melville portrays his hero as knowing what to do, in critical moments, only when he comes to see who he is—when he has been shocked into a recognition of self-knowledge.

In the end, however, Tommo comes to see beyond himself as well as into himself. The knowledge he gains is universal, not simply personal. At the end of his "descent," he recognizes that the Polynesian world he had come to regard as ideal is, in truth, a false paradise; it too, he sees, is mutable, subject to the forces of time and death. This, Frye argues, is "the darkest knowledge at the bottom of the world" that the romance hero has revealed to him, the knowledge that death is inevitable, inescapable.[35] Typee valley has all the appearances of an idyllic place; the land is rich and beautiful, the climate is temperate, the people are happy. As Kory-Kory says, the islanders can hardly imagine that the Polynesian heaven is "much pleasanter" (172–73). But as the simple fact of their faith in an afterlife indicates, the Typees are not immune to disease or age or death. What is even more important, Melville goes on to argue, as the so-called civilized nations encroach more and more on the island culture, as they have elsewhere in Polynesia, the Typees will become more and more susceptible to these insidious fatal powers. Increasingly, as time passes, theirs will become a culture in decline.

To be sure, during the time of his captivity, Tommo shows no concern about the coming destruction of the islanders; he is understandably more concerned about the threat of his own destruction at the hands of his hosts. However, by the time Melville sat down to write *Typee*, some months after his adventure, he had found his motive, his purpose, for becoming a writer.[36] He would throw his whole weight into the effort to slow down the Typees' destruction by disclosing their plight to the very nations that were destroying them. Like Jonah, the Melville who wrote *Typee* came to see that if identity is

destiny, if he was to accept who he was—namely, a man of the Western civilized nations who found himself possessed of the knowledge that the West was slowly killing the cultures of Polynesia—he would have to become a kind of prophet. And like the Old Testament figure described by Father Mapple in *Moby-Dick*, Melville would have to become one who, though he lived in the very heart of "wicked Ninevah," had the courage to preach "the Truth in the face of falsehood."[37]

Before Melville could fulfill his destiny, however, his autobiographical character had to be made to play out his role to the very end. As the hero of romance, Tommo had to be made to suffer the pain of his imprisonment with new force, and then he had to manage somehow to free himself from his captors. It would not be enough for him to break the spell of enchantment that held him in the lower world. There had to be a rousing escape; the hero had to make his ascent out of the confining lower world by a series of remarkable adventures and acts of derring-do. Typically there is first a suspenseful trial scene where the hero's guilt concerning some vaguely defined crime is debated—as there is near the end when the Typees split into factions and argue over Tommo's fate, while he tries to get away to meet his friend Toby, recently rumored to have landed in a distant bay. Typically, too, there is a miraculous rescue scene—as there is when Tommo, seizing the moment when his trial erupts into a brawl, manages to drag himself, leg wound and all, the "four or five miles" to the English whaleboat waiting to snatch him away (246).

Finally, at the climax of the hero's escape, there is usually a moment of bloody violence—as there is when Tommo and his rescuers are driven to use a boat hook and other murderous weapons to keep Mow-Mow and his savage crew from capsizing the rescue boat before it reaches the *Julia*. Like Odysseus, the ancient prototype of the romance hero imprisoned by Polyphemus, Melville's Tommo gains his freedom only after he has done violence to a menacing one-eyed cannibal giant. If all this plotting at the conclusion of *Typee* seems transparently melodramatic, the lurid stuff of every romancer's dreams, it but highlights the fact that Melville had been following the popular formulas all along in his narrative of Polynesian adventure.

Beyond the melodrama of its final scenes, *Typee* ends, like all good romances, with the return of its hero to his proper identity and sphere. The figure who had come to be known as Tommo becomes, once again, an American sailor. As he struggles to reach the bay where he hopes to be rescued, he is suddenly overcome by a rush of pleasure at the sound of the surf and the sight of the ocean's waves, and he hails with delight these "familiar friends"— the same forces which, in the beginning of his story, he had been so eager to escape (248). What Tommo had come to regard as the "prison" of Typee cul-

ture, a place as confining as the belly of a whale, turns out, in the end, therefore, to have been a kind of womb of rebirth as well, for it has returned him
to his true self.

It returns him to his true self, but, it has to be said, it returns him to
himself a profoundly changed man. For through his experience, Melville's
hero, indeed Melville himself, has come to know the world more deeply, more
completely, and to see it as a place he felt compelled to take a hand in reshap-
ing. Like the returning hero described by Joseph Campbell, Melville found
that, through his adventures, he had acquired a "boon" or treasure, but it was
the kind that would have value only if he shared it with his own community.

That boon is the story of Melville's "captivity" and transformation and of
his discovery of the impending destruction of the island people he had come
to know firsthand. With his story, he would try to check the calamitous course
of events in that distant corner of the South Seas, and in that way do what he
could to keep the world from becoming a diminished thing.

∾

"On the Move"
in Polynesia:
Omoo as Picaresque Novel

Because *Typee* and its successor, *Omoo: A Narrative of Adventures in the South Seas* (1847), are both presented as travel narratives based on the author's own experiences in Polynesia, critics have usually judged the two works by the same formal standards, even when acknowledging that there are important differences between them. Some commentators have preferred Melville's second book to his first for its sharply drawn characters, its racy humor, or its free-spirited bonhomie. But the Aristotelian standard of unity has had such a firm hold on critics of Melville's early fiction that most have finally judged *Omoo* to be a lesser artistic achievement than *Typee*. For them, Melville's first book, whatever its other faults might be, is sufficiently unified to be considered an artistic success, while his second is so loosely structured and episodic as to be considered an artistic failure, in spite of its charms.[1]

Yet the two books are radically different—not just in structure but in incident and character, style and tone—enough so to suggest that Melville was working in each case from different models and with distinct aims. Unlike the captivity romance *Typee*, which is by definition suspenseful, melodramatic, and end-dominated, *Omoo* is rambling, leisurely, and open-ended, its title character not the wide-eyed, sometimes dreamy, sometimes anxious adventurer of *Typee* but a carefree, down-at-the-heels wanderer—a nineteenth-century American version of the picaro. Autobiographical works of quite different design and intention, these narratives should not be measured by the same Aristotelian standard. The conventional test of unity is appropriate for *Typee*, but it is hardly the right standard to apply to a picaresque work like *Omoo*.

In his own remarks about *Omoo,* Melville more than once emphasized that, as he wrote to his English publisher John Murray, it was "of a totally different character than 'Typee.'" Anxious to secure the favor of Murray for his new work by promoting it as a worthy sequel to his popular first one, Melville asserted that "This new book begins exactly where Typee [sic] leaves off," but he then went on to declare that it "has no further connection with my first work," and in his preface he repeated both claims almost verbatim. In the same letter to Murray, he went on to say that "It embraces adventures in the South Seas ... and includes an eventful cruise in an English Colonial Whaleman (A Sydney Ship) and a comical residence on the island of Tahiti. The time is about four months, but I & my narrative are both on the move during that short period."[2] To be sure, these remarks hardly constitute a systematic assessment of the author's intentions, but Melville's emphasis on the episodic nature of his adventures, on the comic mood of the piece, and, most significantly, on his own free-spirited movement from place to place in the narrative, all provide important clues to the distinctive character of his second book and to his ruling conception of it as well. Together they suggest that Melville thought of *Omoo* as a narrative in the popular picaresque mode.[3]

Since D. H. Lawrence first used the word to describe *Omoo* in the early 1920s, the book itself and any number of its features have been characterized by the term "picaresque," but critics have always employed the word casually, never in any systematic or theoretical way.[4] Though its title and subtitle, with references to "roving" and "adventures," would seem rather naturally to point to *Omoo's* place in the picaresque genre, the critical reception of the book includes no detailed examination of its similarities with the many prominent works in this form, a form that constitutes one of the oldest, most vital traditions in the history of narrative.[5] Yet the similarities are many and substantial—beyond the episodic, loosely ordered plot, which most commentators have recognized.

What is just as telling, but rarely mentioned, is that it also features lusty, peripatetic characters with a powerful aversion to work—down-and-out types who live by their wits rather than their diligence or strength, take great pleasure in playing crude tricks, and excel (if they can be said to excel at anything at all) only at outfoxing an array of foolish authority figures. The book also maintains a typically comic, fun-loving mood throughout most of the story and takes a satiric view of the quirks and foibles, the excesses and iniquities of the people they encounter in the host culture. And, like many of the early, generally rawer picaresque novels, it more than hints at a darker side, too, as its heroes are shown to be living on the edge of disorder and corruption and to be threatened with ruin and death.

To be sure, the autobiographical basis of Melville's story forced him to depart from certain conventions of the genre and to tone down or reformulate others. To be consistent with his own experience in the South Seas, he had, for example, to abbreviate the customary "life" of the picaro to a brief period in his own life story. And as a recently established and at least marginally respectable author of travel narrative, he had to portray himself in the complex guise of a rather well-scrubbed version of the rogue. However, the resemblances of Melville's second book to earlier picaresque narratives are otherwise deep and pervasive, so much so as to place *Omoo* securely in the picaresque tradition.

What did Melville know about the picaresque form? Beyond what can be deduced about the subject from a close reading of *Omoo* itself, it can be determined, by piecing together various bits of evidence, that Melville's familiarity with the literature of the picaresque tradition, at the time he wrote his second novel, was quite extensive—surprisingly so, given that it has been so little noticed. Melville apparently never kept a regular record of his reading or a journal or notebook, but in general it is known that, from his early youth onward, he was an avid, wide-ranging reader with a special fondness for standard authors—American, British, and Continental (in translation). It is known, too, that, lacking the means to compile a sizable library of his own, he made a habit of raiding the shelves of his relatives and friends and gained access, either on his own or with the help of others, to a series of membership libraries and reading rooms in Albany, Lansingburgh, New York City, and Boston.[6]

More to the point, it is clear from several references in his early works and other sources that he was familiar with several important titles in the picaresque genre. Besides an incidental allusion in *Omoo* to Cervantes's *Don Quixote*, the most famous example of the form, there is a significant reference to Butler's *Hudibras*, which had been modeled after Cervantes's work (one sign of Long Ghost's learning, it is said, is his "repeating poetry by the canto, especially Hudibras"). More importantly, there is a reference to "three volumes" of Smollett's picaresque novels, which the Partoowye host of Omoo and the Doctor offered the two wanderers to help while away their time.[7] Expressing joy at the memory of having "these romances" on hand during their idle stay there, the narrator exclaims: "Amelia!—Peregrine!—you hero of rogues, Count Fathom!—what a debt we owe you!"[8] Since he knew enough about Smollett's novels to suggest they had prompted the Doctor's decision to "lay siege to the heart of little Loo" during their stay in Partoowye, it seems certain that Melville had more than a passing acquaintance with these works (293).

It is equally telling, I believe, that Melville's interest in the writings of Smollett, the most prominent British writer of picaresque fiction, surfaced

again several times in the years immediately following the publication of *Omoo*. This can be seen in the fact that Melville refers knowingly, in *Redburn*, to "the exaggerated sailors of Smollett" (presumably in *Peregrine* but perhaps also in *The Adventures of Roderick Random*) and, in *White-Jacket*, to Count Fathom and to *Peregrine Pickle*. It cannot be determined whether Melville owned any of these works in the early years of his career, but in 1850, according to Merton Sealts, he did borrow Smollett's *Roderick Random* from the well-stocked library of his friend, Evert Duyckinck.[9]

In the same year, Melville also borrowed from Duyckinck the anonymous *Lazarillo de Tormes*, widely recognized as the first picaresque novel. Just the year before, while on his London trip, Melville had picked up a translation of an early successor to *Lazarillo*, namely, Mateo Aleman's *Guzman de Alfarache*, so he obviously had an interest in early Spanish examples of the form, too, an interest that may, of course, have developed even before these titles enter the Melville record. Still another, and, I think, more promising, source is Alain René Lesage's *The Adventures of Gil Blas of Santillane*, the best known of the French picaresque novels and cited by Melville in *White-Jacket*, along with *Peregrine Pickle* and an unspecified volume of Goldsmith, as an example of the kind of "merrily-bound" book that is capable of driving off the spleen just by looking at it.[10] If Melville read *Gil Blas*, as it seems he did, it is possible, of course, that he had done so by the time he wrote *Omoo*. As I will be arguing shortly, Melville's book has closer parallels with the lighter, more upbeat, middle- and upper-class tales of Smollett and Lesage than with the dark and despairing, low-life stories of their Spanish precursors, whose protagonists typically mirror, in their own lives and personalities, the chaos of their wretched environments.

Like most picaresque stories, *Omoo* is an autobiographical tale narrated from a first-person, retrospective point of view. In his preface, Melville emphasizes this fact, saying that the first of his two subjects, namely, the life of sperm-whale fishery sailors in the South Seas, is presented by means of "a circumstantial history of adventures befalling the author," and that his second, the "present condition of the converted Polynesians" after half a century of contact with foreigners, is set forth by means of "a familiar [i.e., personal] account" (xiii). Melville's relation to his picaresque subject matter, however, is complex. He was himself both an insider, a wandering rogue or "omoo" who actually knocked about for a while in the South Seas, and an outsider, an American gentleman who never lost touch with his home and returned to it with his principles and class standing still more or less intact. As a result, he had to build an all-but-contradictory case for his credibility as an observer and reformer: without losing hold of the fundamental values of his Anglo-American

audience—respectability, honesty, sexual virtue—he had to adopt the foot-
loose picaro's experiential test of truth. Otherwise he would have no hope of
effectively undercutting the orthodox or official version of the truth. These
two positions, which are more or less continuously in conflict in the narrative, constitute the principal tension that defines the narrator's voice. For what
Melville's experience had taught him—namely, that foreign influence was
corrupting, indeed destroying, the inhabitants of Polynesia—is at odds with
the official version of the truth held by most of his readership.

The job Melville set for himself in writing this book, then, was to reshape
public opinion in such a way as to diminish the force of previous foreign
influence in the South Sea Islands by substituting his own version of the truth
for the popular, authorized one. It is because Melville managed at least some
of the time to exercise the restraint typical of his class that he never perfectly
fits the mold of the lusty picaro. But it is because he also permitted himself a
certain freedom from this same restraint while engaged in his adventures—
because he always allowed himself to live at the edge of the amoral picaresque
experience—that he was able to put together something more accurate, and
telling, than the orthodox version of the truth concerning the course of events
in Polynesia in the years leading up to his own visit there.

Narrative stance aside, Melville's hero follows in the footsteps of the picaro
or low-life "scamp" in several key ways. Most important is the simple fact of
his poverty, which forces him into a life of aimless wandering and menial tasks
as he tries to keep body and soul together. A rootless "sailor before the mast"
and South Sea Island "rover," he is financially destitute and, like the picaro,
lacks the advantages of *hidalgo*—the inheritance or family connections one
needs to gain a position or trade and the means of financial independence (3,
xiv).[11] To survive, therefore, he has to learn to live by his wits and to take life
more or less as it comes, never worrying overmuch about the right and wrong
of his own behavior. While the life of a sailor does hold the potential for steady
work, and some hope for advancement, Melville's autobiographical hero demonstrates the typical picaro's resistance to authority and curiosity about the
wider world, and this combination keeps him from staying in any one job for
very long. Thus like the standard picaro, Omoo remains entrenched in the
lower classes, living a virtually hand-to-mouth existence. He may never actually starve, but he never knows real plenty, either on the *Julia,* where the foul
provisions are strictly rationed by a mean-spirited captain, or on the seemingly abundant islands of Tahiti and Imeeo, where he must work or steal or
ingratiate himself with one of his local hosts if he wants a square meal.

It is true that Omoo, early in his story, reveals he has a home and friends
and claims it was his "most ardent hope" at the time of his rescue from Typee

valley to return to them (7). But it cannot be said that he therefore voluntarily subjects himself to the precarious way of life he encounters in the South Seas. He is not simply "slumming," safe in the knowledge that he has a home where his needs will be taken care of once he tires of his adventures in Polynesia. Like the true picaro, he is forced, by circumstance and his own willful personality, to live a rootless life in search of some means of survival.

Why he wishes to return to the United States—to renew old ties? to make a try at settling down? or to begin a career?—and whether he wishes to go back for good or just for a short visit, these are questions that are never answered in *Omoo,* and neither the facts of Melville's biography nor the data of his other autobiographical writings shed much light on them, important as they are to an understanding of his decision to become a writer. Certainly by the end of *Omoo,* when he signs on the *Leviathan* "for the coming cruise" and no more, thus leaving open the possibility of "journeying home by short and easy stages," the title character is in no rush to return to America (315). Because, therefore, the advantages of returning home are nowhere spelled out, and because, too, his desire to get back cools considerably once he regains his freedom, Omoo's early hope of getting back to America seems essentially a remnant of the intense longing he experienced while imprisoned by the Typees. There is no sign that he expects his homecoming will lead to financial security or otherwise give him reason to quit his rovings.[12]

Like the picaro, who shows striking similarities to the "isolatoes" of Melville's fiction generally, Omoo tries repeatedly to bring an end to his poverty and alienation; this is, in fact, what prompts his Polynesian adventures in the first place. But, again like the picaro, he never manages to achieve the stability he longs for. Only in the end, when he escapes the South Sea Islands on an American whaler, is there even a hint that the cycle of his chaotic adventuring might be broken. But without going outside the narrative and looking at Melville's own biography, readers of the book can hardly be sure that it will be.

In other respects, Omoo's character follows the script of the conventional rogue—not its earlier, harder incarnation as "evil liver" but its later, softer one as "lovable scamp." For example, he shows a typical aversion to work, as seen in the comic episode at Zeke's potato plantation on Imeeo and in his eagerness to rely on the hospitality of a series of island hosts, sometimes for days at a time, for bed and board.[13] And, like Huck Finn, he even on occasion turns thief, as when he and Long Ghost make a "sly, nocturnal visit" to a whaleship anchored in Papeetee harbor to retrieve some contraband for a picnic or when they are forced to "kidnap" some pigs to satisfy their hunger (160–61, 197). But he is hardly a dyed-in-the-wool thief, and he never engages in confidence games or other criminal behavior, except of the most marginal kind, like the

picaro. In this latter category, he does take part in the illegal "strike" of the *Julia*'s crew, and he spends some time in the Calabooza Beretanee on Tahiti as a result. He has a hearty taste for the liquor then forbidden on the islands, and he shows a real eagerness to witness the outlawed "hevar," or native dance, in the village of Tamai. But these instances aside, he pretty much abides by the law throughout his adventures. On a few occasions he does try to gull people, as when he joins his fellow prisoners in claiming to be Catholic so they might gain "a mouthful to eat, and something generous to drink" from the French priest on Tahiti (144). But these relatively few instances do not really make him the practiced liar familiar to readers of picaresque fiction.

Melville's Omoo may be a "bad boy" on occasion, practicing harmless peccadilloes and casting an excited eye on native beauties when he gets the opportunity, but there is another side to him—a bit straitlaced, even prudish—that is at odds with the spirited, fun-loving manner he sometimes shows. D. H. Lawrence's well-known portrayal of the Melville of *Omoo* as "the gallant rascally epicurian, eating the world like a snipe," is not far from the mark, but it is an exaggeration. While Melville probably was at "his happiest, in *Omoo*," as Lawrence claimed, I think it's not quite true, as Lawrence also said, that "For once he is careless of his actions, careless of his morals, careless of his ideals."[14]

One clear measure of Lawrence's overstatement is the fact that Melville's autobiographical character is not so careless a figure as Long Ghost, the companion and friend whose love of pranks, shifting personality, and devil-may-care attitude make him the true picaresque center of the novel. While he takes pleasure in the Doctor's many capers, as when he hoists the men aloft during their sleep, Omoo is never seen to initiate such pranks himself. It is clear he feels too tenderly for the suffering of his fellows ever to want to cause them harm or pain, even in good fun. By his own admission, for instance, he "always made a point of befriending poor Ropey," the soft-hearted landlubber on the *Julia*, when he sees he is the butt of the others' jokes (55). And he goes out of his way to make it known that he objects to the merrymaking of the healthy members of the crew as long as there are invalids on board the ship. Such sensitivity is hardly to be discovered in the typical picaro, especially the early Spanish picaro, whose daily experience is so threatening, and whose personality, as a consequence, is so unstable, as to make any display of concern for others impossible. Such displays are, however, in evidence in the later French and English picaros of Lesage and Smollett, particulary Gil Blas and Roderick Random, who in fact can be distinguished from their Spanish predecessors by their capacity for love.[15]

Omoo's preoccupation with the feelings of others is just one sign of a ruling mindfulness or prudence that is almost everywhere apparent in his character.

Several times, in fact, he is shown (sometimes along with the generally more prankish Long Ghost) to be more sober-minded than almost everyone else around him. He is the only one, for instance, to rouse himself from sleep and save the *Julia* on the night when Bembo, still fuming over an altercation earlier in the day, furiously tries to crash the ship on a coral reef. And when the crew threatens mutiny at one point, after learning of their dying captain's plan to have himself dropped off on shore before sending them all back out to sea without him, it is Omoo, with assistance from the Doctor, who "labored hard to diffuse the right spirit among the crew; impressing upon them that a little patience and management would, in the end, accomplish all that their violence could" (73). When these remonstrations fail to quiet the sailors, it is Omoo who proposes that a "Round Robin" detailing their grievances should be prepared and sent ashore to the consul with the hope that he would intervene on their behalf (74). And when this tactic brings no results, and the drunken crew moves to go out on "strike," it is Omoo who steps in to propose a more temperate course of action. Knowing that "if anything untoward happened to the vessel," the crew could be brought to trial, he attempts to exercise a leaderly role by openly declaring his intention to do what he could to bring the *Julia* safely into harbor, an action that is soon seconded by Long Ghost (98). It can hardly be said that Melville portrays Omoo as a devil-may-care picaro in such scenes; on the contrary, he is shown to be the most level-headed figure of all, the major proponent, along with the Doctor, of sanity and order.[16]

Even so, Omoo and Long Ghost are not so removed from the spirit of the picaro as to lend their support to the foolish and unjust officials who rule their world. They maintain their independence socially and politically, at the margins of the dominant culture. When they choose to become voices of moderation and good sense, or what passes for such in this sometimes absurd and topsy-turvy world, they do so for purely practical, self-interested reasons: they want no "trouble" with the authorities (70). As Omoo explains, "I felt that I was under a foreign flag; that an English consul was close at hand, and that sailors seldom obtain justice. It was best to be prudent." Like conventional picaros, he and Long Ghost use their wits not to uphold the law but to stay clear of it.[17]

Here, too, however, Omoo is a somewhat more complex figure than the standard heroes of earlier picaresque fiction. For, while it is true that in several instances he tries to stay out of trouble with the law, in others, and under other circumstances, he feels compelled to go out of his way to oppose it, even though by doing so he is likely to get into hot water. Indeed, in the instance discussed above concerning the threat of mutiny, he admits to sympathizing so deeply with the men, "so far, at least, as their real grievances are

concerned," that "if need be" he "stood ready to raise a hand" with them (73).

He does not simply move with the flow of life, "becoming what life asks of him at each moment," as Stuart Miller, in *The Picaresque Novel,* says of the conventional picaro.[18] He is willing to take a stand on principle, on his inherent sense of what is right and just. Though obviously concerned for the survival of himself and his fellows, should the badly decaying *Julia* be forced back to sea without a proper commander, Omoo concludes that in this case "unconditional submission" to the will of Captain Guy and the British consul was "out of the question" on moral grounds (84). Like the picaresque heroes of Smollett and Lesage, Omoo departs from the earlier Spanish models in possessing noble qualities in addition to roguish ones.[19]

As events turn out, however, Melville's title character is never required to sacrifice himself to the sailors' cause. The world of *Omoo* is finally too comic, and too benign, to hold any real potential for tragic sacrifice. Except in this episode of the threatened mutiny, and one or two other smaller incidents, Melville's hero pretty much "takes life as it comes," as Lawrence observed.[20] Among the important signs of Omoo's acquiescence is the fact that, like some of the best known picaros, he engages in a good deal of shape-shifting in response to new opportunities or circumstances. In the beginning, to cite the most dramatic example, he is forced, following his rescue at Typee bay, to undergo a disorienting transformation from the wild-looking, hirsute "king of the cannibals" to a properly attired, properly barbered sailor (8).

Though known throughout the *Julia* episode by the fictitious name of "Typee" (sailors, Melville explains in connection with the signing of the Round Robin, often take their name from "the name of the place from which they hailed"), Omoo's identity in the first half of the book remains that of an unusually literate and intelligent sailor and the "chosen associate" of the popular Long Ghost (74, 37). However, when he and the Doctor decide to make their way to Zeke's plantation on Imeeo, the first stop in their careers as "omoos," they adopt new identities with the absurdly inapt names of Paul and Peter. As "mutineers" on the *Julia,* escapees from the local calabooza, and enemies of the English consul, Omoo and the Doctor have the conventional picaro's reasons for wanting to be sure to cover their trail. In taking the names of two of Christ's Apostles to hide their identities from the local authorities, it is clear they also have the conventional picaro's irreverent love of satire and mischievous fun.

Omoo, however, does not change names, or wardrobes, often enough to qualify as a "failed identity," to borrow the term coined by Alexander Blackburn in *The Myth of the Picaro* to describe the breakdown in personality that sometimes occurs as a result of the picaresque hero's relentless shape-shifting.[21]

The only other time Melville's narrator assumes a new role is when he and the Doctor, after tiring of the work on Zeke's plantation, decide to travel to Taloo to offer themselves as candidates for "some splendid opening" in the official court of the Queen (246). It is on this occasion that Long Ghost, with his old Panama hat shaped like a "Spanish sombrero" and a native "Roora" fashioned like a "poncho," adopts the look of "a mendicant grandee"—a look that places him squarely in the classical picaresque tradition. Omoo, on the other hand, decides on a very different look, donning instead an "Eastern turban" made out of a gay calico frock of the Doctor's, an outlandish creation with pendant sleeves that earns him the humorous sobriquet of "the Bashaw with Two Tails" (235-36).[22]

His costume aside, because he assumes just a few distinct identities in the course of his adventures, Omoo is more akin to Lesage's relatively integrated picaresque hero, Gil Blas, than he is to the early Spanish picaros or even the later protean figures of Smollett. Though he modifies his appearance from time to time, and even changes names and occupations, he still remains— whether as sailor, day laborer, beachcomber, or court supplicant—entirely recognizable to the reader as the same personality.[23]

As already hinted, it is because he is a reasonably stable personality that Melville's narrator has the capacity for friendship, even love, so lacking in the more desperate, early Spanish picaros. The two—stability and friendworthi-ness—are closely related. Certainly it is true that Cervantes's famous examples, Don Quixote and Sancho Panza, have given the picaro the reputation of be-ing an amiable, as well as loyal and loving, sort of character; but Cervantes's creations are a relatively late development in the history of the picaro. In fact the first picaros, starting with Lazarillo de Tormes, were such alienated and unstable figures, and the worlds they lived in were so threatening and danger-ous, as to make them wary of any kind of potential companionship or mutual dependence.

By contrast, Omoo is neither deeply alienated nor emotionally undepend-able. Despite his learning and his sometimes cautious manner—traits that tend to distinguish him from the rest of the Julia's crew—Melville's narrator is readily accepted into their ranks from the start, a fact that is symbolized by an old sailor's "politely" offering to share his pipe with him on his first night on board ship (7). And he quickly finds himself on unusually good terms with the cosmopolitan Doctor, whose companionship, among the rude sail-ors, he finds "an absolute godsend" (12). He is not above trying to trick his new friend now and then, as when he convinces the inexperienced Long Ghost to do all the hard work of paddling their canoe on one memorable occasion, while he himself sits in the stern idly steering. But at other times during their

rovings, he shows genuine brotherliness by helping to keep the rakish Doctor out of harm's way and, in the end, after signing on the *Leviathan*, by splitting his advance wages with him.

As important as the fact of their friendship is the spirit in which the two men enter into it. Omoo and the Doctor come together not out of any weakness but out of strength; they have no neurotic need for one another, nothing beyond the natural desire for good fellowship. They enjoy each other's company and, despite the tricks they sometimes play on one another, they show mutual kindness and respect. Yet each has enough independence to go his own way, either briefly, as at Tamai—where Omoo's impetuous curiosity leads him into an "inglorious" adventure with a little old clothesman who approaches them one night, while the Doctor, who is much annoyed by the old man, goes his separate way—or permanently, as at the end (244). Unlike Zeke and Shorty, and other more famous picaresque pairs, Omoo and Long Ghost seem the exception which proves the rule that, as Omoo says, "no two men were ever united in any enterprise, without one getting the upper hand of the other" (204).

Sometimes the Doctor is the one who initiates their adventures, and sometimes it is Omoo who does so. Yet whenever either of them begins to lord it over the other, as when the Doctor assumes "airs of superiority" over Omoo to gain a soft superintendent's post with Zeke, they are quick to mend their differences (231–32). Through their loyalty to one another, they form a bond that saves them from the lonely fate of the early picaros and strengthens them to meet the difficulties that life throws in their way. But it is never the kind of bond that constrains either man's natural identity or forces him to compromise his personal integrity.

In his portrayal of his fun-loving pair of heroes, Melville seems to have followed the example of Lesage's *Gil Blas* more closely than any other earlier picaresque novel. Like *Gil Blas, Omoo* tells the story of a relatively stable title character who finally escapes the life of chaos that threatens to overwhelm him and of a second, more conventional picaro, like Lesage's Don Raphael, who seems destined never to extricate himself from it. Here as elsewhere, then, Long Ghost, more than Omoo, follows in the tradition of the earlier, darker picaresque heroes. Among other things, like these earlier figures, he has a highly embroidered, generally questionable past. While he "threw out hints of a patrimonial estate, a nabob uncle, and an unfortunate affair which sent him a-roving," his early history, we are told, "was enveloped in the profoundest obscurity." A professed world traveler, he was also a great raconteur: in "the easiest way imaginable, he could refer to an amour he had in Palermo, his lion hunting before breakfast among the Caffres, and the quality of the coffee to be

drunk in Muscat" (12). Most important of all, he is seen to be an unusually accomplished shape-shifter. Repeatedly he responds to new circumstances by calling up new talents, both real and feigned, and these inspire him to lay claim to an almost unimaginable array of identities and occupations—as doctor, "gentleman in distress" (78), devoted "gallant" (178), cook, island trader, navigator, lecturer, English teacher, manufacturer, landscape gardener, festival promoter, gentleman pensioner of state, fiddler, "pious young man" (282), and sailor—though, as might be expected, he regards anything involving honest toil, such as the field work on Zeke's plantation, as "a scrape" to be avoided at all cost (205).

Besides being a wonderfully inventive prankster, in the *Julia* and the calabooza episodes especially, the Doctor also plays the lecherous rake and freeloader in practically every village they visit on Tahiti and Imeeo. More of a sensualist generally than Omoo (who seems to be driven by simple curiosity as much as anything), Long Ghost "was always on the alert" for something to eat, and, though hardly a lush like Jermin, he is not above getting "mellow" on an old hermit's "Arva Tee," despite its offensive smell (132, 174). And in the end, when he decides to "tarry awhile" in Imeeo, he seems fated to follow his picaresque career forever, never quite taking hold anywhere or striking out purposefully in any single direction, while Omoo, by contrast, begins his leisurely return home (315).

Melville evidently sensed that an amusing figure like Long Ghost might run away with his tale, for he at one point voices reluctance to bring him "too often upon the stage" (193–94). But even so, the Doctor serves an indispensable function. As the book's principal example of "evil living," he is the one who provides most of its picaresque entertainment.[24] His presence thus frees Melville's narrator to maintain a relatively respectable demeanor, the kind required of a credible commentator on South Sea Island life. Melville's intention in *Omoo*, as he announced in his preface, was to delight *and* to instruct, and in particular to instruct about "the present condition of the converted Polynesians, as affected by their promiscuous intercourse with foreigners, and the teachings of the missionaries, combined" (xiii). Clearly it would not do for a bona fide scamp or wastrel to be the one to carry out the latter of these two functions. No matter that Melville's strategy of dividing his objectives between his two protagonists seems generally to have failed, for readers in his own time and since. So compelling has his portrayal of the raffish Long Ghost proved to be that Omoo himself, and Melville along with him, has usually been judged not on his own terms but by the company he kept, precisely as he felt Wilson and the other foreigners in Papeetee had judged him (103, 166–67).

As I have taken some pains to show, Omoo's own actions during his adventures are not exactly above reproach; he was, and had to be, like Whitman in "Song of Myself," "both in and out of the game."[25] But he is hardly guilty of the picaresque kind of loose living that William O. Bourne accused him of in an outraged letter to the *New-York Daily Tribune* of October 2, 1847, an attack that, though more heated than most, captures the most common early objections to Melville's book. As Bourne's exaggerations and a single attempt at bitter irony make clear, Melville had good reason to want to guard his public image in *Omoo* by carefully presenting himself as the relatively respectable, prudent young man he in fact appears to have been. For his treatment of the missionaries in Polynesia, which constituted this reviewer's chief complaint against Melville's work, soon led Bourne to erupt in a convulsive *ad hominem* attack:

> From a consideration of the whole subject I pronounce Mr. Melville's book, so far as its pretended facts are concerned, a tissue of uninformed misrepresentations, of prejudiced ignorance, and of hostility characteristic of one who loves South Sea adventure for South Sea abandonment and "*independence.*" His caricatures of the Missionaries, whether in the pulpit or surrounded by a crowd of gaping natives—his contempt for constituted authorities and the consuls and officers—his insubordination—his skulking in the dark where he could not be seen by decent men—his choice of low society—his frequent draughts of "Pisco" or other liquors—his gentle associations with Tahitian and Marquesan damsels—and the unsullied purity of his life and conversation, all entitle him to rank as a man, where his absurdities and misstatements place him as a writer—the shameless herald of his own wantonness, and the pertinacious traducer of loftier and better men.[26]

Omoo does *seem* to have more of a picaro's loose spirit than he turns out, in point of fact, to have, for the simple reason that he is usually seen in the company of the mischievous Doctor. But it is true, too, that he seems even more like one of those picaresque figures who indulge in "evil living" because the world he moves through is so clearly "fallen," so deteriorated and corrupt, so blighted by mischief-making and falsity. Both the *Julia*, the scene of the early chapters, and the South Sea Islands, the scene of the later ones, are portrayed as being in such advanced states of disorder and decay as to abound in subjects fit for satire, and satire is the picaresque writer's stock in trade. Images of chaos

in *Omoo* are, in fact, so pervasive and exaggerated, so deeply comic, as to reveal that Melville possessed a more sophisticated artistic consciousness at this early stage of his career than has generally been thought. For although he has been widely recognized, since the publication of Edward H. Rosenberry's *Melville and the Comic Spirit* in 1957, to have possessed a rich comic sensibility, Melville's talents as a satiric writer have usually been thought to be a development of the period immediately after *Omoo*, that is, starting with the publication of *Mardi* (1848).

From the moment of his first sighting of the *Julia* as it lies off the bay of Typee, Omoo calls attention to the fact that everything about her suggests "an ill state of affairs aboard" (5). The ship itself, once an American privateer but since condemned, sold at auction, and fitted out in Sydney as a whaler, is "very old" (older by several years, in Melville's retelling, than the *Lucy Ann*, the boat that had rescued him), a "slatternly looking craft," and, despite some repairs, "still in a miserable plight," various parts of her being described as "unsound," "worn," "rotten," "patched," and "blistered" (5, 9).[27] The bunks are "mere wrecks" (38); the provisions are old and worm infested, having been sold at auction as "condemned" sometime earlier in Sydney (14); and the crew's quarters are overrun with rats and cockroaches. What time and nature and the skinflinty ways of the ship's owners have not yet ruined with their corrupting touch, the reckless crew is busily destroying, the cook, for example, "frequently helping himself to splinters for kindling-wood from the bitts and beams" of the decaying forecastle (39).

The crew, too, is in a terribly deteriorated, disordered state. Nearly a dozen of the original thirty-two have deserted; and of the rest, more than half are in poor health. Indeed, two of the latter soon die, thus escalating the fear among the others about remaining at sea in a dilapidated craft under an invalided captain. (Here, too, Melville seems to have exaggerated the historical facts of his story to dramatize the chaotic state of affairs on the *Julia*, for these same two sailors are known later to have been very much alive as Melville's shipmates on the *United States*.)[28] Because the captain, too, is sick and confined to his cabin, and generally incompetent besides (as Melville caricatures him, he gained his position through "favoritism" and was "no more meant for the sea than a hair-dresser"), life on the vessel is frequently "in a state of the greatest uproar" (10, 13).

Not only is there no regular discipline on board, but the captain's corrupt policy further excites the already mutinous mood of the crew by keeping them in a permanent state of drunkenness. For, out of fear of the men, he orders a steady supply of the ruinous Pisco for them in the hope that they will not cause trouble about the *Julia*'s many deficiencies. Even the officers who are

left in charge contribute to the general chaos: Jermin, the hearty first mate, often runs about the decks in an intoxicated state "making himself heard at all hours"; and Bembo, the New Zealand harpooner, frequently wakes the others in the middle of the night by "dancing some cannibal fandango" on the deck of the forecastle (13). Though Jermin's bluff manner manages, most of the time, to hold the crew "in some sort of noisy subjection," fights break out, desertions continue, and the unruly crew erupts at the slightest provocation with insolent talk, derisive shouts, irreverant pranks, and even blatant acts of insubordination (14).

While the absence of discipline, the debilitated state of the ship and the crew, and the unpredictable navigation of Jermin are all cause for alarm for Omoo and Long Ghost, the disorder on the *Julia* tends to be presented in the fun-loving mood of low comedy. Pranks and pratfalls, quarrels and shouting, drunken outbursts and noisy merrymaking all occur so frequently as to keep up an almost endless round of crazy, slapstick activity on the ship. When, for example, a party of sailors suddenly deserts ship at Hytyhoo under the cover of Jermin's sotted snoring, they scuttle one boat and cut the tackles on the other, so when Bembo leaps into it the next morning to give chase, his weight drops it crashing to the sea and he gets a good dunking. Later, when Jermin hauls out his rusty quadrant to try to make a reckoning that requires two observers rather than just one, he is said to be so pie-eyed that he can manage the operation all by himself, "inasmuch as he generally saw things double" (61–62). And later still, when Jermin and the consul leave the ship off Papeetee, after informing the men that they must soon return to sea without a proper captain, the sailors run "about deck like madmen" and perform all manner of pranks—some chopping the fastenings of the mainstay with an axe, others smashing a handspike through the cabin skylight, and still others dancing a hornpipe on the forecastle (84–85).

As such scenes of low comedy make clear, the world of *Omoo* is of a piece with the fallen world of picaresque fiction, in action, character, and mood. Here are found men whose consciousness has been so altered by drink or sensuality, by madness or despair, that they take on the grotesque shapes of dreams and nightmares, the natural province of the picaresque mode. In *Omoo* the alteration is frequently represented by characters assuming the forms of animals. Thus the bluff Jermin has a laugh that "looked absolutely sharkish" (11); the ugly sailor called Beauty is described as being "like a couple of yards of boa-constrictor" (17); the landlubber named Ropey is said to be treated "like a dog" by the rest of the crew; and the Dane is portrayed as "a mule of a man" (53, 57). Similarly, Baltimore, the cook, is at one point likened to a porpoise (59), Long Ghost to a land crane "consorting with petrels" (78), a nameless

sailor to "an old sea-bear" (54), and the crew in the calabooza to a collection of creatures in the "Zoological Gardens" of a large metropolis (127).

A more significant example of such brutish equations is Lem Hardy, a "renegado from Christendom and humanity" whom the men of the *Julia* encounter in the bay of Hannamanoo. Once a "dog" before the mast, Hardy has abandoned the lowly sailor's life, and in the process of settling on one of the Islands has transformed himself into a "shark," or at least a symbol of one. For in passing himself off among the natives as the war god of Hivarhoo, Hardy has caused a blue shark to be indelibly tattooed on his forehead (27–28). A similar, more melancholy fate—a permanent, dehumanizing metamorphosis into an animal—is experienced by a sailor they encounter on Roorootoo who is wasting away with the mysterious Fa-Fa, or elephantiasis (127–28). Both of these latter figures serve as sobering examples of the potential fate that awaits those who take up the rootless life of the picaro in the South Seas. They become isolated, "taboo" figures who, as a result of the change they undergo, are forever alienated from their true selves and forever banished from their true homes. Like Omoo's friend the Doctor, who is also dehumanized—changed, not into an animal, but into a "ghost," as his nickname repeatedly reminds us—they serve as a warning against what Melville's hero might become if he were to stay too long in the false paradise of Polynesia. Like Long Ghost, they are examples of the strange doppelgänger figure typically found in fiction, such as the picaresque, where "descent" themes are prominent—incarnations, to quote Frye, of "the hero's shadow and the portent of his own death or isolation."[29] It is as Omoo's "shadow" or "double" in Frye's sense—a meaning that is entirely in keeping with the picaresque formula—that the Long Doctor's function in the story can be most fully appreciated.

In the South Sea Islands portion of the narrative, the theme of disorder, so important to the definition of picaresque fiction, is given an equally prominent place as it was in the first part. In fact, it is quite loudly trumpeted at the very outset of this section, when Melville, altering the time of his own arrival at Tahiti to make it coincide with the dramatic moment of the French takeover of the island under Rear Admiral DuPetit Thouars, asserts that, "Owing to the proceedings of the French, every thing in Tahiti was in an uproar" (69, 75).[30] While it is clear he had little sympathy for the role of the French in this whole affair, Melville gives relatively little emphasis to the immediate turmoil caused by the "forced cession" of Tahiti, a fact that can probably be attributed to his not being present at the event (69). Instead, he turns his attention to the crew's comic difficulties with the posturing English consul, Wilson, and uses this scene as the basis for a lengthy polemic on the progressive dete-

rioration of Tahitian life over the course of half a century of foreign rule and
missionary presence generally.

Like other examples of picaresque fiction, *Omoo* contains a deep vein of
social criticism. Throughout the calabooza and island-hopping sections of the
book, Melville sharply satirizes the foibles and malfeasance of a string of authority figures, but he also vigorously protests, in a way entirely free of humor,
the many evidences of decay in the daily life of the natives that he witnessed at
the time of his own visit. While much of the action in the island chapters is in
keeping with the mood of low comedy that characterizes the *Julia* chapters,
much of it, too, is presented in a serious, even at times elegiac, mood in keeping
with Melville's feeling that the original paradisal order of Polynesia, a thing of
real and inimitable value, was slowly being destroyed. Though it is not widely
recognized as such, a vision of paradise, or of a lost order—such as is implied
throughout Melville's assessment of the contemporary South Sea Island scene
(or such as his hero actually encounters when he travels to the village of Tamai,
where Tahitian life remains as it was in Cook's time)—is a standard feature of
picaresque writing. For such a vision is one means by which the general lack of
order in the picaro's world can be dramatically highlighted.

Throughout the island chapters, Melville adopts other stylized motifs commonly used to accentuate the social chaos of the picaresque world. The quack
doctor motif, for example, which Melville would have encountered in *Roderick
Random* in the figure of the self-serving Doctor Mackshane, appears in *Omoo*
in the form of a "mercenary apothecary" named Doctor Johnson, who laces
his prescriptions with liquor to assure their being consumed by the crew so
he can "run up a bill" with the consulate (193, 133). The motif of the polluted
priest, on the other hand, makes its appearance several times, most notably in
Melville's claim that "in most cases" conversions of the islanders have been
compromised by promises of "some worldly benefit" to their chiefs or in his
hinting that the French priests have taken their first converts, "a set of trim
little native handmaidens," for concubines (187, 142).

Still another popular motif, that of the evil or incompetent magistrate,
which serves to parody the rule of law and propriety, turns up in references to
the economic exploitation of the natives by the French consul, Merenhout
(63), and to the chicanery of DuPetit Thouars and the French governor, Bruat
(123–25). And of course it is evident in the several scenes involving the "unprincipled and dissipated" English consul, Wilson, whose conceit and favoritism toward Captain Guy and Jermin are matched by the fear and impotence
he shows in trying to manage the *Julia*'s headstrong crew (75–76, 113, 146).[31] In
keeping with the picaresque mode, Melville often seizes on a single distinctive

trait in the appearance of a given authority figure and exaggerates it to the point of caricature. Thus all the physical vitality of the skinny first lieutenant of the *Reine Blanche* "seemed exhausted in the production of one enormous moustache," and the French priests wore hats "so preposterously big" that they "seemed extinguishing themselves" (105, 142). Satirical motifs and comic exaggerations such as these provide ludicrously dissonant notes that expose the pretense of official thrummings about the superiority of European culture and its fitness for export to Polynesia.

Melville's chief concern in *Omoo* is not, however, the villainy or foolishness of the Europeans per se but the real harm he believes their presence has caused for the natives of the region and their way of life. The only improvements that European culture has brought to the islands, so far as Melville is able to see, are the new Broom Road, which circumscribes much of Tahiti, and the few new varieties of fruit and cattle left on the island by the expeditions of Cook and Vancouver as well as the improved spiritual prospects of the island population resulting from the missionaries' translation of the Bible into its native tongue.

Wherever else the European touch has been felt by these people, the narrator sees only evidences of decay from a once-thriving and healthy way of life. Alcoholism and diseases of foreign origin, particularly venereal disease, "which now taints the blood of at least two thirds of the common people of the island" of Tahiti, have made for an "amazing decrease" in the population, he says, to just nine thousand people since Cook estimated it (probably erroneously), in 1777, at two hundred thousand (191).[32] Where the natives were once prosperously engaged in a variety of useful occupations, such as the making of tappa, they are now generally idle and suffer a "wretched and destitute mode of life" (189–90). For while they quickly became convinced of the superiority of more costly wares made available by the Europeans, they usually lacked the means to acquire them, and as a consequence they generally had to learn to do without. Even those native arts that have not been abandoned, such as canoe building, have "greatly deteriorated" in the time of the European presence; as Omoo and Long Ghost learn by their own experience one day when they take a spill in such a craft, these canoes "are now the most inelegant, as well as the most insecure of any in the South Seas" (160).

On the other hand, wherever the natives have actively adopted European ways, whether in matters of dress, public decorum, or morality, the result has been simply ludicrous. The women of Tahiti, for instance, following the example of the local missionaries' wives, have taken to wearing "horrid hats" that look like coal scuttles (181), while the men favor a crazy, hodge-podge look. Some might be seen to sport a European-style coat, for example, but no

pantaloons, while others wear a bell-crowned hat and a "girdle," but nothing
in between (182).

Other European values, or systems of values, are shown to be just as incongruous when placed in the context of the islands. In the Cathedral of Papoar
on Tahiti, where Christian services are conducted for the local population, the inhabitants are observed to keep up "an incessant buzzing" on any given Sunday, even during the sermon (171). At the trial of an infamous former naval officer in Partoowye, about five hundred eager witnesses are said to take turns shouting out evidence, while the rest keep up "an incessant jabbering" (300). And mass conversions, such as the famed Great Revival at the Sandwich Islands in 1836, are often known, Melville says, to be followed by "an almost instantaneous relapse into every kind of licentiousness" (174).

In short, rather than being saved by exposure to European ways, the Tahitians are "far worse off now, than formerly," in Melville's view. Arguing that their "prospects are hopeless"—that indeed, in the words of an old Tahitian chant, "man shall cease"—Melville offers an explanation for the widespread, increasing instability of Tahitian culture that is a complete reversal of Leo Marx's well-known "middle ground" theory of the sentimental pastoral ideal when he says that the islanders furnish "a marked illustration of a principle, which history has always exemplified," whereby "all that is corrupt in barbarism and civilization unite, to the exclusion of the virtues of either state." Thus, "like other uncivilized beings, brought into contact with Europeans, they must here remain stationary until utterly extinct" (192).[33]

Without any hope of restoring the old Edenic order among the islands, Omoo sees no prospect of a life for himself there either. The picaresque world of Polynesia is a world in ruins. It promises an outsider like himself nothing but the chance to succumb to its chaos, as the conventional picaro mirrors, internally, the chaos of his social environment. Though he takes great pleasure in his days in the sun, drifting and having fun, and though he shows that—like the later, more up-beat picaresque heroes of Cervantes, Lesage, and Smollett—he can live in a dissolute environment at least for a time without becoming debauched by it, Omoo learns that he cannot stay there without being irrevocably harmed by it.[34]

Without, of course, his quite realizing it, Omoo's Polynesian experience becomes a test of his already-formed character as an American youth of prudence, integrity, and purpose, a test from which he emerges, in the end, more or less unscathed, with his early moral training still intact. Certainly, as a consequence of his adventures, he has learned something important about the world's corruption. He can also be said to have learned something important

about life's pleasure, enough so that he is no longer quite the prude or the worrywart he sometimes shows himself to be early in his adventure. But he cannot be said to have engaged in such "evil living" as to require that he reform his ways; he has no need to try to escape the fate of the hardened picaro. Rather, like the later, sunnier picaros, Gil Blas and Roderick Random, whose status as heroes in a romance is miraculously restored to them at the end of their adventures, Omoo quickly returns to himself and then simply closes the book on the Polynesian chapter of his life. His real identity as a worthy man of noble blood—an American!—is fortuitously recognized, and his escape assured, when the one true authority figure in the book, the "free-hearted" American captain of the "good ship" *Leviathan,* then anchored in Taloo harbor and in need of crew, makes a simple, first-hand test of the strength of Omoo's heartbeat and proclaims him "a Yankee, every beat of my [i.e., Omoo's] pulse!" (289, 314–15). Any doubts about his identity thus removed, the Captain then permits Melville's hero to sign onto his ship for the coming cruise.

This scene of recognition, which reverses the opening scene wherein Omoo began his descent into chaos by signing on the ill-starred *Julia,* provides the kind of romantic moral to the story that Melville's youthful American audience would have greatly favored. But in portraying the release of a good man from threatening circumstances, it also mirrors the ending of such picaresque writings as Lesage's and Smollett's, wherein the hero enjoys a newfound freedom and the promise of some success, though everything around him moves toward tragic dissolution. In ending on the optimistic note of its title character's escape from trouble, *Omoo* marks its departure from the open-ended form of the early Spanish picaresque novel, which typically leaves its hero stranded, face to face with life's anarchy, to be released only in death.[35]

Though the form of Melville's novel is picaresque in being episodic from the first chapter to the last, it does not simply come to a stop at some arbitrary point. With Omoo's escape from the South Sea Islands in the final pages and the prospect of his soon returning home, it comes to a "proper" or conventional conclusion. His role as an American sailor restored, he can give up the temporary identity that had been thrust on him as a poor "omoo." His hope of working his way back home renewed, he can resist the fading enchantments of South Sea Island culture. His memory of home and friends revitalized, he can separate himself from his companion, Long Ghost, the "shadow" figure of folklore, who tempts him to stay and live an irresponsible existence in endless pursuit of pleasure.[36]

Surely the ending of *Omoo* recaptures Melville's own exhilaration at his release from the islands and the restoration of his old self, and not just that of his fictive persona. In his final description of himself, heading out into the

wide Pacific in the *Leviathan,* he suggests that he is already, at least psychologically, happily at home. "Once more," he writes, in a line that anticipates
Whitman's famous "Cradle" poem, "the sailor's cradle rocked under me, and
I found myself rolling in my gait" (316). What Melville could not have known
at the time of his deliverance, yet what informs his writing about the event, is
that, after a short stop in the Hawaiian Islands and another change of ships, he
would return home to marry and rather quickly establish a home of his own.
Composing *Omoo* during the fall of 1846 while quietly courting Elizabeth
Shaw, who was then making a two-month visit at his family's Lansingburgh
house, the young Melville invested his second book with a mood of fond
farewell to his picaresque bachelorhood and of growing love and yearning for
the quiet domestic bliss that has always been the luckless picaro's dream.[37]

Because, as several critics have observed, *Omoo* rambles, even wanders,
from one episode to another, it has usually been regarded as being less unified
and deliberated than Melville's first book—winning in subject and style but
weak in artistic design, a potboiler written to capitalize on the popularity of
Typee. Certainly its plot is not that of the "single, whole, and complete" action
favored by Aristotle, with a causally integrated beginning, middle, and end,
such as is found in the tragedies of Aeschylus, say, or the architectonic novels
of Jane Austen or even Melville's apprentice work *Typee.* Rather, it is that of
the seemingly plotless picaresque narrative that—since it blossomed in
sixteenth-century Spain, though its roots are as old as Homer's *Odyssey*—has
provided an alternative tradition of storytelling, even an anti-tradition, to the
one codified in the widely respected Aristotelian ideal.

The structure of *Omoo,* while not so apparent, is not necessarily inferior to
that of *Typee;* it is simply different, and different in such ways as to have its
own artistic functions and demands. Instead of being organized around one
grand action, formed by the arts of complication, climax, and resolution,
Omoo is ordered in a series of minor actions, formed by the arts of repetition,
variation, and accumulation, like the musical suite. Expansive rather than
intensive in design, the episodic structure of the book is as purposeful in its
own way as the Aristotelian model is in its. Not only did it enable Melville to
provide a panoramic, eyewitness view of a varied island culture that his readership was eager to learn more about, but it also permitted him to reveal what
no single action could—that the title character, the "soul of sensibility" that
was Melville's self-proclaimed persona, and the seemingly inviting, yet ever-
forbidding, Polynesian world he travels through are mutually, radically, irrec-
oncilably incompatible (166).

Melville's Omoo is "on the move" in Polynesia as much for the reason that
it will not bend to his will or satisfy his desires for order as for the reason that

he will not bend to its will or succumb to its chaos. Until the very end, when intention and opportunity come together for the first and only significant time and he is miraculously delivered by the *Leviathan,* the South Sea Islands offer him neither a permanent home nor a means of getting away. Whether he tries to settle down or attempts to escape, his plans always go awry, and he is forced—or feels compelled—to move on to a new adventure.[38] Like the conventional picaresque novel, *Omoo* seems formless because the desires of the central character are repeatedly frustrated. It seems muddled and loosely ordered—always in the process of beginning and always in the process of ending—because it is doing what picaresque novels do: chronicling the series of false starts and defeated hopes that define the hero and his world and the reasons for their misalliance.

Omoo is not a profound book; certainly it lacks the philosophical probing of even Melville's next work, *Mardi.* But it is not so relaxed or heedless in its construction as its commentators have thought, and it in no way represents a falling-off in Melville's artistic control or intelligence. Instead it shows a shift in purpose, a shift in genre, and perhaps even an advance over the melodramatic *Typee* in the author's ability to match intention and performance. Writing to his English publisher, Murray, with a mixture of chagrin at his first effort and content at the one he was then completing, Melville ventured to declare that "A little experience in this art of book-craft has done wonders."[39] Though he was speaking specifically about the state of the manuscript he would soon be sending to the press, and not the level of his artistic accomplishment in that work, Melville's remark nonetheless serves as a reminder that he, for one, felt he was not the novice he was the first time around.

Chapter Three

ᕲ

Breaking Away:
Mardi as Imaginary Voyage

Students of Melville's fiction have long asserted that, early in the composition of *Mardi, and a Voyage Thither* (1849), Melville made a sudden break from the sort of travel writing found in his first two books, only to launch into a disjointed and rather bizarre allegory. But they have not been able to agree about what kind of book *Mardi* is, finally, and their disagreement has added to the uncertainty and misunderstanding, not to mention the disfavor, that mark most critical discussions of Melville's third novel.

While a good many critics agree about several of the important literary precedents of the book, particularly the satiric writings of Lucian, Rabelais, Cyrano de Bergerac, and Swift, those who have used generic terms at all to describe the novel have applied them impressionistically, at best, and at cross-purposes with one another. Thus, when it has not been regarded as full of "incoherencies and disunities" (Branch) or an unreadable "mess" (Beaver), *Mardi* has been called a whole host of things, from "allegorical romance" (Anderson, Dillingham) and "imaginary South Sea travel book" (Chase), to "romantic or transcendental allegory" (Arvin), "psychological allegory" (Johnson), "allegorical voyage" (Howard, Berthoff), "symbolic voyage" (Mason), "fantasy" (Howard), and "philosophic voyage" (Rosenberry).[1] Yet even most of the relatively few scholars who have used generic terms tend to assume that, because Melville wrote unconventional books, he had little or no interest in the traditional forms of the novel or that, as Warner Berthoff has asserted, he absorbed the earlier examples imperfectly.[2] In fact, the large majority of critics would seem to share the view of Richard H. Brodhead that *Mardi* has no "easily recognizable formal model" whatsoever, for either they avoid the

~

question entirely and call it nothing at all, or they see it as a work of sheer improvisation.[3]

To be sure, some disorder in the application of literary terminology in this case is understandable. *Mardi is* an unwieldly book, as loose and baggy a monster as ever a novelist wrote. But one sign of the primitive state of genre study in Melville scholarship, and in criticism on the American novel generally, is the fact that critics have not recognized *Mardi* to be a prime example of what used to be known as the "imaginary voyage," one of the principal forms of the novel before the twentieth century. The precursor of the modern genre of science fiction, which proposes to describe life in a distant *time,* the imaginary voyage pretended to describe life in a distant *place.* At one time a highly popular form, which flourished from the age of world discovery late in the medieval period until the nineteenth century, the imaginary voyage is sufficiently big-bellied to accommodate a wide variety of purposes, most of which Melville was all too eager to include in his extraordinarily ambitious third novel. In what is still a standard reference work, the ten-volume *History of the English Novel* (1924–39), Earnest A. Baker described the antiquity and range of the genre:

> Fabulous voyages have always played a momentous part in the establishment of prose fiction as a new literary genre. They appear as attested records of travel in the vast regions known to all mankind; and then merely as the picturesque framework for a Utopia, as in Plato's account of Atlantis in the *Timaeus;* for love adventures, as in [Antonius Diogenes's] *The Incredible Things beyond Thule;* or for satire, as in Lucian's *True History.* Mediaeval fiction had its Mandeville, not to mention the wondrous adventures by land and sea that provide a similar sort of entertainment in many of the romances. Defoe concocted a small library of travel books, mingled of fact and unabashed invention, before he wrote *Robinson Crusoe;* his later stories, moreover, are largely compounded of imaginary adventures about the globe. Swift, prompted by Cyrano de Bergerac, who was merely frivolous, used the imaginary voyage as a medium for profoundly serious philosophic satire.
>
> The ancients likewise had their Mandevilles and their Defoes, as well as their Swifts and their earnest delineators of various kinds of Utopias . . . [4]

Nonetheless, while *Mardi* combines all of these variations of the form—travel, utopia, love adventure, and satire—it is more than a many-layered version of an imaginary voyage. So rapid was Melville's development during this critical period in his career and so transparently does his growth show through, that

it serves as both a record of the intellectual voyage he himself was making at the time he wrote the book and an assessment of the imaginary voyage genre—a commentary on the uses of fantasy. It is also, therefore, if fitfully, both an interior autobiography and, that most modern of forms, a novel about writing a novel.

Virtually everything Melville wrote about *Mardi* while the book was taking shape reveals that in composing it he was acting out a deep-seated urge to break the popular travel-narrative mold he had relied on to gain his reputation in *Typee* and *Omoo*. At the same time, it is evident that he was also acting out a more fundamental longing to burst the confines of the public identity he had acquired in those books as a rather ordinary if outspoken young man with a breezy prose style and a penchant for stretching the truth. From his letters to his English publishers, it is clear that in *Mardi* Melville wanted to compose a more ambitous and lasting form of literature than he had written before and that he was eagerly feeling his way toward literary greatness.[5]

To accomplish his aims, Melville knew he had to convince John Murray to publish his new book in some other format than the nonfictional Home and Colonial Library series—either that, or he would have to sever relations with Murray altogether and take his chances with another, less eminent publisher. In the beginning, Melville decided to try to stick with Murray. Writing to him on October 29, 1847, shortly after he had begun his book in earnest, Melville was already trying to distance *Mardi,* in novelty and heft, from his previous work, without suggesting a radical change in mode, when he said, "As you may possibly imagine, I am engaged upon another book of South Sea Adventure (continued from, tho' wholly independent of, "Omoo")—The new work will enter into scenes altogether new, & will, I think, possess more interest than the former, which treated of subjects comparatively trite." After hinting that another London firm (presumably Richard Bentley, if we are to trust Melville at this point) had recently inquired about publishing his next book, he went on to predict its certain success, arguing not just the uncommonness of his Polynesian subject but his domination of his end of the market as well as his growing mastery of his own literary skill and power. "I can not but be conscious," he wrote, "that the feild [sic] where I garner is troubled but with few & inconsiderable intruders (in my own peculiar province I mean)—that it is wide & fresh;—indeed, I only but begin, as it were, to feel my hand."[6]

When Melville wrote Murray two months later, on January 1, 1848, his main objective was to inform him that he could not accept the publisher's previous offer of terms, namely, one hundred guineas at the time of publication plus half the profits. But as he went on to make the case for doubling the amount of his advance, Melville conceded that *Mardi* had become sufficiently different

from his first two books on the South Seas that his publisher would hardly be prepared to appreciate its merits. Contrary to what Murray might think, the subject was not "barren of novelty." The "plan I have pursued in the composition of the book now in hand," Melville explained, "clothes the whole subject in new attractions & combines in one cluster all that is romantic, whimsical & poetic in Polynusia [sic]. It is yet a continuous narrative," he asserted, thus calling attention to what has been clear to readers since the book was first published, namely, that *Mardi* is *not* a continuous narrative; rather, it suffers a radical break at the point where the ethereal Yillah enters the story. Surely if the question of the continuity of his narrative was nothing to worry about, Melville would have had no reason to mention it. Further revealing that he had proceeded far enough in the composition of the story, in just two months, to have moved into the imaginary part of the voyage that follows on Yillah's entrance, Melville offered a defense of the change in his story that unveils the ambition behind his effort. "I doubt not that—if it makes the hit I mean it to—it will be counted a rather bold aim; but nevertheless, it shall have the right stuff in it, to redeem its faults, tho' they were legion."[7]

Nearly three months later, on March 25, 1848, Melville wrote Murray again. *Mardi* was still nine months from completion, though he thought it was much closer, even speculating later in his letter that he might be able to place the manuscript in the publisher's hands "by the middle of July next." Beginning with the admission that he had not been precise, or perhaps even candid, about his plans earlier, he now put Murray on notice that he was no longer the writer of travel adventure stories he had earlier claimed himself to be but a romancer—in the broad sense, a novelist, a fabulist, a fiction writer.

> —I beleive [sic] that a letter I wrote you some time ago—I think my last but one—gave you to understand, or implied, that the work I then had in view was a bona-vide narrative of my adventures in the Pacific, continued from "Omoo"—My object in now writing you—I should have done so ere this—is to inform you of a change in my determinations. To be blunt: the work I shall next publish will in downright earnest be a "Romance of Polynisian [sic] Adventure"—

When he came to the point of trying to account for this change, Melville offered three explanations, all of which speak to the growing importance, for him, of the imagination. First, in a statement he repeated later in his brief preface to *Mardi*, he confessed it was a matter of pride with him to be able to show his detractors that he was capable of an even greater, more elevated effort of the imagination than they had supposed. "The truth is, Sir," he said,

"that the reiterated imputation of being a romancer in disguise has at last pricked me into a resolution to show those who may take any interest in the matter, that a *real* romance of mine is no Typee or Omoo, & is made of different stuff altogether." Second, he felt that the "rich poetical material" of Polynesia had never been adequately exploited before in "works of fancy; and which to bring out suitably, required only that play of freedom & invention accorded only to the Romancer & poet." And third, he had grown tired of the mundane realm of his own outward history. As he said, "proceeding in my narrative of *facts* I began to feel an incurible distaste for the same; & a longing to plume my pinions for a flight, & felt irked, cramped & fettered by plodding along with dull common places,—So suddenly standing [abandoning?] the thing alltogether, I went to work heart & soul at a romance which is now in fair progress, since I had worked at it under an earnest ardor."[8]

The confession that he felt he had been challenged to become a writer of fiction, or "romance," by the reviewers of his first two books is, perhaps, the most important clue to Melville's decision to break from his past as a self-proclaimed travel writer and to become, quite openly, a practitioner of the novel. It was the explanation he admitted to here as being "the main inducement in altering my plans." It is not, perhaps, perfectly clear just what Melville meant by this; Ronald Mason, for one, has said Melville's public version of this explanation, in his preface to *Mardi,* is "unilluminating."[9] But later in this same letter to Murray, dated March 25, 1848, Melville offered an elaboration of what was in his mind: "I think . . . it is possible for me to write such a romance, that it shall afford the strongest presumptive evidence of the truth of Typee & Omoo by the sheer force of contrast—not that the Romance is to sink in the comparison, but shall be better—I mean as a literary acheivement [sic], & so essentially different from those two books." What Melville reveals here is simply that he had come to think of the romance as superior to the travel narrative as an art form (however romanticized he himself had made the latter in practice), as he would soon come to think of the writing of Nathaniel Hawthorne as superior to the work of Richard Henry Dana, Jr.

Typical of the young Melville, he was concerned not so much that there had been confusion among his readers about the difference between fact and fiction in his first two books as he was that they had underrated his capacities as an artist by thinking *Typee* and *Omoo* to be works of the imagination. The story that came from his own mind, he suggested here, would be so much bolder and more deeply human than the accounts of his travels could ever be that his critics would immediately recognize the error of their ways; they would see that such a powerful imagination as the one that wrote *Mardi* had not really been engaged at all in the composition of his first two books. While this

may be putting the case too baldly, it is symptomatic of Melville's youthful personality that the crucial factor for him in becoming a novelist was the feeling that his powers had been grossly underestimated. Not to be taken seriously was finally what provoked him to make the extraordinary effort required to write *Mardi*. That it turned out not to be a better book than it is can be explained by the fact that it was simply premature as a work of art.

John Murray never did agree to publish *Mardi*. J. R. Brodhead, the young friend in the U.S. legation who assumed the duties of Melville's London agent when his brother Gansevoort suddenly died, explained in his diary that *Mardi* "is a fiction & Mr Murray says it don't suit him."[10] Though Melville knew that Richard Bentley was waiting in the wings, anxious to meet the author's terms, he persisted in his attempt to secure a contract with Murray. Whether he did so out of loyalty or faith in Murray's imprimatur or as a result of the inertia that familiarity brings, it is hard to say on the basis of the slim existing record. But Melville seems to have been quite eager to maintain the connection, despite his determination to break into a new form of writing.

In the end, it was Murray who broke from Melville. In his last letter to Murray, dated January 28, 1849, which accompanied the manuscript of *Mardi*, Melville increased the amount of the advance he said he would find acceptable to two hundred guineas and then asked Murray to consider his own earlier notion of publishing the book "in handsome style, & independently of any series." In light of this suggestion, along with what I take to be the evident sincerity of Melville's tone elsewhere in the letter—if Murray would agree to his terms, he said, "I should feel exceedingly gratified to continue our connection, & should equally regret to be obliged to leave you"—it appears that Melville was simply trying to drive the hardest bargain possible. It does not seem, finally, that he was trying to force Murray to make the break *for* him. The alacrity, however, with which Bentley agreed to Melville's terms, doing so less than a week after Murray had declined, confirms that Melville must have felt sure enough of Bentley's interest in publishing his third book that he thought he had an ace up his sleeve in his showdown with Murray and could thus confidently try to force him to play on his terms or not at all.[11]

Apparently Melville was determined to increase the ante in his negotiations with John Murray because the stakes had grown unexpectedly high. Writers of course like to be paid by the page; and by that measure, *Mardi* had become a very expensive book. Requiring almost twice the time to finish than Melville had originally planned, it had ballooned to several hundred pages and three volumes in its published form—more than double the length of *Typee* and a bit longer even than *Moby-Dick*. This is one clue to its nature and to its weak-

ness as a work of fiction. As an imaginary voyage, it was infinitely expandable. According to Philip Gove, the chief historian of the genre, the imaginary voyage is so unstructured a form as to be virtually incapable of precise definition. What unifies such works, he claims, is not even so much that they are voyages as that they are "evidence of the activity of the human mind"—an almost laughably apt description of *Mardi*, which offers more than ample testimony to the fact that Melville's mind, at the time he wrote this novel, was in the process of awakening as few others ever have. As Babbalanja says of the fictional author of the apocryphal Koztanza, which serves as an internal parody of *Mardi*, "When Lombardo set about his work, he knew not what it would become. He did not build himself in with plans; he wrote right on; and so doing, got deeper and deeper into himself."[12] The imaginary voyage form, says Gove, who concentrates on its heyday during the eighteenth century, "was basically an often-employed vehicle which took all knowledge to be its province." In practice, its scope included "the realms of geographic knowledge and discovery, of philosophy, of political science, of sociology, of religion, and, in addition, of such a comparatively minor matter as the development of fiction from folklore and geographic myth through romance of adventure to novel."[13]

A more exacting, if somewhat tautological definition of the imaginary voyage, one provided by an earlier student of the form, is that it is "a narrative, usually autobiographic, of a supposed journey into an imaginary country written either for the pleasure or for the profit of the reader, or for both."[14] One important proviso was added by another early scholar, who pointed out that the voyage is "not credible and not intended to be accepted by readers as authentic."[15] This much, of course, is everywhere obvious in *Mardi*, once the reader gets past the early quasi-realistic chapters. But Melville also announced as much in his preface, calling the book "a romance of Polynesian adventure," a "fiction," which in the metaphysical sense only, he hoped, might be taken as a "verity." Such definitions, however, though useful up to a point, fail to suggest why an author would choose to employ a form in which the happenings are not credible. They fail to supply a compelling rationale for the form or to suggest the overriding advantages—psychological, literary, or commercial— of employing it. They therefore say little about its essential nature.

What has been little recognized, even among students of the form, is that the imaginary voyage is but one among many types within a broader mode known as the fantastic. Only in this context can the advantages of the form, and important elements of its essential nature, be properly understood and appreciated. *Mardi*, it should be said, is not a bona fide fantasy; it should still be called by the narrower term of imaginary voyage. It is not like pure examples

of fantastic fiction, such as *Alice in Wonderland*, in that it does not repeatedly engender a sense of astonishment in the reader; it does not continually violate its own ground rules, as Lewis Carroll's book does when it shows nature to be always changing, either growing unexpectedly larger or smaller, like Alice, or suddenly materializing and then vanishing, like the Cheshire Cat.[16] *Mardi* violates its own ground rules only once, when its hero moves from the actual geographical world of the Kingsmill Islands in the South Pacific to the imaginary islands of the Mardian archipelago, where he remains for the rest of the narrative. If, however, it is understood that fantasy, like irony, satire, or realism, is a matter of degrees—that it exists, in practice, over a wide spectrum of possibilities, with the pure form at one end, its absence at the other, and gradations in between—then *Mardi* can be said to partake of the fantastic without being a fantasy, and we can come to understand it in a way that should prove useful.

Mardi, like Melville's first two books, opens in the realistic mode, with its narrator, the central character, on a ship sailing the known world of the South Pacific in search of whales, from Ravavai, near Tahiti, to the Gallipagos Islands off the Ecuadorian coast. However, rather than serving as evidence that Melville started to write one kind of book and then unaccountably shifted to another, the realistic opening ought to be seen as a necessary prelude to the imaginary voyage of the narrator—a ploy, as in *Gulliver's Travels*, for moving the story from the everyday world of the reader to the fantastic world of the storyteller. From the very first page, Melville's novel shows signs of slipping into the fantastic, as the narrator and his fellow sailors long to escape the tedium of their months at sea. Besides the fact that their destination is known as the "Enchanted Islands," and that one must take, as we are told, an astonishingly roundabout way to get there, what the narrator emphasizes in this initial scene is the deadly monotony of the ocean and the wearisomeness of life on ship. The opening pages are rife with signs of the narrator's feeling of confinement and his yearning to be free. There are telling references, for example, to the convict island of Massafuero and to the mutiny on the *Bounty;* and there are reiterated expressions of frustration with the dull reading matter made available by the captain and the stale stories and songs repeated endlessly by the rest of the crew.

Eric Rabkin, in his excellent study, *The Fantastic in Literature* (1976), offers something of a truism when he says that the vision of escape is the most common mark of the literature of fantasy. However, it is a truism worth repeating here, because it captures the spirit not just of the opening chapter but of the whole first quarter of Melville's novel. After the fickle captain announces his decision suddenly to change course and take the *Arcturion* to Kamschatka Bay, in the North Pacific, the narrator protests that he feels he is being carried

off to purgatory; and when his request is refused to put him ashore somewhere en route, he weighs the possibility of jumping ship. Justifying this felo-
nious action on the grounds that the captain was violating his original agreement with him, the narrator one day has a fantastic vision while taking his
turn at the masthead. It is with this remarkably prescient, and moving, fantasy—a preview of the narrator's later leap into the Mardian "world of mind,"
complete with a premonitory sighting of the fair Yillah—that the first chapter
of the book comes to an end:

> It was toward the close of a day, serene and beautiful. There I stood, high
> upon the mast, and away, away, illimitably rolled the ocean beneath. Where
> we then were was perhaps the most unfrequented and least known portion
> of these seas. Westward, however, lay numerous groups of islands, loosely
> laid down upon the charts, and invested with all the charms of dream-
> land. But soon these regions would be past; the mild equatorial breeze
> exchanged for cold, fierce squalls, and all the horrors of northern voyag-
> ing. I cast my eyes downward to the brown planks of the dull, plodding
> ship, silent from stem to stern; then abroad. In the distance what visions
> were spread! The entire western horizon high piled with gold and crimson
> clouds; airy arches, domes, and minarets; as if the yellow, Moorish sun
> were setting behind some vast Alhambra. Vistas seemed leading to worlds
> beyond. To and fro, and all over the towers of this Nineveh in the sky, flew
> troops of birds. Watching them long, one crossed my sight, flew through a
> low arch, and was lost to view. My spirit must have sailed in with it; for
> directly, as in a trance, came upon me the cadence of mild billows laving a
> beach of shells, the waving of boughs, and the voices of maidens, and the
> lulled beatings of my own dissolved heart, all blended together. Now, all
> this, to be plain, was but one of the many visions one has up aloft. But
> coming upon me at this time, it wrought upon me so, that thenceforth my
> desire to quit the Arcturion became little short of a frenzy. (7–8)

As frivolous as such a fantasy might at first seem, Melville shows, in this
opening chapter, that such imaginings have a practical side that can hardly be
dismissed. For, if heeded, the intuitive workings of the imagination can be
truly life saving, while their denial can prove destructive indeed, as is hinted
when the narrator later explains that the *Arcturion* went down, apparently
with all hands on board, not long after he had acted on his inner prompting
and jumped ship (5).

The flight into imaginary worlds begins, then, with the desire to escape the
confining present. But what is the origin of the desire to escape? What are the

feelings that give birth to it? And why does the desire assert itself more urgently at some times than at others? Melville's narrator, it should be emphasized, speaks repeatedly of the monotony and boredom of life on the *Arcturion*—feelings that are typical of the ones experienced by the heroes of imaginary voyages in the early stages of their adventures. However, behind that sense of boredom with the present moment there usually lies a deeper feeling of despair, one that Melville's narrator comes to experience as a result of the deadly calm they encounter on the day after he has his remarkable vision. Though like most other sailors he has, over time, grown somewhat inured to the strange phenomenon, he admits that this particular calm "added not a little to my impatience of the ship" by reviving his early impressions of his first experience of it. Thus, he explains, "to the landsman a calm is no joke. It not only revolutionizes his abdomen, but unsettles his mind; tempts him to recant his belief in the eternal fitness of things; in short, almost makes an infidel of him" (9).

Long before Sartre or Camus, Melville captured a version of the modern existentialist state when he characterized the calm as "a state of existence where existence itself seems suspended." In a calm, one becomes totally alienated from the world; he "grows madly skeptical" about all matters of geography, so convinced is he that the world is imaginary. He can even become alienated from himself, as in the later fables of Kafka, to the point where he seems to take on the characteristics of some odd creature, as Melville's narrator says he suddenly finds a "strange and portentous" voice within himself that keeps up "a sort of involuntary interior humming . . . like a live beetle." Drawing out the litany of evidences of the despair experienced by someone trapped in a calm, the narrator confesses that "more than all else is the consciousness of his utter helplessness. Succor or sympathy there is none." Even the "final satisfaction of despairing" may be beyond him, for he is compelled to give all his attention simply to enduring the calm (10).

The dialectic nature of the relationship between despair and fantasy is hardly unique to *Mardi,* and neither is it unique to the genre of the imaginary voyage. According to Seiji Nuita, a comparative anthropologist who has written provocatively on the origins of utopia, it is universal. Indeed, at the bottom of every manifestation of what Bergson called man's "energy of consciousness," or the activity of the mind as it struggles to be free, there lies despair. "By despair," Nuita explains, "I mean the ultimate condition of man: faced with the certainty of a complete end of time—namely, with death—he aspires to the uncertainty that is life." Despair, then, is the awareness of loneliness, and true loneliness is intolerable—so much so that it leads necessarily to intense imaginative activity. Thus, Nuita concludes, "we may also say that the begin-

ning of utopia [in particular] lies in an awareness of solitude."¹⁷ Such a con-

nection clearly holds true in *Mardi*, where the escape of Melville's narrator

from the *Arcturion* springs precisely from his intolerable sense of solitude in
the midst of an energy-sapping calm. Later, and more emphatically, after the
disappearance of his beloved Yillah, the narrator's quest through the Mardian
archipelago to find her and restore his earlier utopian feeling arises from a
still-more-powerful feeling of despair and loneliness born of loss.

Fantasy is a healthy and natural response to an unendurable situation, the
first step toward one's achieving emotional equilibrium again after an upset
or imbalance of some kind. Fantasy offers a world where the ground rules of
life are diametrically reversed, as Rabkin says.¹⁸ It does more than provide a
much-needed psychological release. It points the way toward some scheme
for corrective action. When Melville's narrator begins to plan his flight from
the *Arcturion,* he imagines himself escaping not alone but with a companion,
the aged Skyman, Jarl, and by a means that he himself can control, a whaleboat.
He shows no concern for the peril of such an undertaking. Because physical
danger is not what was threatening his spirit, it is of no importance here.
What the narrator needs most is freedom, some control over his own movement, and a "chummy," as he says, to share his journey (14).

While the narrator's dream of escape hardly qualifies as a full-fledged fantasy—it is not impossible, we know, for a man to survive a thousand-mile
trip at sea in an open boat—it is sufficiently perilous that Jarl initially "declared that the scheme was a crazy one," having "never known of such a thing
but thrice before," and in each case the runaways were never heard from again
(17). More important, the narrator's dream of escape meets with the kind of
success that encourages him, as Mark Twain said at the end of his fantasy, *The
Mysterious Stranger,* to "Dream other dreams, and better!"¹⁹ It thus prepares
the reader for the truly fantastic leap into the Mardian world later in the story
and for the hero's imaginary voyage through the archipelago of the mind, as
he grapples with the profound despair that comes on him following the disappearance of his beloved Yillah.

Although critics of *Mardi* have emphasized the inconsistency between the
realism of the opening fifth of the novel, the events of which can be plotted on
a map of the known world, and the fancifulness of the rest of it, there are other
features of the opening section that seem designed to prepare the reader for
making the jump into the imaginary world of Mardi later on. Most significantly, in the chapters leading up to the discovery of the exotic Yillah, the reader
is presented with several characters who are themselves accustomed to inhab-
iting imaginary worlds. Jarl, the narrator's old sailing companion, for example,

seems eminently practical-minded for much of their journey together—methodically keeping a calendar, carefully repairing their clothing, worrying over the water supply. But when they encounter the *Parki*, he is suddenly overcome by superstitious fantasies. He takes the *Parki* to be "a shade of a ship, full of sailors' ghosts" and shows himself to be full of "all manner of Valhalla marvels concerning the land of goblins" (63–64).

Similarly, Samoa and Annatoo, the Polynesian couple found operating the *Parki*, are remarkably adept at practical matters of survival on the high seas; but they, too, are wildly superstitious and fly off into imaginary worlds at the slightest provocation. When, for instance, the narrator and his Viking friend come on board their little brig, Samoa and Annatoo take them to be a pair of ghosts from a phantom ship or, more incredibly still, "a couple of men from the moon" (86). Annatoo, especially, is portrayed as a "marvelous" figure, who in a series of comic moments is seen to disappear below deck with a ship's compass or other pilfered items, where she proceeds to act out her inscrutable fantasies (101–02, 114).

Still another technique Melville uses in the opening section to prepare his readers for the leap into the Mardian world of fantasy is to portray several of the more amazing natural wonders one might encounter at sea. Virtually entire chapters are devoted to descriptions of marvelous creatures and other seemingly incredible phenomena of the deep. We are told of the strange devil fish, an "enormous crescent with antlers, like a reindeer, and a Delta of mouths" (39), and of the curious shovel-nosed shark, which is guided to its prey by mysterious pilot fish (53). We learn about the incredible Indian swordfish, which skewers its foes, even an occasional ship, with its "Toledo" (103) and about such strange natural phenomena as shifting equatorial currents or such "remarkable spectacle[s]" as the sea on fire (121). Melville's portraits of all such phenomena seem designed to stretch our notion of what is possible and inure us to what might otherwise seem simply incredible—to blur the distinction between the everyday world and the world of imagination, and in that way ease us into the realm of fantasy. As Melville's narrator says at one point, once one has grown really familiar with the deep, the "sea-serpent is not a fable; and in the sea, that snake is but a garden worm. There are more wonders than the wonders rejected, and more sights unrevealed than you or I ever dreamt of" (39).

For Melville, however, the sea is more than a place of natural wonders, a means to ease his reader's transition into the imaginary realm of Mardi. It is also a distinct *other* world, one diametrically opposed to the familiar world of the land. Like the realm of pure fantasy, it offers a means of reversing perspec-

tives on the *known* world, the world we inhabit, from inside to outside. It
provides the distant point of view we need in order to see, and understand,
our own world with fresh eyes—the distant point of view required for any
critique of culture. As Melville's narrator observes philosophically, after his
beloved Yillah has mysteriously vanished, "happiness seldom seems happiness, except when looked back upon from woes. A flowery landscape, you
must come out of, to behold" (193). Melville had not yet met Hawthorne, or
read his fiction, when he wrote *Mardi,* but he had come to understand something of the aesthetic issue of perspective that Hawthorne would soon seek to
explain in the prefaces to his romances. On his own, Melville had discovered
that the imaginary voyage could supply the "latitude" Hawthorne said the
writer of romance had to have in order to bring into focus his central subject,
what Hawthorne called the "truth of the human heart."[20]

Melville's principal concern in *Mardi* is to reveal just this romancer's view
of the truth of the human heart. He is not so concerned, as the realist is, with
the *appearance* of things in the known world as he is with their *essence.* His
aim is to show what James called "the deeper psychology," the buried life of
the emotions. Thus, when the *Parki* sinks following a storm and the three
survivors—Jarl, Samoa, and the narrator—take to the sea again in the little
Chamois, Melville's hero admits that his heart "sunk" too (116, 120). He has
reached another emotional low point, and nothing but his imagination can
deliver him from it.

Subsequent events indicate that the narrator's imagination does indeed
come to his rescue, catapulting him into a world of wish-fulfillment dreams
(and nightmares), where "visions," "imaginings," "fancies," and "spells" follow
one another in quick succession (139, 144, 152–53, 158). When the three mariners encounter the strange spectacle of the sea on fire, it is said to cast on them
such a "cadaverous" glow as to make them look "like ghosts" (121). Melville
thus signals that his characters are being translated into a fantastic world of
spirits and other dreamlike figures. Though in the distance they see signs of
land, the narrator wonders whether they have somehow run past the expansive chain of islands that had been their destination (125). In this way, Melville
suggests they are moving beyond the charted waters of the Pacific and into an
imaginary sphere. Finally, when, on this deadly quiet afternoon at sea, the three
of them encounter the strange canoe carrying the ethereal Yillah from a non-
existent island named Amma to another such place called Tedaidee for a ritual
sacrifice, all the earlier hints that we have been slowly slipping into a melancholy sailor's daydream seem confirmed.[21] Now suddenly imagining himself
as the hero of a flashy melodrama, the narrator rushes to the maiden's rescue,

slays the villainous priest, and routs the rest of her captors—all fifteen of them (with modest assistance, to be sure, from his two "chummies"). Like a swashbuckling matinee idol, he slashes open the tent where the beautiful maiden has been held prisoner and, gazing at the lovely figure crouching help-lessly before him, exclaims to himself in disbelief, "Did I dream?" (136).

What the fatal encounter with Yillah evinces is precisely what the young narrator had most deeply desired all along as he struggled to escape the lone-liness born of boredom and despair. Without the least bit of conscious effort on his part, his imagination has suggested to him the remedy of romantic love, and from that point on his powers of fancy have concocted a full scenario, complete with a dreamy leading lady and a sizable supporting cast. This is the point where the reader permanently enters the world of Mardi, what Melville later in the narrative identifies as "the world of mind" (557). Although his hero is not such a clichéd figure as to be shown actually falling asleep just before his marvelous adventures begin, Melville's story may nonetheless be regarded as a romantic version of the kind of dream vision found in Chaucer and Bunyan.

In "The Dream begins to fade" (chapter 51), where the narrator explains to Yillah that his professed knowledge of her native isle "had been revealed to me in dreams," he says as much himself. Eagerly trying to convince the reader of the veracity of his explanation to the innocent girl, he argues, like a young Jay Gatsby who has finally found the Daisy of his dreams, "And true it was to say so; and right it was to swear it, upon her white arms crossed. For oh, Yillah; were you not the earthly semblance of that sweet vision, that haunted my earliest thoughts?" (158) Significantly, Yillah herself has not "the remotest conception of her real origin" (153). In fact, she is nothing more than the narrator's youthful fantasy, the image of womanhood he has been seeking in the flesh all his life, over all the "wide watery world" (143). As a character, she thus perfectly accomplishes what Eric Rabkin has said is one of the chief pur-poses of fantasy: She helps to reveal the truth of the human heart—the heart of *Mardi*'s hero, and of his creator as well.

For a writer like Melville, however, the truth of the human heart is a com-plicated business. As revealed in the scenario centering on Yillah's rescue, the narrator is not permitted a simple daydream, as would be the case if he had imagined himself happening on a beautiful maiden floating helplessly alone at sea. Instead, his fantasy is peopled by threatening figures and tainted with anxiety and dread. To gain the girl of his dreams, he must put his own life in peril, and he must kill another man. The narrator's dream of rescuing the strange maiden thus represents more than a persistent male fantasy; it repre-sents the evil a man can, or must, do to accomplish it. It captures what the

male of the species, in its essential nature, amounts to. A creature of seemingly innocent longings, Melville's hero has a Cain-like capacity to slay his brother to gain the thing he deeply desires. Even at this early stage of his career, then, Melville held to the conviction that there was, as he would later say in his review of Hawthorne's *Mosses* (1852), "something, somehow like Original Sin," some "blackness," in the heart of man.[22] The "fall" is universal.

This conviction, complicating though it is, was one to which Melville, even as early as *Mardi*, was beginning to lend his own peculiar contours. For what characterizes his conception of the human heart, finally, is the appearance of ambivalence in the "blackness" of its motives. As in *Pierre; or, The Ambiguities*, in *Mardi* Melville presents the central action of the story, the hero's decision to rescue a damsel in distress, in a morally equivocal light. Confronted with the shrill cries and curses of the priest Aleema's sons, the narrator is suddenly struck hard with remorse, as the truth of the fact is brought home to him that it was by *his* hand that "the dead man had died." Immediately seeking to unburden his guilt, he asks himself "whether the death-deed I had done was sprung of a virtuous motive, the rescuing a captive from thrall; or whether beneath that pretense, I had engaged in this fatal affray for some other, and selfish purpose; the companionship of a beautiful maid" (135). Although he soon senses that "my motives to this enterprise justified not the mad deed, which, in a moment of rage, I had done" (140), we know that, since his own life had been threatened by the menacing priest, a strong case could be made for his having reacted, as Billy Budd will later, in self-defense. Many pages later, moreover, he describes himself as still deeply brooding over the question of his guilt, unable to sleep and imploring the stars to tell him whether he is a "murderer" (179).

If we keep in mind that this episode is all part of a dream, we can see that, as the story progresses, the narrator's guilt anxiety periodically returns to him in the form of Aleema's avenging sons, only to disappear again without ever finally resolving the question of his culpability one way or another. The narrator's decision, therefore, to rescue Yillah, like Pierre's decision to save Isabel, becomes the impetus for a typically ironic Melvillean situation—not a chance for virtuous self-congratulation but an occasion for agonizing self-scrutiny, a crisis in the history of the heart's awakening.

Despite the profound soul-searching prompted by the narrator's murder of Aleema, the true identity of Melville's hero remains unusually vague, even problematic. Lacking even a name or the rudiments of a personal, familial, or cultural history, he is presented as little more than an exceptionally active capacity for imagining alternatives to his own unhappy present, a master of the imaginative art of metamorphosis. Yet indefiniteness of character is typical of the

heroes of the imaginary voyage genre, as such figures as Swift's Gulliver or Lucian's nameless storyteller attest. In the land of dreams, where wishes automatically convert into what seem like realities, fluidity of personality, including the personality of the dreamer, is the rule. Thus from the beginning, the narrator is pictured as straining against the limits of the self, trying to assert a greater freedom than his station in life and circumstances permit, as when he conceives the idea of jumping ship in the middle of the Pacific. Though still a young man, he longs to be the kind of person who can direct his own fate to a far greater degree than a common sailor of the nineteenth century was typically permitted. Indeed, the conventional view of the matter is provided to us by sensible old Jarl, who entreats him "to renounce [his] determination, not be a boy, pause and reflect, stick to the ship, and go home in her like a man" (17). However, not only does the narrator convince Jarl to join him, he also engineers their escape; and, when the little whaleboat drops away from the *Arcturion*, he is the one who assumes command. At every turning point thereafter, moreover, he is the one who takes charge. When they sight the *Parki*, he is the one who sets their course; when they encounter Aleema, he is the one who decides to rescue Yillah; and when they land near Odo, he is the one who takes on the leader's role as Taji, the white demigod and "gentleman from the sun" (165).

Once they enter the Mardian archipelago, however, Taji immediately senses how presumptuous he has been in assuming the identity of a demigod. Though he does not at first understand it as such, Mardi is a house of mirrors, a fantastic world where every lie, every deception one practices is reflected back to him with startling precision. Here, spurious gods and demidivines of various kinds are so commonplace that Taji can hardly escape recognizing the falsity of his own pretensions. Received into Mardi by an imposing delegation of kings from various islands, Melville's narrator jumps to the conclusion that the game is up before it has even begun; "it seemed preposterous," he admits to himself, "to assume a divine dignity in the presence of these undoubted potentates of *terra firma*. Taji seemed oozing from my fingers' ends" (165). Questioned by one old potentate about his origins and future plans, Taji, in a moment of comic lucidity, is forced to wonder whether he may not have gone a bit too far in the outlandish claims he has made about himself. "Much I mourned," he confesses, feeling the distress of a man caught in a giant deception, "that I had not previously studied better my part" (166).

Only when Taji tries to bluff his way through the king's interrogation do the doubts of the royal assemblage disappear. For only then do they recognize him to be acting in a way that is consistent with the conduct of all the other crackpot deities in their topsy-turvy world. Like these other self-inflated figures, Taji at last assumes a lofty demeanor and dismisses the questions of his in-

quisitor as an impertinence, saying, "'Taji comes, old man, because it pleases him to come. And Taji will depart when it suits him'" (166). At the end of this lofty pronouncement, the sham kings of Mardi eagerly welcome the equally sham Taji into their midst, and he and the others are immediately carried off to Odo for a rousing celebration of his visit.

In this scene of the travelers' reception in Mardi, the tone of the novel takes a decidedly comic turn. *Mardi* is about to become a freewheeling satire, where virtually everything is exposed as being the reverse of what it should be. While Taji is pictured at his welcome feast worrying over such mundane questions as "Did deities dine?" we learn that his host, King Media of Odo, is completely indifferent even to the most extravagant and nonsensical of his visitor's claims. Exasperated by Media's failure to appreciate just how arduous interplanetary travel can be, Taji says that what surprised him most was Media's "unaffected indifference to my amazing voyage from the sun; his indifference to the sun itself; and all the wonderful circumstances that must have attended my departure." To the inhabitants of Mardi, anything seems possible, because here people are always making fantastic claims about themselves. As Taji soon learns on his quest through the archipelago, "these Mardians were familiar with still greater marvels than mine; verily believing in prodigies of all sorts. Any one of them put my exploits to the blush" (176). Mardi, the world we live in, is, most ironically, a fantastic world, one worthy of being laughed to scorn.

While for strategic purposes Taji decides to keep up his masquerade as a visiting avatar from the sun, it is important to note that he never deludes himself as to his true identity, as the other demidivines and pasteboard sovereigns do. Unlike these others, Taji knows he has a split personality, one imaginary and one real. In chapter 57, "Taji takes Counsel with himself," where the split is explicit, the narrator reveals that his brief sojourn in Mardi has shocked him into self-awareness. Giving himself the kind of cautionary advice that is all too rare in Mardi, Taji warns himself against the universal infirmity of pride. "Look to thy ways then, Taji," he says, "and carry not thy crest too high. Of a surety, thou hast more peers than inferiors. Thou art overtopped all round. Bear thyself discreetly and not haughtily, Taji. It will not answer to give thyself airs" (176–77).

By contrast, Media, the book's central example of an established demigod and king, has so thoroughly taken on the status of a sovereign as to have lost his humanity. This is dramatized quite baldly on the first day of the voyagers' stay on Odo when several beggarly old petitioners approach their ruler with a request to replace his autocratic juridical verdicts with a system of trial by jury of one's peers. Ordering the rheumatic old supplicants to their knees, Media dismisses their pleas in the angry tones of a despot: "I am king: ye are slaves. Mine

to command: yours to obey" (185). Like the other rulers of Mardi, Media is blind to the fact of his own dual nature; while he lives his private dream of lording it over his subjects, he fails to recognize that he is as needy and mortal as they are. Only in the end, when he sees how a true prince—Alma, god of love, of brotherhood—rules on Serenia, does he see the error of his ways; only then does he renounce his kingship and embrace the humble status of a man, if of one whose lot in life it is to bear the responsibilities of a governor (630).

Always the object of Melville's attack on the kings of Mardi is their blindness to their common humanity. Everywhere he insists, as he does most succinctly in the mock-heroic paean to kingship titled "Belshazzar on the Bench" (chapter 60), that though "a fine king on a throne is a very fine sight to behold," he is, "after all, but a gentleman seated" (182–83). Kingly pride is the universal failing in Mardi, the cause of all mischief, all evil, in Melville's view. Conversely, self-understanding, a monarch's humble acceptance of his truly mortal nature, is seen again and again as the key to any corrective action, the first step in the establishment of a sane and just government.

Taji, the would-be demigod from the sun, does try to be honest with himself, particularly in the evening hours when the quest for Yillah must be halted and he has a chance to look inside himself. However, he never does make a final accounting of his guilty deed. When day returns, he gives all his attention to the quest for the lost maiden, and he ceases to consider the state of his soul. Even when a mysterious incognito, later revealed to be the avenging Hautia, begins to haunt the lovers' retreat and, with its "fathomless eye," pry into his soul, Taji resists its searching gaze (186). But there is nothing he can do, resist though he may, to escape the wrong he has done in taking another man's life. His edenic interlude with Yillah remains blighted by sin and, as a consequence, it is fated to be short lived. As Babbalanja later explains to Taji, "an evil deed gained you your Yillah: no wonder she is lost" (423).

One morning, then, shortly after a ghostlike canoe is seen hovering about their islet near Odo, Yillah suddenly disappears. "Gone!" Taji exclaims. "A *dream*. I closed my eyes, and would have *dreamed* her back. In vain" (194; emphasis added). Several days later, after his anguish has begun to die down, he vows to search the whole archipelago for his lost love. At Media's urging, a new group of voyagers is formed, one made up of characters who are better equipped intellectually than the simple Samoa and Jarl to contribute to the globe-trotting symposium that makes up the remaining three-quarters of the book. Joining Taji and Media are the historian named Mohi, a philosopher known as Babbalanja, and a poet named Yoomy. While Taji's search for Yillah provides the impetus for the imaginary voyage that follows, it soon becomes clear that Melville's real purpose in establishing such a story line was to create

an occasion for conducting a protracted discourse on utopianism and the failures of existing governments throughout the world.

In the remaining chapters, of which there are more than a hundred, Melville devotes most of his energies to the construction of a rollicking satire of kingship, a wild and woolly allegory of the mismanagement of nations by an all-but-endless string of pompous, corrupt, and generally foolish rulers. Of the fifteen islands visited by Taji and his friends—not counting the utopian Serenia or Flozella-a-Nina, where the evil Queen Hautia dwells— the misrule of the reigning monarch is a major point of focus in Melville's treatment of twelve of them. Clearly Media was speaking for Melville when he asserts, late in the story, that on a map of the spheres, Mardi is marked "the world of kings" (542). While *Mardi* has often been said to be an unusually private book, an autobiographical work that was hatched before its time, it should be kept in mind that, in focusing on the follies of the world's potentates, Melville's novel was intended as an examination of current world history—a study, in the common nineteenth-century mode, of the actions of a few, centrally important public figures.[23]

The scene on King Media's own Odo serves to foreshadow the fantastically topsy-turvy world that the questers will encounter elsewhere in Mardi, once their imaginary voyage gets underway. "To look at, and to roam about of holidays, Odo seemed a happy land," we are told. But of course it is in truth a deeply divided place. Only a very few of its inhabitants enjoy the dream-life of freedom and plenty, while the vast majority are made to suffer an endless nightmare of servitude and deprivation. The "chiefs and merry men of mark" live comfortably in cool groves or sylvan nooks, but the "common sort, including serfs, and Helots, war-captives held in bondage," are made to live in foul caves and rotting shelters, hidden from view.

So completely are the rulers of Odo caught up in their selfish fantasies that in their own minds they transform their subjects into animals and then stand amazed at how these "swine could grovel in the mire." More ironic still, they are totally unaware that they themselves are the major cause of their people's suffering. In fact, their very own mandates have "condemned their drudges to a life of death." Out of sheer self-interest, they have forbidden the people to build their homes from anything but the crudest materials; have taxed their serfs to the killing point; and have punished, until they "shriek," all who dare to speak the "heresy" that "Media was no demi-god" (191–92).

While on most of the other islands the suffering of the people is not portrayed so graphically, the central irony of virtually every episode is that the folly of the country's rulers is responsible for the misery of the common man and woman. As a political satirist, Melville consistently takes the populist

point of view one would expect from the author of *Typee* and *Omoo*. On the island of Valapee, for instance, all is said to be in "legislative uproar and confusion" because its monarch is a ten-year-old boy whose mind is a battleground for the inherited spirits of "some twenty heroes, sages, simpletons, and demi-gods, previously lodged in his sire"—a preposterous situation in its own right but one that is made truly dangerous by the fact that the local parliament has declared the boy to be incapable of doing any wrong (202–04). On Diranda, the mindless lord seigniors Hello and Piko are shown celebrating their famous war games, where numberless men are induced "to kill off one another voluntarily, in a peaceable manner," all in the interest of keeping the island's population in equilibrium (439).

In these and most of the other episodes in *Mardi*, Melville set out to show his readers fantastic versions of themselves, of their world of 1848–49, which had in fact been erupting into violence, just recently, with unprecedented force. Arch democrat though he was, Melville did not, however, believe that the world's few republics were especially favored among nations or that their arrival on the world's stage, in the decades just past, necessarily boded well for the future course of humanity. As he says in the anonymous scroll addressed to the "Sovereign-kings of Vivenza" (a thinly veiled allegory referring to all the freemen of the United States):

> The grand error of this age, sovereign-kings! is the general supposition, that the very special Diabolus is abroad; whereas, the very special Diabolus has been abroad ever since Mardi began.
>
> And the grand error of your nation, sovereign-kings! seems this:—The conceit that Mardi is now in the last scene of the last act of her drama; and that all preceding events were ordained, to bring about the catastrophe you believe at hand,—a universal and permanent Republic.
>
> May it please you, those who hold to these things are fools, and not wise. (525)

Showing a heavyhandedness that is a frequent weakness of *Mardi*, but also an independence of mind that is one of the strengths of his work from *Typee* forward, Melville took issue with the fashionable liberal view of his day, explaining that "in themselves, monarchies are not utterly evil. For many nations, they are better than republics; for many, they will ever so remain" (527). Though Vivenza (the United States) is "the best and happiest land under the sun" (528), its claim to being a republican nation where all are born free and

equal is "nullified," as King Media is quick to point out, by the fact that there the members of the tribe of "Hamo" are denied their fundamental rights.

Moreover, in Vivenza, where people "are free to hunt down him who dissents" from majority rule, even freemen, such as the anonymous scroll-writer himself, know the fear of living under a form of despotism, the tyranny of the mob (524). Even in the progressive world of the mid–nineteenth century, kings are not dying out. As Media says, "My children's children will be kings; though, haply, called by other titles." Neither is the last day soon at hand. For again as Media asserts, though "old kingdoms may be on the wane . . . new dynasties advance." Even Vivenza, though still in her childhood, already "lusts for empire like a czar." Melville, to be sure, does not side entirely with Media's point of view here. In the end, he seems to adopt a more complex position, on the one hand saying with the youthful Yoomy that "Our hopes are not wild dreams: Vivenza cheers our hearts. She is a rainbow to the isles!" and, on the other hand saying, with the more cautious Babbalanja, that one should never try to predict the future, for "Fate laughs at prophets" (541–42).

In engineering the shift, near the end of *Mardi*, from a wholly imaginary realm to an allegorical realm of geographically recognizable islands such as Dominora (England), Porpheero (continental Europe), and Vivenza (the United States), Melville is clearly signaling that he wanted his English and American readers to recognize that their countries, too, had failed to live up to their own ideals. But just as clearly he was trying to drive home the point that, despite significant progress in one country or another, there would never be a utopian place in which one might find true happiness. It is one thing to say, as Melville did with increasing urgency in the late chapters of *Mardi*, that true happiness is a thing of the imagination and spirit, that it comes from within. It is quite another to say that, in the pursuit of happiness, politics are irrelevant, at least beyond a certain point. Yet, both explicitly and implicitly, that seems to be the central message of *Mardi*. For as the scroll-writer says matter of factly, "It is not the prime end, and chief blessing, to be politically free. And freedom is only good as a means; is no end in itself . . . freedom is more social than political. And its real felicity is not to be shared. *That* is of a man's own individual getting and holding" (527–29).

In projecting Taji's quest through the Mardian isles, Melville clearly had something very much like this conclusion in mind. For what he demonstrates is that while any number of the islands may seem promising at a distance, none is in fact a suitable dwelling place for Yillah. Time and again we are told the same thing that is said after the voyagers witness the misery of the slaves in the southern regions of Vivenza: "as in Dominora,—so, throughout Vivenza,

North and South,—Yillah harbored not" (535). In the satire of *Mardi,* what we learn, finally, is that all the islands of the imaginary archipelago, like all the nations of the terrestrial globe, are dystopias rather than utopias. All are models of culture to be shunned rather than emulated—all, that is, except one.[24]

The lone exception that Melville provides in *Mardi* is an imaginary place called Serenia—the next-to-last island on Taji's itinerary. Although there is necessarily a kind of political order here, what distinguishes Melville's utopian community from Plato's or Sir Thomas More's is that its political structure is essentially a nullity. Unlike the situation even on Vivenza, where all are said to be kings, and "all equal" (521), on Serenia "there dwells no king" whatsoever. Here people are left to themselves, as Media observes incredulously; here "mystic Love" is ruler (627). Here there are no systematic means of social control, no hierarchy of authority. Thus only on Serenia are Taji and his companions welcomed as "brothers," in strict accordance with the teachings of the Christlike Alma, rather than as demigods. Here people make no boastful claims about the precepts they hold or about the practices they follow; here, says the humble old man who is their guide, "we but earnestly endeavor" (626).

Everywhere on Serenia a distinctively Melvillean kind of skepticism holds sway. All knowledge—of the world, of the self, of other people—is recognized to be incomplete, imperfect, relativistic. On this unique island the reigning assumption is that no one person or party has a corner on the truth. When one dissents from the majority view, it is not said that "he is wrong, and we are right; for this we know not, absolutely," as the old guide explains. Here it is remembered always that "if [any person] dissent from us, we then equally dissent from him." Such relativism is neither the product of grudging tolerance nor the consequence of conscious restraint; it is instead a natural expression of "world-wide love and charity" in action (626).

Every work of utopian literature, Northrop Frye has said, "presents an imaginative vision of the *telos* or end at which social life aims."[25] Inevitably, this will be an end that reflects the writer's own most deeply felt emotional needs, though what those needs are will have been shaped, at least to some degree, by the ideals of the writer's own culture. It should come as no surprise, then, to discover that, for Melville, the most perfect society he could imagine is one where all truth is recognized to be uncertain and relativistic, where imperfection is acknowledged to be the mark of all things human, and where people manage to live together peacefully in spite of their differences. Unsure himself about what constitutes the truth in any absolute sense, whatever the area of human inquiry or endeavor, Melville wanted a society wherein no one would suffer at the hands of a powerful authority because he or she had refused to subscribe to some prevailing, autocratic formulation of what is true.

For a strong-minded American author like Melville, who was just beginning to discover that what he was moved to write and what would sell in the literary marketplace were two very different articles, it naturally follows that this principle would be accorded the central place in his quasi-utopian program. However, Melville also recognized the need to build a great deal of human diversity into his ideal community, simply because of the endless variety of personalities that constitute human nature. After explaining that the Serenians believe neither in human perfection nor in the perfection of their own social state, the old interpreter acknowledges that there are limits to what social engineering can accomplish because there are ineluctable differences in the makeup of individual people. While the Serenians, as he says, "make not the miserable many support the happy few," as is usually the case with monarchies, neither do they, "by annulling reason's laws, seek to breed equality, by breeding anarchy," as would be the case with an egalitarian, communist form of government such as Marx was then proposing in Europe. "In all things," the aged guide explains, "equality is not for all. Each has his own. Some have wider groves of palms than others; fare better; dwell in more tasteful arbors; oftener renew their fragrant thatch. Such differences must be" (627).

While a certain amount of social engineering is necessary to isolate what Melville calls "the vicious," at least until they can be reclaimed, he otherwise emphasizes the voluntary nature of all human endeavor on Serenia, and its natural conformity to the teachings of Alma. Thus on Serenia, no one starves, for example, because "by the abounding, the needy are supplied." This system of mutual support is accomplished, the old guide says, "not by statute, but from dictates, born half dormant in us, and warmed into life by Alma." Melville was not a traditional Christian believer, but he did believe in a natural religion inspired and guided by the example of Christ. The source of right action, he suggests here, is the heart of man, but it is the heart as it has been educated by the example of Alma. When the old guide asserts that "we are all immortal," he does so with the explanation that "Here, Alma joins with our own hearts, confirming nature's promptings." True faith, for Melville, consists of the belief in the coincidence of the two, not in one to the exclusion of the other.

Significantly, it is at this moment in the aged interpreter's rehearsal of Serenia's utopian program that Babbalanja starts to experience his conversion. "I begin to see," the philosopher exclaims. "I come out in light. The sharp fang [of the devilish Azzageddi, his repressed self] tears me less." Melville's heterodoxy is most clearly seen when the old man explains that the Serenians' "faith jars [not] with reason." On the contrary, he says, "Right-reason, and Alma, are the same; else Alma, not reason, would we reject" (629). Only then does the old man quote Alma as exclaiming, "In *me* is that heart of

mild content, which in vain ye seek in rank and title. I am Love: love ye then me." And in response, Babbalanja, Yoomy, Mohi, and even Media all kneel and own Alma as "prince divine" (630).

As its name implies, Serenia is not really a place but a state of mind. In suggesting such an interiorized conception of utopia, Melville was placing himself in the tradition of virtually all idealist utopian thinkers, but especially the one that runs from Plato through Thomas More. It was the idealist More, in fact, who coined the term "utopia," meaning "no place." Like the imagined realms of these other utopianists, Melville's Serenia is not a future ideal but what Frye calls a "hypothetical" ideal; it is "the kind of model of justice and common sense which, once established in the mind," serves to clarify its standards and values.[26] Utopian writing that imagines a "hypothetical" ideal is intended only for those who might find their lives informed by its example, nothing more. Unlike the other kind, which plots out a future ideal, it is not intended for social engineers and others who might be inclined to take its form literally.[27] Thus, when the most talkative member of Taji's group, the aptly named Babbalanja, announces his decision to remain on the island of Serenia rather than continue the quest for Yillah, he explains that his voyage is ended, "Not because what I sought is found; but that I now possess all which may be had of what I sought in Mardi." Turning to Taji, he declares that he now knows the hunt for the beautiful maiden is "vain" because she is a "phantom"; he recognizes that, as an ideal, she exists only in the quester's imagination. "Wise counsel take," he exclaims. "Within our hearts is all we seek, though in that search, many need a prompter" such as Alma (637).

It is important that the wisdom shown here suddenly strikes Babbalanja all at once, in the form of a vision that comes to him while deep in meditation following his conversion. "I have dreamed of wondrous things," he explains to his companions, and then goes on to relate to them the details of a marvelous *E.T.*-like adventure, in which a dazzling extraterrestrial figure suddenly materializes to convey Babbalanja up into the air, past "systems, suns, and moons," and on into more ethereal realms inhabited by higher creatures. The opportunity to witness the structure of the entire universe and to behold the great chain of being is granted him as a reward for adopting an attitude of humility toward all knowledge at the time he took Alma to his heart. "This I have learned, oh! spirit!" he exclaims, responding to the questioning of his celestial guide, "—In things mysterious to seek no more; but rest content, with knowing naught but Love" (632–33).

Having showed such humility, Babbalanja, the book's most energetic seeker of truth, is then given the chance to learn a higher wisdom still, namely that,

as the guide tells him, "No mind but Oro's can know all; no mind that knows not all can be content: content alone approximates to happiness" (634).

Despite such wisdom, Melville clearly knew himself well enough to recognize that he himself was not yet ready to rest content in such knowledge. Ironized though he may be, Taji, the narrator-hero, is Melville's most thoroughly autobiographical character in this novel, and Taji finally refuses to try to live by such wisdom. In continuing his search for Yillah after the others have given up, he seeks a happiness beyond that intended for the inhabitants of Mardi. He seeks fulfillment, an earthly love that will match his transcendent ideal, when in fact the "only Mardian happiness," as the celestial guide tells Babbalanja, "is but exemption from great woes—no more" (636).

In pursuing his impossible dream, Taji seeks to unriddle what is for him the last mystery, the mystery of Yillah's disappearance. If he is not guilty of such pride as attempting to "know all," as only Oro can, he is at least guilty of such pride as seeking to know more than it is given man to know. For in aiming to unravel the mystery of Yillah's vanishing, Taji is in effect trying to solve the mystery of death. Not until the penultimate chapter, in his final confrontation with Hautia, does Taji actually learn of Yillah's demise. But once he does, he immediately takes a suicidal plunge past the reef of Mardi and into the deep beyond, from which "no voyager ever puts back." In doing so, he does no more than any young hero of romance is bound to do when he finds his loved one is gone forever. He chooses death as a last desperate chance at reunion with her rather than suffer "a life of dying" without her (654).

Death is the key to the mystery of Yillah's disappearance, but the cause of her death remains a mystery even at the very end. Yillah's initial disappearance, we are led to believe, was the result of Taji's corruption of the ideal by the sin of murdering Aleema, and presumably her demise is to be attributed to the same cause. Such a conclusion seems to be supported by the allegorical portion of the narrative focusing on Hautia, whose name implies that she is the embodiment of the hero's own destructive pride, the source of all sin.

However, it is also emphasized in the course of the story that death is universal and inescapable. All life is subject to decay and destruction, and this complicates the suggestion that Taji's actions are responsible for the death of the beautiful maiden. In chapter 48, aptly titled "Something under the Surface," Melville interrupts a series of chapters devoted to the character of Yillah to remind his readers that death—here in the form of a rapacious swordfish then seen trailing the *Chamois*—always lurks just out of sight and can destroy at any time. Chapter 185, "L'Ultima sera," provides a later, more expansive example of Melville's preoccupation with the same idea. Here, on "the last

evening" before the travelers suddenly sail into the daylight of Serenia, Babbalanja speaks of his being weary with the mutability of life in such a way as to suggest that Taji's experience of loss is the inevitable result of the passing of time and the universal process of decay:

> . . . why, why live? Life is wearisome to all: the same dull round. Day and night, summer and winter, round about us revolving for aye. One moment lived, is a life. No new stars appear in the sky; no new lights in the soul. Yet, of changes there are many. For though, with rapt sight, in childhood, we behold many strange things beneath the moon, and all Mardi looks a tented fair—how soon every thing fades. All of us, in our very bodies, outlive our ownselves. I think of green youth as of a merry playmate departed; and to shake hands and be pleasant with my old age, seems in prospect even harder, than to draw a cold stranger to my bosom. But old age is not for me. I am not of the stuff that grows old. This Mardi is not our home. Up and down we wander, like exiles transported to a planet afar:—'tis not the world *we* were born in; not the world once so lightsome and gay; not the world where we once merrily danced, dined, and supped; and wooed, and wedded our long-buried wives. Then let us depart. But whither? (619)

Further obscuring our understanding of the causes of Yillah's demise is the fact that, as a character in an imaginary voyage, Yillah is simply a fleeting image in the dream life of the story's narrator-hero. Like all the other characters in the book, including the fabrication called Taji, she is a figment of the storyteller/dreamer's imagination. Melville more than hints at such a conception of her status, and of that of the other characters in *Mardi*, too, in the chapter titled "Dreams" (chapter 119), where his narrator proclaims, in words that seem to point to the unconscious sources of Melville's own bursting creative energies, that, "like a frigate, I am full with a thousand souls; and as on, on, on, I scud before the wind, many mariners rush up from the orlog below, like miners from caves; running shouting across my decks . . . and boisterous speaking-trumpets are heard; and contending orders, to save the good ship from the shoals" (367). Later, much the same idea is dramatized when Melville introduces into the book an analogue for himself named Lombardo, the fictional author of the equally fictional "Koztanza," itself an analogue for *Mardi*. As Babbalanja explains the origins of the characters to be found in Lombardo's work, he "first met them in his reveries; they were walking about in him, sour and moody" and often recalcitrant (596). Like these imaginary characters, or like the figures in dreams generally, Yillah may be coaxed into making an

appearance now and then, but she is not a slave to the dreamer's wishes and cannot be made to appear on command. Instead, she comes and goes according to some peculiar logic of the unconscious mind of the dreamer, some repressed yet powerful emotion of guilt, anxiety, or need.

Because Yillah cannot be brought back to life by the narrator's imagination, Taji, the narrator's dream persona, must ultimately give up the ghost, too, at least for this dream, and this book. And so he does, at the end, when the narrator awakens and returns to the everyday world. Ever faithful to the memory of Yillah, Taji himself has been gradually dying away, becoming less and less a figural presence in the second half of the narrative and more and more a disembodied observer.

In the concluding chapter, when Taji and Hautia have their last confrontation, we witness his virtual demise, as Hautia, the jealous queen of the fallen world we all inhabit, "slowly drank up [his] soul," and the narrator begins to reassert conscious control over the operations of his mind. Using biblical imagery that reveals Hautia's true nature as the serpent of destruction, Taji captures the corrosive effect that the waking world always has on the realm of dreams when he says, "Thus we stood:—snake and victim: life ebbing out from me, to her" (652). Having learned at last of the death of Yillah, and witnessed her form as a "revolving shade" being swept out to sea, Taji confesses to feeling a hellish despair, one more profound than the despair the narrator had felt during the calm on the *Arcturion* in the opening chapters. But he is powerless to free himself. As his own life ebbs away, he feels his dream become a nightmare in which he is held prisoner: "As somnambulists fast-frozen in some horrid dream, ghost-like glide abroad, and fright the wakeful world; so that night, with death-glazed eyes, to and fro I flitted on the damp and weedy beach" (653).

In his final moments, Taji grows almost unrecognizable, imperceptible, even to Mohi and Yoomy, who question him when they find him near the shore the next morning. "Is this specter, Taji?" they ask, and in reply he says, "Taji lives no more. So dead, he has no ghost. I am his spirit's phantom's phantom." Dragged to the water's edge by his friends and carried out to sea in a canoe, Taji says vaguely, "as in a dream, I hearkened to a voice." It is the voice of the historian Mohi, who tells him of King Media's return to Odo and of Media's efforts to help his people there at long last. Once Melville has hurriedly tied up this loose end, Taji, still obsessed with the memory of Yillah, seizes the helm of the little craft and announces his intention to make a suicidal thrust outside of Mardi, the world of mind, of dreams, in a last desperate effort to be reunited with her. As Mohi and Yoomy jump for their lives, Taji exclaims fiercely, "Now I am my own soul's emperor; and my first act is abdication! Hail! realm of

shades!" Immediately, Aleema's sons—"three fixed specters"—reappear, hungering as always for vengeance (653–54).

While virtually the whole book—from the moment of Taji's naming in chapter 53 through the next to the last paragraph in the final chapter—is spoken in the voice of Taji, the narrator's imaginary alter-ego, the last paragraph is uttered by the nameless narrator himself, who has the perspective of one who lives among the waking, in the world of the reader. It is only a single sentence—"And thus, pursuers and pursued flew on, over an endless sea"—but it is enough to mark the return of the anonymous figure whose voice had opened the novel and to reestablish his role as the framing storyteller.[28] Like T. S. Eliot's loveless Prufrock, the narrator of *Mardi* awakens at the end of his imaginary voyage with the knowledge that a part of him has died in a dream that knows no dying. Though Taji is a defiant figure, ever clinging to his faith in a redeeming love, where Prufrock is passive and defeated, the narrator of Melville's novel also might say, as Prufrock says to his repressed double at the end of "The Love Song,"

> We have lingered in the chambers of the sea
> By sea-girls wreathed with seaweed red and brown
> Till human voices wake us, and we drown.[29]

Unlike Eliot, an Anglican who placed no faith in the unconscious, but like the other great moderns of this century—Yeats and Joyce, Miro and Picasso, Freud and Jung—Melville could not, in the end, bring himself to deny the claims of the dream life once he had taken the step of setting it free in what at the time was his most ambitious book. It is true that several important wisdom figures in *Mardi*—the old guide from Serenia; the angelic spirit who assists Babbalanja in his dream vision; Babbalanja himself as well as the other voyagers who choose to settle on Serenia—all reject the claims of the buried self in favor of the dictates of right reason, with its insistence on patience, humility, and acceptance. The piling up of so many examples of renunciation near the end, in combination with Taji's suicide, has led several critics to conclude that Melville must have felt the demands of the deeper self needed to be kept under lock and key. But such a view is predicated on the assumption that Taji is a flesh-and-blood character, in all important respects the same as the narrator. Once it is recognized that he is simply the narrator's alter-ego, an imaginary figure in a wish-fulfillment fantasy turned nightmare, then the objections to Taji's suicide ought to lose their force. Then Taji's end can be seen to signify Melville's feeling that the claims of the deeper self are indisputable and incapable of compromise, that the demands of the natural

man for a transcendent love have a validity not to be denied, despite all the bright wisdom to the contrary that Babbalanja and the others can muster in the concluding chapters.

Mardi is a young man's book, and, at least tangentially, a young woman's, too. It tells the common story, in an uncommonly protracted and imaginative way, of the author's disappointment with love—in Melville's case, of his disappointment with his marriage to Elizabeth Shaw. More than this, however, it reveals that Melville had not been completely disenchanted with love as the result of the one major affair of the heart he is known to have had in his entire life. By the late 1840s, when Mardi was written, he still retained a decidedly romantic view of the subject.[30] At least the part of him represented by Taji refused to give up his belief that the love of his life was so important she was even worth dying for. Part of him, that is to say, defiant as only the young can be, continued to reject the advice of those who spoke of the contentment that comes with a wise acceptance of fate or who advocated a Christ-like self-restraint in the face of disillusionment with the things of this world.

An unusually complicated man, Melville of course did not hold an uncomplicated view of love, even at the end of Mardi, where one might expect a firm resolution of the question. Wise beyond his years, yet urgent with a young man's yearning, he seems to have fought the issue to a standstill and then let it remain unresolved, Taji going his way and Babbalanja and the others going theirs. As has already been seen, Melville endorsed the wisdom of Babbalanja, who came to believe that "Within our hearts is all we seek." However, as a young man, married little more than a year and not yet thoroughly demystified of love, he knew also just how hard it was to be so self-contained. In Babbalanja's next breath, we see him pleading with Taji to stay, all the while realizing, it seems, that his counsel will have no effect: "Then rove no more," he advises. "Gain now, in flush of youth, that last wise thought, too often purchased, by a life of woe. Be wise: be wise" (637).

Whether Melville himself ever resolved this most important of the heart's questions after he finished Mardi, whether he managed to grow content or suffered instead a lifetime of disappointment, it would be impossible to say in a study of the author's fiction such as this. Certainly Melville continued to live with Elizabeth Shaw and to father her children, though in recent years it has come to light that it was a marriage with such problems as to have reached the breaking point nearly two decades later when a separation was threatened. Then, however, it was Elizabeth who came to the verge of breaking away.[31] For Melville himself, the crisis had come and gone long before that, possibly even without his wife knowing it, in the first year of their marriage while he wrote Mardi.[32] If, still in those early months of his marriage, Melville was able

to address his own despair privately, even silently, and with a certain equanimity, it is because the imaginary voyage he himself had taken while writing *Mardi* had helped to clarify his dilemma and brought him some measure of self-understanding. In the process, jumbled and contradictory though his effort sometimes was in this book, he reached beyond the achievement of *Typee* and *Omoo* and began to discover his true calling as a poet of the imagination, that rarest of writers whose task it is, as Wallace Stevens has said, to "represent the mind in the act of defending us against itself."[33]

❧

"Gentleman Forger":
Redburn as Bildungsroman

Since William H. Gilman's *Melville's Early Life and "Redburn"* (1951) launched the scholarly discussion of Melville's fourth novel as something more than a minor chapter in the author's life story, critics of *Redburn* have been sharply divided about the questions of whether and how the title character matures in the course of the narrative. Until James Schroeter challenged the prevailing "mythic" interpretations of the novel in 1967, most commentators accepted the notion that Redburn's growth follows the typically "American" pattern of the "initiation of innocence into evil" described by Newton Arvin in 1950.[1] While Schroeter, too, argued that Redburn shows clear signs of moral and intellectual development, the "progressive" school of opinion, as it might be called, has had an increasing number of detractors, nearly all of whom share H. Bruce Franklin's view that Redburn betrays Harry Bolton in the last chapter and thus fails to act in accord with the mature principle of brotherly love he had come to profess in the second half of the novel.[2]

The debate over Redburn's maturity concerns a vitally important issue in its own right, to be sure, but it has larger consequences as well. For until we can answer the question of whether the title character shows some measurable emotional or psychological growth in the end, we cannot be sure what kind of a book *Redburn* is or what Melville's larger intentions might have been in writing it. There is general agreement that *Redburn* is a work of fiction, despite the fact that its story line is based generally on Melville's own boyhood voyage to

This chapter appeared in a different version as "Melville's Gentleman Forger: The Struggle for Identity in *Redburn*" in *Texas Studies in Literature and Language* 21 (September 1979): 347–67. Reprinted by permission of the University of Texas Press.

Liverpool. But the question of what kind of novel it is, or what novelistic conventions Melville might have relied on in shaping it, has never really been explored before. If Redburn can be shown to mature, we would then be on much firmer ground in regarding it as an "education novel" or bildungsroman, particularly a nautical bildungsroman like Frederick Marryat's *Peter Simple* (1834), rather than the "beggarly" work or "botch" it is still widely assumed to be.[3]

Wellingborough Redburn's treatment of Harry Bolton, while important to any consideration of his maturity, has been exaggerated (if not misjudged) at the expense of the slow and difficult maturing process that the young title character has undergone, though by no means completed, by the end of the novel. Furthermore, this process can be understood more accurately in terms of identity formation than in those of the simpler process of initiation. For, whereas initiation is a relatively straightforward occurrence defined by a crisis of brief duration, and stands as a more or less fixed achievement in the life of the adolescent, identity formation is a complicated and fluid, uncertain process. It implies an extended critical period as well as a tenuous accomplishment that remains subject to the influences of the youth's personal and cultural past, present, and future.

Moreover, because it constitutes only one of several essentially distinct stages in the maturing process, identity formation is also part of a more comprehensive theory of human development than the one provided by the notion of initiation.[4] Certainly Redburn experiences disillusionment about the world and himself during the four months of his "first voyage." But to use the initiation idea of a shift from an unconscious state of innocence to a consciousness of evil as a description of the transition from youth to adulthood is to forget that most of us are lucky to make this transition in less than twice that many years, to oversimplify the complexity of the social and psychological processes of the growth of the self in American culture, and to disregard the precariousness of its accomplishments. Most importantly, it is also to underestimate Melville's understanding of the maturing process—his own, I would say, as much as the one he imagines for his title character.

According to Erik Erikson, arguably the foremost theorist of identity formation, the struggle for identity is the major psychosocial activity of adolescence. In theory, it is the struggle to gain a sense of selfhood that grows out of one's social and psychological past, reflects accurately one's present circumstances, and promises a future that will nourish the continued growth of the self. In psychological terms, Erikson writes, "identity formation employs a process of simultaneous reflection and observation, a process taking place on all levels of mental functioning, by which the individual judges himself in the

light of what he perceives to be the way in which others judge him in comparison to themselves and to a typology significant to them; while he judges their way of judging him in the light of how he perceives himself in comparison to them and to types that have become relevant to him."[5]

Erikson's definition, though cumbersome, has a roundness and precision that more than adequately describe Redburn's actions and mental operations during most of the narrative, particularly when he is the active young protagonist rather than the passive, somewhat older narrator-observer. Thus Redburn, who at the start believes himself to be a gentleman like his father, before his bankruptcy and death, must either modify his conception of himself as he discovers that others, such as Captain Riga of the *Highlander,* take him to be the desperate, impoverished youth that he is or else rationalize his illusion of himself by dismissing their way of judging him, as he does briefly when he concludes that Captain Riga is "a sort of impostor," because "no gentleman would have treated another gentleman as he did me."[6]

In practice, the process of forming an identity, Erikson adds, "is, luckily, and necessarily, for the most part unconscious except where inner conditions and outer circumstances combine to aggravate a painful, or elated, 'identity-consciousness.'"[7] Unhappily for Redburn, it is the exception rather than the rule that applies most often to him, for the novel's major source of dramatic tension, and a good deal of its comedy, is the endlessly repeated aggravation of his painful "identity-consciousness." His story, therefore, is in large part the record of an "identity crisis." In his case, as in Peter Simple's, the aggravation and the crisis result from a conflict between the inner condition of his desire to be recognized as the born "son-of-a-gentleman" and the outer circumstance of his serving as a green and lowly "sailor-boy" in a rigidly heirarchical institution where ease and respect, responsibility and remuneration—significant marks of the life of privilege Redburn craves and among the chief sources of identity strength in American culture—must be earned, if they can be earned at all, by pluck and luck, toughness or meanness, and long years of hard training.

On just two occasions, each time while high in the rigging, does Redburn experience anything like an "elated" form of identity consciousness, such as William James described when he wrote that a man's character is discernible in the "mental or moral attitude in which, when it came upon him, he felt himself most deeply and intensely active and alive. At such moments there is a voice inside which speaks and says: '*This* is the real me!'"[8] For Redburn, one such occasion is when, to appropriate the title of chapter 24, "He Begins to Hop About in the Rigging Like a Saint Jago's Monkey." Yet only a moment's

reflection tells us that a Saint Jago's monkey is a very limited form of identity and thus cause for what is at best an equivocal kind of elation.

From the beginning, Redburn does not actually set out to become a sailor, though a sailor in earnest he becomes as we learn only on the last page when he refers to himself on a later voyage as "a sailor in the Pacific, on board of a whaler" (312). In chapter 1, titled "How Wellingborough Redburn's Taste for the Sea Was Born and Bred in Him," he tells us that "during my early life, most of my thoughts of the sea were connected with the land; but with fine old lands, full of mossy cathedrals and churches, and long, narrow, crooked streets without sidewalks, and lined with strange houses." As he grew older, he says, "my thoughts took a larger flight, and I frequently fell into long reveries about distant voyages and travels." His early objective, then, is to become a world traveler—not because such a life offers novelty or education but because it promises to satisfy his identity ideal. This Redburn reveals in swelling tones when reminiscing that he "thought how fine it would be, to be able to talk about remote and barbarous countries; with what reverence and wonder people would regard me, if I had just returned from the coast of Africa or New Zealand; how dark and romantic my sunburnt cheeks would look; how I would bring home with me foreign clothes of a rich fabric and princely make, and wear them up and down the streets, and how grocers' boys would turn back their heads to look at me, as I went by" (5).

One of Redburn's chief identity models in this early boyhood stage was the nameless man with big eyes who "had been in Stony Arabia, and passed through strange adventures there." So strong is the boy's identification with this exotic stranger that not only did his own eyes seem to become magnified as he stared at him one Sunday in church, but also, Redburn says, "he long haunted me; and several times I dreamt of him" (5–6). Naturally, his identification with this man is ultimately narcissistic, for he wants the grocers' boys to stare at him as he had stared at the Arabian traveler. He wants to love and admire himself.

The other identity model in Redburn's early years, a still more compelling one, was of course his father, who "had several times crossed the Atlantic on business affairs" and used to tell his sons "of the monstrous waves at sea . . . and all about Havre, and Liverpool, and about going up into the ball of St. Paul's in London" (5).[9] Young Wellingborough's desire to imitate his father is seen in the ardent interest he displays in all of the foreign objects the elder Redburn had brought home from Europe—the furniture, the oil paintings and rare old engravings, the large French portfolios of colored prints, the long rows of old books that had been printed in Paris and London and Leipzig, and the old-fashioned glass ship. Indeed, the boy's "continual dwelling upon

foreign associations," he confesses, "bred in me a vague prophetic thought, that I was fated ... to be a great voyager; and that just as my father used to entertain strange gentlemen over their wine after dinner, I would hereafter be telling my own adventures to an eager auditory" (7).

These articles encourage Redburn to identify himself ever more strongly with his father, for while they are the tangible signs of what is foreign about the father to the boy, they are also the means by which he can gain identity with him—if only their "foreignness" can be domesticated, if only these things can be fully understood, as Redburn dreams of mastering the French language by foreign travel in order to "be able to read straight along without stopping" out of the copy of D'Alembert, "which now was a riddle to every one in the house but my father" (7). In short, Redburn wants, at least unconsciously, to become his father, not only because, from the point of view of his wounded young psyche, he can in that way restore him to life, but (pathology aside) because a boy's father is a natural identity model. For these reasons, then, he ships for Liverpool, where he can retrace his father's footsteps with the aid of the elder Redburn's "Prosy Old Guide-Book."

Although at the time of his departure Redburn claims to have formed "a definite purpose of seeking my fortune on the sea," he regards himself, rather comically, to be "as unambitious as a man of sixty," bitter and heavyhearted, a "misanthrope," whose "young mounting dreams of glory" had left him following the loss of his family's wealth (7, 10). But he has not yet abandoned his presumed identity as a young gentleman. Like the aristocratic moleskin shooting jacket, the gift of Redburn's brother, his wealthy past still clings to him, and he to it. The jacket is a complex symbol, however; while it is to Redburn the last proud emblem of the leisure class that earlier had been his destiny, it is now a sign also of the destitution of his family, which can no longer even afford a proper sailor's jacket for its voyaging son. Significantly, this latter meaning never occurs to him. Even though rain shrinks it to the point where Redburn jokingly worries that "it would completely exhale, and leave nothing but the bare seams, by way of a skeleton," on his back, he never finally gives it up (74).

The irony of his being the son of a gentleman with the "scent and savor of poverty" on him does not, to be sure, escape the young Wellingborough. But rather than accept his current state and put his former identity behind him (an all-but-impossible achievement, for it is the only positive identity he has), Redburn does the predictable thing of youth and wallows in self-pity for his fallen condition. With a heart that "aches" in his bosom and "a few hot tears" on his cheeks, he walks "with a slouching, dogged gait" to the Hudson steamer. "Talk not of the bitterness of middle-age and after life," Redburn lectures

melodramatically, in the mildly ironic yet also sympathetic tones of the older narrator, "a boy can feel all that, and much more, when upon his young soul the mildew has fallen" (10–12).

Moreover, once out in the world beyond his family village, Redburn immediately experiences the painful form of identity-consciousness, as revealed in his slightly paranoid speculation that some of his fellow passengers on the boat to New York were, like himself, silently "speculating . . . as to who each other might be" (11). In addition, he attempts self-consciously to conceal his poverty and put a proud appearance before the world, as when he "studiously endeavored to hide" the big patch on his trousers leg with the skirts of his shooting jacket, from what he regards to be the "cold suspicious glances" of the other passengers (12).

But when the inner conditions of hunger and "that desperation and recklessness of poverty which only a pauper knows" begin to conspire with the outer circumstance of the others' stares, Redburn becomes so keenly aware of the inauthenticity of his presumed identity that he grimly taunts them to confirm what he feels to be all too true about himself. Now, he says, "I stretched out my leg boldly, and thrust the patch under their noses, and looked at them so, that they soon looked away." The breaking point is all but reached when the fashionably dressed young ticket collector, after taking Redburn's last dollar (though it is but half the standard fare), denies his presumed identity by "saying something about sportsmen going on shooting expeditions, without having money to pay their expenses." Suddenly sensing "every eye" to be fastened on him, Redburn reacts with pathological violence, like young Robin in Hawthorne's "My Kinsman, Major Molineux." He turns to one of the gazers and, clicking his gunlock, "deliberately" points his fowling-piece at him (12–13).

Chapter 3, "He Arrives in Town," continues the process of exposing the folly of Redburn's attempt to maintain the image of a gentleman in the face of his reduced circumstances and the penetrating eye of others, here chiefly that of the sly Captain Riga. That Redburn, by the opening of this chapter, has already begun reluctantly to see himself as others see him, however, is signaled by his willingness simply to "stalk off" from the grocery where he has stopped for water, rather than use his gun to challenge the "rough looking fellows" there who banter him (14). Still, this adjustment in his self-image becomes clear only in the next scene when we witness the growing distance between Redburn and the well-intentioned Mr. Jones, his older brother's college friend who accompanies him to the docks to help him secure a position on ship. Indeed, in his humorous attempts to win Riga's respect, Mr. Jones misguidedly encourages the boy's pretensions at a false identity by promoting him as the son of a "gentleman of one of the first families in America"—to

Redburn's increasing consternation and the eventual dashing of his hope to gain an advance on his salary (16). That it is the young Redburn, not the wise older narrator, who draws the moral is seen in Melville's use of the past tense: "I said nothing, though I thought the more; and particularly, how that it would have been much better for me, to have gone on board alone, accosted the captain on my own account, and told him the plain truth. Poor people make a very poor business of it when they try to seem rich" (17).

This is the first of several important lessons that Redburn is to learn from Captain Riga, his early self-appointed "tutor" in the business of identity formation (16). Riga is an unsympathetic figure, mainly because he cheats Redburn out of his wages at the end and seems as duplistic in his manner as he is in his attire; "splendidly dressed" and marked by "extreme civility" while on shore, he wears "nothing but old shabby clothes" at sea and flies into a rage when Redburn, in a severe breach of sea decorum, strikes up a conversation with him one day on the quarterdeck (15, 70–71).

However, Riga is a more complicated character than most critics have recognized, an early avatar of the charming, preternaturally shrewd cosmopolitan in *The Confidence-Man*. Perhaps because he himself is something of an "impostor," as Redburn claims, he is capable of exposing the pretensions of others; and, in a sardonic way, he is a truth-teller and wisdom figure. He repeatedly admonishes the young would-be sailor to be honest in his dealings with others and realistic in his judgments about himself. Immediately perceiving Redburn to be a "country lad," he cautions him that a sailor's life is "hard" (15–16). And in his parting words to the boy on their first encounter, Riga warns him not to "get home-sick before you sail, because that will make you very sea-sick when you get to sea," a seemingly indifferent remark that nonetheless carries with it a serious reminder of Redburn's need to come to terms with who he is before undertaking his first voyage (18). The fact that Redburn's great-uncle had been a Senator, Riga knows, will be nothing but a hindrance to the boy's learning to stand on his own legs. "'But his great-uncle don't want to go to sea too?' said the captain, looking funny," in response to the name-dropping of Mr. Jones (16).

Although Redburn comes to dismiss Riga as an unsuitable father substitute because he fails to "prove a kind friend and benefactor," he is in fact one of those fathers such as "Solomon's precepts tend to make—severe and chastising fathers, fathers whose sense of duty overcomes the sense of love" (67). That he is not a worthy identity model, however, can be concluded from the facts of his dualism, or duplicity, and selfishness. Riga's example reveals what one becomes when he sets out to achieve the status of a "gentleman" in the cruel economy of the merchant service. He must develop a double identity,

one for the land and one for the sea. To stay free of pawnbrokers and still pay his "wine bills at the City Hotel" (the false address given by the young thief whom Redburn encounters in a New York pawnshop), he must use technicalities to cheat sailor-boys out of their wages and be miserly with the crew's "allowance of bread and beef" while at sea (307–08, 22).

Unaware of the real difficulties of becoming a sailor before the mast, Redburn at first presumes that it is sufficient to achieve the appearance of a sailor before the mirror. In the amusing, narcissistic scene when he tries on his motley new sailor's outfit, after carefully locking the door of his room in the Joneses' house and hanging a towel over the keyhole, Redburn reveals acute anxiety about his newly adopted identity. His uncertainty as to who he is, unselfconscious though it is, is well-founded, for not until he has completed the first leg of his first voyage can he have a true sense of what it means to be a sailor.

Melville further emphasizes the fact that one's identity is gained slowly and painfully, and not simply chosen, by providing several instances wherein Redburn suffers from mistaken identity during the period when the *Highlander* is being prepared for its Atlantic crossing. Even though he is now down officially in the ship's articles as a "sailor-boy," no one on ship recognizes Wellingborough as such. Indeed, he is variously misjudged to be a "tailor," a "hay-seed," a "loafer," a thief, a "barber's clerk," a "clod-hopper," a stowaway, and even a "pig" (24–29). And a little later, when the crew is divided into watches, Redburn is passed over as though he were an invisible man, until finally he stands alone, "like a silly sheep, over whom two butchers are bargaining" (39).

Still, Redburn is hardly a tabula rasa. It is because he necessarily retains the little wisdom of his past as a gentleman's son that every early experience in the radically new environment of the ship is a shock to the boy's expectations. But, much to his chagrin, Redburn learns that his showy use of a tobacco box is not a practice subscribed to by the true "salt"; that sailors must forego all independent reasoning and *"Obey orders, though you break owners"* (29); that the crew must address each mate as "sir," just as though he were "a born gentleman" (39); that seasick or no, a sailor must do his duty; that infractions of table etiquette are not tolerated.

Moreover, again like Marryat's Peter Simple, Redburn is forced to learn that people and things can have peculiar names on a ship at sea: a young boy may be called "Buttons" (28) or "Jimmy Dux" (49); pails are not pails but "buckets" (65); and "traps" are not the undoing of rats but a tar's baggage (24). What is more disconcerting still, Redburn discovers that at sea practically everyone and everything is capable of taking on an unexpected identity. A man such as Max, who has not one wife but two, can still be an "old bachelor of a

sailor" (79); demon rum can be an effective medicine for a seasick member of
the Juvenile Total Abstinence Association; and the cook's coffee *will* taste like
anything but coffee, from Dutch herrings to old stocking-heels (43).

Through it all Redburn manages to develop the identity of a sailor-boy, in
spite of his reluctance, by being forced by his new condition to judge himself
in the light of what he perceives to be the way in which the rest of the crew
judge him in comparison to themselves and to the seaman's typology, which
includes such terms as "green-horn," "soger," and "sailor man." Although the
process seems more or less inexorable, given Redburn's fundamentally healthy
flexibility and the others' endless "fault-finding," its advance is fitful and marked
by both crises and regressions, as evidenced in a comic instance as late as
chapter 14, when Redburn "Comtemplates Making a Social Call on the Captain in His Cabin" (79). The first major crisis and regression occur simultaneously in chapter 10, significantly the first night at sea, when the drunken
sailor who had been occupying Redburn's bunk throws himself over the side.
Despite the fact that Redburn refers to him as a "suicide," his end seems the
unintended result of the temporary loss of his identity as a seaman (51). "One
of the sailors who had been brought aboard dead drunk, and tumbled into
his bunk by his landlord," it is speculated that he "must have suddenly waked
up . . . raging mad with the delirium tremens . . . and finding himself in a
strange silent place, and knowing not how he had got there, he had rushed on
deck, and so, in a fit of frenzy, put an end to himself" (50). Thus his example
serves, in a symbolic way, as a solemn warning about how hazardous even a
temporary experience of identity confusion can be.

It is the aftermath of this incident, when the other crew members taunt
Redburn for showing his fear, that constitutes the first real crisis in his identity formation. That he immediately regresses to the role of the child is seen
in his vain declaration that he "would have given the whole world" to be safe
back in his home. Of course Redburn rightly argues, first to himself and then
to the others' faces, that the rest of the crew were also frightened by the incident of the "suicide." But he wrongly assumes that they mock him simply
because they are "false-hearted and insincere." Judging from the ultimate effect
of their persecution on him, it seems that they harass Wellingborough for a
constructive purpose. They try to force him to overcome his childlike vulnerability and self-pity by making him so "mad" that he will stand up to them,
and thereby discover his own strength (51). This is, at any rate, what happens.

Even though they turn on Redburn more mercilessly still in repayment for
his forwardness, asking "whether I ever dreamed of becoming a captain, since
I was a gentleman with white hands," they are simply reasserting their natural
superiority over him and in the process egging him on to a peak of anger that

carries him through this critical episode: "I loathed, detested, and hated them with all that was left of my bursting heart and soul," Redburn confesses, "and I thought myself the most forlorn and miserable wretch that ever breathed. May I never be a *man*, thought I, if to be a *boy* is to be such a wretch. And I wailed and wept, and my heart cracked within me, but all the time I defied them through my teeth, and dared them to do their worst" (52; emphasis added). Yet he is soon on his way to becoming a man, and their worst they never do.

These sailors may not be master psychologists (the exception is Jackson, who "understood human nature to a kink"), but neither are they wicked fools; they know that if Redburn is to conquer his fear and self-doubt and become a man in the world, he must receive no mothering from them (57). Moreover, despite Redburn's feeling that he was "a sort of Ishmael in the ship, without a single friend or companion," the others generally treat him with care and kindness (62). The Greenlander shares his Jamaica spirits with him when he becomes seasick; Ned includes him when offering cigars to the rest of the crew; the cook respects his intelligence and education enough to ask him to interpret a mysterious biblical passage for him; and Max gives "something like a compliment" after the boy performs his first feat in the rigging, and otherwise "sometimes manifested some little interest" in his welfare (79).

Only when Redburn acts the "greenhorn" or the pompous fool—roles for which he shows some talent, in the early days of their voyage especially—do the other crew members make him the butt of their jokes and criticism. Virtually all of their actions toward him, in fact, seem designed to make him a man and a sailor. As Redburn himself comes to admit, "As I began to learn my sailor duties, and show activity in running aloft, the men, I observed, treated me with a little more consideration, though not at all relaxing in a certain air of professional superiority" (120). Still, they condemn and compliment him, finally, not simply out of brotherly concern; they know that unless he becomes a true sailor, his example might corrupt them, as is hilariously suggested when Redburn is accused of being a sort of Circe figure who, by his bad table manners, would reduce his messmates to "no better than swine" (55). More seriously, they know there might well be times when his competence as a sailor will be called on to help keep them all out of harm's way.

The lone exception to this collective portrait of the *Highlander*'s crew is the "great bully" Jackson, whose "infernal looking eye," the more mature Redburn says, "haunts me to this day" (57). This man has a deeper impact on Redburn than any other character except his father, for he is the strongest identity model of a sailor among the crew. Not even Max, finally, can stand up to him (79). Moreover, there is a secret sympathy between the two of them, for, like Redburn, Jackson is a reluctant sailor. Though "the best seaman on

board," he was "a notorious old *soger*" and "despised the ordinary sailor-rig," signs that he also despises what he is (56–59). In fact, self-contempt is his master trait. Acute self-hatred explains his "dissipation and abandonment" (57), his perverse joy at the suffering of others, and his "hatred and gall against every thing and every body in the world." It was "as if all the world was one person," Redburn remarks, "and had done him some dreadful harm, that was rankling and festering in his heart" (61).

In psychological terms, Jackson's behavior is marked by a pathological level of "projection," one of the ego's mechanisms of defense against anxiety, in Freud's scheme, whereby an internal danger is attributed to an external source. It is impossible, of course, to determine the historical origin of Jackson's malady, so little is known of him, but it seems to be connected to his being a mere sailor rather than the "General Jackson of New Orleans," whom he claims to have been his "near relation," for he "swore terribly, if any one ventured to question what he asserted on that head" (57). What is more, it is evident that he has become caught in the vicious cycle of compulsive behavior. Because he hates himself, he engages in dissipating behavior; and the more he becomes dissipated, the more he has reason to hate who and what he is. Thus burdened with self-contempt, his conscience exerts such pressure on his ego that Jackson must reform or else project what he experiences unconsciously as an internal evil onto some target in the external world—in his case, "all the world."

Projection, however, can relieve anxiety only if, to the knowing eye of the ego, there is some objective evidence of the evil of the world and of the relative worth of the self. Thus, to cope with his acute sense of inferiority and with the evidence of his own wasting body that he has time and again played the fool, Jackson makes a practice of turning others into fools, as for instance when he once told his mates a "truly funny story, but with a grave face," so they knew not how to respond, "till at last Jackson roared out upon them for a parcel of fools and idiots . . . and laughed them to scorn" (61). For the same reason, too, he "would enter into arguments, to prove that there was nothing to be believed; nothing to be loved, and nothing worth living for" (104). That Jackson's despair is not absolute is revealed in his uncharacteristic attempt to befriend the young stowaway; but that it is finally incurable is seen in the hatred he seemed to feel for him when the little boy shrank from him in spite of his efforts to come to his aid (113).

Jackson's relationship with Redburn marks a critical stage in the formation of Redburn's identity, because Jackson is what Redburn would become over time if he continued to deny his sailor-boy identity on the grounds that it is beneath his fantasy of being a gentleman. In short, Redburn seems to be headed down the spiraling path of self-hatred, like Jackson. Unknowingly he

admits as much when he finds himself "a sort of Ishmael on the ship" after having attracted Jackson's enmity, on the night of the suicide, by exposing Jackson's fear of death: "I began to feel a hatred growing up in me against the whole crew—so much so, that I prayed against it, that it might not master my heart completely, and so make a fiend of me, something like Jackson" (62).

As will be seen, however, what comes to master Redburn's heart instead is the sea and his consequent sense of belonging to the "All." But Jackson's warning to Redburn—that "if ever I crossed his path . . . he would be the death of me"—seems a guarded admonition to avoid the temptation of following his evil example (52). It is because he has such power as a negative identity model, as an inverted Christ, that only in Jackson's death can Redburn and the rest of the crew find "*their* deliverance" (297).

By the second day out of port, Redburn has made some advance in his struggle for identity, for at least he feels "very well" physically. But his "heart was far from feeling right," and he still desires the leisure to "think of home." The change from night to day and from a "black and forbidding" to a "beautiful and blue" sea, however, signals a similar sea change in the boy. Awed by the rising and falling of the surrounding sea swell, Redburn is no longer self-pitying or defiant; rather, he "felt as if in a dream all the time" and "did not exactly know where, or what I was; every thing was so strange and new" (63–65). Then, with the breeze blowing harder and harder and the ship under additional sail, "Every mast and timber seemed to have a pulse in it that was beating with life and joy; and I felt a wild exulting in my own heart, and felt as if I would be glad to bound along so round the world" (66).

Suddenly, in this transcendental moment, Redburn discovers his own heart beating with that of the ship and the sea, and he comes alive as a true sailor. "Then was I first conscious of a wonderful thing in me, that responded to all the wild commotion of the outer world; and went reeling on and on with the planets in their orbits, and was lost in one delirious throb at the center of the All. A wild bubbling and bursting was at my heart, as if a hidden spring had just gushed out there; and my blood ran tingling along my frame, like mountain brooks in spring freshets." Just as suddenly, however, this elated form of identity-consciousness is forced to give way to the painful form by the "vile commission to clean out the chicken coops, and make up the beds of the pigs." "Miserable dog's life is this of the sea!" he now wails, not realizing that in this fallen world, no matter how perfect one's job may seem, he must earn his bread by the sweat of his brow: "commanded like a slave, and set to work like an ass! . . . Yes, yes, blow on, ye breezes, and make a speedy end to this abominable voyage!" (66).

Nevertheless, well before the ship reaches Liverpool, Redburn finds himself free of such farmboy jobs and able to take pride in "the feeling of mastering the rebellious canvas, and tying it down like a slave to the spar." Indeed, here he feels so content as to compare himself, his tongue only part way in his cheek, with the "young King Richard . . . when he trampled down the insurgents of Wat Tyler" (116). What is just as important is that, for the first time, he is willing to admit his limitations, to take disappointments "coolly, in the spirit of Seneca and the stoics," and to stand almost in awe at the sailor's calling, as when he explains that he is given little chance to take the helm because "I was quite young and raw, and steering a ship is a great art" as well as a job of such responsibility that the man to whom it is awarded is to be regarded with "reverence" (116–17, 122). Chapter 26, "A Sailor a Jack of All Trades," a veritable paean to the sailor's calling, offers further evidence of a dramatic change in Redburn's attitude toward his new line of work, and toward himself.

But of course a sailor is more than what he does. He is also what his society views him to be, as Redburn learns with disappointment and even horror in Liverpool, where he is barred from entering both a newsroom and the Lyceum, where former sailors are seen to constitute a large portion of the "army of paupers" in the streets near the docks (186), and where sailors, in the practice of their "two great vices," readily fall prey to "a company of miscreant misanthropes" (176, 191). Thus when Redburn now admits to being "nothing but a poor sailor boy," he has a legitimate reason to be unhappy with his lot (133). It holds out only a limited prospect for future identity development, for "by their very vocation," he observes, sailors "are shunned by the better classes of people, and cut off from all access to respectable and improving society" (138).

Remarkably, however, when he makes this discovery, Redburn does not retreat into his young gentleman's self-image of the past. Instead, he comes to identify himself with the lowly classes the world over, as seen when (speaking in the voice of the mature narrator) he pronounces the radical theory that the evils of the sailors' condition "can only be ameliorated . . . by ameliorating the moral organization of all civilization." The problem is truly pandemic because sailors are among those "classes of men in the world, who bear the same relation to society at large, that the wheels do to a coach: and are just as indispensable." Despite continued improvement in the comforts of the wealthy who ride inside, "no contrivance, no sagacity can lift [the working classes] out of the mire; for upon something the coach must be bottomed; on something the insiders must roll" (138–39).

It is small solace that because "sailors form one of these wheels . . . they are the true importers, and exporters of spices and silks . . . the *primum*

mobile of all commerce" (139). But at least in this conclusion, Redburn sees there is reason to view the wealthy "importer" who had been his father with less idolizing eyes than formerly, and thus reason not to identify with him so heedlessly as he had earlier (5). More important still, however, is the fact that Redburn's assessment of the social predicament of his fellow sailors, like that of the Liverpool poor and of the emigrants on the return voyage, is made possible not simply by his newfound identity as a lowly sailor but also by his *initial* identity as a gentleman's son, with its attendant virtues of cultivated values and educational training—the capacities of perception, understanding, and expression. As becomes increasingly clear in the Liverpool chapters, where the reflective mind of the adult narrator takes over more and more, Redburn has not simply exchanged one identity for another. Rather, his sailor identity has developed in the midst of his continuing identity as a gentleman's son; only the pretensions of the latter have been abandoned. He cannot erase the advantages in education and social training that his father's wealth and station had earlier granted him. Indeed, only the combination of his aristocratic upbringing and his rude sailor apprenticeship could have provided Redburn, as it did Melville, with his full identity as a writer of the sea, an "artist in the rigging" (121).

While still a youth in Liverpool, however, Redburn continues for a while to identify himself with his father. In fact, his voyage there, like his abortive trip to Riddough's Hotel, is a "filial pilgrimage" (154). With the aid of the very guidebook his father had used, and the assurance that "thereby it had been thoroughly tested," the boy sets out to follow his father's earlier paths "through all the town," only to discover that "the thing that had guided the father, could not guide the son" thirty years later. "This world . . . is a moving world," Redburn moralizes; "its Riddough's Hotels are forever being pulled down . . . and its sands are forever shifting" (152–57).

This scene is most often regarded as the turning point in Wellingborough's coming of age, the occasion when he comes to understand that he must leave his father's example behind him. But it is not generally recognized that, despite many disappointing reminders of the fact that the world is always changing, Redburn never finally gives up "old Morocco," and he never does so because he comes to see that in some instances the town's past does survive, as his own past survives in himself. Thus the old book "will yet prove a trusty conductor through many old streets in the old parts of town," he at one point concludes. And, like old guidebooks generally, it will continue to inform him reliably about "the ways our fathers went" (157), as it does in the last instance in which it is mentioned, when Redburn faces the Lyceum and finds that "sure enough, the building before me corresponded stone for stone" with the

book's plate (207; see also 178). Still, that he has by this time already achieved psychological independence from his father without forfeiting his love of his memory is seen in chapter 41, when he explains that "after I had visited all the noted places I could discover, of those marked down upon my father's map; I began to extend my rovings indefinitely" throughout the town (200).

As much as Redburn's discovery of the guidebook's limited value impresses on him the need to form an identity that is appropriate to the conditions of his own present, what releases him from his identity fixation on his father is his nearly simultaneous recognition that his father once had an identity independent of him. In a poignant scene, while standing in a street where his finely dressed father had once walked and pitying himself for his own "sorry apparel," he suddenly realizes that "my own father did not know me then; and had never seen, or heard, or so much as dreamed of me." And if this was once so, he wonders, "how might it be with me hereafter?"—an apprehension that he conquers in the next scene, fittingly at the site of Nelson's Victory Statue, where, after a momentary impulse to run after and overtake his father around the corner, Redburn recalls that he "had gone whither no son's search could find him in this world" (154–55). Finally, thinking of all that must have happened to his parent since he was last there, "how he had been shaken by many storms of adversity, and at last died a bankrupt," a man as poor as Wellingborough himself, he perceives the fallibility and mortality of his father, and the father ceases to be the boy's identity ideal, the "marvelous being . . . who could not by any possibility do wrong" (34). By the end of the chapter, after suffering additional disappointments and frustration at the poverty that prevents him from visiting the antiquities beyond Liverpool, Redburn has reached the point of identity clarity necessary to admit, "I am not the traveler my father was. I am only a common-carrier across the Atlantic" (160).

Accomplishments in identity formation, however, are never perfectly secure. Under altered circumstances, a person can revert to an earlier stage or take on a new self-image, and such self-images can cause identity confusion. Moreover, according to Erikson, "the strength acquired at any stage is tested by the necessity to transcend it in such a way that the individual can take chances in the next stage with what was most vulnerably precious in the previous one. Thus the young adult, emerging from the search for and insistence on identity, is eager and willing to fuse his identity with that of others. He is ready for intimacy—that is, the capacity to commit himself to concrete affiliations and partnerships and to develop the ethical strength to abide by such commitments, even though they may call for significant sacrifices and compromises."[10]

Thus the entrance of Harry Bolton initiates another major crisis, the final one, in Redburn's struggle for identity. At the time of their meeting, Redburn's

"whole soul . . . in its loneliness . . . was yearning to throw itself into the unbounded bosom of some immaculate friend" (223). However, because Harry is initially presumed to be an "incontrovertible son of a gentleman," Redburn's "eagerness to enjoy [his] society" leads to an irreducible conflict: only by regressing to his boyish self-image as a gentleman can Redburn hope to advance to the point of gaining the intimacy with Harry that he longs for (216). That he ultimately refuses to play Harry's hectic game of gentlemanly pretensions is a sign of the strength of Redburn's recent identity development. But the question remains whether he holds back his "whole soul" from Harry simply because he suspects him to be a "gentleman forger" who sometimes spins out "imperial reminiscences of high life" not his own (223, 226).[11] If this is the sole cause, Redburn would seem to be unwilling to make the sacrifices and compromises necessary for the achievement of real intimacy, and his engagement in the maturing process would seem to have come to a halt.

On several occasions Redburn allays his own suspicions of his friend with evidence of Harry's aristocratic background: "his manners are polished, he has a mighty easy address," Redburn argues to himself at one point. And when Harry suddenly appears with "money to rig [Redburn] all out" for the London venture, Redburn rather eagerly concludes that "he was then indeed what he seems" (223–24). More frequently, however, he finds that "all he said was enveloped in a mystery that I did not much like" (225). Twice during the London trip Harry vehemently refuses to explain his unaccountable behavior in Aladdin's Palace, the gambling house (and possibly homosexual club) from which he unaccountably disappears, leaving Redburn to spend the night alone in wonderment; and, at the very end, his "secrets" lie forever in his "ocean grave" (252).

Little can be proved about Harry's past, however. The only time he seems caught in a lie is when he admits that "his nerves would not hear of" his going aloft on the *Highlander*. For as Redburn reminds him, "Did you not tell me that you made no doubt you would acquit yourself well in the rigging? Did you not say that you had been two voyages to Bombay [as a guinea-pig sailor]?" Still, rather than pass moral judgment here, Redburn only expresses concern for his friend's welfare: "Harry, you were mad to ship" (255). Redburn thus seems true to his earlier word that he "ever cherished toward Harry a heart, loving and true," despite his reservations (223). What prevents Redburn from giving his "whole soul" to him is not his friend's pretensions or his presumed prevarications per se but Harry's refusal, in spite of his obvious love for Redburn, to open his true self to him. For, like the early Redburn, he is forever striving to proclaim to himself and the world an identity as a gentleman that is not his—or is no longer his, if it ever was. To his sorrow, then, Redburn dis-

covers that authentic intimacy can be achieved only between parties who are themselves authentic and mutually willing to open themselves to one another.

Bona fide son of a gentleman or no, Harry lacks the necessary means of a gentleman's identity. Thus, just as Jackson is the model of what Redburn might have become at sea, so Harry Bolton, who is "some years" Redburn's senior, is the model of what he might have become had he stayed on land—a posturing "blade" frenetically trying to keep up the appearance of an outworn self-image, a moody and vulnerable youth whose fear of exposure isolates him from any true connection with the rest of humanity (225, 253). Such is the lesson of the London episode for Redburn. Entering the boisterous city in a cab, seated beside his newly bewhiskered friend, and himself dressed in stylish new clothes, Redburn suddenly thought himself "somebody else" (227). And at Aladdin's Palace, though he "tried to assume a careless and lordly air . . . like a young Prince Esterhazy," he confesses that "all the time I felt my face burning with embarrassment, and for the time, I must have looked very guilty of something" (229). When a "terrible revulsion" unexpectedly comes over him on his sensing the obscure falsity and evil of this house, Redburn's achieved identity as a sailor comes back to him. Now he admits, "I would have given the world had I been safe back in Liverpool, fast asleep in my old bunk in Prince's Dock"—much as he had wished to be safe at home on the night of the "suicide" (233). But there is a difference: Redburn no longer acts like a child; now he accepts what he is.

Contrary to the view that Redburn betrays Harry Bolton, it seems that it is Harry who betrays Redburn—as a consequence of an even more fundamental betrayal of himself. Nonetheless, the recurring issue concerning the ending of this book is whether the title character acts out of immature expediency, "that charming call of the world," in H. Bruce Franklin's memorable phrase, when he leaves Harry in New York and returns to his own home. According to Franklin, what Redburn has to gain by abandoning his friend is freedom from the responsibilities of being a "brother" to him (312). In transferring those responsibilities "from his own neck" to that of his New York friend Goodwell, "Redburn has . . . forcefully acted out the answer to a question about the 'friendless' common sailor which much earlier he had shoved in the reader's face: 'Will you throw open your parlors to him; invite him to dinner?'"[12]

There are two immediate problems with this argument. First, Harry is not a common sailor. This is far from a hairsplitting distinction, for Melville's whole object in attacking the closed-door policy of the rich is specifically to improve the sorry prospects of sailors—men, he says, whose "recklessness and sensualism of character, ignorance and depravity" cut them off "from all access to respectable and improving society" (138). The issue is not the sailors'

financial poverty, but their cultural poverty. Thus Harry hardly qualifies; his failings and his needs are of another order. The second problem is that, aside from the question of how Harry would pay for a 180-mile trip to Redburn's home (how Redburn is going to pay for it is not even made clear), it is a little uncertain whether there would be much of a "parlor" there into which Harry might be invited, let alone "dinner" enough to share with a friend. Invocation of the familiar folly of carrying coals to Newcastle seems appropriate here. For although Melville fails to explain what was contained in the letters conveyed by Mr. Jones that "compelled" Redburn to return home, presumably it was not good news (304). When Redburn had left home only four months earlier, his family was so impoverished as not to be able to afford powder for the rifle that he pawned for sailor clothes in New York.

Moreover, given the presence of autobiographical details elsewhere in the book, it seems pertinent to recall that on Melville's own return from his Liverpool voyage he was greeted with the news that the family furniture had been advertised for auction to prevent foreclosure on the mortgage—a detail that Melville might have had qualms about advertising still further in his book and one that perhaps he simply suppressed rather than fabricate an explanation that would not have been autobiographically true. Despite William Gilman's thorough examination of the subject, we are a long way from knowing in every detail where autobiography in this novel ends and fiction begins.[13]

In addition, it should be noted that Harry does not travel to America in order to be a guest in Redburn's home. Although at the time of his departure from Liverpool Harry had "resolved upon the sea" for his future, when it is discovered that he is not a sailor at heart he tells his friend that "somewhere in America he must work out his temporal felicity" (238, 279). When Redburn last sees him, Harry is waiting for an opening "in a mercantile house, where he might flourish his pen" (282). "Dull" times and "multitudes" of other qualified young men, however, prevent him from securing such a place, in spite of the efforts of Goodwell. Redburn, therefore, hardly could have anticipated that, as Goodwell informs him, Harry's "melancholy could bring him to the insanity of throwing himself away in a whaler" (311). Harry's problem, so to speak, is his failure to develop an identity with a future, and for this both the dull times and Harry himself are to blame. Significantly, it is Redburn, not Harry, who dreams up jobs that might be suitable for Harry to undertake when they reach America (279–82).

But these qualifications and mitigating circumstances aside, there is perhaps still a lingering doubt as to whether Redburn acts out of immature expediency in taking leave of Harry. An answer seems necessary for a full appre-

ciation of Melville's portrayal of the trials of the maturing process. Harry's end is not the result of Redburn's negligence; rather, it is the product of chance operating in frightful conspiracy with Harry's own lack of self-knowledge and consequent identity confusion. When Redburn says at the end, as Ishmael will later say at the conclusion of his narrative, "I . . . chance to survive," he is making a distinction between his own fate and that of his friend, who "fell over the side" of a whaler and "was jammed between the ship, and a whale" (312). In a world where it is possible for a young man, such as one Redburn once knew at home, to leave "his cottage one morning in high spirits" and be "brought back at noon with his right side paralyzed from head to foot," the element of chance must figure mightily in the explanation of any individual's fate (93). But self-knowledge is at least potentially within one's control, and self-knowledge—a sense of identity—is what Harry Bolton lacks. It is known from Harry's conduct during the London episode that he was liable "to yield to the most sudden, crazy, and contrary impulses" under duress; and given Harry's fear of going aloft on the merchant ship, Redburn has every reason to agree with Goodwell that it would have been "insanity" for him to ship on an even more dangerous whaler (311). In fact, Redburn knows his friend better than Harry knows himself, for he is the one to suggest that it would be better for him to "cross the sea as a steerage passenger, since he could procure enough money for that" (220–21).

But Redburn knows, too, that everyone must finally get on his own legs. Indeed, this is the hardest lesson of his whole maturing process, and it explains why there is "a secret sympathy" between himself and the little glass ship's fallen figurehead, which he will not have "put on his legs again," as he says in the beginning, "till I get on my own" (9). As Redburn laments when Harry refuses to pay his passage to New York, "After all, every one in this world has his own fate intrusted to himself; and though we may warn, and forewarn, and give sage advice, and indulge in many apprehensions touching our friends; yet our friends, for the most part, will *'gang their ain gate;'* and the most we can do is, to hope for the best" (220). I do not believe this is the language of expediency, but if it is, then it is that of an expediency which must be reached at some point in all human relations if one is to have any hope of gaining an identity worth having. Brotherly love is not, unfortunately, the answer to every human problem or personal difficulty.

Redburn, like his creator, was one of the lucky ones. Not only did he survive; he also escaped the destructive identities of Jackson and Harry Bolton. Although he went on to pass "through far more perilous scenes than any narrated" in the record of his first voyage, he ended neither as a lowly sailor nor as

a pretending gentleman (312). The one identity had as little future as the other. But having been nurtured as the son of a gentleman and reshaped as a sailor-boy, Redburn, like Melville, was freed to make for himself an identity of ever-expanding possibility and a career in which he, too, "might flourish his pen." "Would that a man could do something & then say—It is finished," Melville wrote to his friend Evert Duyckinck in the month before he sat down to compose *Redburn;* "—not that one thing only, but all others—that he has reached his uttermost, & can never exceed it. But live & push—tho' we put one leg forward ten miles—its no reason the other must lag behind—no, *that* must again distance the other—& so we go till we get the cramp & die."[14] Though written in a tone that conveys Melville's frustration at the difficulties of the growth of the self, this statement makes explicit what we know from the books he went on to write after *Redburn*—that he had committed his whole life to the process of becoming a new kind of "gentleman forger," one who would forge in the smithy of his soul a remarkable identity as the novel-writing sailor and gentleman's son.

Redburn is not a pure example of the bildungsroman.[15] It lacks the scope and fullness of the classic instances of the genre, such as Goethe's *Wilhelm Meisters Lehrjahre,* Dickens's *Great Expectations,* or Charlotte Brontë's *Jane Eyre.* It tells us relatively little about the hero's childhood (though it does reveal something, particularly in the first chapter), and offers only a few hints about his later life, hardly more than the fact that "years" later he found himself "a sailor in the Pacific, on board of a whaler" (312) and that, later still, he wrote *Redburn.* Even so, it still qualifies as an abbreviated version of the form, particularly if it is accepted that, as Jerome Buckley has observed, the typical bildungsroman is "strongly autobiographical," as *Redburn* is, and that it has close ties to the "confession," as Melville more than hints at in the subtitle.[16] If it fails to give us even so much as the single *lehrjahre* of Goethe's hero, it at least provides the critical four months of Redburn's "first voyage." And it focuses not simply on an important chapter in the young protagonist's life, but on what is clearly the *most* important chapter in that life, when he leaves the protection of his home and family to venture into the world for the first time on his own.

It is true that Redburn does not advance socially or economically; in the final chapter, he still has "an empty pocket" (311) and no job or vocational prospect in sight. But he achieves a new level of psychological independence and realism and develops a capacity for friendship and caring that were impossible at the start when he was full of youthful illusions and self-pity.[17] And he manages to bring his conception of himself into line with the painful truth of his own, and his family's, reduced circumstances. Though still too young

and malleable to have found his place in society by the end of the narrative, he has lost his social pretensions and otherwise matured to the point where he can be honest with others and himself, about who he is, where he comes from, and what his future holds. He is chastened but hardly defeated, a bit older and considerably wiser, and ready to move on to the next stage of his life, whatever it might bring.

∾

Power & Dignity

in a Man-of-War World:

White-Jacket as Political Novel

While several of Melville's narratives, from *Typee* and *Omoo* through *Billy Budd*, have an obvious political subtext, *White-Jacket* is his one sustained meditation on a political theme and his purest attempt at writing a political novel. Whereas in *Typee*, the most politically charged of his narratives after *White-Jacket*, Melville's interest in arguing for the preservation of the South Sea Island natives had to compete with his interest in writing a captivity romance, in *White-Jacket* his effort to bring about a reform of abuses of power in the U.S. Navy is far and away his chief object. More than anything, he wanted this book to have political consequences; he wanted, above all, to put an end to the hated flogging laws.[1] Yet from a novelistic standpoint, the single-mindedness of his attempt is something of a problem. For politics—Melville's portrayal of the exercise of power in an American man-of-war at midcentury and his polemical attack on its degrading abuses—so dominates his concerns in this book that it can make only a slight claim to being a novel at all.[2] To be sure, politics and the novel can be made to harmonize, as Tolstoy's *War and Peace*, George Eliot's *Felix Holt*, and Hawthorne's *The Blithedale Romance* all demonstrate; but the difficulty of the attempt for every writer was explained by Stendhal when he observed that "Politics in a work of literature is like a pistol shot in the midst of a concert, something loud and rude, yet a thing to which it is not possible to refuse one's attention."[3]

That Melville made less than a satisfactory fusion of the two in *White-Jacket* is explained only in part by the fact that he composed the book in just two months and, as he confessed later, "almost entirely for 'lucre'";[4] for *Redburn* (1849), a notably better novel—its characters more fully realized, its incremental

story line more compelling than the later work's serial one—was written in about the same length of time, under the same financial exigency, and even a bit earlier in Melville's development. At least as important an explanation for *White-Jacket's* relative weakness as a novel is the fact that Melville's objective in writing it was deeply, even profoundly, political. For unlike the "many worthy old chroniclers" to whom his narrator at one point compares himself, Melville desired to do more than preserve a detailed picture of the man-of-war world before it passed away; he sought to exercise power—the power of the word, in the public mind and in the U.S. Congress—to destroy the very world he chronicled. His "humble narrative," he prayed, would become "the history of an obsolete barbarism."[5]

In his joy at finding an occasion to fire volley after volley at the enemy, wielding the writer's imaginary power over his real (or remembered) adversaries, while at the same time reliving the indignities of his year and more of utter powerlessness on an American fighting ship, Melville allowed his attention to be diverted from the business of crafting the kind of book he claimed in retrospect to have been "most moved to write."[6] In short, the author's own political excitement, the chief source of the book's liveliness, is also the cause of the book's deficiency as a novel. Not until *Moby-Dick* (1851), his next book, did he admit that a writer needed not only time, strength, and cash but patience, too, to write at his best.[7]

Yet hurry though he did to get *White-Jacket* into print, it is one of the larger ironies of America's literary history that the book was published too late to have any real impact on the naval abuses, particularly the flogging practices, it so vehemently attacked. As Anderson was the first to point out, the flogging laws had been the subject of debate in Congress for some time when Melville began work on his account of "the World in a Man-of-War," and although it was published in its American edition before the legislation outlawing flogging was actually passed by Congress in late September 1850, the debates in Washington were just concluding when *White-Jacket* appeared late in March of that year.[8]

Melville's political views and his hunger to wield political power are so much in evidence in *White-Jacket* not simply because he had never before experienced such a highly charged political atmosphere as the one he found on the *United States,* but because that atmosphere so threatened his own identity and self-worth. When he signed on the American frigate in Honolulu in 1843 for the voyage home, he was not in the "jelly of youth," unlike the young midshipmen in his novel, whom he treats with a mixture of brotherly captiousness and concern (346). He was two days shy of his twenty-fourth birthday, years past the ideal age for entrance into military service; he was an expe-

rienced sailor, having already served on both a merchant ship and a whaler; and he was fresh from a year of such independence—beachcombing and roving the Polynesian isles—as most men know only in their dreams. Moreover, the ideology he found reigning in the American navy, a throwback to the despotism of the Middle Ages, ran absolutely counter to his own, which had been nurtured on the standard political ideals of American democracy—liberty of conscience, freedom of action, equality of opportunity.

The importance of Melville's experience of this ideological discord to his motives for writing *White-Jacket*, to its sometimes strident tone, and to its meaning, can best be appreciated, I think, by invoking the definition of ideology coined by Erik Erikson as "the social institution which [in the normal course of things] is the guardian of identity."[9] For when Melville stepped onto the *United States*, he suddenly became subject to an autocratic ideology that did everything it could to erase his previous identity, both by systematically intimidating him and by arbitrarily imposing on him a much-diminished sense of himself as a "cog" in a military machine, as a set of numbers in a highly regimented bureaucracy, or as a "prisoner," a "serf," and a "slave" (194, 174, 295).[10] For more than a year he suffered indignities and lived under the threat of flogging at the masthead. When it came time to write his book, he responded in kind in an intense effort to even the score—publicly shaming the U.S. Navy, lashing it with the word—and make it comply not simply with his own ideology but with the ideology of the nation as spelled out in the Declaration of Independence and the Bill of Rights. He himself admitted, in a letter to Richard Henry Dana, Jr., whose *Two Years Before the Mast* (1840) also was intended as an anti-flogging tale, that his motives in writing the book had been personal, as well as humanitarian, and that he feared he might be charged with having reacted too vindictively. "This man-of-war book, My Dear Sir," he wrote a little sheepishly, not long before it had appeared, "is in some parts rather man-of-*warish* in style—rather aggressive I fear.—But you, who like myself, have experienced in person the usages to which a sailor is subjected, will not wonder, perhaps, at any thing in the book. Would to God, that every man who shall read it, had been before the mast in an armed ship, that he might know something himself of what he shall only read of"—an odd wish that reveals not so much Melville's desire to have the book accepted for an authentic record as his desire to have his readers realize, through firsthand experience of the sort of indignities he himself had suffered on the *United States*, that his aggressive tone was warranted.[11]

For White-Jacket, and for Melville, the most difficult problem of life under the totalitarian regime of an American man-of-war was how to preserve personal autonomy, identity, and dignity. Everything else, other than the simple

need to keep alive in what was sometimes an extremely dangerous line of work, was dwarfed by this. To regard White-Jacket's attempts to solve the intricacies of that problem, in particular his determination to remain "aloof" from much of the rest of the crew, as evidence of a "superior" attitude toward "the people" or of an "antidemocratic" feeling on Melville's part, as more than one critic has done in recent years, is to narrow the needs of the self to the maintenance of a set of moral attitudes or stands, to overlook the autocratic power structure of an American frigate in the middle of the last century, and to restrict rather too severely the meaning of "democratic" ideology. It is also to confuse "the people" on ship and "the people" on shore. Most importantly, it is to disregard the fundamental rationale for Melville's indictment of the man-of-war world—the central thesis of *White-Jacket*—namely, that the "general depravity of the man-of-war's-man" could be reformed only by reforming the corrupting conditions under which he lived (142). If, as Larry J. Reynolds has suggested, Melville "emphasizes the depravity and vulgarity of the mass of men, the 'mob,'" while also affirming "the revolutionary ideals of liberty, equality, and fraternity," he does so not because he was of a "divided nature . . . both a democratic idealist at times and an antidemocratic realist at others"; he does so because he was a reformer who had become convinced, as he says quite emphatically, that "it can not admit of a reasonable doubt, in any unbiased mind conversant with the interior life of a man-of-war, that most of the sailor iniquities practiced therein are indirectly to be ascribed to the morally debasing effects of the unjust, despotic, and degrading laws under which the man-of-war's-man lives" (304).[12] Perhaps it needs to be added that, in Melville's view, naval reforms would be forthcoming only if his readers could be convinced they were necessary and would have a salutary effect on the lives of sailors like those he portrayed in his narrative.

From the very start of the common sailor's service, as we see in White-Jacket's own example, the workings of the man-of-war world conspire to strip away his personality, all for the purpose of putting his energies at the command of the hierarchy of power. Given "the great number of men [about 500], and the necessity of precision and discipline," the whole frigate must be run like a vast machine (8). So demanding are its myriad regulations and so alienating its organization into various divisions that even an experienced merchant sailor must wipe clean the slate of his identity as he takes his place in a man-of-war for the first time: "he must begin anew; he knows nothing; Greek and Hebrew could not help him, for the language he must learn has neither grammar nor lexicon." Significantly, the title character's only name, a nickname not officially recognized, is the one he acquires on shipboard. Officially he is hardly more than a set of numbers, as White-Jacket discovers

to his horror later when arraigned at the mast—"the *number of his mess* . . . his *ship's number* . . . the number of his hammock . . . the number of the gun to which he was assigned; besides a variety of other numbers; all of which would have taken Jedediah Buxton himself some time to arrange in battalions, previous to adding up." What is just as important, the accomplished sailor's identity suddenly having been erased, he must begin not only "wholly nonplused, and confounded," but painfully conscious of his insignificance. Thus, White-Jacket implores, indirectly speaking of his own pitiful initiation, "Mark him, as he advances along the files of old ocean-warriors; mark his debased attitude, his deprecating gestures, his Sawney stare, like a Scotchman in London in King James's time" (11–12).

Because even the most routine operations of life on ship are designed for the convenience and pleasure of those in command, "the people" are forced to remain virtual integers—to remain "equal" indeed—throughout their service. As White-Jacket learns one hot, windless night while struggling to move his hammock from the close quarters of its assigned tier, life for the common sailor is so hemmed in that there are, really, no alternatives to the prescribed way of doing things. Thus he is at last forced to return to his "own level," he says, his tongue only part way in his cheek, "and moralize upon the folly, in all arbitrary governments, of striving to get either *below* or *above* those whom legislation has placed upon an equality with yourself" (81). Where the men's lives have no value beyond their service to the ship's functioning, their personal desires— the natural assertions of their personal worth or dignity—become dispensible luxuries. Even the little solaces of privacy become superfluities: "It is almost a physical impossibility," White-Jacket observes, "that you can ever be alone. You dine at a vast *table d'hôte;* sleep in commons, and make your toilet where and when you can. There is no calling for a mutton chop and a pint of claret by yourself. . . . It is something like life in a large manufactory. The bell strikes to dinner, and hungry or not, you must dine" (35).

If the sailors' three meals must be "crowded into a space of less than eight" hours, or if they must mess not at tables but on the deck "and peck up their broken biscuit . . . like fowls in a barn-yard," it is because "this arrangement makes a neater and cleaner thing of it for the officers," or because "this unobstructedness in an American fighting-ship" is so valued by those in command (29–30, 87). If the men must suffer "chills, colds, and agues" as a result of scrubbing out the ship even on mornings when the thermometer is at zero or engage in the "wearisome, dog-like, galley-slave employment" of holystoning the decks, it is because of an American officer's love of "neatness" or a lieutenant's desire to inflict "punishment" on the crew (86–87). If the people are not allowed use of their hammocks during the day while off duty,

even though "every other night, [they regularly] have but three hours' sleep," it is because "such a proceeding would mar the uniformity of daily events in a man-of-war" (82, 84). For "the people," there can be no dignity or comfort to life on such terms; and there will be none, Melville argues, as long as those who hold power, from the youngest midshipmen to the most experienced captains, can so readily inflate their own sense of dignity by degrading those farther down the hierarchy. What is more mournful still, because the common sailor lacks access to the public sources of dignity and personal comfort, or the power to gain either, he typically turns to the self-forgetfulness of illicit pleasure, and thus all but ensures his permanent debasement.

To be sure, there are a few sailors, generally either one of two types, who escape this almost irremediable fate. One type, represented by Quoin (the poet Lemsford's nemesis) and the foretopman Landless (otherwise known as "Happy Jack"), willingly subordinates his identity to his official function and gives up his inherent dignity to the man-of-war enterprise. Little more than survivors, such men are the true "cornerstones" (as Quoin's name suggests) of the totalitarian system in a man-of-war. Thus for the quarter gunner Quoin, for whom "the honor and dignity of the United States of America seemed indissolubly linked with the keeping his guns unspotted and glossy," it was "a thousand pities he was not able to dwarf himself still more" than his stunted height would permit, "so as to creep in at the touch-hole" and personally inspect the gun's interior (42).

The other type to escape permanent decadence is, in contrast, the sailor who "exhibits traits of moral sensitiveness, whose demeanor shows some dignity within." Unlike the soulless Quoins or "Happy Jacks" whom "most sea-officers profess to admire," the second type is "the man they, in many cases, instinctively dislike." They do so, White-Jacket explains, because they "feel such a man to be a continual reproach to them, as being mentally superior to their power. . . . To them there is an insolence in his manly freedom, contempt in his very carriage" (384–85). This latter type, which includes Jack Chase, Mad Jack, Ushant, and White-Jacket himself, even Lemsford and the "hermit" Nord, manages—through a combination of forcefulness or simple determination, ingenuity, and luck—to retain some dignity and sense of identity in spite of the depersonalizing forces at work on the *Neversink*. More than survivors, these men are the benevolent leaders or even the potential redeemers of the man-of-war world.

These exceptions aside, "the people" in general are desperate or defeated in spirit—like the *"steady-cooks,"* who are "of no mark or consideration whatever in the ship; lost to all noble promptings; sighing for no worlds to conquer"—and thus susceptible to further degradation and manipulation (63).

Lacking faith in themselves, and in their future, many deteriorate so far as to regard their "great 'prospect in life'" to be their official allowance of daily "*tots*," described by Melville, sardonically, as "a perpetual perspective of ravishing landscapes, indefinitely receding in the distance" (53).

If portions of *White-Jacket* read like excerpts from a conventional temperance tract (at one point, for instance, the narrator observes that on special Fourth of July celebrations "all roll together in the same muddy trough of drunkenness"), perhaps it is because Melville was capable of having conventional reactions to seeing his fellow sailors degrading themselves, losing their wages, and ruining their lives as a result of worshiping at the fountain of their "old arch-enemy, the ever-devilish god of grog" (89, 176). Even so, unlike more conventional temperance writers, Melville recognized that intemperance, at least among American man-of-war's men, had a political dimension to its complex of causes. He recognized that the daily rationing of grog not only served to control the men's "love for ardent spirits," it served to control and ease exploitation of the men; he recognized, to borrow from Marx, that grog on a frigate was almost literally "the opium of the people" (54).[13] Not only does White-Jacket know "several forlorn individuals, shipping as landsmen, who have confessed" to him that they entered the navy because of the government's assurance of daily grog rations, but he also is certain that this assurance is "the controlling inducement which keeps many men" in the service (53–54). What is more, the men are kept relatively tractable by the threat that their grog may be "stopped" for a day or a week, as "one of the most common punishments for very trivial offences." Most insidious of all, even naturally sober men often are induced, against their better judgment, to draw their regular allotment of grog, rather than the money for it, "by the thought of receiving a scourging for some inconsiderable offence, as a substitute for the stopping of their spirits" (140).

Abject, exploited, bored with routine, unlettered if not illiterate, living "under lock and key," sexually frustrated, and addicted to drink—the wonder is not that various of the crew would resort to getting drunk on eau de cologne or risk life and limb to sneak ashore while in harbor or hazard a flogging to smuggle spirits aboard or gamble, fight, pilfer, and pursue "other evils, so direful that they will hardly bear even so much as an allusion" (though Melville, not wanting any reader to puzzle unnecessarily, provides not one but four allusions explaining that he is indeed referring to illicit sexual activity [174, 375]). The real wonder is that some members of the crew could resist such temptations at all. For the only pleasures permitted man-of-war's men in Melville's time—reading, checkers, embroidery, theatricals, swapping yarns, social drinking—are the ones most favored by celibates and septuagenarians. Yet White-Jacket, together with some of the men who become his friends,

does manage to resist the seductions of forbidden activities, and he does so not simply because such activities offend his Victorian sense of morality, or are beneath his personal sense of dignity (important as these considerations may be in the long run), but because every one of these activities could end in his being publicly flogged at the gangway.

For the same reason, White-Jacket decides not to mix casually with the many "roughs" among the crew, but instead to restrict his friendships to his more judicious "comrades of the main-top," plus Nord and Lemsford (both after-guardsmen with ardent literary interests) and the "laughing philosopher," Williams. As he explains, in a statement that reveals his natural inclination to be openly sociable and suggests how circumstances, not class bias, forced him to exercise caution in the choice of his companions, "I had not been long on board ere I found that it would not do to be intimate with every body. An indiscriminate intimacy with all hands leads to sundry annoyances and scrapes, too often ending with a dozen at the gang-way" (50, 52). That the fear of trouble and physical punishment is a bona fide concern, not a convenient rationalization, is clear from the book's first flogging scene, an object lesson wherein the innocent-hearted Mark and Antone—"two steady, middle-aged men, whom [White-Jacket] had often admired for their sobriety"—and the handsome young Peter, an early incarnation of Billy Budd, are drawn into a fracas by the "brutal bully" John and suffer public scourging (136).

In keeping with this view, it is important to recognize that White-Jacket is not alone in his fear of entangling alliances. Nord, "a reader of good books" and "an earnest thinker" whose portrait as "A Man-of-war Hermit in a Mob" reveals him to be an extremist version or even an alter ego of White-Jacket, becomes a "wandering recluse," and he does so not because of any social finicalness on his part, but because, as White-Jacket speculates rather coyly, "Doubtless, he took the same view of the thing that another of the crew did; and had early resolved, so to conduct himself as never to run the risk of the scourge." Thus, though ignorant of sailing, Nord "faithfully discharged what-ever special duties devolved upon him; and was so fortunate as never to render himself liable to a reprimand." Even so, White-Jacket concludes, with obvious empathy for the man he calls his "friend," "several events that took place must have horrified him, at times, with the thought that, however he might isolate and entomb himself, yet for all this, the improbability of his being overtaken by what he most dreaded never advanced to the infallibility of the impossible."

Though White-Jacket's description of him is couched in speculative terms (Nord is hard to know, never speaking of his past), that description is impor-tant at least for what it reveals, as a projection, about White-Jacket himself, particularly his preoccupation with the mystery of how Nord "managed to

preserve his dignity, as he did, among such a rabble rout." Not that Nord's was
the dignity of a fallen aristocrat, like Harry Bolton in *Redburn*, struggling to
maintain the appearance of a gentleman amid paupers. Instead, his was the
dignity of a learned man with a profound heart trying to preserve his identity
in the midst of the common herd. So great was Nord's knowledge of books
and so deep his feeling for their authors that "He amazed me," White-Jacket
says with obvious admiration, "as much as Coleridge did the troopers among
whom he enlisted" (50–52).

White-Jacket never forgets that he is one of "the people"; he could hardly
do so even if he wanted to, for he eats and sleeps with them in common and is
ordered about the ship just as they are. But he does regard his topmates, with
whom he is "on the best possible terms," as constituting a kind of aristocracy
among the crew. "Whatever the other seamen might have been," he remarks,
"these were a noble set of tars, and well worthy an introduction to the reader"
(13). To a degree, their superior status is self-appointed: "We accounted ourselves the best seamen in the ship," White-Jacket says with playful self-congratulation; "and from our airy perch, literally looked down upon the
landlopers below, sneaking about the deck." But this feeling of *"esprit de corps,"*
he explains, was "always pervading, more or less, the various sections of a
man-of-war's crew" (15). More importantly, their special status, unofficial
though it may be—indeed, the whole task-based hierarchy within the crew—
is necessarily acknowledged by "the people" at large and reinforced by the
commander's exercise of the power of promotion and demotion. It is not a
fabrication of White-Jacket's allegedly aristocratic frame of mind.[14] For while
the topmen "are always made up of active sailors" in the prime of life, the
other four major divisions of a man-of-war's crew bear some stigma widely
acknowledged on ship and otherwise more or less objectively verifiable: the
sheet-anchor-men, though all veterans and worthy of reverence, are "an old
weather-beaten set" who live more in the past than in the present; the after-
guardsmen, reluctant sailors whose duties require little seamanship, are "composed chiefly of landsmen" who come to be called *"sea-dandies"*; *"waisters,"*
unfortunate sorts, must perform the "ignoble duties" of "attending to the
drainage and sewerage below hatches"; and the *"holders,"* who toil in isolation
three decks down, seldom see the light of day (9–10). Thus after Bland, the
master-at-arms, was caught smuggling liquor aboard the *Neversink,* he was
cashiered, imprisoned, and then, "by way of disgracing him still more . . .
thrust into the *waist,* the most inglorious division of the ship" (185).

Furthermore, both by official appointment and by popular acclamation
the beau ideal of a man-of-war's man is the captain of the maintop, the "noble"
Jack Chase. As the epitome of what a common sailor might be, he is not a

"snob" or an "elitist," and he is never regarded as such by anyone on the *Neversink*. Rather, he "was loved by the seamen and admired by the officers; and even when the Captain spoke to him, it was with a slight air of respect" (13). It is because they live through this maintop captain (whose initials are the same as the Christian savior's) and see their own noble potential realized through him that the men carry him "in triumph" on their shoulders after the captain reinstates him, without ado, in the position he abandoned when he went ashore to fight for the rights of man in Peru (19). It is for this reason, too, that they respond so thunderously—their desire for liberation and justice all but breaking through the dramatic form designed to contain it—when Jack Chase appears in the man-of-war theatrical as "Percy Royal-Mast," the hero who frees fifteen "oppressed sailors" from the watchhouse. Indeed, this "chivalric character" is but a melodramatic version of Jack Chase in his actual role on the *Neversink* as the people's "tribune" when they seek shore liberty in Rio de Janeiro (94, 225).

Melville's faithfulness to a doctrine of literary realism—his fear of duplicating the melodrama of the man-of-war theatrical in the later drama of White-Jacket's arraignment at the mast—seems to have dictated that Colbrook, the corporal of the marines, rather than Jack Chase, would be the first to step forward to save White-Jacket from flogging. But it is still Jack Chase, the "universally regarded" Delphic oracle in "all things pertaining to a man-of-war," who guards the seamen's ideal against every form of corruption or attack. If a fellow maintopman's hat is out of tilt, he is the one who takes the man to task; and if his mates ever suffer criticism, as they do when the ex-whaleman Tubbs heaps scorn on the maintopmen in general, he is the one who flies to their defense. In short, Jack Chase serves redeeming psychic and political functions for "the people": as one who "had a high conceit of his profession as a seaman," he stands as an example of dignity and accomplishment to his defeated and degraded comrades, and as their leader and spokesman he represents their chief access to power in the man-of-war world (13).

If, then, White-Jacket and his fellow topmen form an aristocracy among the seamen, it is a natural aristocracy based not on inheritance or privilege but on merit, and on merit that is recognized by virtually everyone on the *Neversink* (the lone exception being the former whaleman Tubbs). If they have anything of an attitude of superiority toward the rest of the crew, it is a moral superiority based not on class or wealth or arrogance but on a belief in values—diligence, sobriety, honesty, vitality, independence—that are widely respected in the American navy and in American culture at large. If those values are not so widely honored among the crew of the *Neversink*, Melville argued, it is be-

cause so many of the men have been so degraded by their life in the man-of-war world that they have lost all faith in their transforming, ennobling power.

When White-Jacket condemns the behavior of the men, he does not do so to make himself look good. On the occasion, for example, when he remonstrated, like the young Ben Franklin, with an old toper of a topman about his "daily dram-drinking," telling him "it was ruining him, and advised him to *stop his grog* and receive the money for it" instead, he is not trying to establish any social or moral distance between them (54). Rather, he is attempting to reduce the distance that already separates them by proposing ways of improving the man's health and sense of self-worth. More generally, when White-Jacket emphasizes the depravity and degradation of much of the crew, he does so for the purpose of shaming the powerful classes ashore who are responsible for the crew's plight, and in that way try to force the kind of legislation that would ameliorate it. One of the things that made Melville a writer of the first rank was his ability to see the whole of the world he portrayed—to understand that the debased ways of oppressed people are in large part the product of debasing treatment by stronger powers, not a symptom of their inherent lack of dignity.

Even so, Melville seems to have been sensitive to the possibility that the reader might misconstrue White-Jacket's attempts to maintain his dignity and see them as signaling an attitude of superiority. In chapter 12, for instance, wherein White-Jacket describes Quoin's ill-natured character and then offers (with deceptive lightheartedness) some common-sense advice to the young on choosing a vocation, Melville's narrator spells out the behaviorist theory identified by the chapter title, "The Good or Bad Temper of Men-of-war's men, in a great Degree, attributable to their Particular Stations and Duties aboard Ship." To support this theory, he cites the example of a "fine [former] top-mate of ours, a most merry and companionable fellow," who soon became ill-tempered and quarrelsome like the other quarter gunners when he was promoted to a petty officer's position among them (45). That Melville also guarded, scrupulously if not always successfully, against developing the reality of a superiority complex is suggested by his confession to having discovered an attitude of latent racism in himself while being forced to watch the mulatto Rose-Water's public scourging. Instantly feeling himself thankful for being white—and thus assuming an inherently justified immunity to such degradation himself—he suddenly realizes that all men on a man-of-war are liable to such punishment. "Still, there is something in us, somehow," he soberly observes, "that, in the most degraded condition, we snatch at a chance to deceive ourselves into a fancied superiority to others, whom we suppose

lower in the scale than ourselves" (277).[15] While such an admission could, of course, be viewed as a sign that Melville was capable of concealing more than a faint streak of "elitism" even from himself, his willingness to make the admission, his recognition of the eagerly self-pleasing ways of the mind generally, and the censorious tone in which his confession is made, all argue that his was an unusually sensitive conscience on this issue.

What is just as telling is that White-Jacket, like his creator, shows a healthy sense of self-irony on several occasions when his character threatens to fall off the track. He is able equally to mock the "wounding" of his "self-conceit" on the occasion of being blackballed from his first "mess" and to satirize the pretense to superiority in himself and his second group of messmates after he has been accepted into their fold (57). When the evil Bland, broken of his command after the exposure of his elaborate smuggling operation, is accepted into White-Jacket's new Mess No. 1, the famed "Forty-two-pounder Club," White-Jacket waxes eloquent on the impunity with which the fine men of his distinguished mess "could do so many equivocal things, utterly inadmissible for messes of inferior pretension." Yet the irony of his brief disquisition is all the more remarkable for its double edge: while puncturing the puffed-up self-satisfaction of the men of his new mess (himself included), he also deflates the ethical relativism of those who refuse—out of generous liberalism, the faith (like Emerson's) that evil is but good in the making, or fear of "elitism"—to call a sin a sin, or a sinner a sinner. "Besides," he intones, explaining, with broad irony, their ready adoption of Bland,

> though we all abhorred the monster of Sin itself, yet, from our social superiority, highly rarified education in our lofty top, and large and liberal sweep of the aggregate of things, we were in a good degree free from those useless, personal prejudices, and galling hatreds, against conspicuous *sinners*— not *Sin*—which so widely prevail among men of warped understandings and unchristian and uncharitable hearts. No; the superstitions and dogmas concerning Sin had not laid their withering maxims upon our hearts. We perceived how that evil was but good disguised, and a knave a saint in his way; how that in other planets, perhaps, what we deem wrong, may there be deemed right; even as some substances, without undergoing any mutations in themselves, utterly change their color, according to the light thrown upon them. We perceived that the anticipated millennium must have begun upon the morning the first worlds were created; and that, taken all in all our man-of-war world itself was as eligible a round-sterned craft as any to be found in the Milky Way. And we fancied that though some of us, of the gun-deck, were at times condemned to sufferings and slights,

and all manner of tribulation and anguish, yet, no doubt, it was only our 127 misapprehension of these things that made us take them for woeful pains instead of the most agreeable pleasures. (186)

Nowhere else in his early writings is the utilitarian basis of Melville's own ethical thinking, particularly the belief that pleasure and pain are the measures of right and wrong, or his quarrel with the "coolness" of Transcendentalist ethics more evident than here.[16] He had not yet reached the point, as he did later in "The Whiteness of the Whale" chapter of *Moby-Dick,* where he was willing to entertain the possibility of absolute relativity in all things.

Yet the "woeful pains" that he regarded as the real basis of his fellow sailors' grievances were more psychological than physical, if we are to judge from the whole of White-Jacket's own behavior. Even his determination to make "a hermit of myself in some things, in order to avoid the possibility of the scourge," arises not so much from his fear of the repeated ripping of his flesh or of the days of agonizing recovery that would follow a flogging as it does from his anticipation of the naked display of his own powerlessness and the permanence of the reminding scars (279–80).[17]

White-Jacket's fear of flogging is but a symptom of a deeper fear of shaming and of an exceptionally strong, if also perhaps insecure, sense of personal dignity. It is for this reason that, although he was "not at all singular in having but comparatively few acquaintances on board," he "certainly" carried his "fastidiousness to an unusual extent" (50). For in the performance of every one of his duties, White-Jacket does more than is required of him; he shows the eagerness of a young man desperate to please. In the beginning, he "flies to obey" the order to loose the mainroyal (8); later, he reveals that he kept his "bright-work" in such perfect order that he "received the most extravagant encomiums from the officers; one of whom offered to match me against any brasier or brass-polisher in her British majesty's Navy" (171). By the end, he has made such a habit of showing his "sharpsightedness, skill, and celerity" that Jack Chase chooses him for the dangerous, and much-honored, job of reeving the halyards (391).

Perhaps the most unequivocal instance of White-Jacket's determination to protect his ego even more than his flesh—of his desire to avoid any criticism or humiliation whatsoever—is provided by the comic scene in which White-Jacket takes his turn as *"cook of the mess."* Having already observed the freedom of the other sailors in criticizing the shortcomings of the week's cook, he had resolved, when his turn came, to protect his "reputation and credit" by approving himself "an unexceptionable caterer, and the most impartial of stewards." Therefore, upon making his first *"duff"* (a sad mixture of flour, water,

beef fat, and raisins), he says with the resolution of a brave but vulnerable young perfectionist, "I made up my mind to lay myself out on that *duff*; to centre all my energies upon it; to put the very soul of art into it, and achieve an unrivaled *duff*—a *duff* that should put out of conceit all other *duffs*, and forever make my administration memorable" (59–61).

But White-Jacket's determination to maintain his dignity at all costs is not always shown in such a humorous, self-mocking light. Sometimes, especially when the Captain is party to the situation, instead of trying to protect his dignity by pleasing those in command, he tries to preserve or strengthen it by taking a wholly independent course. When asked to serve in the Captain's gig, for example, a position deemed "a great honor" by some, he fast procures a substitute, because he "did not relish the idea of being a sort of body-servant to Captain Claret—since his gigmen were often called upon to scrub his cabin floor, and perform other duties for him" (161, 163). When he learns that a "sumptuary edict" limits the crew's smoking privileges to the galley and to the brief period after meals, he decides to quit the luxury altogether—"though I smoked like an Indian summer ere I entered the Neversink"—rather than "enslave it to a time and a place" (387). And in the book's most critical episode, when he is threatened with a flogging for failing to be at his assigned station during an unusual "tacking" maneuver, not only does he refuse "to stand obsequiously touching" his hat while addressing the Captain, as is the custom, but he comes to the verge of committing simultaneous suicide and murder of the Captain because, he says, "No other way could I escape the scourge" (though, of course, if this were in fact his only objective, suicide alone would have been sufficient). Disclaiming the capacity to "analyze" his heart as it stood at the time, he nonetheless goes on to offer two justifications for his contemplated action—the need to defend his self-respect from the gross indignity of a flogging and the desire to assert his self-worth by actively seeking justice at what is truly the court of last resort:

> the thing that swayed me to my purpose was not altogether the thought that Captain Claret was about to degrade me, and that I had taken an oath with my soul that he should not. No, I felt my man's manhood so bottomless within me, that no word, no blow, no scourge of Captain Claret could cut me deep enough for that. I but swung to an instinct in me—the instinct diffused through all animated nature, the same that prompts even a worm to turn under the heel. Locking souls with him, I meant to drag Captain Claret from this earthly tribunal of his to that of Jehovah, and let Him decide between us. (279–80)

Ironically, what saves him the indignity of the scourge, and the ignominy of murder and suicide, is the impeccable reputation he had earned as a responsible sailor, one who would never be absent from his post if he had been properly informed at the start about where he was supposed to be. One's dignity, he discovers, can be a kind of power.

Unconvincing though this melodramatic scene may be as autobiography, it reveals the deep sense of pride, the incipient Ahabism, of Melville's central character: his refusal passively to accept a degrading fate; his willingness, despite the deep strain of pacifism in his character, to fight with his very life to preserve his identity and his sense of justice. Still, these qualities are shown in less operatic ways, too, most importantly in the symbolism of the jacket itself. It should be said that most readings of the symbolic meaning of the white jacket seem strained or incomplete because they fail to consider either its practical and symbolic values for White-Jacket himself or the many clues Melville has provided as to what its practical and symbolic values would have been for sailors on an American frigate at the time he was writing. This is especially true of the prevailing "humanistic" reading, according to which the jacket is not a jacket so much as it is a "sign" of the title character's aloofness and arrogance before he finally sheds it in his celebrated fall from the maintop.[18] Given the fact that the *Neversink* is bound for the bitter cold of Cape Horn, and also that no regular pea jackets were available from the purser's steward (or so Melville says), the simple white duck shirt, which White-Jacket has to remake as a substitute for a heavy coat, becomes a constant, public reminder of how insignificant he is to the ship, and to the larger military force, he serves. One symptom, among many, of the man-of-war world's practical disregard for the well-being of "the people," it symbolizes, first and foremost, an institutional insult or slight.

However, the duck shirt, like the more famous scarlet letter in Hawthorne's romance, changes symbolic meaning, as the protagonist reworks it to suit his pleasure. Like Hester Prynne, who embroiders over her simple letter, quietly needling her Puritan elders in the process, White-Jacket converts the symbol of his powerlessness and shame into a bold and humorous "advertisement for myself" that flaunts the stupidity of America's navy brass, exposing their carelessness and ineptitude and their insensitivity to the needs of the common sailor. It was, he says, "a strange-looking coat, to be sure; of a Quakerish amplitude about the skirts; with an infirm, tumble-down collar; and a clumsy fullness about the wrist-bands; and white, yea, white as a shroud." The inside was "bedarned and bequilted" with "many odds and ends of patches—old socks, old trowser-legs, and the like . . . till it became, all over, stiff and padded, as King James's cotton-stuffed and dagger-proof doublet." And the whole

was provided with "a great variety of pockets, pantries, clothes-presses, and cupboards" for the convenient storage of its owner's personal effects—everything from a shirt or two and a pair of trousers to a small library and a snack of biscuits (3–4, 36). Was there ever before such a garment? Was there ever such insouciance in the United States Navy?[19] Thus transformed into "an outlandish garment of [his] own devising," the shirt-cum-jacket becomes a consciously crafted symbol of White-Jacket's determination to establish the dignity of an identity amid the depersonalizing forces of the man-of-war world—a comic instance of Ahab's much grimmer effort personally to count for something, when he exclaims, "In the midst of the personified impersonal, a personality stands here" (3).[20] Indeed, so compelling is this expression of the narrator's identity to the rest of the crew that they soon identify him by his white jacket and make it the principal feature of his public self.

Of course such a bold and Chaplinesque assertion of his self-regard is bound to have its liabilities, as well as a comic side more generally. It invites a good deal of teasing from his fun-loving shipmates, and it sometimes prompts more recognition from the ship's command than he would like to have. But except for the threatened flogging, the treatment White-Jacket receives from the others on ship—as distinct from the treatment he suffers as a consequence of the miserable conditions of shipboard life—is all the stuff of comedy. When his many pockets are picked of their conspicuous contents, for instance, he reports that, while sailors will often steal a thing from someone they dislike, "where the theft involves something funny, as in the case of the white jacket, they only steal for the sake of the joke" (38).

Even his ostracism by the mates of his first mess is hardly the embittering experience it is usually taken to be, determined though his new messmates seem to have been to blackball him. Although he explains that "all along they had nourished a prejudice against my white jacket" because they "must have harbored the silly fancy that in it I gave myself airs, and wore it in order to look consequential," it is clear he is slyly trying to shift the blame, here, for his miserable failures as "cook of the mess." For he admits, in passing, that his messmates "gradually changed their behavior" toward him only after his week in office, a week that began with a memorable "duff" that would have done service as a "mill-stone" to ensure the drowning that one wag proposes as a just desert for White-Jacket himself (61). Unless they banish him forever, they know they will have to put up with his cooking when his turn comes again. More unhappily still, while his watchmates are free to go "skulking and 'sogering' about the decks, secure from detection—their identity undiscoverable," White-Jacket is awarded "many a hard job" because it is so easy for an officer, "in that mob of incognitoes, to individualize *that white jacket*,'

and dispatch him on the errand." "Indeed," he mourns, "upon all these occasions, such alacrity and cheerfulness was I obliged to display, that I was frequently held up as an illustrious example of activity, which the rest were called
upon to emulate" (20–21).

When it finally dawns on him that his new identity is a kind of evil fate,
White-Jacket naturally rebels and tries to change it or escape from it completely. "Oh! how I execrated my luckless garment," he exclaims melodramatically; "how often I scoured the deck with it to give it a tawny hue; how
often I supplicated the inexorable Brush, captain of the paint-room, for just
one brushful of his invaluable pigment" (121). However, by the time they reach
a mild climate where he can dispense with his jacket altogether, as he does
when he tries to pass it off at an auction of the belongings of a deceased sailor,
the garment has achieved such notoriety as to be immediately recognized,
and a chorus of fifty voices cries out in mock derision, "The white jacket!"
After listening in speechless horror as the assembled bidders banter back and
forth about its worthlessness ("bunch of old swabs," "cleaning-rags," "reg'lar
herring-net"), White-Jacket is forced to reclaim the odious badge of his identity (202–03). Not until the *Neversink* nears the end of its voyage, when White-
Jacket falls from the yardarm and cuts away the constricting article in a life
struggle, could Melville have allowed him to divest himself of it once and for
all. For only at the end is he free of the man-of-war world that called into
existence his "White-Jacket" identity as one systematically slighted (if also
insouciant), degraded (if also defiant), and powerless (yet not lacking in the
resources of a mighty self-regard).

White-Jacket's climactic fall is only the last, most dramatic instance of the
many dangers he is needlessly subjected to simply because the faceless, indifferent man-of-war world fails to provide him with a regulation, government-
issue pea coat. His underwater escape from the makeshift jacket, then, a sort
of rebirth by caesarean section, is the clearest evidence of the fact that he also
possesses an identity of his own—a capacity not quite like anyone else's for
meeting circumstances not quite like anyone else's—that is deeper and more
permanent than the public identity he is forced to assume on the *Neversink*.
We are, Melville's narrator says, in a statement that defines the very essence of
identity, "precisely what we worship. Ourselves are Fate" (321). More than
anything, what White-Jacket can be said to "worship" or value is his own dignity or self-regard.

Presumably much the same can be said about Melville himself. Not that
White-Jacket, or his creator, demonstrates the kind of hubris to be seen later
in Ahab. On the contrary. Melville knew when to stop, when to treat his autobiographical character with irony, when to cast his self-regard in a comic form,

as seen earlier. As much as anything else, it is that irony, that sense of comedy, that keeps White-Jacket from being the monster of aristocratic egotism he is sometimes taken to be by Melville's critics.

For Melville, personal dignity was a centrally important matter for all of humanity. It was not the special preserve of the aristocratic or privileged classes, whether on land or on ship. As seen most emphatically in the examples of old Ushant, in the episode of the "massacre of the beards," and of White-Jacket himself, in the episode of his arraignment before the mast, Melville adamantly supported, and promoted, what might be termed the democratization of dignity. Something like a process of this sort, after all, is what was involved in the political revolutions that had occurred in America and Europe during the several decades before *White-Jacket* was written. Melville *was* a democrat, a pragmatic one, not an elitist, in his political attitudes. But he could not be called a "leveler," or anything like it. The "discreet, but democratic, legislation" he called for in this book was intended to bring down naval officers, as he said, "without affecting their legitimate dignity and authority" and at the same time to elevate the common sailor "without relaxing the subordination, in which he should by all means be retained" (166).

While Melville did profess not to share the "certain vague, republican scruples" that had prevented America from having admirals in 1850, this was because—his pacifism to the contrary notwithstanding—he thought it likely that "as her ships of war increase," flag officers "may become indispensable" (20). Given the man-of-war character of the world, he had little objection to a hierarchy of power per se or to the granting of extensive powers to American naval officers. He understood that without regulations, and the authority to execute them, "a man-of-war's crew would be nothing but a mob" (9).

But Melville wanted to limit the discretionary powers that commanding officers and their quarterdeck subordinates then held over "the people." For as matters then stood, he argued, the well-known "fiction" that "the king . . . can do no wrong" had been magnified on a man-of-war "by indirectly extending it" from the captain to all of his officers, including even the greenest midshipmen (217). And in practice this meant that any officer was free to abuse any common sailor for his own purely personal ends, as happens in one memorable instance when a young midshipman, out of "mere wanton spite and unscrupulousness," caused "a forlorn, broken-down, miserable object" of a middle-aged landsman to be flogged at the gangway (216). Melville recognized that a naval officer's position has a "requisite dignity," which he was careful to define in democratic terms as that which benefits the state (166). But he perceived also that anyone in a position of authority who confuses the dignity of his position with that of his person is likely to be sufficiently pride-

ful as to be careless of the well-being of those under his command. Thus many of the ceremonials and other practices in a man-of-war—the all-night races and sail-stowing rivalries between ships, the grand receptions of visiting commodores, the deck polishings in the foulest weather, the honorific terms of address, even certain heedless naval engagements—not only minister merely to the "arrogance" and "glory" of the officers but are also injurious to the sailors' health and generate "a feeling of servility and debasement" in their hearts (166, 197, 314). It is a mark of the man-of war world that the power and dignity one typically finds there seem to be finite commodities in a closed economy; for when one man tries to make a gain in either respect, some other man seems always to lose.

Melville, however, was a romantic democrat as well as a pragmatic one. He knew that power and dignity only *seem* to be finite commodities, and that it was just this kind of fearful, self-protective thinking that kept the man-of-war world alive. "True dignity," what Melville also called "the common dignity of manhood," is religious in nature—infinite, invisible, untouchable—and so, too, is true power (142, 21). This "feeling of the innate dignity remaining untouched," he wrote in "Some of the Evil Effects of Flogging," chapter 34, "though outwardly the body be scarred for the whole term of the natural life, is one of the hushed things, buried among the holiest privacies of the soul; a thing between a man's God and himself; and forever undiscernible by our fellowmen, who account *that* a degradation which seems so to the corporal eye" (142). As old Ushant explains to the master-at-arms after being flogged for refusing to comply with Captain Claret's orders for a general "massacre of the beards," "'tis no dishonor when he who would dishonor you, only dishonors himself" (366). In the end, it is significant that what White-Jacket takes away from his experience on the *Neversink* is not the outlandish jacket that temporarily defines his identity there but "a blessing of old Ushant, and one precious hair of his beard for a keepsake." For Ushant, like his beard, is the living symbol of the power of dignity in passive resistance—the only power the man-of-war world cannot conquer; the only power it cannot see (395).

∽

Sounding the Self:
Moby-Dick as Epic Novel

At the end of his now famous review, written in the late summer of 1850 while composing *Moby-Dick*, Melville predicted that Hawthorne's *Mosses from an Old Manse* would one day be regarded as his masterpiece. "For," he explained, "there is a sure, though a secret sign in some works which prove the culmination of the powers (only the developable ones, however) that produced them." Whether Melville had read any of Hawthorne's other works at this time is unclear. Still unacquainted with the man himself, or so he professed, he apparently did not know that Hawthorne had published *The Scarlet Letter* earlier that same year.[1] Even so, Melville had the good sense to hedge his bets by adding that he hoped the older writer would yet prove his prediction wrong, "Especially," he explained, "as I somehow cling to the strange fancy, that, in all men, hiddenly reside certain wondrous, occult properties—as in some plants and minerals—which by some happy but very rare accident (as bronze was discovered by the melting of the iron and brass in the burning of Corinth) may chance to be called forth here on earth; not entirely waiting for their better discovery in the more congenial, blessed atmosphere of heaven."[2]

What is remarkable about this rather droll version of Emersonian philosophy is that it captures the same conviction regarding the potency of transcendent powers, the same conception of life, even the same theory of art that Melville was then trying to infuse into his own masterwork. The calling forth of wondrous, occult properties, that rare but happy accident in the life of humankind, is the central subject of Melville's great story. In its most heightened form, it is also the subject of the world's great modern epics, particularly spiritual epics, such as the *Divine Comedy* and *Paradise Lost*, that tell the story

of a hero who makes a life-transforming journey into the deepest realms of the self and back out again.

Since 1950, when Newton Arvin and Henry F. Pommer first examined the matter in some detail, many critics have gone on record as calling *Moby-Dick* an epic or acknowledging it has significant ties with the epic tradition.[3] But there have also been many who have questioned such a designation and argued instead for the influence of some other genre, particularly tragedy, romance, or anatomy, or some heterogeneous combination of genres. Even some who advocate reading the book as an epic, such as Arvin or, more recently, John P. McWilliams, have expressed reservations about the term or claimed the book finally eludes generic classification. Clearly, Melville's critics are far from agreement on the matter, despite the fact that it is one of the most analyzed texts in all of American literature. Even among critics who are predisposed to see the book as an epic, there is some disagreement about the qualities that make it so.

While there are several reasons for such disagreement, much of it, I would say, stems from the fact that even as an epic *Moby-Dick* is an unusually ambitious work that brings together two epic traditions rather than one: the ancient or primitive national epic of combat or conflict, as in the *Iliad* or *Beowulf,* and the modern universal epic of spiritual quest, of the search for a transcendent order or significance to human life, as in the *Divine Comedy* or *Paradise Lost.* Though in Melville's treatment the two are in fact woven together to form a single story, with each of the two major characters crossing the line into the other's epic territory, the first can be said to focus generally on Ahab and the second on Ishmael.

While much of my discussion centers on Ahab and the ancient epic of combat, my principal point of focus throughout is on *Moby-Dick* as a spiritual epic. The later tradition envelopes the earlier one, as Ishmael's story envelopes Ahab's. As more and more critics in the twentieth century have testified, this is Ishmael's story even more than it is Ahab's, important as Ahab's is, and so the parallels with the spiritual epic are more pervasive, and more profound, than the parallels with the primitive epic of physical courage. Moreover, given Melville's symbolic technique, which in an epic work is designed to infuse the quotidian world with significance and elevate mundane matters to the supernatural plane, the theme of the quest for the soul takes on an overriding importance. The ancient epics, too, of course had a spiritual dimension in that they were intended to explain the intrusions of the gods into the affairs of humankind; they were, as Arthur Hutson and Patricia McCoy, among others, have said, concerned in a fundamental way with mythology.[4] But, beginning with Dante, the epic became essentially inward, and not sim-

ply psychological but spiritual, centering on the search for the soul or the soul's salvation. As an epic of the universal story of mankind, therefore, *Moby-Dick* is more than a local instance of mythmaking or nation-building, comparable for its time and place to the *Odyssey* of ancient Greece or the *Aeneid* of early Rome. It is also Melville's attempt to show that the powers behind the great spiritual epics of the world are the same powers that propelled its major religious mythologies—Judeo-Christian, Hindu, Egyptian, among others Melville knew quite thoroughly[5]—and that they were as alive in his own day as they had been in those earlier times.[6]

My understanding of Melville's conception of epic writing has been much informed by several searching studies of the epic poem, especially work by Lascelles Abercrombie, Albert Cook, and John Kevin Newman.[7] However, my understanding of Melville's conception of the epic journey or quest in particular is even more deeply indebted to the work of several modern students of psychology, religion, and myth, especially C. G. Jung, Mircea Eliade, and Joseph Campbell, who define life, and the quest, in terms of individuation or spiritual awakening and otherwise explore, from a modern, broadly psychological point of view, the gap between the seen and the unseen, the known and the unknown worlds. Campbell offers the classic formulation, in *The Hero with a Thousand Faces,* though he in no way restricts his discussion to the epic per se, when he says that the hero's journey is structured like the "monomyth" found in rites of passage, with their three-part structure of separation, initiation or trial, and return. As Campbell says, "A hero ventures forth from the world of common day into a region of supernatural wonder: fabulous forces are there encountered and a decisive victory is won: the hero comes back from this mysterious adventure with the power to bestow boons on his fellow man."[8] The Greek legends of Prometheus and Jason, the biblical narratives of Moses and Christ, the legend of the Buddha, and the epic stories of Odysseus and Aeneas all follow this basic pattern, typically represented in terms of the hero's being swallowed by a monster and then being reborn.

When seen in relation to *Moby-Dick,* such a scheme, with its emphasis on transformation and the turning toward spiritual self-knowledge, naturally points to Ishmael as the true hero of the book; he alone completes an initiatory test and returns to tell about it, though the nature of his "boon" may at first seem problematic. By contrast, Ahab resists the test, even as he resists all reminders of his mortality. In Eliade's terms, he clings to his existence as a "natural" man and is never "born to the spirit."[9] As is often the case, however, there are larger social and political consequences to such resistance. Entrusted with the power to rule others, Ahab is an instance of the public man turned private person. Like the king who becomes a tyrant, a dangerous figure known in myth

and folklore as "Holdfast," he sacrifices the public good for his own benefit.[10] Unredeemed and unreborn, Ahab is incapable of recognizing anything beyond his own egoistic needs, and as a consequence he brings not health nor treasure nor sacred knowledge but ruin and death to his people and to himself.

In the following discussion, I have taken a cue from Ishmael, a model anatomist, and dissected *Moby-Dick* into pieces, in this case five sections of nearly equal length. I have done so for practical reasons and as a convenience to the reader, who would no doubt otherwise find this an impossibly long discussion. But I have done so also to call attention to a five-part structure that I believe is inherent to the narrative itself. This structure takes its definition from the stages in the whale hunt that forms the basic story line of the book: (1) preparations for the hunt (chapters 1–23); (2) presentation of the lore of the whaling industry (chapters 24–47); (3) the pursuit of the whale (chapters 48–76); (4) capturing the whale (chapters 77–105); and (5) the trial in the whale's "belly" (chapters 106–35). For each of these parts, I have appropriated a corresponding section title from T. S. Eliot's *The Waste Land* to indicate in a shorthand form how Melville unfolds the central themes of the hunt for the great White Whale. Both works, in fact, the one for the nineteenth century and the other for the twentieth, make extensive use of many of the same central images, of death and burial, of games and the hunt, of fire and water, of lightning, thunder, and rain. More importantly, both are epic works that tell much the same story of a devastated land, a wounded fisher king, and the search for a holy elixir or precious fluid, whether of whale oil or water.[11]

The first clues that *Moby-Dick* belongs with the world's great epics are to be found in the etymology and extracts sections of the book's frontmatter. Here, Melville creates the impression that his subject is universal and that, like the old oral epics, his story is a work of bricolage. To appropriate a distinction first made by Lascelles Abercrombie, one of the pioneering students of the form, the extracts are the epic material—"fragmentary, scattered, loosely related, sometimes contradictory"—out of which Melville's epic poetry was made.[12] Even before the current storyteller, in this case Ishmael, had come along to put together the pieces, there had been earlier bards, in sundry cultures and languages, who sang of his subject. By implication, the whale is everywhere and immortal. The etymologies and extracts help to establish the epic stature, formidableness, and inexhaustibility of Ishmael's subject, and they serve to place the reader in an appropriate mood of awe or wonder.

Yet they also help to establish the character of Melville's storyteller, even before he introduces himself. They suggest the compiler himself to be a broken, searching, strangely modern figure, sometimes a lexicographer, sometimes

a sub-sub-librarian, and at other times an author or a whaler, whose world is fragmented almost beyond repair—a man so preoccupied with the beast of destruction as to be at once possessed and at the same time paralyzed. Like Tiresias, the narrator of Eliot's poem, he is all but overwhelmed by the oppressiveness of death and destruction, trapped in a past without change, and can therefore do little more than murmur, "These fragments I have shored against my ruins."[13] Together, the extracts reveal the compiler's fixation on Leviathan, the ancient initiator of the Last Things, at the same time they reveal his numbness, or shock, and his inability to make sense of what he has lived through.

But the opening extracts have a redemptive function as well.[14] Like the scattered pieces of a fertility god, they await the water that will restore life to the dead land, and its people, in some distant spring. In effect, they are like seeds of the hero's renewal, as the writings of the past often are. But their mystery first must be unlocked; a worthy hero who can show the way must make himself known. Even before the story begins, then, Melville hints at important parallels between his story of the wounded Ahab, named for a despised Old Testament king, and the ancient myth of the impotent Fisher King, whose land has been devastated by his own selfishness and who now awaits a cure.

One final word of introduction: As almost anyone who has ever looked closely into Melville's novel knows, *Moby-Dick* is an incredibly rich and complex work with as intricate a set of symbols, image patterns, and motifs as is to be found in a work of literature anywhere in the world. One of the things I hope to show in the succeeding pages is that there is a logic to Melville's patterning, a logic driven by his understanding of and excitement for the epic genre but given form by a language of nature that is universal—of decay and rebirth, of seasonal cycles, of water, fire, thunder, lightning. I cannot, of course, say whether Melville himself was fully conscious of the intricate web of relations I trace in this chapter. But I believe that, as he himself said in his review of Hawthorne's *Mosses,* there is something "wondrous" or "occult" about certain instances of the creative process that make them transcend what can normally be expected in such matters. Certainly to those of us who have never written an epic, particularly one of such depth and grandeur and richness as *Moby-Dick,* there is something preternatural about the form itself. Perhaps it is true, too, that there is something preternatural also about the effort required to produce one.

I. THE BURIAL OF THE DEAD

Like the *Divine Comedy, The Waste Land,* and other spiritual epics, *Moby-Dick* opens with its hero in a fallen state of emotional torpor and confusion. Starting

his story before his transforming experience on the *Pequod,* Ishmael says he is like a spiritually dead man in a spiritually dead land, seeking the relief of the condemned everywhere. He has grown weary of existence, as one does when his youth is spent and he finds himself, as Dante said at the start of his story, "In the middle of the journey of our life." He experiences depression, morbidness, even thoughts of suicide, and he hungers for change or escape.

Like Ahab, Ishmael suffers from a malaise or schism in the soul, an aggression so intense as to prove deadly to himself and others. As Ishmael confesses, it is only by holding to "a strong moral principle" that he can keep himself from "deliberately stepping into the street, and methodically knocking people's hats off." Whenever he finds himself overtaken by such an urge, he knows it is "high time to get to sea as soon as I can." However, whether this is to be viewed as a still surer means of realizing a deep-seated death wish or as an alternative to it, a means of regaining his health, Ishmael himself seems a little unsure. Going to sea, he says equivocally, "is my substitute for pistol and ball."[15] Even if he himself is unsure, his unconscious knows there must be a dying to the world before there can be a rebirth. That is the only way one can ever hope to overcome the death of the spirit. Ahab's example attests to that by his failure, as Ishmael's example does by his success. For the hero to come back as one reborn, filled with creative energy, as Ishmael does when he returns to tell his tale at the end, he must first give up the world and everything in it.

It is significant, but not widely recognized, that Ishmael is not alone in his suffering, that he is a representative figure or exemplary hero. "If they but knew it," he writes, "almost all men in their degree, some time or other, cherish very nearly the same feelings towards the ocean with me," and as proof he has to look no further than his own fellow "Manhattoes." Everywhere he looks, on a dreamy Sunday afternoon, he sees "crowds of water-gazers," thirsting for the adventure that will free them from the land and the deadly routine of their lives. All of them, "thousands upon thousands of mortal men fixed in ocean reveries," hunger for that deeper, vivifying knowledge of the spirit that going to sea makes possible. "Meditation and water," Ishmael explains, "are wedded forever" because, as the Greeks were the first to learn, introspection is the way to self-understanding (3–4). However, as the example of Narcissus warns, such inwardness can be a dangerous business; it must not lead simply to a love for the self or a fascinated preoccupation. It has to be conducted as an active search for and testing of the self; it has to involve a trial. Few people get beyond the stage of being weekend water-gazers because they are afraid of the challenge of the new, afraid of what the unfamiliar might hold. They thus remain among the dead, "victims" whom one day a more adventurous soul, like Ishmael, will come back to try to rescue, and so on, in an endless cycle.

What distinguishes Ishmael from these more timid Manhattanites is simply that he accepts the call to the sea. He does so, to be sure, without full understanding of what he is doing or why, but he is the sort of man who lives intuitively and knows to trust his inner promptings wherever they might lead him. Because the episodes in his journey represent trials of the spirit, psychological trials, his passage is inward as much as it is across land or water—"into depths where obscure resistances are overcome," as Campbell explains, "and long lost, forgotten powers are revivified, to be made available for the transfiguration of the world."[16]

In *Moby-Dick* this inner realm is of course represented by the sea, a universal image of the unconscious, where all the monsters and helping figures of childhood are to be found, along with the many talents and other powers that lie dormant within every adult. Chief among these, in Ishmael's case, is the complicated image of the Whale itself, which is all these things and more and also serves as the "herald" that calls him to his adventure. At the end of chapter 1, "Loomings," with its promise of some distant, portentous engagement, Ishmael reveals that his chief motive for wanting to go whaling "was the overwhelming idea of the great whale himself." But that he is responding as much to a lure from within the self as from without is suggested in the final lines of this opening chapter, when he asserts that, having examined his motives and finding the idea of going whaling to his liking, "the great flood-gates of the wonder-world swung open, and in the wild conceits that swayed me to my purpose, two and two there floated in my inmost soul, endless processions of the whale, and, midmost of them all, one grand hooded phantom, like a snow hill in the air" (7). For Melville's hero, this phantom whale that is later incarnated as the great White Whale is the beginning and the end, and it represents all the instinctual vitality locked deep within the self. It is in this sense that the Whale is synonymous with "the ungraspable phantom of life" that is "the key to it all" (5).

Because the way of the hero is through a strange realm filled with danger and hardship, he requires the help of a guide or wisdom figure, some master of the world beyond who can provide the kind of assistance that, to the neophyte, seems magical. As in any initiatory experience, the novice has to be instructed in the rules of the game and have the way pointed out to him. Also, usually the guide supplies a charm or fetish that will serve to ward off danger or insulate the hero from the dark forces unleashed during this process. While the guide is sometimes a woman, like Beatrice in Dante's vision, more typically it is a man, as in the *Divine Comedy* again, where Virgil assumes the role in the early stages. So in *Moby-Dick* Ishmael is guided through the early episodes of his journey by the masterful harpooner and mystagogue, Queequeg,

a deeply if comically religious man whose home is a mythical island called Kokovoko. In keeping with such mysterious figures generally, Queequeg is both protective and forbidding, nurturing and threatening, like the complex powers of the unconscious that he symbolizes.[17]

When Ishmael meets Queequeg, on his first night at the Spouter-Inn, while en route to his initial whaling adventure, the unlettered cannibal seems a most unlikely candidate for a mentor in any regard, except possibly the art of embalming. Queequeg, who has been out late peddling shrunken heads in the streets of New Bedford, looks like something out of a nightmare (Ishmael, it will be noted, had been struggling to fall asleep when the savage makes his entrance into his room), with strange tattoos all over his body, a hideous scalp-knot on his head, and a frightful tomahawk at his side. Ishmael, who admits to being "as much afraid of him as if it was the devil himself" when he first glimpses him, is initially horror-struck that he might lose his own head to this "abominable savage" (22). As it turns out, of course, Queequeg is not a cannibal; but, in the logic of the book, his reputation as a man-eater does make him an appropriate guide for a novice like Ishmael, whose initiation will require that he be swallowed by a Whale. Though Ishmael "ain't insured!" as he exclaims in desperation to the landlord, he could hardly do better than to trust himself to this implausible guide who will one day save him from the wrath of the great White Whale. Even on this first night, after all the proper introductions have been made, he comes somehow to sense that this peculiar figure is a kind of blessing in disguise, so much so that, after dismissing Peter Coffin, he turned in, as he says, "and never slept better in my life" (24). Having once before that evening gone to bed commending himself "to the care of heaven" (20), he can do so now with a true sense of security. To the hero who can bring himself to believe in the ultimate benevolence of the creation, all the security of an assisting providence will be given.

Still, if Ishmael knew how to read the signs, he would know his destiny had brought him to the one man who can lead him through the maze of his future trials and on to the final, life-changing encounter with the beast of destruction. The next morning, waking to find Queequeg's arm thrown over him in a loving, protective embrace, he sees only that "this arm of his [was] tattooed all over with an interminable Cretan labyrinth of a figure" (25). Ishmael is too green at this point to recognize that this figure represents a map of the path in and out of the maze of the Minotaur, the beast he must slay to gain whatever treasure awaits him. He can hardly be expected to know, at this early stage of the hunt, that he himself will become an American version of Theseus. However, much later in the narrative, in "A Bower in the Arsacides" (chapter 102), he will turn up with a tattoo on his own right arm bearing the dimensions of

a gigantic whale, whose labyrinthine skeleton he has wandered into and out
of again. An experienced whaler himself by this time, Ishmael is then ready to
lead his readers into the belly of the whale and out again. In the end, he becomes their guide and protector, the hero who shows the way.

The next morning, though, when Ishmael ventures into the streets of New
Bedford, he is startled to find himself in the midst of an entire society completely devoted to the business of whaling. Virtually all the males of the town
are living at a stage much in advance of the Manhattanites who manage to get
only as far as the water's edge in their longing to go to sea. As Ishmael goes out
to survey the local scene, he is astonished to discover the streets are full of
seasoned whalers just like Queequeg, not simply "the queerest looking non-
descripts from foreign parts," but "savages outright"—Feegeeans, Tongata-
booans, Erromanggoans—as well as "scores of green Vermonters and New
Hampshire men, all athirst for gain and glory in the fishery" (31). The whole
town, the entire industry, it seems, is set up to initiate young men into the
ways of the hunt.

But such appearances are deceptive. The rites of passage of New England
farmboys are only incidental to the basic mission of America's foremost whaling
town, namely, the accumulation of huge fortunes. "Nowhere in all America,"
Ishmael writes, "will you find more patrician-like houses; parks and gardens
more opulent, than in New Bedford." A virtual "land of oil," the "town itself is
perhaps the dearest place to live in, in all New England," its wealth all "har-
pooned and dragged up hither from the bottom of the sea" (32). The whole
town, in other words, is dedicated to acquiring only the lowest form of treasure that whaling can bring. Fortunately, Ishmael, who only the night before
had escaped the ashy, Gomorrah-like inn called "The Trap," somehow knows
not to undertake the hunt for material gain only. Intuitively, he recognizes he
must push on to Nantucket, the one place in the world where the simple
values of the original whale hunters are still practiced, and embark from there.

Melville spells out the dangers of the hero's quest, particularly the dangers
of his seeking only earthly profits, in "The Chapel." Here Ishmael, still a relatively conventional hero seeking a conventional form of strength in a conventional place, becomes one of "a small scattered congregation of sailors, and
sailors' wives and widows" who sit in silence contemplating the burial of the
dead at sea. On his way to the chapel, he had experienced a sudden change in
the weather, from "sunny cold" to "driving sleet and mist," a change that em-
blematizes the changeability of the earthly realm that is the theme of this chapter
(34). Once inside, Ishmael sits with the others staring at a series of marble
tablets, which flank the pulpit, bearing the names and other details of the lives
of sailors lost at sea—stark reminders of the mutability of human existence

and human fortune. Although later, when he signs on the *Pequod,* Ishmael shows a healthy regard for the advantages of earning a good wage, in this scene he comes to recognize that to be paid can never be the chief object of the hunt. For he discovers his own mortality and witnesses the folly of a life dedicated to heaping up material riches. In the chapel, he sees that one must choose between death as an ultimate end and faith in some afterlife or spiritual principle. But he also sees that, for a thinking man like himself, the choice is always tenuous and that true faith is never free of entanglements with the world. As he says, in an odd, haunting image, "Faith, like a jackal, feeds among the tombs, and even from these dead doubts she gathers her most vital hope" (37). Still, the need to conquer death, or look beyond it, to seek the soul and live out of it, is at last clear. This is the true reason for undertaking the hunt for the whale, and in the chapel scene this becomes Ishmael's overriding motive.

Although initially sobered by the many memento mori in the chapel, Ishmael somehow manages to grow "merry" again and jokes that he can even consider a stove boat as a "fine chance for promotion" to a higher realm. "Methinks we have hugely mistaken this matter of Life and Death," he exclaims. "Methinks that what they call my shadow here on earth is my true substance.... Methinks my body is but the lees of my better being. In fact," he says, unconsciously contrasting himself with his future captain, Ahab, who regards every limb as sacred, "take my body who will, take it I say, it is not me. And therefore three cheers for Nantucket; and come a stove boat and stove body when they will, for stave my soul, Jove himself cannot" (37). Despite the obvious bravado of this outburst, Ishmael here makes it clear that he has survived his first test and will emerge from this curious Chapel Perilous a profoundly changed man.

Before looking at the sermon that serves as a gloss on this all-important first step in Ishmael's transformation, it is necessary to look briefly at Father Mapple, the complex, sometimes baffling chaplain who delivers it. A man of God, and agent of the Father (as his Catholic-sounding nickname rather obviously implies), he too had gone to sea in his youth and served as a harpooner in the whaling industry. Old in years and experience, then, yet forever young in appearance, he is thus a fit guide for young petitioners. But unlike Queequeg, Mapple counsels caution and obedience. He is in fact an example of a special kind of guide, called in Jung's term a "threshold guardian," who stands at the gateway to the realm of supernatural power and warns the tender or fainthearted to stay away. Conservative and cautious by nature, like the parents of young children, such a figure purposely tries to delimit the hero's world on every side, in accordance with the abilities of the aspirant. When Mapple speaks, therefore, he is like the ancient oracles who guarded the path of the supplicant; he warns the would-be adventurer to stay within the confines

of the known world and to flee all fearful encounters with the great powers beyond. To be sure, as a threshold guardian, it is not Mapple's job to frighten away *all* comers; on the contrary, his function is to make sure that the few who finally do come forward are truly ready to take the plunge, that they have the courage and skill to survive the challenges of the next stage of the journey.

After Father Mapple climbs up to his pulpit, he stands to deliver his sermon from behind a copy of the Bible. Immediately sizing him up, Ishmael senses that what he is about to speak is the truth, not because it conforms to the standard Judaeo-Christian view, but because what the chaplain brings to his congregation is the water of renewal. Mapple himself speaks from the very midst of it. "[R]eplenished with the meat and wine of the word," Ishmael explains, "to the faithful man of God, this pulpit, I see, is a self-containing stronghold—a lofty Ehrenbreitstein, with a perennial well of water within the walls" (39). Mapple's sermon, however, is deceptive, as dual-edged as the man himself. What he preaches is indeed a "two-stranded lesson" (42). While on the one hand he speaks to the many whose hearts are not yet ready, preaching against sin and disobedience, and counseling repentance and submission to the will of God; on the other, he also speaks to the few, like Ishmael, who may at that very moment be on the threshold of the potentially deadly yet also potentially glorious adventure of the hero.

Properly understood, the story of Jonah, though couched in the familiar biblical language of sin and trial and deliverance, is a universal tale of one who actively refuses the call to the soul's awakening. It thus serves as a warning, and an invitation, to those who might be resisting or wavering on the brink. What Mapple says is paradoxical: the call is irresistible; the call must be freely accepted. Clearly there is no escaping the experience of being trapped in the belly of the whale, if that is one's destiny. Whether one refuses, like Jonah, or accepts the call, as Ishmael does, there is no avoiding the experience of death and burial, of suffering and dismemberment, when it finally comes.[18] There is only the hope of surviving it in some new form, the hope of some ultimate redemption or miraculous return from the dead, as Jonah returns in the end.

In Melville's conception, the call to adventure, the call to spiritual awakening, was equivalent to the Puritan experience of grace; and, to the rational mind, it entailed the same contradictory dynamic of fate and free will. Like his Calvinist forebears, Melville understood the call as an invitation to experience the woe and delight of the loss of ego that leads to the discovery of the self or the soul, one's core identity. Though one of the smallest books in the Scriptures, Mapple exclaims of Jonah's story, while underscoring the sermon's true theme, "what depths of the soul does Jonah's deep sea-line sound!" (42). The chaplain's rendering of Jonah's tale constitutes a paradigm of the central

situation of Melville's epic as a whole, of the trials of the self and its transformation, its breakup and recovery in the belly of the beast. As such, it deserves careful scrutiny.

In Mapple's rendering, the story of Jonah is the story of a man bent on escaping his identity, the identity of his destiny. Jonah's every move, every encounter, reveals this to be so. As he steps onto the ship bound for Tarshish, all the sailors stop to stare at him and wonder *who he is*. And almost immediately, as if in answer to their question, someone calls him a "parricide," a seemingly offhand remark that, ironically, provides an important clue to his identity (43). For in refusing the call to do his Father's bidding, Jonah in effect "kills the father" in himself, the source of spiritual life, of empowering identity, at his center. He refuses to grow up. When the Captain, hearing Jonah coming toward his cabin, calls out "Who's there?" the innocent request to identify himself "mangles" Jonah, an early sign that, for Melville, Jonah's story is linked with Ahab's, as well as Ishmael's, and that the process of dismemberment is symbolic of the pain of personal transformation (44).

It is only when the "hard hand of God" presses on Jonah, forcing him to answer the crew's demands to reveal who he is, that the object of his trial is defined as nothing more or less than the acceptance of his identity. It is only when he begins to confess who he is—first tentatively, "I am a Hebrew," he cries at the height of the storm, thus identifying himself as one of the chosen; then more emphatically, "I fear the Lord the God of Heaven"—that the process of recovering his true self can begin in earnest. For it is then that his shipmates throw him into the sea, where he is carried down "into the yawning jaws awaiting him" (46). There, having owned up to his earthly identity as "one who fears the Lord," he finally accepts God's call, repents his waywardness, and discovers his spiritual identity as one who is delivered by the Lord. In Hebrew Jonah means "dove." And as we know from the story of Noah and elsewhere, the dove carries the sign of peace; it brings news of deliverance from death.

Mapple's sermon does more than warn against refusing the call, however. It also defines the marks of those who do and those who do not refuse it, and as such it provides a means for judging Ishmael's motives, his readiness to undertake the journey, and for determining why Ahab's quest is destined to fail. First of all, until the adventurer owns who he is and recognizes the need to make the journey he is called to, he lives as a man who is already dead, as Jonah does when he "sleeps" with a "dead ear" in his tomblike berth below the ship's waterline (45). That is to say, he feels trapped in his own ego. Secondly, he must "pay" for his own passage. As Mapple says, in this world it is "sin that pays its way" (44). Like Ahab, who in the end pays for his passage on the *Pequod* with

the gold doubloon, the "God-fugitive" Jonah is willing to pay much more than the standard fare if that will permit him to escape his destiny (46). But of course those who refuse the call cannot escape having to pay spiritually, too, for their waywardness. That is why they die. Without an infinite source of vitality to sustain them, without a soul, their lives eventually run out.

As it is for Jonah, so it is for these others; the guilty conscience of the resisting hero "is a wound, and there's naught to staunch it" (45). His spiritual lifeblood would all eventually leak away, leaving him dead. Only if it were replenished endlessly, as it would be if he possessed the oil of the whale, would the lamp of his soul burn eternally.[19] In sum, the marks of those who refuse the call, who remain imprisoned by their earthly identity, are these: a feeling of spiritual deadness and entrapment; a sense of life's meagerness, and apprehension at its eventually running out; a desperate desire to hold on, to pay any price but the one required of them; a great fear of God and of not being chosen; and the profound dread that there will be no boon or prize at the end of the game.[20]

In the end, after being reborn "out of the belly of hell," when Jonah is commanded a second time, he answers the call to do "the Almighty's bidding." He agrees to do his duty by preaching "the Truth to the Face of Falsehood"; he goes to Nineveh and brings the prophecy of the deliverance from death of the people there (47–48). Following his own deliverance, Jonah thus becomes an instance of the returning hero, an image of the many figures in *Moby-Dick* who speak as prophets to the dead—of Father Mapple, Elijah, Pip, and finally Ishmael. Melville, however, shows us little of the returning Jonah. Instead, it is Father Mapple who fills out the image of the returning hero in his role as boon-carrier.[21] Significantly, he is a man of the word, an artist, a truth-teller, like Melville himself. When he speaks, the signs are on him that God speaks through him; the "light" that leaps from his eye, the "thunders" that roll away from his brow, these make his listeners look on him with the sense they are looking on the Godhead itself, "with a quick fear that was strange to them" (47).

Yet even Mapple is a reluctant hero; what he shows by his example is how difficult it is to return to the human fold after the intense inwardness and sublimity of the hunt. As he explains to his congregation, "[while] God has laid but one hand upon you; both his hands press upon me." The boon becomes a terrible burden; to be a "speaker of true things," to sound "unwelcome truths in the ears of a wicked Nineveh," to speak to the dead of their deadness and suffer the enmity of the damned is a hard thing.

Fortunately, there is a power to sustain the returning quester—the power of God, of the deepest self. In an image that defines the central meaning of Melville's great symbol of the Whale, there is the power of Leviathan itself, its

breeching a trope for the birth of the soul out of the depths of its imprison-ment, as it is in Mapple's sermon. Instantaneously, when Jonah finally speaks his own name, when he cries out his identity for the first time, "Then God spake unto the fish [that confined him]; and from the shuddering cold and blackness of the sea, the whale came breeching up towards the warm and pleas-ant sun, and all the delights of air and earth" (47–48). As this image powerfully suggests, the birth of the self is an occurrence of incredible force, and of tran-scendent beauty and joy. Though there is a burden to the hero's return, a "woe," it is more than compensated by the "delight" he experiences in performing his true calling. At the culminating moment, when Mapple begins his peroration on the theme of "delight," the chaplain speaks the overriding thesis of his ser-mon, and of the whole first section of *Moby-Dick*, when he exclaims, "Delight is to him,—a far, far upward, and inward delight—who against the proud gods and commodores of this earth, ever stands forth his own inexorable self" (48).

Chapter 10, "A Bosom Friend," the first of several in the portrait of Queequeg, presents another imposing, yet this time also comic, example of a character who knows how to stand forth "his own inexorable self." Like the New Bedford chaplain, Queequeg is at one with his god and seems to command all the powers of the earth. Where Mapple moves easily through the driving rain (the water that restores or destroys) on his way to the Whalemen's Chapel, Queequeg sits comfortably before the hearth fire (the fire that revives or kills) in the Spouter-Inn. Where Mapple refashions the word of God to suit his ministerial purpose, Queequeg reworks the countenance of his little surrogate god, Yojo, to suit his inner vision. Neither man's action is sacrilegious because both work out of the inner necessity of the returning hero. Both have seen the face of the Father, and now, each in his independent way, they have come back to the fold to relate what they have witnessed, and to do the work they are bidden to do.

Yet as the title of this chapter suggests, Queequeg is more than the guide who will show Ishmael the way to the hidden god. He *is* the god, an image of that "inexorable self" at the center of every successful hero. A pagan, savage and illiterate, he had a "hideously marred" face with "something in it," Ishmael says vaguely, "which was by no means disagreeable." Yet what that something is he then proceeds to identify, with deadpan irony, when he exclaims, "You cannot hide the soul" (49). Though on the way to Nantucket a greenhorn mistakes Queequeg for "the devil," Ishmael has already gone far enough in his initiation to be able to see in the Polynesian's deep, dark eyes "tokens of a spirit that would dare a thousand devils" (60, 50). If he "looked like a man who had never cringed and never had had a creditor," as Ishmael observes of him, no doubt it is because he never had a cause to fear anything and never had a need to borrow. Wholly centered in himself, he has "no desire to enlarge his circle of

acquaintances"; but when his friends come to him, as Ishmael does, he is happy to reciprocate, and more (50). Possessing more of the world's wealth than he himself will ever need, he gives half his thirty pieces of silver, and more, to his new friend, Ishmael. In his own example, he thus makes clear that the world will always provide the initiate whatever he needs to make his journey. To the poor hero like Ishmael, who has the courage to make the first step, life becomes a veritable cornucopia, supplying both bed and counterpane, an evening of good talk, a long smoke, and a friend who "would gladly die for me, if need should be" (51). If he also has to be forced to take an embalmed head into the bargain, that is because, unlike Queequeg, he still has no more desire to be reminded of his mortality than any other poor mortal.

Still, more important than these outward signs of the warming of the world, in the midst of New Bedford's arctic winter, are the signs of warming taking place within Ishmael himself, now that he has made friends with Queequeg. Sitting in their room, the "fire burning low," watching the cannibal count the pages of a "marvelous book" (presumably the Bible), he suddenly became "sensible of strange feelings. I felt a melting in me. No more my splintered heart and maddened hand were turned against the wolfish world. This soothing savage had redeemed it" (50–51).

Later, after the two have formally declared their friendship, Ishmael shows the powerful effect of his transformation when, unlike Jonah before him, he jumps at the chance to do the Lord's bidding. In a comic scene, Ishmael shows he is, if anything, a little too quick to preach his own religion, his "particular Presbyterian form of worship," to a real pagan. For, the way he sees it, he has to "turn idolator" and become a pagan himself first if he is to have any influence with Queequeg (52). Still, as the result of his efforts, Ishmael goes to bed not alone, as Jonah did, but with a friend; not with a conscience wracked by guilt, as Jonah had, but with one "at peace"; not to sleep like a dead man but to lie abed "chatting and napping" at intervals and then to awake refreshed long before daybreak (53). There, in the cold and the dark, after the fire has gone out, Ishmael speaks for the first time not simply of feeling his "identity" but of feeling it "aright," as if "darkness were indeed the proper element of our essences," he theorizes, "though light be more congenial to our clayey part" (54). Now, warmed by an interior fire, Ishmael has no need for any other kind of flame.

The next day, as the two of them glide down the Acushnet River on the way out of town toward Nantucket, they see ice-crusted New Bedford off to one side, "huge hills and mountains of casks on casks piled upon her wharves" (60). These casks are of course intended to hold the precious whale oil that is the town's principal source of wealth. However, they are really more like stacks

of coffins, or caskets, that lie there mutely waiting to serve the burial of the dead instead. To the mind prepared to look for the "meaning" of things, as Ishmael does with comic self-consciousness in the New Bedford chapters, and acknowledge the pervasiveness of death in this wintry landscape, they serve as reminders that America's most affluent town is, after all, a land of the dead and must be abandoned.

By contrast, Nantucket seems impoverished and unpromising. To the worldly eye, it is a wasteland, a desert of sand—"all beach, without a background." But despite the barrenness of the landscape, the people of Nantucket enjoy a wealth and power that those of New Bedford and other whaling centers can hardly appreciate. For like "sea hermits, issuing from their ant-hill in the sea," these "naked Nantucketers" have "overrun and conquered the watery world like so many Alexanders; parcelling out among them the Atlantic, Pacific, and Indian oceans, as the three pirate powers did Poland." As is soon evident in Ishmael's dealings with the Quaker Bildad, the Nantucketers can be shrewd, grasping materialists, but they possess a wealth beyond material riches, too. So at home is the Nantucket whaler while at sea, so attuned to its powerful rhythms, that at night, like the landless gull, he "furls his sails, and lays him to his rest, while under his very pillow rush herds of walruses and whales" (63–64). A nation of adventuring heroes, the people of Nantucket command the wealth of all the seas, the wealth of dreams and the unconscious, as this oceanic image of natural power makes clear.

Like most chapter titles in *Moby-Dick*, "Chowder," the title of the next chapter, is a metaphor or conceit. Besides suggesting something of the mixed character of Ishmael's initial experience of Nantucket, it offers a preview, in miniature, of the mixed nature of the whaling life generally. Arriving at the Try-Pots Inn, Ishmael is immediately reminded by the gallows on the sign outside that there is death and damnation in the whaleman's calling. If one is not killed or maimed in the hunt, the despair at failure can be just as devastating and lead to the same result. Mistress Hussey lectures Queequeg about a recent suicide in her apartments, a young man named Stiggs, who, "coming from that unfort'nt v'y'ge of his," as she says, "when he was gone four years and a half, with ony three barrels of *ile*, was found dead in my first floor back, with his harpoon in his side," a would-be Christ but one forsaken by the Father (67).

However, just as there is both clam and cod on the bill of fare at the Try-Pots Inn, so is there both death and life in the business of whaling. The cook in the kitchen will sometimes mix up the order and serve "clam" (symbol of the recalcitrance of life, of the withholding side of the dual-edged female principle): "that's a rather cold and clammy reception in the winter time, ain't it, Mrs. Hussey?" complains Ishmael facetiously, when his dinner order arrives.

But the boldest adventurer will generally get "cod" (symbol of the potency of life, of the providential side of the dual-edged male principle), as Ishmael discovers when he steps to the kitchen window and barks out his order to be sure there will be no mistake about it. "Ask," saith the Lord, according to the well-known proverb, "and ye shall be given." In this world, even the adventuring hero sometimes has to take potluck; but if he is truly fearless about tapping its wealth, he will be rewarded beyond even his wildest dreams. When asked, at the end of this chapter, whether he and Queequeg will take clam or cod the next morning for breakfast, Ishmael responds with the boldness of one who has learned to stand forth his own inexorable self, "Both; and let's have a couple of smoked herring by way of variety," he adds cheekily (67).

"God helps those who help themselves"—that is the unwritten motto of the successful adventurer, and that is the surprising lesson of the following chapter, "The Ship." Though the hero can hardly know such a thing in the beginning, the person who serves as a guide is simply a symbol of the assisting power that dwells within everyone. He is, as in the case of Queequeg, an image of the soul of the adventurer, his task being to instill in his new friend an abiding confidence in his own powers. Thus Ishmael, despite the newfound brazenness displayed at the end of the previous chapter, expresses "surprise and no small concern" when Queequeg informs him that the little god Yojo wants Ishmael himself to be the one to select their ship. Speaking like the novice he is, Ishmael nervously admits that "I did not like that plan at all. I had not a little relied upon Queequeg's sagacity to point out the whaler best fitted to carry us and our fortunes securely." Yet the next morning, his courage screwed up to a pitch, he accomplishes his task quickly and with little worry or internal debate. Ostensibly entrusting everything to the little god Yojo, the comic fetish or charm that seems to protect Ishmael in Queequeg's absence, he in fact falls back on his own intuition in choosing the *Pequod* over the several other ships then in port (67–68). Though in the course of his adventures he sometimes claims to be a victim of the mysterious Fates, it should be recognized that, for the most part, in important ways Ishmael really is the master of his own destiny.

The first part of his day's work successfully completed, Ishmael is nonetheless little wiser than when he began. Boarding the *Pequod* to propose himself as a "candidate" for the voyage, his first response is to look around the quarterdeck "for some one having authority" (70). Clearly, he has not yet figured out that all authority comes from within. Several pages later, though he has by then met with both Captains Peleg and Bildad and taken care of all necessary details, he ends the scene still hungering to see the man who is really in charge. Having only heard about Captain Ahab at this point, Ishmael feels the

mystery of his authority deepen. For at this point he learns only that there is much more to know about him. Not until much later are we shown that, behind Ahab, there is a higher authority still, and that Ahab, the son of a "crazy, widowed mother," also seeks the Father (79). Here, however, everything that transpires demonstrates, in an understated way, what Ishmael is not yet prepared to know—namely, that in all essential matters the final authority must reside within the adventurer's own soul.

The encounter with Peleg and Bildad is structured as a second major threshold scene, where Ishmael's resolve and worthiness are tested and he is revealed to be one of the chosen few. Almost literally, in stepping onto the *Pequod,* Ishmael steps into the mouth of the whale, the entrance to the place of trial. For the ship has been rebuilt out of various parts of the whalemen's catch over a long span of years, and the curious wigwam in which he is subjected to Peleg's rigorous questioning is actually supported by the jawbones of a right whale.

Like Father Mapple, Peleg has the job of separating false aspirants from true ones. Those who are not yet ready to follow the path, he tries to dissuade, or intimidate, while those of pure heart and steady purpose he tries to encourage or help smooth their way. Like a holy man conducting an inquest of a heretic, Peleg questions Ishmael about his previous experience at sea. And like a true master, he begins by asking the key question concerning the ultimate test of the whale-hunting hero: "ever been in a stove boat?" Immediately sensing in the politeness of Ishmael's reply ("No, Sir, I never have") that he is a perfect neophyte, Peleg goes back to the beginning and inquires, with the disgust of one who is prepared to hear the worst, "Dost know nothing at all about whaling, I dare say—eh?" When Ishmael confesses his complete ignorance, but then proceeds to mention his previous experience in the merchant service, Peleg cuts him off in disgust and then offers a hint as to the peculiar nature of the whaling enterprise that might help to set him back on track: "Marchant service be damned," he exclaims. "Talk not that lingo to me. Dost see that leg?—I'll take that leg away from thy stern, if ever thou talkest of the marchant service to me again. Marchant service indeed!" (71).

What Peleg hints at here is that those who stray from the true spirit of whaling, who engage in the hunt for worldly, selfish purposes, will suffer the loss of their "standpoint" or leg, symbolic of the phallus or life force, as the captain of the *Pequod* does. It seems hardly a coincidence that, when Peleg hears of such heresy, he suspects Ishmael of being a kind of parricide, accusing him of thinking about "murdering the officers" when he gets to sea. To be sure, Peleg is stringing him along, playing him for the greenhorn he is, as Ishmael eventually comes to realize. But when he returns to the questioning in earnest, asking about Ishmael's motives in wanting to go "a-whaling," Peleg begins to see a

little into his heart, and what he finds wins him over to the novice's side: "Well, sir, I want to see what whaling is," Ishmael replies. "I want to see the world" (71). Demonstrating the simple curiosity and innocent wonder of the true aspirant, Ishmael here reveals none of the covetousness or sensualism typical of the men in the merchant service, and none of the egotism that will later emerge in Ahab. After more of Peleg's tough questioning, which Ishmael gets through with relative ease, he is invited "below deck into the cabin," there to sign the ship's papers, and to meet Bildad, in the last test of this early series (73).

Bildad is made of sterner stuff than Peleg, however, and poses a stiffer challenge. Originally "educated according to the strictest sect of Nantucket Quakerism," he is a man who in his later years has resisted all the world's temptations, even "the sight of many unclad, lovely island creatures, round the Horn," as Ulysses resisted the sirens. Known chiefly for his "immutableness," he is one who has himself passed the true whaleman's test, and as such he is thus best suited to administer it to others (74). Like an old sachem or rabbi confronting a young initiate, he asks Ishmael just a single question, composed of two well-chosen words. So masterful is this high priest of whaling—who throughout the interview sits holding the Scriptures in his hands—that he formulates his query using the words of his friend, simply redirecting them to this supplicant. When Peleg informs him that Ishmael says "he's our man, . . . he wants to ship," Bildad masterfully turns to the would-be hero and asks him to testify on his own behalf, "Dost thee?" He thus puts to him the one essential question: he asks Ishmael to search his heart and speak his fitness for signing on. That Ishmael speaks truly when he replies "I *dost*" is attested to by the fact that in doing so he slips into the idiom of the old Quaker whaleman, exemplar of Nantucket's great adventurers, and that he does so "unconsciously." For as is repeatedly revealed in *Moby-Dick,* to speak unconsciously is to speak out of the authority of the divine self. In saying "I *dost,*" Ishmael does more than assert his readiness, however. He also proclaims his own mortality and thus confesses his dependence on the divine energy to sustain him: "I am dust," he seems to say. At the end of their brief interview, then, Ishmael receives Bildad's laconic blessing or approval. When Peleg asks his friend what he thinks of their young prospect, Bildad responds only with a slightly exasperated but neatly ambiguous, "He'll do" (75).

That Bildad also proves to be exceedingly tight-fisted when it comes to assigning Ishmael his share of the ship's profits may not be so much a sign of hypocrisy in the end, as is generally thought, as it is a sign of consistency. Bildad does have a weaker side, but a case can also be made that he drives a hard bargain because he knows that any worldiness, any sign of hunger for "a princely fortune" (76), may so contaminate the initiate's efforts as to lead him to ruin.

Bildad knows that the initiate must put all ideas of making an earthly fortune out of his mind if he is to have any hope of gaining the ultimate reward. As he says, "where your treasure is, there will your heart be also" (77). Indeed, one's heart, or soul, as Melville explains throughout *Moby-Dick*, is one's treasure.

Having affirmed his readiness for the voyage of the *Pequod*, Ishmael is now prepared to speak the name of the "I" who uttered "I *dost*." Returning to his room in the Try-Pots Inn, where Queequeg has been observing his "Ramadan," practicing the sort of asceticism or indifference to the world that Bildad had been trying to instill in Ishmael, Ishmael tries to rouse the Polynesian by speaking softly through the keyhole. In doing so, he announces his identity for the first time in the chronology of the book's events. "Queequeg," he whispers, as though still seeking some external confirmation of himself. "I say, Queequeg! why don't you speak? It's I—Ishmael" (82). Ironically, at the very moment he wants Queequeg to confirm his presence, Ishmael is giving voice to his own deepest self. Here, for the first time, we can begin to appreciate the significance of Ishmael's name, which in Hebrew means "God shall hear," for the biblical Ishmael was more than an outcast or rejected son; he was also one whose name contained the promise of divine redemption. To identify oneself as "Ishmael" is to speak one's faith that the self contains within it all the strength of God the Father. Of course, Queequeg, who is both a simple savage from Kokovoko and an image of the eternal soul within each person, does not stir until he is ready. The soul will not respond simply because it is summoned. At times we may assume that it will succumb to our "polite arts and blandishments," as Ishmael wrongly assumes Queequeg will do in this same scene (84). But generally it comes alive in its own good time, according to a rhythm of its own, as Queequeg finally does the next morning, long after Ishmael has given up trying to rouse him, and the sun first enters their room.

Brief as this scene is, Ishmael nonetheless shows that he has learned to respect the independence of the soul that bides its time. Confident, finally, that Queequeg will eventually follow him to bed, Ishmael takes his own bearskin jacket and, in his last act before retiring, throws it over his new friend, "as it promised to be a very cold night" (84). It is not a gesture that shows much respect for the savage's own wishes, to be sure. But it is an act of real tenderness just the same, one that shows Ishmael to have made a big advance over the smug tolerance he had claimed at the start of this chapter.

As if to confirm that at least a small opening has been made in Ishmael's religious temper, the chapter ends with a reversal of the beginning. Instead of congratulating himself for his noblesse oblige, as he did when he first met Queequeg and learned of his bizarre religious practices, he ends with the sudden recognition that an illiterate savage like Queequeg was capable of feeling

much the same way toward himself, thinking that "he knew a good deal more about the true religion than I did" and felt "a sort of condescending concern and compassion" for Ishmael because of his great ignorance (86). Thus, while Ishmael opens the chapter with only a tiny "key-hole prospect" onto Queequeg's Ramadan (and a "crooked and sinister one" at that, as he says), he ends it with the light of day finally dawning on him, literally and figuratively (82). Still a good Presbyterian, garrulously proselytizing to Queequeg even in the last paragraphs of this chapter, Ishmael at least shows signs of becoming more understanding of the religious beliefs and practices of his companion and of learning to appreciate the universal conditions underlying the world's many religions.

Having grown more tolerant himself, now, the naturally loquacious Ishmael finds it but a small step to preaching toleration to others. Chapter 18, "His Mark," ostensibly concerns Queequeg's demonstration of prowess with a harpoon (hitting "his mark") and signing the ship's papers (making "his mark"). But, less obviously, it also concerns Ishmael's growing ecumenicalism, even to the point of showing him in the outrageously funny, unexpected role of Queequeg's evangelist—not his Matthew, Luke, or John, but "His Mark." From the time he enters the story, Queequeg has been something of a Christ-figure to Ishmael, prompting his spiritual awakening, guiding the recovery of his soul, pointing the way to renewed health and happiness. Of course there is a good deal of leg-pulling in Ishmael's exorbitant claim to the Quaker captains that "Queequeg here is a born member of the First Congregational Church. He is a deacon himself, Queequeg is" (88). But beneath the humor of his prevarication and wordplay, the gospel truth of Ishmael's universalism shines through.

Contrary to those, such as H. Bruce Franklin, who argue that *Moby-Dick* shows Melville's preoccupation with one or another religious mythology, I would emphasize the importance of Ishmael's growing ecumenicalism, an ecumenicalism that reaches its high point in this scene. Pressed hard by Bildad to explain himself, Ishmael responds facetiously, "I mean, sir, the same ancient Catholic Church to which you and I, and Captain Peleg there, and Queequeg here, and all of us, and every mother's son and soul of us belong; the great and everlasting First Congregation of this whole worshipping world; we all belong to that . . . in *that* we all join hands." "Splice, thou mean'st *splice* hands," Peleg corrects him, thus emphasizing his own recognition, under the sway of Ishmael's rhetoric, of the powerful human bonds, the equality and goodwill, that everyone celebrates in the simple gesture of joining hands (later celebrated in "A Squeeze of the Hand"). Ironically, it is Peleg, then, and not Queequeg, who comes to be converted in this chapter. His heart is changed by the upstart evangelist Ishmael, as he himself humorously confesses. "Young

man," Peleg exclaims, at the same time telling them to forget about the cannibal's so-called "conversion" papers and inviting the two of them on board, "you'd better ship for a missionary, instead of a fore-mast hand; I never heard a better sermon" (88).

Bildad is not so easily won over, however. "Eyeing" Queequeg during the signing of the *Pequod*'s papers, afterward he stands and places a tract entitled "The Latter Day Coming; or No Time to Lose," in the cannibal's hands. Only then does he join hands with him, grasping both the little book and Queequeg's hands in his own. Looking "earnestly into his eyes," he warns him to "mind thine eye" and "turn from the wrath to come." But clearly these are wasted words, like the words in the tract that the illiterate Queequeg will never read (nor needs to). As the incarnation of the soul, Queequeg has no ego involvement in the life he leads; unlike Ahab, he does not have to mind his "I." Neither does he have to concern himself with the Last Things, for he has nothing to lose in the end. Instead, as demonstrated earlier, Queequeg keeps his eye on the eye of the whale, the incarnation of the self. For the whale is an image of all Nature, what Emerson called the "Other Me." Like a Buddhist archer, who trains himself to think of nothing but his target, Queequeg is a perfect master, one who can hit the "spot" at will, because he and the whale's eye are one (88–89).

Elijah, the "Prophet" of the next chapter, mysteriously materializes to provide Ishmael his final test before he ships out, asking him whether he has any fear for his soul and darkly hinting that he has committed himself to a fatal undertaking. As the last guardian of the threshold to the magic realm, the prophet tries to shake the initiate's resolve by casting doubt on the ship's whole enterprise; by claiming to know all about its strange past and the captain he enigmaticly refers to as "Old Thunder"; and by pretending to have knowledge of the *Pequod*'s future (92). After determining that Ishmael and his friend have just signed the ship's articles, the old sailor inquires ominously, "Anything down there about your souls?" Ironically, Ishmael seems not to comprehend: "About what?" he replies (91). In this case, he is fortunate not to understand Elijah, for we see here by how thin a thread the fate of the would-be adventurer hangs; if Ishmael had comprehended the old prophet, he might have been scared away, or so we are led to assume. However, Ishmael does continue to resist Elijah's sly insinuations, and in the end the old man intimates that Ishmael is made of the true stuff: "I like to hear a chap talk up that way," he says, pretending to call an end to their talk; "you are just the man for him [i.e., Ahab]—the likes of ye. Morning to ye, shipmates, morning!" (93). Despite some lingering doubts after he learns the name of this stranger,

Ishmael dismisses them almost entirely by the end of the scene, just a trace of uncertainty remaining to show his mortality.

In the concluding three chapters of this long opening section of *Moby-Dick,* Melville brings to a close the themes of the preparation for the hunt that are his chief concern. "All Astir," which focuses on the preparation of the ship—the purchasing and collecting and the fetching, hauling, and stowing down of its stores—conveys the idea of the world's richness or fecundity, its boundless capacity to provide for the hero's material needs so he can get on with the important business of the quest. Like Mother Nature, the figure called Aunt Charity, who is the *Pequod*'s chief provisioner, is "a lean old lady of a most determined and indefatigable spirit, but withal very kindhearted." She is an image of the eternal woman, always up and doing, forever eager to lend her "hand and heart to anything that promised to yield safety, comfort, and consolation" to the ship's officers and crew. But, even so, there are some needs that even the eternal female cannot supply, some accidents or losses she cannot anticipate or protect against. While the whale ship has been provisioned with "spare boats, spare spars, and spare lines and harpoons, and spare everythings, almost," there can be no supplying, as Ishmael says with both humor and seriousness, of a "spare Captain and duplicate ship" (96). For some things, the men must supply their own insurance; they must be their own protection. How they might accomplish that all-important task is the subject of the next chapter, "Going Aboard," the title of which reiterates a timeless call to adventure.

The next day, when Ishmael and Queequeg make their way past crazy Elijah one last time and step aboard the *Pequod,* it is still early morning, and all is quiet, "not a soul moving." The only person they encounter is a sleeper, a man down in the forecastle spread "at whole length upon two chests" [a fore-image of Ishmael on the coffin/life-buoy at the end], "his face downwards and inclosed in his folded arms," a pose symbolizing self-protection. An old rigger, "wrapped in a tattered pea-jacket," a variation of the earlier image of Queequeg at his Ramadan with Ishmael's coat thrown over him, this curious figure is another likeness of the soul, but the soul in a state of sleep (99). Taking seats at each end of the man, Ishmael and Queequeg pass the time talking and sharing a smoke from the latter's odd tomahawk-pipe. Unaccountably, whenever Queequeg took his turn with the instrument, "he flourished the hatchet-side of it over the sleeper's head," and when Ishmael asks what he is up to, he says only, "Perry easy, kill-e; oh! perry easy!" Still, the action and the explanation together make it clear that Queequeg is acting out a version of the story of Damocles, and that in his version the sword of Fate hangs over the soul that sleeps. The soul must never let down its guard. Like the sleeper who finally

wakes to the smoke of his own damnation, the soul must be "all alive now"; it must "turn to." It, too, must be forever up and about its business (100).

What that business consists of Ishmael unwittingly explains when he says that Queequeg's tomahawk-pipe "both brained his foes and soothed his soul" (100). Quite simply, it is the soul's job to slay its enemies; only then can it feel "soothed."[22] In fact, such a notion of the soul's duty provides the rationale for the rest of Melville's epic story. It explains why Ishmael, having found his deepest self, must still go to sea—not to slay the White Whale (which is, after all, Melville's great image of the soul) but to destroy its enemies. Despite this long foreground, then, the journey of Ishmael is only now ready to begin.

At various times in the land-based chapters of *Moby-Dick*, Ishmael shows that he is a fearful man, as well as a man of courage. Whether making his way through the pitch-black streets of New Bedford or facing the prospect of sleeping with a savage; whether contemplating the cenotaphs in the Whaleman's Chapel or standing helplessly outside Queequeg's locked room, Ishmael evidences a nervous, morbid imagination. He is a man who fears death and destruction, and premature burial most of all. In the chapters at the end of this section, his fearfulness even intensifies, as he comes closer and closer to the time when he must cross the threshold of the ship for the last time and move irreversibly into Captain Ahab's domain. The first meeting with Elijah stirs up in Ishmael "all kinds of vague wonderments and half-apprehensions" concerning the *Pequod*, its mysterious captain, and the leg he has lost; and when he sees a group of dim, shadowy figures boarding the ship before dawn the next morning, he has to "beat . . . down" his fear when he learns they are nowhere to be found. Significantly, it "seemed," Ishmael says, that "Queequeg had not at all noticed" these strange figures (93, 99). Undoubtedly Queequeg did notice them, and everything else besides. The reason he seems not to observe such things is simply that he has no fears, and so he registers no reactions. Unlike the young Ishmael, he is always the master of himself. In the chapter titled "Merry Christmas," when the *Pequod* is making its way out to sea, Ishmael is given a lesson to this effect, a Christmas present in the form of a swift kick in the pants from Captain Peleg, who commands the ship while it is headed out to sea. Ironically, then, even at the start of his quest, Ishmael is offered a "boon," one of the most valuable to be gleaned from his whole journey. Having stopped in the midst of his sailor duties to worry about the perils of starting the voyage with "such a devil for a pilot" as Peleg, who had taken to shouting out his orders in great oaths, Ishmael feels a "sudden sharp poke in my rear"—a timely warning that he needs to pay attention to his duty and not to his fears (103). Clearly, this is a lesson Ishmael takes to heart, for he is never kicked a second time, not even, in the end, by Moby Dick.

"The Lee Shore" is the capstone (a substitute, Ishmael intimates, for a tomb-stone) of the long opening section of *Moby-Dick* that is so thoroughly perme-ated by themes of death and burial. A memorial to the questing spirit incar-nated in Bulkington, the mariner who hardly lands from one voyage before embarking on another, this chapter offers the promise that the adventuring hero never really dies and is never really buried. "Wonderfullest things are ever the unmentionable," Ishmael exclaims concerning the apparent immor-tality of this eternally restless figure; "deep memories yield no epitaphs; this six-inch chapter is the stoneless grave of Bulkington" (106). It is important that Ishmael mentions Bulkington as a future "sleeping-partner" of his (16), for like the old rigger whom Ishmael and Queequeg found sleeping in the forecastle on the morning of their departure, Bulkington is next seen "all alive" and tending to business up on the deck, indeed "standing at her helm." What makes Bulkington such a remarkable instance of the adventuring hero is not simply that he can put his fears behind him, as Peleg would have Ishmael do, but that he can put all of his needs for every kind of human comfort behind him as well. As his example suggests, the quest is the most strenuous under-taking imaginable, requiring the most heroic discipline and great personal sacrifice. Like the "storm-tossed ship, that miserably drives along the leeward land," all the power of nature seems to force the quester such as Bulkington toward the shore, the land of his mortal being, inviting him to find rest in comforts that are falsely soothing, or in a peace known only to the dead. "The port would fain give succor; the port is pitiful; in the port is safety, comfort, hearthstone, supper, warm blankets, friends, all that's kind to our mortali-ties," Ishmael explains. But in that gale, until the agitated adventurer finds true peace, until he slays his enemies, "the port, the land, is that ship's direst jeopardy." Just "one touch of land" would mean instant destruction (106).

Thus all adventuring, Ishmael argues, "all deep, earnest thinking is but the intrepid effort of *the soul* to keep the open independence of her sea; while the wildest winds of heaven and earth conspire to cast her on the treacherous, slavish shore" (emphasis added). Though the quester cannot know while in the midst of his adventure whether he will ever reach his goal, ever slay his enemies or come face to face with the Father, "better is it to perish in that howling infinite [of landlessness], than be ingloriously dashed upon the lee, even if that were safety!" Even so, Ishmael insists, speaking now as one who has already lived through the adventure and, like Queequeg, knows the re-sult to be a truly divine translation, the "agony" of the journey, and the "ter-rors" of the trial, are not "vain." "Take heart, take heart, O Bulkington! Bear thee grimly, demigod! Up from the spray of thy ocean-perishing—straight up, leaps thy apotheosis!" (107). As in other spiritual epics, Ishmael suggests,

the hero will eventually come to appreciate the apparent paradox that in his death is his life. Only by dying to the world, only by being tried in the belly of the whale endlessly, can he hope to experience the continuous rebirth of the soul that keeps it vital.

II. THE GAME OF CHESS

In "The Advocate," which in the chronology of the story appears after the *Pequod* has reached sea, Ishmael suddenly begins to speak in a new voice. Jumping way ahead and looking back on his life retrospectively, he is now an experienced whaleman addressing an audience of the uninitiated, instructing his readers in the complexities of the whale fishery. He thus begins to speak consistently for the first time as an epic poet, who, as E. M. W. Tillyard has said, combines "abundant content and masterly control," or breadth of knowledge and density of language.[23] Because whaling seems so unpromising and unlikely a subject for an epic, so "unpoetical and disreputable," Ishmael must become an aggressive "advocate." But in doing so he deviates only in tone— exaggerated, straining after effect, comic—from the role of the traditional epic poet such as Homer or Milton, whose job it is to mediate between the lives of his heroes and his audience, explaining to us their arcane activities; promoting their enterprise; and in general trying to make us see that we have an investment in their cause. Like the master of an intricate sport, such as whale fishing can be, he must also instruct his readers in the rules of the game.

However, if he is to convince those readers to take up the game themselves, he must do more than explain how it is played. He must portray the men who are its champions and communicate something of the spirit of their peculiar activity. He must engage the interest of his readers in the lives of exemplary heroes who are themselves caught up in a quintessential contest, and he must raise the stature and importance of their undertaking so that the universal destiny will be seen to be symbolized in their experience. That, more than anything else, according to Abercrombie, is the principal task of the epic poet, and that is what Ishmael attempts to do in chapter 24 and in the several chapters that follow.[24]

Because the whalemen and their legendary antagonist, the great White Whale, must be introduced to the reader and their histories brought up to date; and because, too, the life on an American whaleship needs to be portrayed, this second section of *Moby-Dick* is more essay than narrative. Opening not with one or two but half a dozen or more chapters cast in a polemical

style, including speculative chapters on "Cetology" and "The Whiteness of the Whale," the second part of Melville's epic novel closes, appropriately, at the end of "The Mat-Maker," chapter 47, another speculative chapter, where Ishmael's effort to weave the forces of fate, free will, and chance into a single cosmic theory is unexpectedly interrupted by the sighting of the *Pequod*'s first whale. With the sounding of the whaleman's "There she blows!," Ishmael suddenly realizes that the business of whaling is a thing of destiny. For when the brute fact of the whale abruptly surfaces to interrupt the flow of Ishmael's imagination, "the ball of free will dropped from my hand" (215). And the mat, like the theory it symbolizes, is left behind, unfinished.

Given the inherently unpromising nature of his subject, Melville had to go to great lengths to achieve the epic effect of significance in portraying his chief actors. Heroic action requires heroic characters, and the whalemen are widely thought to be nothing more than "butchers" (108). However, Ishmael, who manages time and again to turn obstacles into challenges to his inventiveness, immediately sets about appropriating epic conventions to his own needs, arguing, for example, with tongue firmly in his cheek, that martial commanders, who are among the most common heroes of epic, have themselves often been the bloodiest butchers in the world. Whatever reservations one might conceive of regarding the fitness of whalemen to serve as heroes for an epic, Ishmael has a mock-logical counterargument. If it is thought that whaling has no power or influence in the ways of the world, or that it has never had a redeeming "peaceful" or civilizing influence on the course of history, he counters with little-known facts showing how fabulously lucrative the whaling enterprise has been, or with outlandish examples of countries, or entire continents, that have been liberated from colonialism through the efforts of the early whalemen (109).

In rejoinder after rejoinder, example after historical example, Ishmael builds a hyperbolic case for the nobility of the whale, for the dignity of the whaling business, and even for the royalty of the whaling man's blood. Repeatedly he calls up outrageous analogies from royal history or custom to place his whaling material in the heroic tradition, as he does, most memorably, when he speaks of the coronation of the heads of kings in terms of oiling a "head of salad" with whale oil (113). Among the most important analogies are the several provided in the two "Knights and Squires" chapters, which elevate the *Pequod*'s motley mates and harpooneers to the level of Arthurian aristocrats, or at least attempt to. And Ishmael does much the same thing in the next chapter, which focuses on Ahab, the crotchety Nantucket captain named for a wicked Old Testament king. Melville has even managed to insert a queen into the dramatis personae introduced here, namely, "Queen Mab" (the subject of chapter 31), the fairy queen of English folklore believed to govern people's dreams.

As the mocking tone of "Postscript," chapter 25, suggests, however, and as Ishmael matter-of-factly maintains at the end of the first "Knights and Squires" chapter, the concern with royalty in the epic genre, the preoccupation with titles and bloodlines and pomp, is a concern merely with the trappings, rather than the essence, of the epic story. Anticipating his portrayal of the sorrowful "fall of valor in the soul" of Starbuck, when the first mate tries to stand up to Ahab, Ishmael states that "this august dignity I treat of, is not the dignity of kings and robes, but that abounding dignity which has no robed investiture." In oxymoronic language characteristic of the epic, Ishmael describes his subject as "that democratic dignity which, on all hands, radiates without end from God; Himself!" He observes that God calls His "selectest champions," including such notorious popular examples as John Bunyan and Andrew Jackson, from "the kingly commons." Repeatedly in these chapters, it is natural, self-made courage, not inherited rank or wealth, that forms the basis of such dignity, in Ishmael's view, and that makes even these "meanest mariners, and renegades and castaways" who serve on the *Pequod* worthy of epic treatment (117). Starbuck possesses such courage, though for him it is "a thing simply useful" in the hunting of whales (116). And Stubb and Flask do, too, though on a lower plane, the one being simply "indifferent" and the other "dead" to any apprehensions of danger (118–19). The higher forms of courage, on the other hand, simple daring and coolness under pressure, are represented in the three harpooneers, Queequeg, Tashtego, and Daggoo, and in the *Pequod*'s captain, who is portrayed memorably the first time we see him, staring out beyond the ship's bow with "an infinity of firmest fortitude, a determinate, unsurrenderable wilfulness," in his search for Moby Dick (124).

All of these examples are early signs that Melville was working self-consciously in the epic tradition, a tradition increasingly recognized as being self-consciousnessly imitative, as Tom Winnifrith has argued, or parodic, as John Kevin Newman has said.[25] In all the major epics, whether oral or literary, the most conspicuous value is simply courage. All the great epics, as Abercrombie has explained, remind us that, while courage may not be the only significant attitude one can hold toward life, "man can achieve nothing until he has first achieved courage." Given the precariousness of life, particularly when the oral epics were being formed, it follows that courage is "the absolutely necessary foundation of any subsequent valuation of life," and so it proved to be, even in the development of the spiritual epic.[26]

More than any other character, Ahab dominates the second part of *Moby-Dick*. As "supreme lord and dictator" of the *Pequod* and the protagonist in Melville's story of the Whale, he is also, of course, the book's central character (122). However, he is not Melville's example of the epic hero, the redemptive

figure of universal mythology. That role has been reserved for Ishmael. Instead, Ahab is Melville's example of the failed hero, the man who refuses the call to adventure. He is the opposite of Melville's narrator, not an incarnation of the self, or soul, but of the selfish ego. Like Minos, the Cretan in Ovid's *Metamorphoses*, a work that at least one critic has called an epic,[27] Ahab is a ruler who forsakes his public duty for his private need and is thus transformed into a tyrant. Rather than serve the group he has been entrusted to lead, he uses his position to force the group to serve him, as Melville makes plain in "The Specksynder" (chapter 33). And in the process he brings everything to ruin.

A psychologically complex figure, "fear-haunted" yet hostile, "alert at every hand to meet and battle back the anticipated aggressions of his environment," the "tyrant-monster," as Campbell calls such a figure, is "the world's messenger of disaster, even though, in his mind, he may entertain himself with humane intentions."[28] Such a man is Ahab, who also believes his aggression is the product of high purpose and in the end brings catastrophe to himself and his men. In his imagination, he "piled upon the whale's white hump the sum of all the general rage and hate felt by his whole race from Adam down" and then set himself the insuperable task of eradicating all evil from the world (184). But his professed intention masks his private fear and hatred. The evil he sees in Moby Dick is a projection, mainly, out of the hell of his own psyche.

Everything about Ahab, as Ishmael initially presents him, hints at his being a man who has repeatedly refused the call to the soul's awakening and who, instead of submitting to the will of God, holds ever more tightly to the little bit of mortality allotted to him. On his first entrance, he is described as one who has somehow escaped a trial by fire but been scarred by it, not as one who calmly submitted and proved himself equal to it: "He looked," as Ishmael says, "like a man cut away from the stake, when the fire has overrunningly wasted all the limbs without consuming them." Of the thin, rodlike mark running down the side of Ahab's face, Ishmael says it resembled the seam in a great tree trunk after a lightning bolt (symbol of Zeus, of the deity) has ripped through it, "leaving the tree still greenly alive, but branded" (123). Only after he has examined these sinister details does Ishmael even notice Ahab's "barbaric white leg," the book's overriding symbol, and symptom, of Ahab's dying and of his inevitable return to the dust he came from. And only then, almost by way of explanation, does he observe that the "moody stricken" Ahab carries the look of a "crucifixion" in his face, emblem of the would-be redeemer who has lost faith and feels himself forsaken by his God (124).

In fact, in the concluding paragraphs of this chapter Ishmael underscores the fact that Ahab has been near death, not only from his recent wound but

also from the ravages of age and winter. As the *Pequod* sails south, therefore, into spring and the whale's customary feeding grounds, Ahab comes up on deck more and more, his face each time more alive, like a "thunder-cloven old oak" that at last sends forth "some few green sprouts" (125). Summoned back for one last meeting with the Father, Ahab believes he is on a mission of destruction that will guarantee him a kind of immortality. Only later will he come to admit his fear that he is the one who will be destroyed. As in the spiritual epics of Dante and Milton, and indeed in all the great religious mythologies of the world, Ahab's refusal of the invitation to come home to God is a refusal to give up his limited, earthly conception of what constitutes his own self-interest. Like the heroes of these other works, he looks at the future not in terms of death and rebirth, but as a relentless threat to his vitality, to his identity and everything he stands for.[29] So fearful of death is he, so desperate to cling to the life he still holds, that soon after his first appearance on deck, as the ship moves into the tropics, he grows reluctant to leave the open air, even at night, and go down to his cabin for sleep: "It feels like going down into one's tomb," he would mutter to himself, ". . . to go to my grave-dug berth" (127).

Fearful of death, ever sensitive to insult, resistant to loss or change, Ahab is incapable of taking even a step, let alone a leap, into the unknown. Indeed, so rigid is he that he contests to the death any will that challenges his own. To the man like Ahab who lives in time, locked in the grasp of the ego, even the divinity becomes an enemy. "Talk not to me of blasphemy, man," he exclaims to Starbuck, when the first mate questions his motives for going after Moby Dick; "I'd strike the sun if it insulted me" (164). He refuses to see that life perpetually enacts the mystery of dismemberment, even as it enacts also the mystery of renewal. Speaking as though he considered his own dismasting to be a unique occurrence rather than but one instance of the common fate, Ahab reminds himself that the "prophecy was that I should be dismembered," and then he tries to bolster his ego by pretending to play prophet himself, claiming boldly that "I now prophesy that I will dismember my dismemberer" (168). He does not understand, what an anonymous Long Island sailor perceives when the latter says enigmatically, in "Midnight, Forecastle" (Chapter 40), "Hoe corn when you may, say I. All legs go to harvest soon" (174).

Despite his blasphemy, Ahab is otherwise a glorious figure, the representative man of his time, the American at midcentury. As the book's epic hero manqué, he contains within him not only the common, universal values of his type but Melville's summation of the cultural values of the United States in 1850—pride, independence, manly determination, pragmatism. These are not the highest values, to be sure, and they are not the only ones found in nine-

teenth-century America, but they are the predominant ones. So, too, Ahab's greatness is a "mortal greatness," a greatness that is "disease," and not the immortal kind that Ishmael comes to exemplify (74). Though Ahab is a powerfully sympathetic figure, it is clear Melville himself did not subscribe to the values he embodies. On the contrary, he saw them as America's doom. What Melville perceived, in looking at the young nation, was a whole culture trapped, as Emerson had said, in the temporal dimension of life; incapable of throwing off the childish ego; sensitive to any threat to its interests, big or small; quick to defend its sovereignty as well as its honor; lacking any real faith in the unseen, the spirit world of the soul, to sustain life and give it transcendent meaning.

Repeatedly in this second part of *Moby-Dick*, Melville portrays characters trading insults, plotting revenge, eagerly jumping into senseless fights, as they do at the end of the long dramatic chapter 40, when a Spanish sailor, bearing some nameless "old grudge," provokes a row with Daggoo by using a sly racial epithet (177). As timely, even culture-bound, as Melville's portrayal of the representative man is, however, it is also timeless, universal, as even this small example of the Spanish sailor suggests. As an old Manx sailor exclaims, in response to a call for the crew to form a ring around the combatants, "Ready formed. There! the ringed horizon. In that ring Cain struck Abel. Sweet work, right work! No? Why then, God, mad'st thou the ring?" (178).

From the start of the *Pequod*'s journey, when Stubb ventures to ask Ahab to muffle his step and Ahab sends him packing, Melville portrays life among the men on ship as a contest of wills, a struggle for supremacy and the spoils of privilege. In the everyday affairs described in "The Specksynder" (chapter 33), and more particularly in "The Cabin-Table" (chapter 34), a symbolic scene in which the captain presides over the apportionment of every dish, Ahab carefully maintains his position by observing the "forms and usages" of the sea. At times he does "mask" his true intentions, as Ishmael explains, "incidentally making use of [these common practices] for other and more private ends than they were legitimately intended to subserve" (147). Ahab does this most obviously in "The Quarter-Deck" (chapter 36), where, to bind the crew to his mad plan, he promises a gold doubloon to the man who first sights Moby Dick and then beats down, by sheer force of will, the first mate's objections. No matter how superior a man's intellect, Ishmael observes in "The Specksynder," he can never assume a position of practical advantage over others "without the aid of some sort of external arts and entrenchments, always, in themselves, more or less paltry and base." This, as Ishmael goes on to explain in a resonant line, is what "for ever keeps God's true princes of the Empire from the world's hustings; and leaves the highest honors that this air can give,

to those men who become famous more through their infinite inferiority to the choice hidden handful of the Divine Inert, than through their undoubted superiority over the dead level of the mass" (148).

This is not to say that the man of soul must forever remain above it all, silently contemplating "the problem of the universe," as Ishmael says he does whenever he takes his turn as lookout (158). He recognizes, at the end of chapter 35, that one must eventually come down from the mast-head and live in the world. There is work to be done, often aggressive, murderous work, in the service of truth and in defense of the soul. But as Stubb's dream makes clear, there is a way of living in the world without being entirely of it, without re-turning insult for insult or demanding "an eye for an eye" each time one feels he has been wounded. As the fairy queen of English folklore who governs people's dreams, Queen Mab speaks the wisdom of the unconscious, the deeper self. And what she says, in effect, is that there is a passive, Christ-like response to a wounding experience that can prove more sensible, and healing, than the furiously vengeful one demanded by the ego.

When Stubb wakes up the next morning after Ahab has ordered him "Down, dog, and kennel," he tells Flask he had a "queer dream" in which the captain kicked him with his ivory leg, "and when I tried to kick back, *upon my soul . . .* I kicked my leg right off! And then, presto! Ahab seemed a pyramid, and I, *like a blazing fool,* kept kicking at it" (127, 131; emphasis added). To be sure, it is Stubb's ego that views Ahab's outburst of the night before as an insult, just as it is his ego that prompts him, in his dream, to try to return the indignity by kicking back. But as seen when Stubb loses his own leg in his dream—a loss that informs Ahab's dismemberment by Moby Dick—any attempt to avenge an insult against a truly superior power is foolish; it is to stub one's toe on a pyramid, to squander one's potency and harm oneself unnecessarily.

This idea is made more emphatically in what Stubb calls the "greatest joke" of his whole dream, when a hump-backed old merman offers his own poste-rior as an alternative target for Stubb's kicking. Once the old man turns away, revealing that "his stern was stuck full of marlinspikes, with the points out," the light begins to dawn on "wise Stubb" that he will only hurt *himself* if he keeps kicking (132). But given that he goes back to kicking the pyramid, it is clear he does not see what the image of the inverted marlinspikes really sug-gests, namely, that the instruments of vengeance will surely be turned back against the aggressor, particularly if wielded out of hate and not out of duty. Such wisdom is finally beyond Stubb, the man whose eleventh command-ment is "think not" (128), just as it is finally beyond Ahab, the man who even-tually comes to believe that "to think's audacity" (563).

What is also beyond Stubb is that he should change his view of the beating
he had taken from Ahab and think of it instead as a source of "great glory."
"Remember what I say," the old dream figure tells him before disappearing;
"*be* kicked by him; account his kicks honors; and on no account kick back;
for you can't help yourself, wise Stubb. Don't you see that pyramid?" (132).
Significantly, Stubb shows some potential for change in the brief moment
after his encounter with Ahab. While making his way below deck, a stray
thought, an unconscious insight into Ahab's true condition as a man of
suffering, breaks through his ego's defenses, and he suddenly wonders whether
he should go back and strike Ahab or possibly get down and pray for him,
though "it would be the first time I ever *did* pray" (128). Stubb, however, never
recognizes that what he takes to be an insult may in fact be the mysterious
operation of a wise Providence working through his tormentor. And in his
failure he mirrors, as his example helps to explain, Ahab's still grander failure.

For Ishmael, the true hero of Melville's story, the crucial question is not
whether he can contain his anger and vengefulness, but whether he can resist
Ahab and the temptation to make Ahab's feud his own. If he is to have a
chance at the epic experience of being swallowed by the whale, he must keep
from being swallowed up in Ahab's rage, as all the others are. For a time,
however, Ishmael does succumb. As he says at the opening of "Moby Dick"
(chapter 41), after the quarterdeck ceremony wherein Ahab impels his men
to join in the hunt for the White Whale, "I, Ishmael, was one of that crew;
my shouts had gone up with the rest; my oath had been welded with theirs. . . .
A wild, mystical, sympathetical feeling was in me; Ahab's quenchless feud
seemed mine." The "dread" he admits to feeling "in my soul" during the ceremony, therefore, is caused by his unconscious fear of Ahab, and not by any
fear of Moby Dick (155).

With Ahab now established as the greatest challenge to the well-being of his
soul, Ishmael has entered into the second, or "purification," stage of the hero's
journey, when, as Campbell says, "the senses are 'cleansed and humbled,' and
the energies and interests 'concentrated upon transcendental things,'" as they
are in "The Mast-Head," one of the key chapters in this part of *Moby-Dick*. In
psychological terms, this is the time when the powerful, ruling images of the
hero's infantile past are finally confronted and defeated or exorcised, as Ishmael
can be seen struggling, throughout the middle three sections of the book, to
free himself from Ahab, his domineering "double."[30] Certainly in the beginning, when Ishmael admits to a compulsion to stepping into the street and
"methodically knocking people's hats off" (3), he is already a man of rage like
the *Pequod*'s captain. It is an easy step for him, then, when the opportunity

presents itself, to transfer all his psychic turmoil to a powerful figure like Ahab, who promises to redirect it toward a single, practically assailable target. It should be added, however, that given the passionate response of the crew generally in the quarterdeck scene, the *Pequod*'s captain is not to be viewed as something dredged up out of Ishmael's psyche alone. Ahab is a universal figure, an image of the infantile rage, and hunger, deep within us all.

Intuitively, Ishmael knows that Ahab will present the greatest trial of his entire journey, and he knows this, if only dimly, from the moment he first lays eyes on him. In "Ahab" (chapter 28), where Ishmael describes the portentous moment when he sees the *Pequod*'s captain for the first time, he admits that "foreboding shivers ran over me" (123). In fact, his response to the physical presence of the man is precisely like that of the innocent Vermont colt (described in "The Whiteness of the Whale" chapter) to the shaking of a buffalo skin from the western prairie—an unpremeditated, reflex action to a mysterious but palpable threat of death. Significantly, Ishmael experiences no such fear when he first sights a whale, not even when he first sights Moby Dick on the final day of the chase. In the single moment of Ishmael's first view of Ahab is epitomized the central problem of the second part of the hero's epic journey, when he is captured, or seduced, by his opposite, his repressed self or ego-image.

In the early days of the *Pequod*'s journey, when Ishmael is willing to make Ahab's feud his own, it is Ishmael's resistances, not Ahab's, that are broken as he puts aside his pride, his own purpose in signing up for the voyage, and even his own safety and submits to "crazy Ahab's" plan (184). At the point where Ahab's feud becomes his own, Ishmael finds that he and this powerful "double" are one. The key questions of the second part of his journey, then, are whether Ishmael can somehow free himself from the feud of the wounded captain, now that he has been powerfully galvanized by him, and where he will find the force, the self-mastery, to do so.

In the early days of the hunt, Ishmael cannot know that the White Whale will be his salvation. He cannot know that Moby Dick will empower him, by the force and magnitude of its vitalizing effect on his own imagination, to throw off Ahab's rage and resume the course of his own adventure; just as he cannot know that his deeper self will empower him to break the stranglehold of his ego. In the first stage of the journey, while under Ahab's influence, Ishmael takes the position that the whale is fundamentally malicious. In "The Affadavit" (chapter 45), for example, he lends his support to the view that the whale is a creature capable of "wilful, deliberate designs of destruction"(209).

But, as caught up in Ahab's design as he is, Ishmael does not share Ahab's totalizing view that "all evil" is "visibly personified, and made practically as-

sailable," in the great whale (184). His own view is subtler and more elusive,

just as his intelligence is rarer and more true. In fact, when in "The Whiteness of the Whale" he attempts to set down what it is that "above all things appalled" him about Moby Dick, Ishmael provides such a searching yet finally uncertain assessment of the subject as to torment his readers with his own sense of bafflement (188). Without being at all sure that what he says is accurate, couching every statement in conditional (or interrogative) terms, Ishmael comes to suspect that it is not the whiteness of the whale he finds so menacing but the indefiniteness of that whiteness—the basal, even existential, meaninglessness of it. What is so appalling to Ishmael about the whale's white color is that it seems to undermine all possibility for faith in the existence of a divine intention or plan in all the operations of the universe. As he haltingly tries to explain, near the end of his long effort to capture his exact feelings,

> Is it that by its indefiniteness it shadows forth the heartless voids and immensities of the universe, and thus stabs us from behind with the thought of annihilation, when beholding the white depths of the milky way? Or is it, that as in essence whiteness is not so much a color as the visible absence of color, and at the same time the concrete of all colors; is it for these reasons that there is such a dumb blankness, full of meaning, in a wide landscape of snows—a colorless, all-color of atheism from which we shrink? (195)

Clearly, in this chapter, where he works so diligently to strip the whale's whiteness of all associations, the positive ones, the negative ones, and those in between, Ishmael senses the wrongheadedness, the subjectivity, of Ahab's view of the whale. But despite his magnificent, epic effort to get at the essence of the matter, Ishmael cannot at this stage get beyond the point of seeing the whale as a hideous blank screen on which every observer projects his own torment. Alert to the contradictions in the whale's whiteness, Ishmael is still incapable of seeing them as coexisting at once in one being. Instead, he concludes that they must have their origin in the subjective consciousness of the observer, each in effect cancelling the other out in a final blank meaninglessness. He is still not prepared to understand the paradoxical character of the whale's whiteness, for he is still not prepared to understand the paradoxical character of his own soul and of the primordial force that governs all life. Though he senses the need to free himself from the monomania of Ahab's view, the best he can do, without supernatural aid, is wonder whether the whiteness of the whale, or by extension the whale itself, has any inherent meaning, any irreducible purpose whatsoever. Having been magnetized by the force of Ahab's personality, and thus having lost touch temporarily with his own

all-comprehending soul, Ishmael is incapable of apprehending the dual nature, the good *and* the evil, of Leviathan.

Only in the end, when Ishmael sees Moby Dick for the first time and comes under its life-changing spell, does he have the full power of his own soul restored to him. Then, using his own eyes instead of Ahab's, he can see the whale to be the incarnation of the life-giving dismemberer, the great God Absolute that is both Creator and Destroyer. Only then can he understand that the White Whale is an image of the divine power that inheres in all things, wreaking destruction on the dying generations, bringing life to those waiting to be reborn. As primordial yet fresh an image as any in the world's literature, Melville's whale is finally but a variation of the age-old image of doubleness—the doubleness of God, and of the world that is God's creation. Like the all-devouring monster, the bull-demon of the labyrinth in the myth of Theseus, the great White Whale has one aspect that is angry, provoking, and destructive and another that is benign, enlightening, and vivifying. Simultaneously a figure of doom and of what Campbell calls the "world navel," the whale is Melville's symbol of the source of all existence, of all harm and all beneficence.[31] Like Moby Dick—rumored to be both "ubiquitous" and "immortal"; supplier of light and of life—the world navel is everywhere and everlasting, yet also double, inexhaustibly supplying both sustenance and death, happiness and sorrow, goodness and iniquity (182–83).

Those who fail to understand the doubleness of nature, and of human experience, will necessarily fear death and resist the inevitable process of dismemberment. Like Ahab, they will focus all their attention on the forces that threaten them and feel so hemmed in as to think they inhabit a prison. "How can the prisoner reach outside," Ahab exclaims to Starbuck, in his first major speech, "except by thrusting through the wall? To me, the white whale is that wall, shoved near to me" (164). Ahab's expression of imprisonment is but a trope for the impotence of the ego. For no matter how large, the ego is always limited in power; it cannot penetrate the wall of the material universe. Only the soul, the deeper self, can do that, and "Ahab's soul," we are told at the end of chapter 34, is in effect dead, sleeping away the winter in the hollow of a tree like an old bear "shut up in the caved trunk of his body," feeding on "the sullen paws of its gloom" (153).

Repeatedly, Melville suggests it is when the soul is inactive, sleeping, or "dead" that one is most sensitive to the threat of dismemberment, or most fearful of life. It is, for instance, after Ahab has overpowered Starbuck's resistance in the quarterdeck scene that the first mate confesses, "with soul beat down," that he feels the "latent horror" in life (170). But it is also clear that his soul has been "overmanned," as Starbuck says, not because Ahab is a monster

of superior force, but because Starbuck has not trusted his own power to resist him. "I would up heart, were it not like lead," he confesses weakly. "But my whole clock's run down; my heart the all-controlling weight. I have no key to lift again." From that moment, Starbuck is defeated, self-defeated. Contrary to what he believes, he does contain the key within himself; however, he is the virtuous man who would fight the horror in life not with the all-powerful soul but "with the soft feeling of the human in me." In the end, he leaves it to God to "wedge aside" Ahab's "heaven-insulting purpose" (169–70). In doing so, he abdicates his responsibility, and he pays for his failure with his life.

Those who do understand the dual nature of nature will have no fear of death; they will in fact embrace death as a necessary part of the whole. Like the hero of the spiritual epic, they will be able to pass back and forth from time into eternity, in and out of the belly of the whale, endlessly and without harm to their soul. Like Ishmael on the masthead, when he loses all attachment to his ego, or on the third day of the chase, when he finally sees Moby Dick for the first time, breaching out of the water in an epiphany of beauty and power, they will find that the material world is not a "wall" of imprisonment but a door, or what Campbell calls a "Wall of Paradise," that opens to reveal the divinity behind all creation.[32] This door or Wall of Paradise is made up of the "coincidence of opposites," all the dyadic forces that define human experience in this world—life and death, land and sea, sickness and health, day and night, male and female, matter and spirit—the same conflicting forces that make up the subject of *Moby-Dick*. Those like Ahab, whose egotism leads them to see the world selfishly, defensively, will never be able to penetrate the wall, no matter how they strain or rage. Like the *Pequod*'s captain, who makes his last appearance bound, literally, to the "wall" of Moby Dick, they will die without knowing that their true selves forever lie waiting on the other side. Like Ahab, who insists on playing the game according to his own rules, they will never garner the victor's prize, never know the triumph that lies beyond life's tragedy.

III. THE FIRE SERMON

On the practical level, part three of *Moby-Dick* focuses on the difficulties of the hunt, on the pursuit, capture, killing, and dismembering of the whale. Opening with "The First Lowering," chapter 48, it runs through chapter 76, "The Battering-Ram," in which Ishmael describes the "dead, impregnable, uninjurable wall" of the whale protecting the buoyant "mass of tremendous life" that swims behind it (337). In other words, it stops just short of "The Great Heidelberg Tun" (chapter 77), in which Ishmael describes the initial

step of the fourth stage, the breaking into the interior of the whale, the practical equivalent of the mythological journey down into its belly. Though the pursuit of the whale has a spiritual dimension, too, it is first and foremost a worldly, carnal business, a hunger of the flesh for the flesh.

Melville defines the hunt as a form of cannibalism, an instance of "the universal cannibalism of the sea" (274). It is but another name for the process of dismemberment encoded in the brutal notion of "eat or be eaten." In the "fiery hunt" for the albino whale, Ahab makes the appetite of the crew burn for satisfaction, as he himself burns for revenge (195). But the desires of the flesh are self-consuming; to heed them, as Ahab does in his mad chase after Moby Dick, leads to death, is itself a form of dying into death. In all the religious mythologies of the world, the way of all flesh is the way of fiery destruction. So too in *Moby-Dick.* What is required is a spiritual view of the hunt, such as Melville's narrator comes to have. But such a view can be achieved only after a rigorous purification, a cleansing of the senses in a trial by fire, such as Ishmael experiences momentarily at the end of "The First Lowering." Only then will the hero find his way to a face-to-face confrontation with the "image of the ungraspable phantom of life," the soul within himself that waits to sound its name.

In the journey of the hero, the third part of *Moby-Dick* corresponds with the crisis, what Campbell calls "the ultimate adventure," the meeting, and marriage, with the alluring figure known as the Queen Goddess of the World. In Melville's handling of this stage of the epic plot, the great whale is an instance of this queenly apparition. Appearing in the book for the first time in "The First Lowering" and "The Spirit Spout" (chapters 48 and 51), Moby Dick proves a tantalizing yet elusive lure. Moreover, there are other whales, lesser versions of the Queen, to be encountered before the "grand hooded phantom" (7) becomes the exclusive object of the *Pequod*'s hunt. In fact, in Melville's novel the crisis is an exceptionally protracted, on-again-off-again affair, stretching beyond the third and into the fourth and fifth parts of the narrative. While Moby Dick is not, of course, a ravishingly beautiful woman or goddess, it is androgynous and in other respects corresponds with the character of this mythical figure. Its "vast milky mass," we are told in "The Town-Ho's Story," has an "appalling beauty" (256); and while its power and aggressiveness are dominant, its conventional female character is evident in the fact that it lures the sailors on at the same time it runs away from them. More important than the whale's gender, however, is the fact that, like the goddess of myth and religion—like Beatrice or the Virgin Mary—the great whale is the embodiment of every perfection. By the simple fact of its mesmerizing power, it assures the soul that the bliss of memory, whether remembered from the womb or imagined as a lost ideal, will be ours once again.[33]

Even so, the Queen Goddess, whether remembered as one's mother or as the Mother Nature that nurtures us all, is a complex, even contradictory, figure. Like the whale, she is both benign and evil, sustaining and punishing, enticing and forbidding. She thus represents all existence, all knowledge, or all that can be known. The false hero, who sees with a fearful eye, will recognize only one dimension of her, as Ahab recognizes only the whale's malice. But the true hero will see and appreciate her totality, as Ishmael comes to see and appreciate the doubleness of the White Whale.

The tale of "The First Lowering," which opens part three, is a prophetic version of the ultimate adventure, an epitome of what the hero's coming home to God will entail and what it will require of him. At the same time, it dramatizes the relative spiritual development of each of the major characters and measures their readiness to meet the great God face to face. Although we are never actually told that the school of whales that prompts this first lowering includes Moby Dick, the idea is suggested symbolically that the one whale featured in this scene is an extraordinary, godlike beast very much like Moby Dick. One clue to Melville's intention is the seemingly innocuous chapter title, which refers not simply to the process of the men going over the side in their whaleboats prior to giving chase but to the scowling or "clouding over" of the face of the godhead whom they would capture. Certainly this pun is intended, for Melville later uses "lowering" with the very same meaning in describing the whale's mighty brow (346). Moreover, it should be noticed that the whale featured here comes and goes in a squall, which is itself preceded by a sudden clouding over. Indeed, the whale is saved by a squall that bursts on the whaleboats right at the instant when Queequeg darts his harpoon into it. For all its gritty realism, it is a moment much like the symbolic moment in *Walden,* when the loon Thoreau has been chasing across the Pond suddenly calls on the "god of loons" to whip up a wind to save him.

After the boats have been lowered, the whales all begin to dive under the surface. Their disappearance provides an opportunity for each of the main characters to strike a typical pose: Starbuck, for example, sits "silently eyeing the vast blue eye of the sea" in cool anticipation of their return; and Flask complains impatiently, "I can't see." It is the Indian, Tashtego, however, whose people were the first to try to interpret the whale's ways, who first spies the school again, though "no whale, nor any sign of a herring," as Ishmael says emphatically, would have been visible to a landsman (221–22).

By contrast, the oarsmen—and this includes Ishmael—are not permitted to see much of anything. With their backs toward the whale, they must "put out their eyes" and give every drop of energy to rowing (223). Like Melville's readers, they can experience the whale only secondhand, "with their eyes on

the intense countenance of the mate in the stern of the boat," reading there their future. To be sure, all their other senses are alive to the "thrilling" experience of the imminent confrontation. To a man such as Ishmael, "who for the first time finds himself pulling into the charmed, churned circle of the hunted sperm whale," it is akin to a visionary experience, producing strange and powerful emotions, like the feelings of "the dead man's ghost encountering the first unknown phantom in the other world" (223–24). But, like any neophyte, he must be careful not to look on the face of the great god directly. For unless he is prepared for the revelation of its full magnificence, he will be overwhelmed; he will become a dead man's ghost in literal fact. As Flask explains, in the sperm-whale fishery it is an "unalterable law" that an oarsman must pull himself "back-foremost into death's jaws." "I should like to see a boat's crew backing water up to a whale face foremost," he exclaims, with more meaning than he knows. "Ha, ha! the whale would give them squint for squint, mind that!" (227). Significantly, Ishmael never sees a live whale, never sees one face to face, free of the distorting effect of the sea, until the very last chapter. There, in the culminating moment of his odyssey, as he watches from a distance, he finally sees Moby Dick breach out of the water in an epiphany of power and beauty, just before it destroys the *Pequod*.[34]

Throughout "The First Lowering," the *Pequod*'s encounter with the whale is described in religious terms. Most tellingly, after the whale escapes in the storm and the boat is wrecked, Ishmael speaks not just of their surviving a test but of their being transformed by it. In language that evokes a ritualistic trial by fire, he says that when the wind increased to a howl, "the whole squall roared, forked, and crackled around us like a white fire upon the prairie, in which, unconsumed, we were burning; immortal in these jaws of death!" (225). This pivotal chapter, then, ends early the next morning, with a stove boat and a rescue ship, in a curious foreshadowing of the final scene of the novel.

"The Hyena" (chapter 49), as its puzzling title implies, confirms that for Ishmael the experience described in "The First Lowering" was a profoundly transfiguring one. The "last man" to be dragged aboard the *Pequod* after the squall, Ishmael immediately shakes off his fear of these perilous events, just as he shakes off the water from his dunking. After confirming with his shipmates that the violence of their recent encounter is anything but a rarity in the sperm-whale fishery, he goes jauntily below deck to make out a draft of his will. In doing so, he shows his readiness, qualified though it may be (it is, after all, only a rough draft he writes), to give up his attachment to the things of this world and make peace with death, even if the best he can manage is a kind of perverse pleasure in the process. Pushed to the brink of disaster in the storm, he returns to the ship with a new outlook on life, a "free and easy sort of

genial, desperado philosophy." Whereas previously he had looked on the prospect of his own death as "a thing most momentous," it now strikes him as simply part of the "vast practical joke" that defines the universal scheme of things. He may be able to see the humor of the joke only "dimly," but, as the title of this chapter suggests, if one is going to enter into "death's jaws" it is best to do so with the grin of the hyena on one's own countenance. For to adopt Ishmael's "genial, desperado philosophy" is to transcend the anguish at the prospect of dismemberment and death that so torments Ahab. It is to reach a state of mind where "nothing dispirits, and nothing seems worth while disputing." One simply "bolts down" everything, "all creeds, and beliefs . . . all hard things visible and invisible" as "an ostrich of potent digestion gobbles down bullets and gun flints"—in effect, "eating" any and all experience, even death, rather than being "eaten" by it (226–27).

While at first glance this seemingly cannibalistic philosophy may seem impious, it is actually based on an implicit faith in God and His wisdom, or so Ishmael suggests. Ishmael may regard the Creator as an "unseen and unaccountable old joker," bestowing such "jolly punches" as death and disaster on his helpless creatures, but Ishmael presumes nonetheless that He still exists, actively presiding over all creation. The problem is simply that man fails to comprehend His ways, fails to understand the nature of the "general joke" (226–27). With a faith, therefore, that everything that happens in this world has some mysterious purpose, Ishmael releases his hold on what few belongings he has (signing them over to Queequeg, his "legatee") and vows to take "a cool, collected dive at death and destruction." Having dispensed with his worldliness, and with it any concern for his ego, Ishmael then experiences an unexpected benefit: he suddenly feels as though "a stone was rolled away from my heart." Like Lazarus, who was lowered into his grave only to be resurrected again, Ishmael can say, "I survived myself; my death and burial were locked up in my chest," there to remain forever, in the keeping of his heart (227–28).

Having proved himself in "The First Lowering," then, Ishmael and the rest of the crew soon encounter a mysterious "silvery jet" that seems to lure them on. "Lit up by the moon, it looked celestial; seemed some plumed and glittering god uprising from the sea" (232). It is "The Spirit-Spout" of chapter 51; and while some of the sailors swear it is Moby Dick, Ishmael never does offer an opinion on the matter. Whatever its true identity, the appearance of the beckoning jet clearly advances the adventure of the hero to a new, and distinctly spiritual, stage. Significantly, when Fedallah cries out at seeing the spout, the crew responds not with terror but with "pleasure," and as Ishmael says, "almost every soul on board instinctively desired a lowering." All of them sense the White Whale to be the incarnation of the soul they all yearn to

discover. At this point, even the *Pequod* seems to be propelled by a new impulse, one that runs counter to its regular movement in the mundane realm of the whaling business. When the unusual order is given to set all sails in pursuit of the strange spout, the ship is said to rush along "as if two antagonistic influences were struggling in her—one to mount direct to heaven, the other to drive yawingly to some horizontal goal." Still, like the Queen Goddess of the World, even the spirit-spout, for all its mighty allure, is a figure of "dread" as well as of pleasure—a thing of doubleness. Appearing sporadically but always at night thereafter, this "flitting apparition" generates great apprehension among the crew, "as if it were treacherously beckoning us on and on, in order that the monster might turn round upon us, and rend us at last in the remotest and most savage seas." Intuitively, these rude, superstitious sailors know they have a spiritual and an earthly nature, a soul and an ego, and that the life of the one is the death of the other. They know, instinctively, that they are akin to Ahab, the dying man of whom Ishmael observes, "on life and death this old man walked" (233).

In most of the remaining chapters of this third part of *Moby-Dick*, Ishmael turns his attention to an exploration of a very different sort of effort to capture the whale, one close to his own concerns as a writer. These chapters center on the wide variety of artistic attempts, by men working in diverse media, to picture the whale as they themselves, supposedly, have seen it. These include chapters 55–57—"Of the Monstrous Pictures of Whales," "Of the Less Erroneous Pictures of Whales," "Of Whales in Paint; in Teeth; &c."—as well as chapters 74–75, which depict the heads of the sperm and right whales. Less obviously, they also include the first three of the "gam" chapters, in which sailors from the *Albatross,* the *Town-Ho,* and the *Jeroboam* relate tales of their encounters with Moby Dick. And they include others as well, such as the chapter on "Brit," on "The Whale as a Dish," and "The Battering Ram." All in all, three-quarters of the chapters in this section concern portraits or representations of the whale, the notable exceptions being those that treat whaling instruments—"The Line," "The Dart," and "The Monkey-Rope"—particularly such instruments as are used to secure, or gain entrance into, the whale.

While the many portraits help generate the sense of variety and density that an epic treatment of the subject requires, they also serve to bring into relief Ishmael's fixation on the question of what distinguishes a true picture from a false one, a report of someone's experience of the genuine article from one that has been adulterated by subjective temperament or point of view. In a world of "fanatic" Shaker prophets like Gabriel (315) and "corrupt" Lima priests (249), of devil-worshiping Parsees and "insane old" whaling captains

(237), there is reason to doubt the testimony of those who claim to know what they have seen when they claim to have seen something as strange as a living whale, particularly a white whale.

What keeps Ishmael from presenting a slanted or distorted view of this creature is that his view is never so simpleminded, or so intractable, as to be unqualified. It is always provisional, the product of what he admits to be personal opinion and not what he claims to know with absolute certainty. Typically, his view is as free of egotism as is humanly possible, short of his reaching the "transparent eyeball" state of Pip, after the cabin boy has become a "castaway." Even though by the time he writes his tale Ishmael has become an experienced whaler, one who has served in "various whalemen of more than one nation" (288), he himself never presents a final, authorized view of the whale or its meaning. He knows how difficult it is to get a clear, unobstructed view of the thing itself in its living, moving form. Most often, all that anyone knows about the whale is derived from its skeleton or from a carcass stranded on shore, and these lifeless forms can hardly be said to give a true idea of the "noble animal itself in all its undashed pride." The living whale, "in his full majesty and significance, is only to be seen at sea in unfathomable waters," Ishmael explains, and even then one can rarely get a totally unobstructed view. Even if one were lucky enough to see a live whale up close and afloat, "the vast bulk of him is out of sight," obscured, even distorted, by the water around him. As for seeing a living whale out of the water, there are precious few opportunities, for "it is a thing eternally impossible for mortal man to hoist him bodily into the air, so as to preserve all his mighty swells and undulations" (263).

Even when it comes time for Ishmael, then, to paint "something like the true form of the whale as he actually appears to the eye of the whaleman," he makes no pretense of depicting a living whale. Instead, he restricts himself to the moment "when in his own absolute body the whale is moored alongside the whale-ship" (260). Because the chance of seeing a living whale out of the water is so slight, therefore, "the great Leviathan is that one creature in the world which must remain unpainted to the last." To the landsman especially, this is a matter of some consequence. For, without an accurate picture, "there is no earthly way of finding out precisely what the whale really looks like." The only alternative is to go to sea in search of the whale yourself. But then, as Ishmael observes, "you run no small risk of being eternally stove and sunk by him" (264). Much the same might be said of the would-be hero's difficulties in capturing a glimpse of the true nature of the self or soul. Either the ego obstructs any view of the soul or it imprisons it, as it does in Ahab's case. The potential hero thus fails to recognize the self for the Leviathan that it is and

dies without experiencing any higher promise to life. If one undertakes the challenge of the journey on his own, he runs the risk of being destroyed or overwhelmed or of being driven cravenly back to land, none the wiser for the effort.

In "Stubb Kills a Whale," chapter 61, the *Pequod* encounters its second whale of the voyage and Ishmael sees a live whale partially out of the water for the first time, enough to get a view of its tail. This, then, continues a carefully developed pattern in the later sections of the book, whereby the whale is revealed to Ishmael in increments or stages. While the whalemen quietly draw nearer, the monster suddenly turns up flukes, flitting its tail "forty feet into the air, and then [sinking] out of sight like a tower swallowed up." Significantly, as one of three men then on the lookout, Ishmael takes part in the sighting of this whale, and he does so, almost paradoxically, while lost in a "spell of sleep" induced by an empty sea—when the unconscious can make contact with its objective correlative, the surrounding ocean. Slipping into a dreamy mood, not long before the sighting, Ishmael observes that "at last my soul went out of my body; though my body still continued to sway" (282). Then instantly, as he explains, using imagery that foreshadows his near-drowning at the end, "bubbles seemed bursting beneath my closed eyes; like vices my hands grasped the shrouds; some invisible, gracious agency preserved me; with a shock I came back to life." Miraculously, in one of the great moments in the novel, when Ishmael opens his eyes, the image that greets him is the image of this invisible, grace-filled, life-preserving agency of the leviathanic self, slightly submerged in the sea but alive and "lazily undulating." "And lo!" he exclaims, "close under our lee . . . a gigantic Sperm Whale lay rolling in the water . . . his broad, glossy back, of an Ethiopian hue, glistening in the sun's rays like a mirror" (283). Somehow it is as though it had always been there, but Ishmael's egoistic defenses had kept him from being aware of it. But now, in this strangely relaxed mood, what meets his startled gaze, as he opens his eyes, is the glistening mirrorlike surface of the whale, the image of his own ungraspable soul reflected back to him.

In contrast to the sublimity of the moment of Ishmael's waking to his first glimpse of a living sperm whale, the next scene, "Stubb's Supper," describing the bloody aftermath of the hunt, is a comic orgy of the senses. Once the beast has been slain, and the "inert, sluggish corpse" hauled back and secured to the ship, all high-mindedness disappears as Ahab and Starbuck make their exit, and the crude second mate, "flushed with conquest," prepares to enjoy a ceremonial steak from the victim's choicest part. Stubb is a "high liver," in the low, ironic sense of the phrase, for he is "somewhat intemperately fond of the whale as a flavorish thing to his palate" (291–92). Given that the whole of this

scene, with the men on deck cutting into the steak and the sharks below feeding on the carcass, captures the central theme of what Melville calls "the horrible vulturism of earth" (308), it is fitting that Stubb should preside here. For as one who combines the fleshly appetites of Flask and the spiritual tendencies of Starbuck, he is just the one to call for the black cook to preach to the sharks and urge them to curb their rapaciousness.

Fleece's sermon is the central rhetorical statement in the third part of *Moby-Dick*, the centerpiece, in fact, of the whole novel. Though it verges on being a piece out of a vaudeville comedy routine, with Stubb as straight man, it has a serious undertone that reflects the entire rationale of the hero's struggle. In his sermon warning against the hungers of the flesh, the old black cook speaks a timeless wisdom. His words may fall on deaf ears, as Melville must have feared his whole narrative might, but Fleece has the right idea when he tries to take into account the fallen nature of his congregation and asks them not to change themselves beyond what is possible. Instead, he enjoins them to acknowledge their dual nature and to use the one side to control the other. "Your woraciousness, fellow-critters," he apostrophizes, "I don't blame ye so much for; dat is nature, and can't be helped; but to gobern dat wicked nature, dat is de pint. You is sharks, sartin; but if you gobern de shark in you, why den you be angel; for all angel is not'ing more dan de shark well goberned" (295).

Despite the simplicity of his appeal, however, Fleece knows his effort will prove futile. Creatures of appetite will not pay attention to good spiritual counsel "till dare bellies is full," and, as even Fleece understands, "dare bellies is bottomless" (295). Yet what neither he nor Stubb seems to realize is that there is but one alternative to a life of the flesh: as the second mate himself says, after he discovers that Fleece has overcooked his whalesteak, "You must go home and be born over again" (296). The way of the hero is the only way, the way of death and rebirth. Clearly this is what Melville meant when he has Stubb tell Fleece in his bantering way, just moments later, that he cannot expect to get to heaven "by crawling through the lubber's hole . . . no, no, cook, you don't get there, except you go the regular way, round by the rigging" (297).

Fleece's "fire sermon" is an epitome of the whole third part of *Moby-Dick*, which brings into sharp focus the author's fixation on the life of the flesh. "Stubb's Supper," "The Whale as a Dish," "The Shark Massacre," "Cutting In," "The Blanket," and "The Funeral" (chapters 64–69) together evidence a deep preoccupation with the body of the whale and its dismemberment. But the chapters also show an equal preoccupation with the body of man, with the pleasures and needs and sins of the flesh of humankind. In fact, Melville has constructed his story in such a way that practically everything about the whale

is symbolic of some fundamental human trait or truth or provides an occasion for examining the parallel ways of humanity. In every detail, it is fraught with human meaning, and in this way, too, it is a profoundly epic work.

Though he claimed not to "oscillate in Emerson's rainbow," Melville agreed with Emerson's famous axiom that "the whole of nature is a metaphor of the human mind." At the time he wrote *Moby-Dick*, he too believed, as Emerson proclaimed in *Nature*, that "the laws of moral nature answer to those of matter as face to face in a glass."[35] The process of "cutting in," or stripping away the whale's flesh, for example, is to be understood as a metaphor for the process of fleshly discipline or self-denial that one must follow to attain spiritual well-being. Similarly, these several chapters, going back to "Stubb Kills a Whale," shadow forth the whole process of life's unfolding, from birth to death, as one of dismemberment and dying. While in the beginning Ishmael sees the whale's body as something holy, glistening in the sun, by the time it has been gouged and chewed by sharks, cut into by the crew and stripped of its "blanket," it lies at its funeral still colossal but "desecrated" (309).

However, as the novel's quintessential metaphor for the soul, the whale is more than a symbol. It is a paradigm of all human behavior, the ultimate guide or authority in the hero's journey to self-understanding. While earlier Ishmael had more than hinted that there is something valuable to be learned from the whale, it is not until the first of the anatomy chapters—particularly "The Blanket," together with "Cutting In"—that he makes explicit the idea that mankind should actually model itself after the whale. It is in this sense that the whale can be understood to embody, like the figure of the Goddess of the World, the totality of what can be known.

In the anatomy chapters such as these, the trials of the hero in his encounters with the whale can be seen to be educative, and his willingness to imperil his life in this bloody business can be seen to pay off handsomely. For it is, after all, only with the firsthand experience of whaling that one can gain the wisdom the whale has to offer. In chapter 68, after deciding that the whale's skin is constituted not of the thin isinglass substance at the outermost surface of the beast but of the whole enveloping layer of its blubber, Ishmael points out that this thick mass is like a "blanket or counterpane," an image that recalls the counterpane Ishmael had shared with Queequeg in the Spouter-Inn. Like that earlier counterpane, the whale's "blanket" permits its inhabitant "to keep himself comfortable" in any weather, in any climate. "Herein we see," Ishmael concludes, in a little "fire sermon" of his own, "the rare virtue of thick walls. . . . Oh, man! admire and model thyself after the whale! Do thou, too, remain warm among ice. Do thou, too, live in this world without being of it" (307).

In a similar fashion, later, when considering the sperm whale's head as it hangs from the side of the ship, Ishmael argues the wisdom of patterning the development of one's mind after the whale's. Hypothesizing that, with one eye on either side of its head, the whale must be able to "attentively examine two distinct prospects, one on one side of him, and the other in an exactly opposite direction" at the same time, Ishmael reasons that the brain of the whale must be "much more comprehensive, combining, and subtle than man's," not more capacious. "Why then do you try to 'enlarge' your mind?" he asks; and then, taking his cue from the example of the whale, he offers the simple injunction to "Subtilize it" instead (331). Given the fundamental doubleness of the world, its goodness and its evil, the ability to take in its contradictions simultaneously is more than an asset; it is a prerequisite to one's seeing it whole, as the hero must learn to do.

More than a subtle brain, however, or thick walls, what one needs in order to survive in this world of dangers, what one needs for the health of his or her soul, is a "battering ram" like the whale's, a mighty, unfeeling instrument for protecting the life force as one goes about one's business. As in other respects, so here, the sperm whale is a model of engineering mastery: simple in design, reliable in operation—above all, effective. Like an enormous forehead, but with padding twenty feet thick covering the cranium, the battering ram of the sperm whale lacks "a single organ or tender prominence of any sort whatsoever." Layered over with an envelope of "boneless toughness," it will resist the sharpest lance darted by the strongest arm. Yet it is more than a means of defense; as Ishmael's term for it suggests, it is intended to be used actively, aggressively, offensively, as a billy goat uses its horns to defeat a foe or clear a path to some goal. What makes this "dead, impregnable, uninjurable wall" so extraordinary, so formidable, Ishmael explains, is that it is "unerringly" impelled by "a mass of tremendous life, only to be adequately estimated as piled wood is—by the cord; and all obedient to one volition, as the smallest insect." With such an instrument, there is virtually nothing the whale's gigantic willpower cannot accomplish. For the whale, to "stove a passage through the Isthmus of Darien," and mix the Atlantic with the Pacific, would hardly be too tall an order (337–38).

Unfortunately, there is no equivalent of this battering ram in the human makeup (except, possibly, the relatively puny nose). However, the important thing is for Melville's readers to be able to believe in the irresistible power of the self that is the human equivalent of the mass of life behind the whale's forehead. For should they be able to do that, should they be able to believe that they have a similar forcefulness within themselves, it would be *as if* they

had a battering ram just like the whale's, and they would then be able to venture out to confront the forbidding truth of human experience without being scared away or overwhelmed. "Unless you own the whale," Ishmael explains, unless you have witnessed his infinite power firsthand and believe in it for yourself, "you are but a provincial and sentimentalist in Truth." But because "clear Truth is a thing for salamander giants only to encounter," one must either *be* a whale, or be *like* a whale, not to be overcome when one confronts such Truth (338). Those who are "provincials"—that is, those who have not undertaken a journey such as Ishmael's—will have no chance of surviving such an encounter when it occurs, for they will lack the faith and self-confidence required to meet the truth of human limitation and mortality.

Speaking at this point as one who has completed the cycle of the hero's adventure and thus knows the Truth, Ishmael signals the end of the third part of *Moby-Dick* by putting to the reader an oracle's sort of question. Employing an image of the aspiring hero at the moment of crisis, he asks rhetorically, "What befel the weakling youth lifting the dread goddess's veil at Sais?" (338). It is a simple question, so simple that even those who do not know the story of the great Egyptian mother of the gods will sense Melville's meaning: it is the unseasoned "provincials" or unbelievers of the world who will lose out in the ultimate test. Lacking the talent, courage, or fortitude of the true hero, they will fail to win the boon of love, or charity, that Campbell defines as "life itself enjoyed as the encasement of eternity."[36] "The encasement of eternity" is an apt description of the central object in the next chapter, "The Great Heidelberg Tun," which begins the fourth part of the novel. For the great "tun" contains the highly prized spermaceti "in its absolutely pure, limpid, and odoriferous state," the "most precious" of all the whale's "oily vintages" (340).

IV. DEATH BY WATER

"The Great Heidelberg Tun" is an important threshold chapter, marking the beginning of the questers' descent into the whale. Having caught, killed, and dragged a sperm whale to the ship and then stripped away the blubber and beheaded it, the crew hoists the head against the *Pequod*'s side in preparation for the difficult maneuver of breaking into the interior case or "tun." Earlier, in chapters 74 and 75, Ishmael had imagined himself going inside the mouths of a sperm whale and a right whale while conducting a tour of the two as they hang on opposite sides of the ship. But chapter 77 signifies the first actual venture inside a whale, literally a cutting through the wall in search of

buried treasure. When such efforts are successful, the end result is "the Baling of the Case," or retrieval of the precious "sperm," from the large reservoir within the whale's head (339).

In this and the following chapter, "Cistern and Buckets," where Queequeg rescues Tashtego from the whale's head after it breaks loose and starts sinking, Melville begins using language that involves a vast conceit whereby the sperm oil stands for the vital "fluid" of the human soul. Repeatedly described as "precious" or "invaluable" and "pure," the sperm is said to be contained in the "sanctuary," or "secret inner chamber and sanctum sanctorum," of the whale. This curiously holy, sexually charged, life-giving substance is Melville's version of the object of the epic quest in its most essential form, the "unalloyed" oil that requires a "marvellous," yet sometimes "fatal," operation to tap it, as Tashtego learns to his horror (339–40, 344). Not all whalemen, of course, succeed even at capturing the sperm whale, let alone at breaking into its tun and retrieving this most valued of prizes. Like the men of the *Virgin*, described in chapter 81, they may spend their days going from ship to ship begging a little oil, forever dependent on others for the light they need to show them the way.

The whole of part four of *Moby-Dick* focuses on the whale's interior. All the world seems rushing to gain entrance there, to search for its riches, to experience its transforming power, to *know* the beast from inside. Opening with Tashtego's accidental entombment in the sperm whale's tun, the fourth section closes with Ishmael's very deliberate venture inside a whale's skeleton, described in "A Bower in the Arsacides," where he has gone to gather measurements for his study of the magnitude of the monster (chapters 102–05). Along the way, Ishmael contemplates the "nut" or brain of the whale, which is buried deep in its head; he discusses the historical likelihood of Jonah's being swallowed into the whale's belly; he offers a chapter on "ambergris," the valuable, waxlike substance found deep in its bowels; and, in still more imaginative variations on this theme, he writes of his own experience of being encircled by a great swirling herd of whales in "The Grand Armada" and then of the ship's mincer encasing himself within the whale's foreskin in "The Cassock."

At least half of the chapters in part four are concerned with sundry methods for gaining access to the whale's interior and the various treasures to be retrieved there. Still other chapters elaborate on the central themes of part four by examining various containers for processing or holding the oil and other prizes once they have been collected from inside the whale. These include chapters on the hold of a whaleship, the *Jungfrau*, which is forever empty; on the hand, which breaks down lumps of spermaceti and ends by holding other hands; on the try-works," with its twin try-pots, each with a capacity for

holding many barrels of oil; on the lamp; and the decanter. Even the chapter on "The Doubloon," a token containing real monetary value for the sailor who first sights Moby Dick, is related to the central theme of this section, as is the chapter on the story of Captain Boomer, of the *Samuel Enderby,* whose right arm was swallowed by the White Whale. Melville's preoccupation with the theme of containment in part four is symptomatic of his interest in the vitalizing boon or treasure, the thing contained that is the object of the hero's quest. But it is also symptomatic of his interest in the process of the hero's being contained or imprisoned, and tried and transformed, as Jonah was alleged to have been, inside the whale.

Throughout part four of the narrative, then, Melville develops themes of death and resurrection, of recovery and rebirth, of the awakening of the self to new life. In the early chapters of this section, Tashtego is miraculously delivered and reborn through the daring "obstetrics" of Queequeg, after the Indian has slipped into the Great Tun and been "coffined, hearsed, and tombed" there (344).[37] Almost a victim of drowning after the head of the whale that confines him rips free of the *Pequod* and sinks into the sea, Tashtego is the first of several characters who experience a kind of "death by water" and live to tell about it. Jonah, first of all, and then Pip, Captain Boomer, and Ishmael all come to know something of this remarkable, life-changing fate. There is a death by land that is the common death; it is the "living death" of those who never venture from shore. But there is also a death by water, which is initiated by an escape from convention and leads to a dying to the world, as in baptism. This death ends in resurrection or rebirth, or in a saving glimpse of the world beyond this one. However, as Pip's example testifies, unless the breakthrough occurs within the ritual of the hunt, the experience can be so overwhelming as to drive the would-be initiate "mad" (414). He may return from his journey a changed man, but he will lack the self-command, or the semblance of sanity, required to make himself understood by others.

In developing the themes of transformation, of the hero's dying and renewal, in this section, Melville continues with the "anatomy" of the whale he had begun earlier. However, in keeping with these themes, he emphasizes, throughout part four, the whale's masculinity and godlike power. If one is to perform the equivalent of miracles and raise the living from the dead, if one is to bring oneself to life as if after a long, long sleep, one must possess the strength and regenerative power that are exemplified in the whale. In "The Prairie," Ishmael sings praises to the "mighty," "sublime" character of the sperm whale's brow, gazing on which "you feel the Deity and the dread powers more forcibly than in beholding any other object in living nature" (346). In "The Nut" he stresses the whale's backbone and hump, "the organ of firm-

ness or indomitableness" (350). And in "The Fountain," "A Squeeze of the Hand," and "The Cassock," he celebrates the procreative powers of the whale, its sexual potency. The one whale that the men of the *Pequod* hunt down in this section, moreover, is a male, "a huge, humped old bull," and they do so after winning a race against the crew of a rival ship called the *Virgin* (352). Most of the book's many instances of so-called "male humor," in fact, are to be found in this section, particularly in "Schools and Schoolmasters," "Fast-Fish and Loose-Fish," "Heads and Tails," "The Pequod Meets the Rose-Bud," and "Ambergris," among others.

Such varied and persistent efforts at suggesting the masculinity of the whale are crucial to Melville's development of the penultimate stage in the hero's adventure. This is the stage represented in traditional religions and mythic stories as the atonement with the Father. Although it is typically cast in confrontational terms, it invariably leads to a reconciliation between the hero and his progenitor or ruler, for the hero must come to recognize that he will never achieve atonement by aggression or simple force of will. The Father, the ruling force of the world, is simply too powerful to be overcome by such means. As in other spiritual epics, so here: atonement results from the hero's renunciation of his own egoistic preoccupations and from his absolute trust in the Father's mercy. Of course Ahab, the man with the mortally wounded ego, lacks such trust, while Ishmael eventually acquires it. Indeed, it is his trust, his faith in the spirit within him, that frees him from Ahab's vengeful search.

Few aspirants ever manage to achieve atonement. The Father admits into His order only those who have shown themselves worthy. For if He fails to prevent those who are not really prepared for the role of authority that awaits them, everything will run to chaos, as it does in the story of the "scaramouch" Gabriel, the crazy Shaker prophet who by fear and cunning manages to gain an upper hand over almost everyone on the *Jeroboam* (314). Ahab's destruction, and the chaos he brings to his crew because of his supreme selfishness, is a variation on this theme. Yet Ahab is only the most spectacular failure in the book, its central paradigm of the false aspirant. There are others, particularly in this fourth part of the narrative. The episode involving the eternally empty German whaleship called the *Virgin* symbolizes this theme. So, too, does the subsequent episode involving the *Rose-Bud,* whose captain is tricked into giving up the ambergris from a foul-smelling old whale carcass. Unlike Ahab, however, these captains are neophytes in the art of whaling; when asked about Moby Dick, neither one can say he has even heard of him before.

Not even all of the *Pequod's* crew, however, successful though they are as a group, are deserving whalemen. When it is discovered, in the episode with the Germans, that the old whale they have captured is diseased, and blind and

crippled as well, Flask shows a malignant side to his character when he deliberately pricks the ulceration on the animal's flank. Flask may be the one who brings in this catch, but his sadistic action taints the spirit of the hunt. Clearly, he is too self-indulgent to deserve his reward, and subsequent events mysteriously preclude him from enjoying it. Almost immediately afterward, the dead whale's body takes on water and starts to go down. Though the crew manages to secure the sinking whale to the ship's side, it threatens to capsize her; the fluke-chains have to be cut, and the corpse disappears, carrying with it "all its treasures unrifled" (358).

Whether because of lack of skill or a corrupt heart, many aspiring whalemen never reap the rewards of the hunt. They are a discredit to their calling and will never know the glory of atonement. But as Ishmael argues in "The Honor and Glory of Whaling" (chapter 82), there have been "many great demi-gods and heroes, prophets of all sorts," over the ages, who have brought great distinction to the whaling profession. They are bona fide heroes, and together they constitute an "emblazoned . . . fraternity" of God's chosen. An improbable collection, to be sure, including Perseus, St. George, Hercules, Jonah, Ishmael himself ("though but subordinately"), and even the Hindu god Vishnu, each qualifies as a "doer of rejoicing good deeds" (361–63). Perseus, especially, the founder of "our brotherhood," is famous for his chivalry. Free of such selfish motives as the Flasks and the Derick De Deers of the world demonstrate, the "gallant Perseus" took up the hunt in order to "succor the distressed" (361).

Even more revealing is the example of Vishnu, the "grandmaster" of the whalemen's order, whom Brahma, the "God of Gods," created to preside over the work of reforming the world after the great deluge. Buried in Melville's abbreviated one-paragraph recreation of this story is the whole cycle of the epic hero's task—the transforming journey that leads to the discovery of a life-saving, world-changing treasure: in order to recover the mystical books known as the Vedas, books that would one day assist him in refashioning the world, Vishnu became incarnate in a whale and, "sounding down in him to the uttermost depths, rescued the sacred volumes" from the bottom of the sea (363). As Vishnu's story exemplifies, the responsibility of even the most divine hero, once he has attained his full powers, is to serve the renovation of the world, not his own personal interests.

The hero who achieves atonement with the Father takes on all the power and responsibility of the Father. This is so because, as Vishnu's story also makes clear, he and the Father are one. The voyage of the hero is thus a passage from sonship to fatherhood, one in which the aspirant discovers that he is his own Father, capable of performing the very same kinds of miracles he had thought

only the Father could accomplish. As Melville suggests in "Jonah Historically Regarded," what the members of the whalemen's fraternity all have in common, besides their utter selflessness, is their capacity to work apparent miracles. However, these are not the sort of miracles that the doubtful old Sag-Harbor man thinks of when he questions the possibility of Jonah's actually fitting down a whale's throat or surviving the action of its powerful stomach juices. Instead, these are what might be called miracles of metaphor, imaginative feats whereby the storyteller jolts his reader into a new understanding of things, a new relation to the truth. As his ironic tone implies, Melville did not share the belief of the simple Portuguese priest that the report of Jonah's traveling to Nineveh all the way around the horn of Africa in just three days, while installed inside the whale, was "a signal magnification of the general miracle." And neither did he believe, with the devoted Turks who built a mosque in Jonah's honor as a sign of their faith in his story, that their holy structure contained "a miraculous lamp that burnt without any oil" (366). His was not the faith of the literal-minded.

However, as a writer, and as a man of imagination, Melville did believe in the transforming power of the *story* of Jonah. He believed that even the skeptical reader could be made to feel the truth and force of the language of metaphor. Certainly as one who himself believed in the undying conscience of the fugitive Jonah in Mapple's sermon, Melville felt there was such a thing, metaphorically speaking, as a "miraculous lamp" that burns without oil (366). As he shows, furthermore, at the beginning of "Pitchpoling" (chapter 84), right after mentioning the miraculous lamp of the Turks, he believed that one could, with the help of the imagination, be made to see all language, all the world even, as perfectly plastic and capable of revealing a figurative truth. In this chapter describing one of the finest of all "the wondrous devices and dexterities" that a whaleman must learn to master, Melville performs something of a miracle himself by turning a simple whaleboat into a lamp of a very unusual kind. Needing a whale for his demonstration of the "fine manoeuvre with the lance called pitchpoling," Melville chose this moment to describe Queequeg's peculiar practice of "anointing" his boat with grease to make it slide through the water, "rubbing in the unctuousness" as one would rub a magic lamp. "He seemed," Ishmael observes, "to be working in obedience to some particular presentiment," and then adds that "Nor did it remain unwarranted by the event." For toward noon of that same day (when the sun, emblem of the Father of all the gods, would have been at its meridian), several whales were "raised," as one might be said to "raise" a host of powerful genii (367–78). To the literal-minded, Queequeg would appear to be a miracle worker in this

scene. But to the mind attuned to metaphor, Queequeg is simply a man who is in touch with the rhythms of nature, or at one with the gods of the deep, even as he is "at one" with his Father on high.

"Pitchpoling" ends with a clean kill and another miracle. Stubb, a man whose "coolness and equanimity in the direst emergencies" make him a master of this art, readies himself in a ritualistic way; and then, "with a rapid, nameless impulse" arching the spearlike pitchpole the necessary distance, he hits the "life spot" of the whale. Immediately the whale "spouts red blood" instead of "sparkling water." But this transubstantiation is hardly the miracle it might have been if Stubb were a bona fide hero. Though he is the one who blurts out the clue as to what his own transformation would require when he shouts that "all fountains must run wine today," he exposes his spiritual unreadiness when he speaks his preference instead for "old Orleans whiskey, or old Ohio, or unspeakably old Monongahela." What he calls "the living stuff" is not, of course, an earthly liquor or "spirit" (367–68). It is not even the blood of the dying god, symbolically apt though that may be. Instead, as the next chapter, "The Fountain," reveals, this "living stuff," which is the very essence of life, is symbolized by the whale's spout or fountain, an image of the Father as the great fountainhead of life (369).

As the scientific rhetoric of "The Fountain" makes clear, however, Ishmael is not one to jump directly to any conclusions as to what the whale's spoutings "mean." As usual, his way is more roundabout, an exercise in anatomy that soon slips into intellectual high jinx, only to end abruptly when a fountain of intuition erupts within Ishmael himself. For him, the question of the exact nature of the whale's spout, whether "really water, or nothing but vapor," seems an insoluble mystery, and he goes on to worry the subject in typical fashion for several pages (370).

Only after Ishmael has laid bare all the difficulties of deciding, and tried out several hypotheses, does he come to the conclusion that the whale's fountain is nothing but "mist" or "vapor." Though his reasoning is circular, and otherwise riddled with logical fallacies, his conclusion is perfectly sound. For it comes to him from one of those "intuitions of some things heavenly," as he says, in which he has come to have faith. It is an expression of the peculiar life-giving fountain that wells within every living thing (373–74). The essence of life, this marvelously inventive chapter demonstrates, is neither water nor air, and it is not some cunning mixture of the two called "mist." Rather, it is what Ishmael shows it to be at the end of his discourse, one of those "divine intuitions" that now and then shoot "through all the thick mists of the dim doubts in my mind," as they rise out of the unconscious into his consciousness—intimations of immortality as they make themselves known to the mortal side of his being.

Ishmael experiences this particular intuition, it should be emphasized, while looking at his own image in a mirror and watching a steamy vapor rise from his head, a little experiment he says he once conducted while in the midst of composing "a little treatise on Eternity," presumably *Moby-Dick* itself (374).

"Divine intuitions" of the truth—snatches, glimpses—these are some of the treasures that can come to the successful adventurer. They help clarify his perceptions; as Ishmael says, his "fog" is enkindled with a "heavenly ray" (374). But for the most part, mankind is cut off from the source of all truth, the Father. Trapped in their own consciousness, enslaved by their ego, people have no memory of God and no capacity for seeing Him in the present, no capacity for wonder and worship. In what Melville, in "The Prairie" (chapter 79), called "the now egotistical sky" of his own century, there is no evidence of the "gods of old." They all seem to have vanished, to be lured back again only by a "highly cultured, poetical nation," such as he himself was trying to inspire in writing *Moby-Dick* (347).

But as Ishmael says in this chapter that focuses on the expansive forehead of the whale, the image of God *can* be recollected, or restored to one, in the "imposing" frontal view of the sperm whale's head. The "high and mighty god-like dignity inherent in the brow" of any number of other creatures is so greatly amplified in the brow of the sperm whale that "gazing on it, in that full front view, you feel the Deity and the dread powers more forcibly than in beholding any other object in living nature." Unfortunately, however, to gain this "sublime" view, one has to place himself in the monster's charging path (346). And even then, one can at best only snatch a glimpse of it, for everyone but the most experienced whalemen—the harpooner and the mate—must actually face backward through all but the very last stages of any encounter with the whale.

Seeing the Father face to face represents the ultimate revelation in the hero's journey toward self-understanding, the supreme test of his readiness and character. Luckily, as we learn in "The Tail" (chapter 86), there are other views of the whale that are almost as inspiring of religious feeling, without being nearly so perilous as the front view. These, too, can have the effect of transforming the aspirant, as Ishmael's sight of the peaking of the whale's flukes transforms him, making him eager to "celebrate" the whale's tail, though it remains shrouded in mystery (375). "Excepting the sublime *breach*," he asserts, the peaking of the whale's flukes "is perhaps the grandest sight to be seen in all animated nature. Out of the bottomless profundities the gigantic tail seems spasmodically snatching at the highest heaven" (378).

Yet as important as this feeling of spiritual excitement, which the sight of the whale's upturned flukes can inspire, is the attitude of reverence for the

Most High that the poised tail itself seems to exemplify. Describing a remark-able scene he once witnessed while standing on the lookout one sunrise, Ishmael testifies that "I once saw a large herd of whales in the east, all heading towards the sun, and for a moment vibrating in concert with peaked flukes. As it seemed to me at the time, such a grand embodiment of adoration of the gods was never beheld, even in Persia, the home of the fire worshippers." He comes away from the experience with the idea that the whale is "the most devout of all beings," and in doing so he identifies yet another reason why all people should model themselves after this remarkable creature (378).

To be sure, there are some gestures of the tail that "remain wholly inexpli-cable" to Ishmael and certain other motions of its body that are "unaccount-able" even to the most experienced hunter. As much as anything, the feature-less face of the beast puzzles him even beyond the last act of his story. However, as is suggested by the biblical language he invokes, particularly from Exodus 33:23, Ishmael has come to believe in the whale as one is sometimes said to believe in a religion, in spite of his great ignorance of it. Thus chapter 86 ends with his confession that "The more I consider this mighty tail, the more do I deplore my inability to express it. . . . But if I know not even the tail of this whale, how understand his head? much more, how comprehend his face, when face he has none? Thou shalt see my back parts, my tail, he seems to say, but my face shall not be seen" (378–79).

In the next chapter, however, Ishmael launches into a broad if indirect series of hints as to the mysterious character of the whale's face, Melville's symbol for the inexpressible face of God. "The Grand Armada" is the center-piece of the fourth part of *Moby-Dick;* it tells the story, first on a grand scale and then in miniature, of the whole epic hunt. What it reveals about the coun-tenance of the whale—here imaginatively portrayed as the collective expres-sion of a whole herd of whales viewed in close proximity to Ishmael's boat—is its moodiness or doubleness, its capacity to be both excited and calm, even at the same time. Ishmael opens the chapter at the moment when the *Pequod* is making its way through the Straits of Sunda into the China seas, the favored haunt of the White Whale. Passing through these straits, Ishmael says, one has the sense of entering "the central gateway opening into some vast walled em-pire"—the fabled East, with its "inexhaustible wealth of spices, and silks, and jewels, and gold, and ivory" (381). It is, of course, remindful of the hero's passage through the "wall" of the whale en route to the treasure. But the wealth that awaits the crew of the *Pequod* at this point is not a material kind of trea-sure, such as the Orient offers; it is instead "a spectacle of singular magnifi-cence"—a great "host of vapory spouts" all spread across half the horizon "up-playing and sparkling in the noon-day air" (382).

Following a hard and lengthy chase in which the crew is made to earn its reward, they suddenly catch up to the whole herd of gallied whales, now seemingly "going mad with consternation." After Queequeg harpoons a lone whale on the edge of the caravan, the wounded beast, Ishmael says, threw "blinding spray in our faces, and then running away with us like light, steered straight for the heart of the herd" (385). Their external eyes thus blinded, the crewmen must instead trust their inner eyes, and what they see approximates a miraculous vision. As they are dragged deeper and deeper into the "frantic shoal," they come upon a great calm or "sleek," generated by the moisture even a quiet whale throws off, at the "innermost heart" of the immense herd. "Yes, we were now in that enchanted calm which they say lurks at the heart of every commotion" (385–87). Within moments, these simple whalemen have experienced the two sides of the Spirit of God that in the opening of Genesis is said to move over the face of the waters.

Now hemmed in by the "living wall" that shuts out all but the most courageous, skillful whalemen (the wall, Ishmael observes, "that had only admitted us in order to shut us up"), they are "visited by small tame cows and calves; the women and children of this routed host" (387). There in this magic circle, inside not a single whale but a whole pod of them, they witness leviathan versions of the same domestic rites of the bridal chamber and nursery that they had left behind on land. There they see images of creation, age-old images out of Genesis—the swelling forms of expectant mother whales and the motionless forms of nursing mothers; even a newborn, recently confined in its mother's belly, the "umbilical cord of Madame Leviathan" still joining them. "Some of the subtlest secrets of the seas," Ishmael exclaims, "seemed divulged to us in this enchanted pond. We saw young Leviathan amours in the deep" (388). Finally, Ishmael suggests that, in viewing this scene, he discovers what the successful hero always finds: the face of the Father and the face of the hero are one and the same.

In a single paragraph Melville captures the whole essence of the epic hunt when he has Ishmael give voice to the feeling of profound happiness that comes to him as he gazes into the enchanted pond at the center of this "grand armada":

And thus, though surrounded by circle upon circle of consternations and affrights, did these inscrutable creatures at the centre freely and fearlessly indulge in all peaceful concernments; yea, serenely revelled in dalliance and delight. But even so, amid the tornadoed Atlantic of my being, do I myself still for ever centrally disport in mute calm; and while ponderous

planets of unwaning woe revolve round me, deep down and deep inland there I still bathe me in eternal mildness of joy. (388–89)

Saying this, Ishmael thus announces that he has at last looked into the same waters in which the young Narcissus had drowned—looked and seen and grasped the "ungraspable phantom of life" and discovered there an image not of wrath but of "eternal mildness of joy."

What it would be like to see the face of God, not as it is reflected in the image of the whale, but directly, is the solemn subject of "The Castaway" (chapter 93). Pip, the black cabin boy who is the central figure in this scene, is not a whaleman but a "ship-keeper," a role reserved for those having little or no standing as sailors (411). At a time of emergency, therefore, when he is rushed into service in one of the boats, he has no experience in the hunt and loses his head at the first moment of contact with the beast. When he leaps from the boat the first time, Stubb takes pity on him and acts immediately, "for God's sake," to save him. However, when he jumps a second time, the cabin boy is left behind on the open sea "like a hurried traveller's trunk," a fore-image of the box that will buoy up Ishmael in the end. Pip turns his face, in an attitude of dumb worship, "out from the centre of the sea" toward the sun, portrayed here as "another lonely castaway, though the loftiest and the brightest" (413). He is therefore one who looks at God face to face, without first going through the whaling ritual. The "awful lonesomeness" of being on an open ocean, Ishmael exclaims, "is intolerable. The intense concentration of self in the middle of such a heartless immensity, my God! who can tell it?" (414).

Having to take the full force of the light of the deity directly, without a medium to mute or channel it, Pip is simply overwhelmed. His earthly personality is destroyed. After a time, his "ringed horizon began to expand around him miserably" until the whole world and his own consciousness became one. In effect, he has opened his soul beyond the initial terror of meeting the Father and, in doing so, come to understand the beginning and the end of all creation. He and the great Father are thus reconciled. But from the hour of his rescue, Ishmael explains,

the little negro went about the deck an idiot; such, at least, they said he was. The sea had jeeringly kept his finite body up, but drowned the infinite of his soul. Not drowned entirely, though. Rather carried down alive to wondrous depths, where strange shapes of the unwarped primal world glided to and fro before his passive eyes; and the miser-merman, Wisdom,

revealed his hoarded heaps; and among the joyous, heartless, ever-juvenile
eternities, Pip saw the multitudinous, God-omnipresent, coral insects, that
out of the firmament of waters heaved the colossal orbs. He saw God's foot
upon the treadle of the loom, and spoke it; and therefore his shipmates
called him mad (414).

More than any other character in the book, Pip knows that the soul and God
are one. Though his ego has been blasted, and with it his capacity for translat-
ing all he has witnessed, he alone among the crew has dived so deep as to
sound the self to its bottom. He alone knows that, in the end, there is no
death; there is really only life. Whether we recognize it or not, whether we will
it or not, "we are all," as Ishmael says before Pip leaps a second time from
Stubb's whaleboat, "in the hands of the Gods" (413).

Although "A Squeeze of the Hand," the next chapter, is radically different in
tone from "The Castaway"—gentle and dreamy where the latter is grave and
mystical—it should be read as a companion piece, for it confirms that the
hand of the Father that holds us, though it may treat us with wrath, is ultimately a hand of forgiveness, mercy, and love. Whether it chastizes or comforts, it is a hand of support, one that acts out of concern for our best interests,
like the so-called "supernatural hand" that the young Ishmael once woke to
find holding his own hand hours after he had been sent to bed for some youthful
misdeed (26). On the face of it, "A Squeeze of the Hand" concerns Ishmael's
mollifying experience of squeezing lumps of spermaceti back into fluid form,
the "hand" of the title, in this case, referring simply to the hand of Ishmael and
of his respective co-laborers. For Ishmael it is a crucial, transforming experience, a pivotal event in his epic journey, for it results in his decision to break
free of Ahab's magnetic hold. However, as an extended trope or pun on life-
giving male sperm, "A Squeeze of the Hand" also celebrates the endless flowing
of the seminal waters of the Creator, the "living stuff," to borrow Stubb's term,
that jets from the eternal fountain to bring forth life out of nothingness.[38]

The hand of the Father that clenches in anger to chastise the child can also
"squeeze" with a gentle firmness to give reassurance of His love, or it can
open wide to release the treasure that promises the renewal of life. Significantly,
Ishmael loses his ego, in this chapter, as well as his sanity, as Pip does in "The
Castaway." "I squeezed that sperm," Ishmael exclaims, "till I myself almost
melted into it; I squeezed that sperm till a strange sort of insanity came over
me." But his transformation has not incapacitated him, as Pip's had incapacitated Pip. Instead, his experience of squeezing case has given birth to an almost mystical illumination that makes him value the common life as never

before. This, then, is the greatest boon of all—not simply the "abounding, affectionate, friendly, loving feeling" Ishmael suddenly feels toward his fellow sailors, but the radically enhanced appreciation he feels for the life he had left behind on shore. "I have perceived," he concludes meditatively, "that in all cases man must eventually lower, or at least shift, his conceit of attainable felicity; not placing it anywhere in the intellect or the fancy; but in the wife, the heart, the bed, the table, the saddle, the fire-side, the country; now that I have perceived all this, I am ready to squeeze case eternally" (416). Yet as Ishmael's own example suggests, one cannot achieve the frame of mind required to appreciate such domestic pleasures, without first leaving the land and going to sea. What is more, unless he engages in the entire ritual of the hunt, the would-be hero will never be able to return home. If, like Pip, he happens on a shortcut to revelation, it will catch him unawares, and he will never be able to recover from the shock of recognition.

After "A Squeeze of the Hand" comes another notorious phallic chapter, "The Cassock," this one treating circumcision. But like its predecessor, "The Cassock" is more than a crude male joke. As Melville's use of religious imagery implies, the outlandish scene described here has thematic significance that links it with the most fundamental purposes of the hero's epic adventure. Chapter 95 sketches the process of the mincer's stripping, refashioning, and donning of the whale's foreskin in preparation for the task of chopping up the blubber to be "tried out" in the pots, much as a priest might be said to don his cassock in preparation for his performance of some holy office. The ritelike quality of these operations emphasizes that the whole process of breaking down the whale's blubber into precious oil, described in the next chapter, "The Try-Works," is a very serious affair indeed, the whalers' equivalent of the ritualistic dismemberment and sacrifice of harvest gods like Osiris to ensure the renewed life of the tribe in spring.

The process portrayed in "The Cassock" is, of course, a form of phallic worship, an ancient and widespread celebration of life that Melville alludes to in referring to the story of Queen Maachah in 1 Kings 15. When the circumciser cuts away the male's foreskin, he removes the protective cover of the phallus, thus exposing the symbol of life itself; that is the chief purpose of the rite. But in this scene from *Moby-Dick*, when the mincer substitutes himself for the phallus by slipping inside its cover, Melville thus symbolizes that man is the source of his own life, that he can attain the state of immortality only by becoming so *like* the whale as to put himself in its place, inside the walls of its magically insulating skin. This "investiture alone," Ishmael says of the foreskin, "will adequately protect him" (420). Without it, the mincer runs the risk of self-mutilation, of dismembering his own toes and more, as Ahab may be said

to do. In this respect, the symbol of the cassock also serves to inform the meaning of all the other protective coverings encountered earlier in the narrative—the counterpane, Mapple's raincoat, the nightgown, Queequeg's poncho, the whale's blanket—all the magic walls and covers that shield what Ishmael early in his story calls the "warm spark" of life from the threat of death (54).

As much as anything, "The Cassock" underscores the need for the protecting rituals of the whale hunt if one is to survive the final stages of the encounter with the Father. At the same time, however, "The Cassock" also captures the Oedipal nature of the human struggle with the Father for domination of the world. In Melville's rendering of this ageless conflict, it is not the initiates who are circumcised, as is usually the case, but the gods themselves, the whales. For in this way the whalemen signify their success at conquering the beast as well as their own fitness for enjoying the fruits of the hunt.

In turn, the whales sometimes appear to conspire with their pursuers, permitting themselves to be captured and sacrificed for the good of the whalemen, as when they become mysteriously "gallied" and suddenly stop, in the chase described in "The Grand Armada," at the very moment when their escape seems assured. So, too, in some early tribes, the elders are known to have sacrificed or bled themselves to supply sustenance for the young during the long period of their initiation. Such self-sacrifice reveals that the transfer of power is to be considered an impersonal process, one designed to guarantee the continued existence of the whole tribe, not that of any particular member or group. Only the fearful, the selfish, or the narcissistic, those who refuse the call to adventure, come in the end to know the gods by their fury rather than by their mercy. Like Ahab, whose severed leg constitutes a mitigated castration, their manhood is constantly threatened in the struggle with the powers that rule the self and the world. Instead of gaining strength or vitality over time, they seem, ineluctably, to be always losing what little life remains to them.

"The Try-Works" stands as the culmination of the process of breaking down the whale's flesh into light-bringing, life-giving oil, the final step in the transfer of power that will eventually result in the initiate's triumph over darkness, temporality, and death. Appropriately, the scene described here is also the turning point in Ishmael's quest for spiritual health, the moment of crisis when he comes to understand, more emphatically than he ever could have before, why he must renounce his part in Ahab's mad plan. The trying out of the whale's blubber is a fiery process comparable to the trying out or testing of the soul of the epic hero. It is an epitome of every man's life. Fittingly, it occurs in a place of special knowledge, the try-pots, where secrets are exchanged among the sailors and where Ishmael discovers a remarkable law of geometry. When the trying-out is allowed to go to completion, a wonderful transformation occurs.

All the impurities are burned off in a "horrible" smoke, leaving a fresh, sweet oil that only whalemen can know in its "unvitiated state" (422, 426).

When Ishmael first describes the operation, it is night, and the only illumination is provided by the hellish flame consuming the flesh of the whale "martyr" (422). Standing duty at the helm, he watches the harpooneers wildly gesticulating with their "huge pronged forks and dippers" as they alternately stoke the pots and stir up the fire. "Wrapped, for that interval, in darkness myself," Ishmael says, he achieves a state of mental clarity whereby "I but the better saw the redness, the madness, the ghastliness of others." In this grim mood, he thus finally penetrates the deeper significance of the scene, observing that "the rushing Pequod, freighted with savages, and laden with fire, and burning a corpse, and plunging into that blackness of darkness, seemed the material counterpart of her monomaniac commander's soul" (423).

After a while, however, Ishmael grows drowsy and loses this mental clarity, until finally the sight of the "fiend shapes" silhouetted against the fire "begat kindred visions in my soul." Under their influence, the influence of sleep, of death, he gets completely turned around and brings the ship to the verge of destruction before suddenly recovering his senses. "Starting from a brief standing sleep," he says, in language that describes also the mesmerizing influence of Ahab, "I was horribly conscious of something fatally wrong" (423). Sensing that the whole ship is headed in the wrong direction and will be destroyed, he wakes with a "stark, bewildered feeling, as of death" coming over him. Having righted the ship, and relieved to find that his "unnatural hallucination of the night" is over, he comes to recognize that, like Ahab, he had been looking "too long in the face of the fire," had in fact become "inverted," and "deadened," by it. "Turn not thy back on the compass," he then sermonizes, anticipating the time when Ahab will do just that; "accept the first hint of the hitching tiller; believe not the artificial fire, when its redness makes all things look ghastly. Tomorrow, in the natural sun, the skies will be bright; those who glared like devils in the forking flames, the morn will show in far other, at least gentler, relief; the glorious, golden, glad sun, the only true lamp—all others but liars!" (424–25).

Again, it is the sun, timeless image of the Father, that is the true guide to life. However, the sun is not simply a thing of glory and gladness in Melville's scheme. As an image of the Godhead, it is contradictory, double, a maddening mystery. Ruler of the known world, of all life, during the daylight hours, it is also lord of the underworld, of the dead, at night. But even during its ascendancy, the sun is bipolar, revealing a world of joy and pain, of benefit as well as loss. As Ishmael observes in a memorable apostrophe, "the sun hides not Virginia's Dismal Swamp, nor Rome's accursed Campagna, nor wide Sahara....

The sun hides not the ocean, which is the dark side of this earth, and which is two thirds of this earth. So therefore, that man who hath more of joy than sorrow in him, that mortal man cannot be true—not true, or undeveloped." Conversely, the man who dwells only on the sorrows of life will become, in wise Solomon's phrase, one of the "congregation of the dead" even while living. Like Ahab, he will spurn the sun and worship instead the "artificial fire," the diminished, refracted, earthly form of the same vital energy that pours forth from the great source of all light and life (424–25).

As the potential hero of Melville's epic, then, Ishmael must learn to recognize the Father by His absence as well as by His glorious presence. In contrast to Starbuck, who professes in the doubloon scene not to believe in the sun at midnight, he must learn to have faith during the dark times of trial as well as during the periods of light. And he must come to see that the two are but parts of a single whole. The god of the sundoor, as Campbell says, is "the fountainhead of all the pairs of opposites." "In him are contained and from him proceed the contradictions, good and evil, death and life, pain and pleasure, boons and deprivation."[39] To the person who comes to understand this complexity, life is no longer a trial but a blessing. If, like the whaleman, he stays his course and seeks only what Ishmael, in "The Lamp" (chapter 97), calls "the food of light," he will meet such success as to "live in light" day and night, such an abundance of oil will be given to him. The light-giving, life-nurturing whale oil will permit him, even while asleep at night in his bunk, to be housed as in "some illuminated shrine of canonized kings and counsellors" (426). For Ishmael, then, this is the be all and end all of the whole whaling adventure: to live in light.

Given its proximity to Ishmael's discussion of the sun as "the only true lamp" at the end of chapter 96, the next chapter, "The Lamp," clearly correlates the light from the sun with the light from the oil of the sperm whale. These images in turn are related to the light that pours forth from the soul, as suggested first in Father Mapple's sermon, where the lamp hanging in Jonah's ship-cabin symbolizes the future prophet's conscience, the inner source of illumination available to all. *This* is the ultimate boon, the discovery that the light of the soul, of truth and immortality, is within oneself, that the hero and the Father are one. Sun, whale oil, soul, and God—all are variations of the same principle of light and life.

By contrast, the doubloon, a graven image of the sun, and the subject of the following chapter, is a false version of the guiding light. A circle of gold that Ahab has affixed high on the mainmast as a reward for the first sailor who sights Moby Dick, the doubloon competes with the sun for the crew's attention and homage. Indeed, it distracts them from the golden globe that the

Creator, in like manner, has set in the heavens to guide all humanity. Rather than generating light, however, the doubloon only reflects it, whatever the source, true or false. It is a mirror and not a lamp, to appropriate M. H. Abrams's well-known terms.[40] As each of the would-be communicants from among the *Pequod*'s crew makes his entrance to gaze on the gold coin, we are shown that the doubloon simply reflects back the subjective outlook of the observer. Leading off the procession, Ahab reveals his own egotism, and that of all the other observers as well, when he says, "There's something ever egotistical in mountain-tops and towers, and all other grand and lofty things; look here,—three peaks as proud as Lucifer" (431).

Still, the doubloon is a double thing—complex, contradictory, elusive in meaning. As the White Whale's "talisman," the doubloon is potentially more than a distraction from the true light. It is also a magical vehicle for raising Moby Dick, a mystical means of achieving the highest form of spiritual illumination. Minted in Ecuador, a country named for the region of the earth closest to the sun, and bearing in its inscription a segment of the zodiac with the "keystone sun" entering Libra, or the scales (the sign of judgment), the gold coin is presented as having powerful affinities with the sun. It is what Ishmael terms a "medal of the sun," or what Ahab calls a "coined sun," and it thus represents the ultimate source of all life (431).

Surely this is what Pip means when he refers to the doubloon as the "ship's navel," a common mythological image of the magical spot or "door" through which the vivifying energies of the spirit life pour into the world. The last to make his entrance in this scene, Pip offers no reading of the coin. Instead he articulates the unconscious motives, the propelling hunger of the *Pequod*'s whole crew, when he observes that the men "are all on fire to unscrew it" (435); all those who come forward to gaze on the doubloon want more than its monetary value as their reward for sighting Moby Dick. Their need is such that all of them, whether they know it or not, yearn to set free the flow of life into the body of the world, to restore vitality and meaning to their lives.

For Ishmael, Melville's single epic hero, this will be the life-saving consequence of his finally gaining a complete and unobstructed view of Moby Dick on the last day of the chase. All the power in the navel of the world, in the whale, will pour into him in the end in the form of spiritual energy or grace and buoy him up in the face of death. For, beneath the spot represented as the navel of the world, as Campbell explains this universal image, is "the earth-supporting head of the cosmic serpent, the dragon, symbolical of the waters of the abyss, which are the divine life-creative energy and substance of the demiurge, the world-generative aspect of immortal being."[41] As the successful hero, then, Ishmael is himself the umbilical point through which life's sus-

taining energies enter into the creation. To be sure, the doubloon is in fact nothing more than a gold coin; in Melville's scheme, it has no special, magical power. But as a symbol, it reveals that anything in the world, no matter how small or insignificant it might seem, is potentially divine. If one but knows how to tap it, and can let go of his ego, he will find that any point in the world is capable of becoming the place of special knowledge and power. For, to the true hero, the life force is everywhere.

Ishmael offers no reading of the doubloon. Like Pip, he has none of the ego involvement in the quest that keeps the other characters from seeing the coin objectively. Unlike the others, he has no selfish motive, nothing beyond simple curiosity, for continuing with the hunt at this point—nothing to prove, as Ahab tries to prove his indomitableness; nothing to gain, as Stubb and Flask think of gaining worldly riches; nothing to protect, as Starbuck tries to salvage his faith in a benevolent God. For Ishmael, the quest is all but over. Having sounded his soul, he has learned to master his ego and thereby achieved mastery of life. As he demonstrates in "A Bower in the Arsacides," where he speaks of making a visit, sometime later in life, to a temple formed of the skeleton of a great sperm whale on an imaginary island, Ishmael is able, finally, to go in and out of the "belly of the whale" without fear or harm, more or less at will. After he has once seen Moby Dick, he will have gone beyond the terrors of meeting the self that the whale signifies and will then understand the interior of the whale to be a holy, life-renewing place, a Chapel Perilous without perils.

It is true that "A Bower in the Arsacides" is the one episode in the book where Ishmael portrays himself as accomplishing the extraordinary feat of entering the whale's "belly." However, the ease with which he breaks through the wall of the ribs, as he says, and makes his winding way into the sanctum sanctorum of the beast and out again, suggests that he could do it again any time he wishes. So, too, of course, can anyone else, so easy is the hero's task, as long as one has the wisdom to do as Ishmael had done in following the example of Theseus, the ancient hero who used a simple string to find his way out of the Cretan labyrinth after venturing inside to kill the Minotaur. Using a "ball of Arsacidean twine" (is this, perhaps, the very same "ball of free will" that had dropped from his hand at the end of "The Mat-Maker"?), Ishmael says he wandered throughout the convoluted interior of the skeleton until his line ran out, and then he retraced his steps (450).

Like any successful epic hero, what Ishmael confronts, in the course of his descent, is his own mortality, the naked fact of death. Emerging from the same opening where he had entered, he says simply, "I saw no living thing within; naught was there but bones" (450). There is wry humor here, to be sure, and irony as well. But the fact remains that, in the metaphoric sense of

the phrase, Ishmael has reached the end of the line. His quest is virtually finished; all that remains is for him to see Moby Dick, to glimpse a vision of God, and then make his return. By this point, he has defeated the hypos that originally sent him to sea; he has seen beyond his own death and is now prepared to do something worthy with the life that is left to him.

Like every epic hero once he has come to his journey's end, Ishmael possesses the power to save others, to guide the chosen few along the path of trials to the same life-transforming spot where he achieved his greatest triumph, the triumph of life over death. And indeed this is what he does, or tries to do. For, at the end of "The Fossil Whale" (chapter 104), Ishmael leads his reader into still another such holy place, a Barbary temple made of whale bones. It is said not only that a prophet who prophesied of Mahomet came from this spot but also that "the Prophet Jonas was cast forth by the Whale at the Base of the Temple" there. Whether coming to it or going away, one will forever find the belly of the whale to be a place of the highest spiritual power. A prophet himself in the end, Ishmael thus awaits the time when his reader, too, will issue forth a prophet of the soul. "In this Afric Temple of the Whale I leave you, reader," he says at the end of this chapter, "and if you be a Nantucketer, and a whaleman, you will silently worship there" (458). Future generations of readers can be assured that they, too, will benefit from Ishmael's example. In "Does the Whale's Magnitude Diminish?—Will He Perish?" the final chapter of the fourth section of *Moby-Dick*, Ishmael testifies that the whale grows larger, more powerful with every generation, that it is immortal in species, though individual bodies die. Clearly, what he says of the whale as a species he, and Melville, too, felt to be true of the human soul as well.

V. WHAT THE THUNDER SAID

Part five belongs to Ahab, the wounded king, or "grand, ungodly, god-like man" whose face bears a savage scar like the mark made by a lightning bolt (79, 123). In the last thirty chapters, he takes over center stage as Ishmael had in part one. Chapter 106, "Ahab's Leg," marks the transition into this final section. Here Melville's attention shifts sharply but deftly from the matter of Ishmael's growing independence and spiritual development to Ahab's earlier dismemberment by the White Whale, the event that precipitated the quest, and his inconsolable grief at his loss.

The previous chapter, "Does the Whale's Magnitude Diminish?—Will He Perish?" had made a firm case for the whale's immortality and thus for its

appropriateness as a symbol for the soul. But "Ahab's Leg" comes as an immediate reminder of mankind's unalterable mortality, and of the inadequacy of
pride or ego as a foundation or "standpoint." As Thomas Greene has argued,
the epic hero must in the end be made to see that, in spite of his awe-inspiring
energy and effort at control, "his inescapable limitations await him."[42] Repeatedly in the chapters of this last section we are told of the destruction and
mutability that attend all Ahab's activities and indeed of the transience of all
life. Ahab's leg, the book's central metaphor for this impermanence, itself
breaks down again and again; several casks of oil in the *Pequod*'s hold inexplicably start leaking; even the robust Queequeg takes sick and comes to the
edge of his grave; various other crewmembers die through accidents or fierce
encounters with the whale; whaleboats are stove and, once repaired, stove
again; the ship's compasses are permanently destroyed in a storm; the log line
deteriorates and snaps; the life-buoy dries out and sinks.

Under the misguided command of the monomaniacal captain known as
"*Old* Thunder" (92, 505; emphasis added), everything on ship runs to decay
and disorder. Unlike the ageless thunder that speaks in the typhoon, Ahab is
dying; his power inexorably "leaks" away (474). He has lost the power to deliver the lightning-bolt, symbol of spiritual illumination, that would free the
heavenly waters and bring life-giving rain. While he never possessed this power
in his own person, the potential was always there, waiting to operate through
him, as it can through anyone. But since his dismemberment, Ahab has been
so blinded by pride and the needs of his own ego as to be incapable of knowing the promise of divine grace within himself. Only the ever-renewing thunder of the true gods—the illusion-shattering energy of nature, of the whale
speaking without, and of the soul speaking within—can restore one to life
and keep life fresh in the midst of the decay that time inevitably brings. As
described in "The Needle," chapter 124, it is this thunder that turns around
the *Pequod*'s compasses on the night of the great storm and leads the crew to
sail away from Moby Dick, toward safety, if only for a time.

"Ahab's Leg" places the *Pequod*'s captain in the tradition of the Fisher King,
the ancient Mesopotamian figure that, as Jessie Weston argued in *From Ritual
to Romance*, formed the basis of the medieval Christian Grail legend. Like the
Fisher King, Ahab is a wounded ruler who seeks to restore his own health and
potency by capturing a fish of miraculous revitalizing power.[43] Part human,
part divine, he stands, like the early fertility cult figures of Osiris, Attis, and
Adonis, between the people he commands and the mysterious forces that
control his destiny. In several versions of the Grail story, there is a causal relation, as there is in *Moby-Dick*, between the vitality of the king and the health

of his land or people: when he is vigorous, they know prosperity; but when his forces have been depleted or destroyed "by wound, sickness, old age, or death," as Weston says, "the land becomes waste, and the task of the hero is that of restoration." The Grail legend thus had its basis in early vegetation rituals or dramatized celebrations of the cycle of the seasons, running from birth through growth and decay and on to birth again.[44]

Because the foot, according to Freud, is an "age-old sexual symbol," Ahab's dismemberment can also be understood as a symbolic emasculation.[45] However, it is an emasculation that becomes almost literal in chapter 106, where Melville details the history of Ahab's trials with various replacements for his severed leg. On one occasion, which occurred on a night just before the ship sailed with Ishmael from Nantucket, Ahab had been discovered lying insensible on the ground with his ivory limb inexplicably broken loose and all but piercing his "groin." What makes Ahab unusual as an exemplar of the Fisher King is that his wounds are, to a significant degree, self-generated, even self-inflicted. As an epic writer of the nineteenth century, Melville provided a modern psychological rendering of the ritualistic sacrifice according to which Ahab, the ruling demigod, unconsciously contributes to his own destruction. He is not the victim of an arbitrary fate so much as he is his own worst enemy. As Ishmael makes the case at the start of "Ahab's Leg," where he describes the most recent instance of the limb's giving way under him, "The precipitating manner in which Captain Ahab had quitted the Samuel Enderby of London, had not been unattended with some small violence to his own person." So eager was he to get on with his mad chase after the White Whale that he gave his ivory leg "a half-splintering shock" when he leaped into his boat and then, after reaching the ship, did still further violence to it when in a fit of fury he "vehemently" turned to give an urgent command to the helmsman to pursue his course more "inflexibly" (463). A "hard-driver," as the carpenter calls him, who persists without caution in his pursuit of the Whale, Ahab thus becomes his own destroyer. He has "driven one leg to death, and spavined the other for life, and now wears out bone legs by the cord," in seemingly endless repetition of the universal fate (472).

In contrast to Ahab, who incarnates the will to destruction, the carpenter, the central figure in the next chapter, incarnates what Melville calls the "unaccountable, cunning life-principle" (468). Where the relentless Ahab destroys, with impunity, legs and anything else he has a mind to, the ship's carpenter humbly makes the repairs that keep the captain, and his men, functioning. In the face of "those thousand nameless mechanical emergencies continually recurring in a large ship," he represents the force that keeps all operations

from grinding to a halt, "repairing stove boats, sprung spars, reforming the shape of clumsy-bladed oars, inserting bull's eyes in the deck, or new tree-nails in the side planks" (466). Like a universal redeemer or practical savior (like Christ, also a humble carpenter), he seems able to prolong the life of mortal materials almost endlessly by refashioning them when they break down. Sixty years old or more himself, he is nonetheless "uncompromised as a new-born babe," his youthfulness a consequence of his lack of ego, for he lived "without premeditated reference to this world or the next." Unlike Ahab, he has no prideful sense of himself to protect and can thus maintain the attitude of "humorousness" he needs to carry him beyond the tragedy of loss and destruction (467–68). Unlike Ahab, the carpenter does not hold to a slanted, pessimistic view of grief; he does not believe, as Ahab does, that "both the ancestry and posterity of Grief go further than the ancestry and posterity of Joy" (464). Able to see beyond the limited tragic view of life, he doggedly persists in the cobbling, halfway measures—the refashioning of coffins into life-buoys—that can result in deliverance from the ravages of time and death. "Ahab's Leg" testifies to the hardness, pain, and brevity of life. But "The Carpenter" testifies to the truth that all mortality is balanced by an endlessly persistent and resourceful life energy.

Not everything, of course, can be forever repaired, as the old Manxman tries to tell Ahab later in "The Log and the Line." When a life finally breaks, there is no refashioning it; when it slips away, there is no carpenter's vise strong enough to hold it in place. One must, therefore, accept death as a new stage in existence, secure in the faith that the Father who makes all things knows what He is doing. Without such faith, even as he is without the knowledge of his own father, Ahab tries to resist the forces of death at the same time that he unconsciously courts them.

By contrast, Queequeg, Ishmael's spiritual guide, in "Queequeg in his Coffin" (chapter 110), shows himself to be as fearless of death as he is capable of conquering it. When a sizable leak is discovered in the *Pequod*'s hold, it is Queequeg who goes down to investigate the source of trouble. There, mysteriously, he is seized with a murderous fever that brings him "close to the very sill of the door of death." He thus becomes, in this chapter, an image of the adventurer going to his "endless end." Unlike Ahab, Queequeg shows no signs of egotism, and no possessiveness regarding his body. As his flesh wastes away "till there seemed but little left of him but his frame and tattooing," he does not rail against his fate, as Ahab does, or jealously guard his dwindling store of vitality. Instead, he accepts his fate, at the same time he grows more spiritual. His eyes "seemed growing fuller and fuller . . . a wondrous testimony to that immortal health in

him which could not die, or be weakened"(476–77). By contrast, Ahab, on the last day of the chase, with Moby Dick bearing down on him for the last time, cries out that he grows "blind." "Is't night?" he exclaims in bewilderment (570).

Calmly accepting the fact of his imminent death, Queequeg quietly makes all of the arrangements for his own burial, unlike Ahab, who resists even the slightest suggestion that he might be mortal. When the appointed hour seems near, for instance, the Polynesian tells Ishmael he would like to be buried in a little "coffin-canoe" made of dark wood, just like the ones the deceased whalemen of Nantucket are placed in, and the ship's carpenter is instructed to make one especially for him (478). In fact, he faces the prospect of death in much the same spirit as he faces life, namely, as an adventure or journey. He already understands what Ishmael eventually comes to see, that even death is "only a launching into the region of the strange Untried; it is but the first salutation to the possibilities of the immense Remote, the Wild, the Watery, the Unshored" (486). When it comes time to make preparations for his pro-jected journey to heaven, Queequeg asks that his coffin be provisioned with food and water and the iron from his harpoon, symbol of all phallic power and of his death-defying commitment to life. In contrast to Ahab, who gives up his spear, hurling it defiantly into Moby Dick at the very moment of his own death, Queequeg never loses faith in the hero's adventure or in the life-sustaining powers of the universe. Once his coffin-canoe is ready to receive him, he makes "trial of its comforts" and then, asking that little Yojo be placed on his chest, he at last pronounces it "'Rarmai' (it will do; it is easy)," a simple yet profound religious utterance that Queequeg seems about to make almost every minute of his life (479).

As Ishmael's guide, Queequeg is more than an examplar of the spiritually whole man confidently confronting his fate. In the end, he is an image of the hero's eventual triumph over death, of the potential for renewal, and of the hero's need to return to the human community with the life-restoring gift of his example. Here also Queequeg incarnates Ishmael's destiny. For Ishmael, too, will come to the verge of his "endless end," only to experience a miracu-lous deliverance and then return home to perform the sort of task typically required of the epic hero. When the Polynesian goes down in the *Pequod*'s hold to inspect the casks believed to be leaking sperm oil, it is as though he becomes infected with the mortality eating away at the barrels down there, the same mortality that is slowly destroying Ahab's vitality.

However, lying in his coffin "as if in a dream," Queequeg reacts in a way that suggests he overhears, and takes to heart, the heavenly ramblings of little Pip, who praises the Polynesian as one who "dies game," while the distraught cabin boy castigates himself for his cowardice. Before long, Queequeg unex-

pectedly recovers from his strange malady, his only explanation being that,
"at a critical moment, he had just recalled a little duty ashore, which he was
leaving undone; and therefore had changed his mind about dying." As Melville
structures this scene, it is as though Pip, the incarnation of the infantile unconscious who, as Starbuck says, "brings heavenly vouchers of all our heavenly homes," gives utterance to Queequeg's unconscious knowledge of the
special responsibility he bears as one of the chosen men of courage. Reminded
by Pip of his own true character and calling, Queequeg is thus also reminded
of his own extraordinary power. He is free as only the hero of the spiritual
epic is free: "to live or die," he believes, "was a matter of his own sovereign will
and pleasure." Certainly "mere sickness could not kill him: nothing but a
whale, or a gale, or some violent, ungovernable, unintelligent destroyer of
that sort," or so he says (479–80).

In the end, though, even Queequeg is destroyed by just such a destroyer.
But having carved on the lid of his coffin a copy of all the "twisted tattooing"
on his body, he bequeathes to Ishmael not only the mysterious duty he had
left unfinished on shore but the means of carrying it out—namely, a complete theory of the heavens and the earth, in "hieroglyphic" form, and a "mystical treatise on the art of attaining truth" that "a departed prophet and seer"
of Queequeg's native island had originally etched on his skin. That theory
and treatise, though they remain "a riddle to unfold," have likewise been preserved in the "wondrous work in one volume" called *Moby-Dick* that Ishmael
writes on his return from the dead (480–81). The duty, and the means of
accomplishing it, are thus passed along to Melville's readers as well.

More than anywhere else in this book, Melville at this moment reveals that
Queequeg, spiritually serene and without regard for himself, is the central
wisdom figure, the key to *Moby-Dick*. Queequeg in his coffin is an image of
the ultimate treasure in the epic hero's quest, a testimonial to the indestructi-
bility of the soul, despite the body's infirmity. Unlike Ahab, who seeks always
to assure himself of his physical immortality, Queequeg knows that the fate of
the body is of no consequence in the journey of the soul, that preoccupation
with the life of the body in fact blinds the eye to the more glorious life of the
spirit. He knows what Ahab will not recognize, that the desire for physical
immortality is misguided; that bodily dismemberment is of necessity the experience of living in time; and that the discovery of the soul, and its immortality, is mankind's greatest treasure.

In "The Pacific" (chapter 111), where the hunt for Moby Dick intensifies, the
Pequod moves into a strangely spiritual realm where the "gently awful stirrings"
of the rolling sea seem, as Ishmael says, the expression of "some hidden soul
beneath." Here, in this tranquil ocean that Ishmael has dreamed of gazing on

since his youth, "millions of mixed shades and shadows, drowned dreams, somnambulisms, reveries; all that we call lives and souls, lie dreaming, dreaming, still; tossing like slumberers in their beds" (482). Yet clearly they are evident only to the spiritual man. Ahab, who is committed only to the task of destroying his destroyer, sees or senses almost none of the spirituality of the South Sea. He is blind to what is truly indestructible. Ishmael explains that where almost anyone else would be inspired by the "eternal swells" of the Pacific to "own" the god of nature, Ahab is so preoccupied as to have "few thoughts of Pan" (483). Even later, in "The Gilder," when the *Pequod* penetrates into the heart of the soothing Japanese cruising ground, where the "tranquil beauty and brilliancy" of the ocean's surface makes the voyager forget "the tiger heart that pants beneath it," Ahab is only temporarily affected by such "gilding." For, explains Ishmael, speaking of the soothing scenes before Ahab and his crew, "if these secret golden keys did seem to open in him his own secret golden treasuries, yet did his breath upon them prove but tarnishing" (492). Ahab knows more of the unseen world than the jolly commander of the *Bachelor,* who proclaims "good-humoredly" that he does not believe in Moby Dick and shrugs off the loss of two of his men as of no consequence (494). But because he holds fast to what he has, resents every loss, and distrusts the powers that support all life, Ahab sees only a fraction of the unseen world that Queequeg and Ishmael and other spiritually minded characters such as Pip are capable of sensing.

"The Pacific," the last threshold chapter of Melville's epic, marks the *Pequod*'s entrance into the realm ruled by Moby Dick. It is the place where the quester finally meets the Father, where he comes home to God. As a symbol of the serenity of the redeemed soul—of Queequeg in his coffin, of Ishmael after his change of heart—the Pacific Ocean serves as a reminder that the object of the quest is spiritual, and the quester's proper attitude is one of faith, not anxiety, hostility, or pride.

Yet because Ahab is committed to the life of the ego and not of the soul, from this point on, as his purpose intensifies, his every move is seen to contribute to his self-destruction. In the several chapters that follow, Melville, using elaborate epic imagery, dramatizes his version of the classic argument concerning the causes of the tragic hero's downfall.[46] In chapters 112 and 113, "The Blacksmith" and "The Forge," where Ahab oversees the manufacture of the harpoon that he imagines to be infallible, he stakes his whole enterprise on the power of the "artificial fire," rather than the sun, to lead him to his prey. Baptizing the finished weapon in the name of the devil, Ahab thus underscores his determination to defy his Maker in every way possible rather than admit his dependence on Him. Yet as Melville implies, he should instead follow the example of reverence and trust that Ahab himself witnesses one evening

in the scene described in "The Dying Whale" (chapter 116). There, after he and his crew have slain several whales, they watch as the last of them, slowly expiring, turns "his homage-rendering and invoking brow" toward the sun.

For a time, even Ahab is strangely affected by this instance of what, among dying sperm whales, is a common occurrence, acknowledging to himself that even at sea "life dies sunwards full of faith." But his suspicion soon returns and he concludes that it is vain for the dying whale to "seek intercedings with yon all-quickening sun," for it "only calls forth life, but gives it not again" (496–97). From here on, Ahab commits himself to a "prouder, if a darker faith," or nihilism. As the next chapter, "The Whale Watch," makes clear, while Ahab's ego still searches blindly for assurances of his immortality "on land and on sea," he has become so swallowed up by fear of his own death that he dreams again and again of hearses (410–11).

"The Whale Watch," chapter 117, shows Ahab moving more and more in a nighttime world, a sunless world of fears and premonitions of his own death. "The Quadrant," the next chapter, makes explicit his final rejection of the sun, and with it his refusal to acknowledge that, like every other living thing, he is a child of the great star. Until the scene described here, Ahab is said to have paid regular obeisance to the sun, taking his observation of it every day, with the ship's quadrant, to determine the latitude of his ship. However, now, in the glassy Japanese sea, the sun shines with such "nakedness of unrelieved radiance" as "the insufferable splendors of God's throne"; and Ahab, pretending to grow impatient with the hunt but secretly overpowered by the sun's sheer glory, swears that he will no longer permit it to serve as his "Pilot." "Thou tellest me truly where I *am*," he exclaims in frustration, "but canst thou cast the least hint where I *shall* be? Or canst thou tell where some other thing besides me is this moment living? Where is Moby Dick?" Again coming to the verge of real insight, Ahab again backs away. Rather than abandon his mad plan, he throws down the quadrant and tramples on it, swearing he will be guided by it no more. Rather than depend on an instrument that casts "man's eyes aloft to that heaven, whose live vividness but scorches him," Ahab says, "as these old eyes are even now scorched with thy light, O sun," he vows from that moment on to be guided only by "the level ship's compass" and the equally "level" log and line (500–501).

Before long, however, Ahab will discover the fallibility of these earthly instruments, as the compass, by a process described in "The Needle" (chapter 124), is discovered to be inverted by the thunder of the great Typhoon, and the log-line, as described in chapter 125, is found to be so weathered as to snap the first time the log and line is put into use. Once having made the pact to take the infernal Fedallah rather than the sun as his "pilot," Ahab finds more

and more that nothing in the world will support him or his mission. Everything goes against him.

Ahab's renunciation of the sun is the turning point in his dying soul's journey and ushers in the crisis of the fifth and final part of Melville's epic novel. Toward evening of the same day on which he had trampled on the quadrant, "the direst of all storms," a Typhoon, bursts on the Japan Sea, stripping the *Pequod* of her sails and leaving the men helpless before its wrath (503). It is as though Ahab's sacrilege has so angered the gods as to cause them to lash out with a great tempest, though the tempest is in fact their most dramatic warning for him to turn back.

The night scene presented in "The Candles" (chapter 119) has a moody, otherwordly atmosphere in keeping with its mysterious, seemingly supernatural happenings. In the midst of the storm, the three masts and yardarms all suddenly burst into pallid flame. While all the crew stand together "enchanted" and in a reverent attitude, intuitively sensing, as Ishmael says, that "God's burning finger has been laid on the ship" (506), Ahab assumes a stance of boldest defiance. Grasping the ship's lightning rod with his hand—not in an effort to absorb the heavenly power that streams through it into himself but out of a vain determination to measure his own power against that of the deity—he swears to the inviolability of his own ego, declaring proudly, "In the midst of the personified impersonal, a personality stands here. Though but a point at best; whencesoe'er I came; wheresoe'er I go; yet while I earthly live, the queenly personality lives in me, and feels her royal rights." When the lightning suddenly flashes and the corpusants flare up to new heights, as though in response to this profane assertion of his independence, Ahab gleefully owns that the flame is his "fiery father." But at the end of his fierce soliloquy he vows nonetheless to worship his "sire" not with reverence but "defyingly" (507–08). Clearly, his feud is now beyond all reason and beyond any possibility of satisfaction; it is indeed "quenchless," as Ishmael had earlier said of it (179).

Blinded as Ahab is by his egomania, it is left to Starbuck to read all the signs of the storm and interpret its general meaning. Thus even before Ahab discovers in "The Needle" that the Typhoon's thunder had turned the *Pequod*'s compasses, forcing the ship away from an encounter with the White Whale, Starbuck understands that the gale, in blowing from the east, was blowing them away from Moby Dick. And he understands, when he witnesses the flame issuing from Ahab's harpoon "like a serpent's tongue," the reverse of the process whereby Ahab and Perth had put fire into it, that it symbolically speaks to them the deity's own gravest warning: "God, God is against thee, old man." Though Ahab tries, at the end of this grand scene, to quiet the fears of his awestruck crew by overpowering the harpoon's mysterious flame with his own

breath, several of the crew run from him, as if he were a giant tree on a level plain during a hurricane, a tree "whose very height and strength but render it so much the more unsafe, because so much the more a mark of thunderbolts" (508).

Ishmael's choice of image, significant in itself as an expression of Melville's conception of tragic hubris, suggests that the pyrotechnics of this scene are intended as a heavenly warning to all on the *Pequod* to ready themselves for an imminent disaster. Turn around, the storm says; unless you are prepared, you will be destroyed by the great White Whale. What the thunder says in *Moby-Dick,* then, is what it has always said to the people of the world everywhere, whether in the mythologies of Zeus, Yahweh, or the Supreme Buddha: those who come to the Father in pride will be struck down, while those who come in true humility will know that His glory is the glory of the redeemed soul. Only those who come to Him without ego, as Ishmael does in the last chapters, where he seems little more than a disembodied voice, will see the Father and recognize Him to be one with the soul of humankind.

On the morning after the storm, the ocean rolls in mighty swells, and the brilliant sun, at once muffled and diffused, spreads its "emblazonings" everywhere, making the sea "a crucible of molten gold" (516). It is as though the same supernatural energy displayed in the lightning the night before has now been quieted and diffused, bathing the whole world in its glory. So compelling, so magnetic an attraction is it that even Ahab, the man of darkness, is moved to fix his gaze on its morning splendor. And when it is discovered that the storm has reversed the compass, Ahab is forced once again to take his bearings by the sun, thus tacitly acknowledging his dependence on it, even though just the day before he had vowed to steer his course with nothing but level, worldly instruments. After righting the ship's path, Ahab pushes on, ignoring or misreading the meaning of the many natural occurrences that warn him to turn back. But while he seems more determined than ever to pursue his fatal course, the debate regarding his mission, and the beliefs that undergird it, rages in his own mind more and more and plagues him with ever-greater intensity.

Ahab's interior debate is brought to the fore in "The Deck" (chapter 127), during his brief exchange with the carpenter, as the latter works at turning Queequeg's coffin into a replacement for the dried-out life-buoy. Every move of the carpenter's, in this chapter, seems to Ahab to raise the unsettling question of whether there is life beyond death, whether one has such a thing as an immortal soul. The scene opens with Ahab offhandedly observing that the coffin is lying near the ship's hatchway, "handy to the vault," in his mordant phrase. To him it symbolizes that there is no transcendence to another world, no life after death, only a simple drop into the crypt. But before long he finds

that the carpenter's every move somehow unsettles him, either by suggesting the inescapability of death or by calling into question Ahab's certainty that all faith is vain. And as a consequence, Ahab banishes him from his sight. "Despatch! and get these traps out of my sight," he exclaims, pointing to various of the carpenter's belongings that seem to trick his imagination into changing his most fundamental beliefs (527–28).

Even so, deep down Ahab recognizes that the true source of all his unsettling thoughts is his own mind. Hearing the "rat-tat!" of the banished carpenter's mallet in the distance, and sensing in the sound the ticking of a clock that reminds him of his mortality, he laments, "Oh! how immaterial are all materials! What things real are there, but imponderable thoughts?" The chapter ends with Ahab wondering whether he should, in the formulation of his own beliefs, follow the example of the carpenter and try to change the coffin, "the very dreaded symbol of grim death," into "an immortality preserver," an imaginative feat that he might be able to accomplish if he could somehow bring himself to believe in the immortality of the soul. Though he immediately dismisses such a possibility with the admission "so far gone am I in the dark side of earth," he nonetheless is made so nervous by the sounds of the carpenter as to feel driven to escape below deck (528). The scene ends ironically, with Ahab seeking Pip, the book's central image of the lost soul and the emblem of what Ahab refuses to acknowledge in himself. Such vacillation, sometimes unconscious, sometimes startlingly conscious, shows the *Pequod*'s captain to be a more fully rounded character than is generally recognized—not a simple madman with a monomaniacal hunger for revenge, but a deeply divided figure whose fixed purpose hides a profound distrust of the mercy of the Father and a fear that he himself might not be worthy.

In the remaining chapters leading up to the final chase, Melville devotes most of his effort to demonstrating that, "stricken, blasted, if he be," as Peleg had earlier told Ishmael, "Ahab has his humanities!" (79). If we are to see Ahab as more than a monster of rage, if we are to feel genuine sympathy for him, we must be made to recognize that his singlemindedness has cost him dearly, and we have to be made to understand that he himself appreciates what he has had to give up in so relentlessly pursing his one object. At the same time, we have to be made to see that Ahab's failure, in the end, is a failure of love, and that he manages to catch at least a glimpse of this idea on his own. In three scenes—Ahab's brief meeting with Captain Gardner of the *Rachel* in chapter 128; his poignant exchange with Pip in chapter 129; and his fluctuating discourse with Starbuck in "The Symphony," chapter 132—Ahab's fixedness of purpose is put to a series of profound tests.

In the first, when an acquaintance from Nantucket, the captain of the *Rachel*, comes aboard the *Pequod* and entreats Ahab to help him search for his lost son, Ahab seems to be completely unmoved by the man's plea. But when he suddenly orders Captain Gardiner from his ship, to prevent him from delaying his own search for Moby Dick, he reveals not only that he feels for his fellow captain but also that he knows he is committing a sin against his own soul. "God bless ye, man," he exclaims, "and may I forgive myself" (532).

In the second scene, Pip, who sees in Ahab's sturdy hand a "man-rope," something "weak souls may hold by" (522), asks nothing more than that he be permitted to accompany his captain wherever he goes on the ship. Ahab, however, finds Pip's fidelity "too curing to my malady." The desire to respond with a fidelity of his own would lead him, he knows, to give up the hunt for the Whale, and so he refuses even this seemingly trifling request. Still, Ahab is so deeply moved by the cabin boy's plea that he confesses his own purpose "keels up in him" unless Pip stops, and he finally has to threaten him with "murder" to make him leave (534).

In the third scene, when the first mate catches Ahab in an unprecedented mood of wistfulness and urges him one last time to turn back to Nantucket and their wives and children, Ahab shows himself suddenly of a mind to protect Starbuck, the only man on the *Pequod* who had ever openly opposed him, by encouraging him to stay on board when they give chase to Moby Dick. In this way, Starbuck might survive the confrontation with the Whale and return to his family. Momentarily moved by Starbuck's enthusiasm at the prospect of returning home, Ahab suddenly stops to wonder, with an air of all but unprecedented detachment, what it is that makes him persist in his quest for the White Whale. Using terms that bring him to the verge of defining his dilemma for himself for the first time, he nonetheless fails to recognize that his conflict is so deeply human as to be universal, a battle between sheer ego and the will to love. "What is it," he pleads with Starbuck, "what nameless, inscrutable, unearthly thing is it; what cozening, hidden lord and master, and cruel, remorseless emperor commands me; that against all natural lovings and longings, I so keep pushing, and crowding, and jamming myself on all the time; recklessly making me ready to do what in my own proper, natural heart, I durst not so much as dare?" (545).

Ahab cannot love because he cannot conquer his ego, and he cannot conquer his ego because he cannot bring himself to admit there is an "invisible power" that rules over all. Though he senses that his own heart could not beat nor his brain think "unless God does that beating, does that thinking, does that living, and not I," he is so jealous of his own power, so egotistical, that he

is incapable of seeing humanity as being ruled by anything more than "Fate" (545). He may possess the potential, but Ahab is far from being the epic hero. Preoccupied more and more with the subjects of sleep and death in these late chapters, Ahab lacks the comprehensive understanding of the true hero, the kind that only the awakened soul can attain.

When seen for the first time early in "The Symphony," Ahab had been leaning over the side, not studying his own reflection, like Narcissus, but watching "how his shadow in the water sank and sank to his gaze," as though he were watching his own soul drown before his very eyes. At the end of the chapter, he is seen for the last time, before the three-day chase, in much the same position. After Starbuck has stolen away in despair, Ahab crosses the deck to gaze over the other side. But this time, instead of seeing his own image, he sees only the reflection of Fedallah, who is there leaning over the same rail. Only Ahab's shadow, the shade or ghost of his soul, and not the soul itself, survives in him now. Immediately at the start of the chase in the next chapter, then, Ahab is referred to as "the old man," one sign among many that he will soon be in his last death throes (543).

Death is the great subject of *Moby-Dick,* death and immortality. Nowhere is this more apparent than in the final section of Melville's epic, where to read of Ahab's quickening pursuit of the White Whale is to witness a man rushing, uncontrollably, into the jaws of destruction. More and more as the *Pequod* moves toward its inevitable confrontation with Moby Dick, it is as though it travels in a realm of death, a wasteland or place of trial, where men disappear or perish without a trace, the young and innocent as well as the seasoned and hearty. As they near the outskirts of the equatorial fishing grounds, on the line closest to the sun, Ishmael's shipmates hear cries just before dawn, cries that sound like the voices of "newly drowned men," as the old Manxman explains (523). At sunrise the next morning, the *Pequod* loses one of its own men when he falls from aloft, a premonition of the many sacrifices to come. And on the following day, they encounter the *Rachel,* whose captain has lost a son and other men as well while hunting the White Whale.

As evidenced by the example of the *Rachel,* and also of the *Delight,* the simple act of sighting Moby Dick can cost a sailor his life. "Hast seen the White Whale?" Ahab cries out to the *Rachel,* the word "seen" here taking on the meaning of a religious experience. "Aye, yesterday. Have ye seen a whale-boat adrift?" comes the ominous reply, as if there were some fatal connection between the act of beholding the great Whale and the sacrifice of a human life. Indeed, the waters inhabited by Moby Dick can be murderous to all but the chosen few. To the five men of the *Delight* who lost their lives to Moby Dick just hours before the *Pequod* crossed its path, the surrounding sea is indeed a sailors' "tomb," the

burial place of the dead. Yet, with the exception of Ahab, those who survive an encounter with the Whale are usually quick to develop a healthy respect for the beast and to turn their thoughts to whatever prospects they might have for life in the next world. For them, a deadly sea can become a place of trial leading to eternal life. As the men of the *Delight* set about burying the one sailor recovered from the previous day's carnage, the captain voices a faith in "the resurrection and the life" that is never heard on the decks of Ahab's ship (541).

The waters inhabited by the great White Whale are the waters of life as well as of death. But to a man such as Ahab, whose pride corrodes all faith, they will never bring renewal. As symbolized by the loss of his hat, or crown, in chapter 130, Ahab is a dying king who is fast losing his power to rule, a type of the Fisher King for whom the living waters will never flow again. On the eve of the first day of the chase, Ahab is preoccupied with his weakness and his age, confessing to Starbuck that he feels "deadly faint" with his burden and "intolerably old," and he even jests that his gray hair must have grown "from out some ashes." Having spent forty years at sea making war on the horrors of the deep, he comes at last to recognize that his life is an emptiness, that he has failed to gain anything of true value. Unlike Moses, whose forty-year trial was eventually rewarded with the discovery of the Promised Land, Ahab wonders now at the end of his time how he might be "the richer or better" for all his struggle and concludes bitterly that he has been "a forty years' fool." For all his adult years he has suffered privation, knowing almost nothing but the solitary life of a whaling captain and feeding "upon dry salted fare—fit emblem," as he tells his first mate, "of the dry nourishment of my soul" (543–44).

Yet only when Ahab sheds a lone tear as he stands gazing into the sea and muses over all he has missed on shore these many years—human sympathy, friendship and family life, the green world—is it clear that he understands the many sacrifices he has had to make. And only then is it clear that he is worthy of our attention and sympathy, that he is fully human, capable of appreciating the common life, and that he feels as we feel. "Nor did all the Pacific contain such wealth as that one wee drop," Ishmael says, for that one drop symbolizes a human soul lost (543–44). More than a sentimental touch, this one tear signals Ahab's one moment of complete self-understanding. Though he will not turn back even now, his tear of self-knowledge symbolizes the "freeing of the waters," to appropriate Jesse Weston's phrase, the release of the life-giving rain or pent-up rivers into the dying world, and the washing away of death and evil and egotism that holds the wasteland in its grip.[47] Before the "great shroud of the sea" can roll on, restored to its equilibrium of five-thousand years before, it must unleash the havoc that will right the disequilibrium brought about by Ahab's immense pride (572).

The three-day chase, powerfully suspenseful though it is as drama, brings no significant surprises for the reader, only a resounding resolution, the most perfect an epic novelist has ever imagined. When at dawn of the first day Ahab senses Moby Dick's proximity and orders Daggoo to "Call all hands!" the black harpooneer wakes the sleeping crew with great thundering "judgment claps" on the forecastle deck, as if summoning them all to their final reckoning (547). Clearly, when judgment is pronounced, Ahab will be found guilty of refusing the call to adventure, the call to bring his will into line with the divine will. Clearly, he and his men are doomed. Yet even at this late hour, Ahab is free, in the way Milton's Satan was free, to decide to live eternally or die; even at this late hour, Ahab holds his fate in his own hands, even as he holds the spear, the masculine symbol of life and instrument of death known from the Grail legend and elsewhere, that will determine his destiny. In *Moby-Dick* the epic question—is humankind fated or free?—returns with the return of the Whale in the book's waning moments and is here resolved once and for all. Melville shows not simply that Ahab's life is taken from him but that Ahab himself, refusing to take life on any terms other than his own misguided ones, deliberately, willfully, tragically gives it up, even as he gives up his harpoon. Although the *Pequod*'s captain, after the nearly fatal second day of the chase, lectures Starbuck that he cannot turn around and head for home, his claim that "This whole act's immutably decreed . . . I am the Fates' lieutenant" is a sign of the advanced state of his *amor fati,* the failed hero's fatal love of fate that masks his yearning to be free of all personal accountability for his actions (561–62). As Ahab had confessed only moments earlier, while being lifted into the *Pequod* after his ivory leg had broken one more time, "Aye, aye, Starbuck, 'tis sweet to lean sometimes" (560). Here, too, he finds it comforting to shift the burden of responsibility for the coming destruction away from himself and to give it instead to the mysterious Fates.

Not until Ahab finally gives up his harpoon, not once but three times, thrusting it into the Whale in his ultimate act of defiance, does the beast turn on him with all its fury. On the first day's chase, Moby Dick simply toys with Ahab's boat, "as a mildly cruel cat her mouse" (550); afterward, an exhausted Ahab desperately asks whether the harpoon is "safe," and he is told by Stubb, "Aye, sir, for it was not darted." Significantly, after making anxious inquiries, Ahab learns also that his crew is safe as well, and for the same reason, namely, the harpoon was not thrown. Significantly, too, Ahab himself, though only moments earlier he had been lying "all crushed" in the bottom of Stubb's boat, quickly revives, "the eternal sap" running up in his bones again (551–52). On the second day it becomes more evident still that the harpoon is a magical instrument, its misuse a crime punishable by death. This time, on learning

that Fedallah is missing, Ahab is forced to recall that he had thrown his iron into Moby Dick in their last encounter. And on the third day the pattern is consummated. Ahab is destroyed, but not until he has darted two more spears into the White Whale and turned his own body, as he says emphatically, away "from the sun" (571). No sooner does he plunge the last of these instruments into his foe than he is caught around the neck by the whaleline and dragged under, a victim, like the Parsee, of Ahab's own weapon. Three times he was given the chance to choose life rather than death, and three times he chose to give up the spear in hatred and defiance. Having failed the test not once but three times, his fate is sealed: he deserves to live no more.

Whether Ishmael, more than any of the rest of the *Pequod*'s crew, deserves to live—more than Queequeg, say, or Pip—is the book's crowning mystery, its lone unanswered question. Ahab's fate is predictable. Even the destruction of all the ship's crew comes as no surprise. The great mystery for Melville, in the end, is not death but life, the unfathomable gratuitousness of it. The "Epilogue," brief yet dense, a little treasure that radically alters the meaning of all the rest of the book, conveys nothing so strongly as Ishmael's own wonder at his continued existence, at his survival of the wrath of the avenging God. Only the slightest attempt is made to explain his escape. All we are told is that "the Fates ordained" that he would be the one called on to assume Fedallah's place in Ahab's boat on the third day of the chase, after the Parsee had gone down with the Whale. From there, it just happened that, of the three oarsmen tossed out of the boat on the next encounter with Moby Dick, Ishmael was the one who was left a castaway, floating beyond the reach of the White Whale's final frenzy. Otherwise, the fact that he alone was specially chosen is presented as a matter beyond human understanding.

Not only did he survive the wrath of Moby Dick and the awful power of the sinking *Pequod*'s whirlpool, but he has also somehow been preserved from the universal cannibalism of the sea. For "one whole day and night" Ishmael is mysteriously protected from the sharks, who "glided by as if with padlocks on their mouths," and from the "savage sea-hawks," who "sailed with sheathed beaks," before he is finally plucked out of the sea by the *Rachel* (573). A lone man somehow persisting in a hostile universe, buoyed up on a miniature version of the world we all inhabit—part life-buoy, part coffin—Ishmael in the end is an image of us all, gifted with life and miraculously surviving, moment by moment.

An everyman figure, Ishmael is also, paradoxically, the specially chosen one. He alone is the universal epic hero of *Moby-Dick*. Though an orphan and outcast, lacking family, wealth, and other conventional forms of legitimacy, he is the one man on the ill-fated *Pequod* whose cry God hears. Indeed, his

name, the name he takes for himself, means "God shall hear." This is the identity he discovers for himself at the climax of his adventure: the one whom God hears. "Ishmael" is not the given name of Melville's narrator; it is the name he appropriates for himself after the fact, because it so aptly captures his experience as a castaway who in the end finds the Father after all. Like other epic stories, therefore, Ishmael's story climaxes with the discovery of the hero's true character and ends with his return to the community of his birth to bear witness to what he has learned. His retelling of that story, in turn, begins with the famous line that announces his identity: "Call me Ishmael." It is the vitalizing declaration of a man who knows from personal experience that God and the soul of the redeemed hero are one.

His identity having been revealed to him in the moment of his soul's greatest test, Ishmael returns to share the wealth of his discovery with the people of his own land, those Sunday "water-gazers" of Manhattan, and elsewhere, who long for the adventure that will liberate the soul.[48] This wealth or treasure is contained within the pages of *Moby-Dick,* the book that records its hero's experience on the *Pequod* and bodies forth the wisdom Ishmael has gained from the events leading up to the fateful confrontation with the Whale. Ishmael does not, of course, capture the White Whale with a harpoon, as Ahab would try to do. Being divine, Moby Dick can never be taken that way. But Ishmael can be said to capture him with his pen in the book called *The Whale* with potentially life-changing consequences to his readers.

Not the Whale, but the grace the Whale embodies—this is what the hero must seek. The Whale's "grace" cannot be destroyed, as Ahab would have it, for it is of the very essence of life; and life, we know from Melville's tale, is the abiding, indestructible mystery. When we read *Moby-Dick,* we have the chance to partake of that grace, if we can bring ourselves to take up the call. Those of us who read Melville's book and discover thereby something of our deeper selves are like the redeemed of Yahweh who, as Campbell says, are "served the inexhaustible, delicious flesh of the monsters Behemoth, Leviathan, and Ziz" at the Messianic banquet.[49] Going into Melville's epic, into the belly of *The Whale,* we find not that we are contained or trapped there but that we are fed and sustained. *Moby-Dick,* that is to say, is more than the story of one man's renewal. It is that still rarer thing, a religious text, a world-redeeming epic.

∾

The Divided Self:

Pierre as Psychological Novel

When it was published in 1852, *Pierre; or, The Ambiguities* was met by public neglect and the loud objections, even contempt, of reviewers. Though widely recognized in recent years as the work of a writer near the peak of his considerable powers, it has nonetheless been regarded by all but a very few critics as a seriously flawed book or an outright mistake—proof that Melville was fast losing his grip.[1] Certainly there are reasons for its failure to generate a receptive audience: to some, the subject of incest was simply scandalous; to others, Melville's portrayal of what the *Literary World* called the "impracticability" of Christian virtue was (somehow) shockingly heterodox; and to still others, those sated on Carlyle or, in more recent years, nurtured on the leaner prose of modern writers, the book's swollen language and sometimes frenzied tone proved to be grossly overdone.[2] More fundamentally, I believe, *Pierre* has not been well received because it is a novel more deeply at odds with itself than readers are accustomed to encountering in a work of fiction. As its subtitle more than hints at, it is a novel that takes division—conflict, irresolution, ambiguity—as its subject.

Of course we all expect novels to contain conflicts and to reflect the author's uncertainties. But, deconstructionists excepted, we expect them also to move toward resolution and to be the product, finally, of a unified intention or vision. While Pierre more than satisfies the first of these expectations, what makes it an unusual, unlovable novel is that it refuses even to begin to meet the second. The spirit of perversity, of division, reigns everywhere. Yet this contrariness is precisely what makes *Pierre* one of the great heuristic novels in American literature. The perversity that rules over it has the potential for an

unusual kind of enlightenment, one that makes possible a reconception of our expectations about the nature of fiction, of the world we inhabit, and of ourselves as psychological beings.

That *Pierre* was written at cross-purposes with itself is apparent in many respects, but none of them is so striking as the fact of its contradictory form, acknowledged as such when Melville called it, with some irony, a "blasphemous rhapsody."[3] In action or plot, it is a tragic melodrama, a work designed to excite intense emotions of pity and fear, amazement and delight, and to *sell*—to compete with the wildly popular domestic novels of the day, such as Susan Warner's *The Wide, Wide World* (1850). As Melville explained in the controversial huckstering letter in which he rejected his British publisher's financial terms, "my new book [is] . . . very much more calculated for popularity than anything you have yet published of mine—being a regular romance, with a mysterious plot to it, & stirring passions at work, and withall, representing a new & elevated aspect of American life."[4] In its presentation of character, however, as his concluding qualification hinted, Melville's book was so unconventional and exacting as to be without precedent, a work designed to puzzle and, in an unexampled way, to educate the reader about the very emotions it aroused. Indeed, so "new & elevated" was Melville's portrayal of character in *Pierre* that in subtlety, complexity, precision, elusiveness, indeed, in what has come to be called psychological realism, nothing like it would appear in English until Henry James reached his mature phase with *The Portrait of a Lady* (1881).

Melville defined what was exceptional about his portrayal of Pierre and at the same time offered a statement of the novel's thesis, when at the opening of Book IV, "Retrospective," he issued a caveat to his assessment of the powerful effect of Isabel's extraordinary letter on his young protagonist. "In their precise tracings-out and subtle causations," he said, with the detachment of one recalling his own actions in a tempest, "the strongest and fiercest emotions of life defy all analytical insight." This is so, he explained, because "every motion of the heart" is the result of "an infinite series of infinitely involved and untraceable foregoing occurrences" that ultimately include one's whole history (67). However, he proceeded to show in the remainder of the novel that this is so also because the heart, which is as much in need of what will bring it earthly happiness as of what will bring it spiritual peace, is capable of conflict with itself and able to enlist the mind to rationalize forbidden desires, while promoting the cause of those more transcendental desires that might otherwise lose their urgency.

Pierre is the history of an irreparably divided self, its genesis and development, its vicissitudes and deconstruction; it is the story of a young man's

awakening to the ambiguity of his own motives and to the tragic consequences of his refusal to diminish himself by limiting his desires to one realm of life or another. But it is the story, too, of his discovery of the impenetrable ambiguity of the world he inhabits, of his beloved father's shadowy past and the mysterious Isabel's claim to be his sister, a discovery that so deepens his conflict as to result in a deadlock to be broken only by his suicide.[5]

Crucial as it is to our understanding of Melville's objectives, the ambiguity of Pierre's motives is not what Melville's readers over the past almost four decades have been led to believe it is, most notably by Dr. Henry A. Murray's well-known psychoanalytic discussion in his introduction to the Hendricks House edition of the novel. At the center of Murray's illuminating and important, yet now doctrinaire, reading of the book is his assertion that, contrary to virtually all previous critical accounts of the young protagonist's desire to come to Isabel's aid, "in Pierre's love for Isabel, Eros is fused with Agape, and, though largely unconscious, Eros, not Agape, is the determining factor."[6] Such a claim does more than reduce the complexities of human motivation to the needs of the sex drive; it also presumes the book's author to have provided certainty where Melville would have us recognize still more ambiguity.

Murray, in fact, sees irony, not ambiguity, as marking the novel's central turning point, when Pierre discovers that he has an erotic and not just a charitable interest in the woman who professes to be his sister. But there is ambiguity, too, at this juncture, not only about whether Pierre's sexual interest in this woman, who may or may not be his sister, is technically incestuous in nature, but about whether his carnal desire actually predates his benevolent motive and even whether his passion is truly paramount, and not just incidental, to his compassion—ambiguity, in short, about the *history* and relative strength of Pierre's erotic attraction to Isabel and about the extent of any rationalizing he may have been practicing to hide it from himself.

Furthermore, Murray and others who have examined Pierre's psychology have failed to recognize that the Eros-Agape distinction, now a critical commonplace in discussions of the book, does not cover the whole subject of Pierre's motivation. Complicating the picture further is a third motive, a third kind of love—namely, self-love, Pierre's desire for an identity that is worthy of his own self-regard. Most telling is the fact that, at the critical moments of his career, when he decides to abandon Lucy to help Isabel and, again in the end, when he chooses to take his own life, Pierre's ultimate concern is not whom he wants to *possess* or what he wants to *accomplish* but what he wants to *be*. It is possible, of course, that Pierre's desire to be one who is worthy of self-love could be just another of the mind's clever ploys for permitting the pursuit of unconscious

illicit desires, whether erotic or destructive. But I find no evidence to suggest that Melville thought he knew that it was. Instead, on this score he seems to have left his readers yet another seemingly impenetrable ambiguity to ponder.

Book I, "Pierre Just Emerging from His Teens," shows the young hero in the beginning of his story to be entirely at one with himself, his world, and his loved ones, enjoying the sort of bliss typically reserved for heroines in the early pages of popular domestic novels. When he and his beloved Lucy stand in the dewy morning "silently but ardently eying each other," they behold "mutual reflections of a boundless admiration and love" (4). For Pierre and his mother, "the pure joined current of life" flowed on "freely and lightsomely." Not yet, the narrator adds ominously, had "the fair river . . . borne its waves to those sideways repelling rocks, where it was thenceforth destined to be forever divided into two unmixing streams" (5). Born and nurtured in the country, Pierre was everywhere surrounded by beautiful scenes that were a perfect complement to his own poetic nature and whose more storied features all bore the names of the old Glendinning family line. In the opening section of the novel, therefore, Pierre experiences not even the slightest hint of trouble or alienation, either from the people who are important to him or from the place and time that constitute his lot in life. All is one.

However, even in this first book of *Pierre,* the seeds of the title character's division can be seen to have been sown, for Pierre was born into a divided culture and raised according to conflicting expectations. With pride in the Revolutionary War exploits of his illustrious ancestors, for example, comes personal pride, a high regard for the rich and promising character he has inherited. Yet Pierre's pride has been shaped also by his father's paradoxical ideal of the Christian male; he is expected to stand firm as "the complete polished steel of the gentleman" but "girded with Religion's silken sash." What his family background, education, and religious upbringing—the shaping influences of the nineteenth century's cult of domesticity—train him to be and do, in turn, is revealed in Pierre's acknowledgment that the only thing missing from his otherwise perfect life is a sister. "He mourned that so delicious a feeling as fraternal love had been denied him," an admission that reveals his unselfish desires as well as his selfish ones. He wants, he says, "some one whom I might love, and protect, and fight for, if need be," and he wants this because he wants honor and reputation for himself. "It must be a glorious thing to engage in a mortal quarrel on a sweet sister's behalf!" he exclaims at one point (6–7). Pierre wants to be one who can love himself for the heroic

actions he has performed in service to a defenseless sibling and for the praise, or self-congratulation, those actions will earn for him.

Mrs. Glendinning's soliloquy at the end of the first book aptly captures the conflicting expectations—to be self-regarding and self-forgetting; self-asserting and self-denying—that Pierre must live up to as he emerges into manhood, expectations that provide their own deconstructionist critique of the nineteenth-century male ideal of domesticity. "A noble boy, and docile," she says repeatedly after he has left her, thus revealing her own contradictory set of values. "Pray God, he never becomes otherwise to me." And then, lifting the historic baton that once belonged to one of Pierre's famous grandfathers, she puzzles to herself, "This is his inheritance—this symbol of command! and I swell out to think it. Yet but just now I fondled the conceit that Pierre was so sweetly docile! Here sure is a most strange inconsistency! For is sweet docility a general's badge? and is this baton but a distaff then?—Here's something widely wrong" (20).

That Mrs. Glendinning loves her son *almost* as much as she loves herself is suggested in her passing thought, "Now I almost wish him otherwise than sweet and docile to me, seeing that it must be hard for man to be an uncompromising hero and a commander among his race, and yet never ruffle any domestic brow." But that she herself, ultimately, has divided feelings is shown in the evasive way she prays to heaven that "he show his heroicness in some smooth way of favoring fortune." "Give him, O God, regardful gales!" she pleads. "Fan him with unwavering prosperities! So shall he remain all docility to me, and yet prove a haughty hero to the world!" (20). As the terms of Mrs. Glendinning's aside suggest, it is because Pierre tries to be both tractable to his mother and heroic to the world, both unoffending and righteous, that he is divided against himself. And because the split that these powerful demands force on him is irreconcileable, he eventually destroys himself.

Isabel's sudden shriek at the Miss Pennies' sewing circle upon the announcement of the arrival of Madam Glendinning and her son (a scene reminiscent of the "bee" in Warner's *The Wide, Wide World*) marks the transition from the potential to the actual bisecting of Pierre's self. "Though he saw not the person from whom it came, and though the voice was wholly strange to him, yet the sudden shriek seemed to split its way clean through his heart, and leave a yawning gap there" (45). Why Isabel's cry should have this sudden effect on Pierre is never explained. At the time it seems unprecedented and without cause.[7] But Pierre has been ripe with the potential for self-division for some time, and once the rent starts, it instantly runs its natural course. Given that Pierre had for some time before this entertained "ten thousand mailed thoughts

of heroicness . . . and glared round for some insulted good cause to defend" (14), it is evident that, when he heard Isabel's cry of distress, he was more than ready to respond, and, with the birth of his response, he immediately knew his heart to be at odds with itself in its love for Lucy.

It needs to be added that at this particular moment Pierre is more than usually susceptible to the supplications of almost any woman besides Lucy. Lucy, who has for some time been away from Saddle Meadows, has not yet returned for the summer, and so Pierre's ardor for her has had a chance to cool a bit. Moreover, his interest in the opposite sex generally had been showing signs of new vitality lately, even before he had heard Isabel's outburst. In fact, earlier in the day, he is said to be "cheered" by his mother's promise of seeing, among the sewing group that evening, "how many really pretty, and naturally-refined dames and girls [he] shall one day be lord of the manor of" (44–45).

When, then, Pierre sees Isabel's face for the first time at the Miss Pennies' gathering, he stands transfixed. As he confesses to his mother later that night, "never before in my whole existence, have I so completely gone wandering in my soul, as at that very moment" (48). What he sees in Isabel's face is the loveliness and loneliness, the beauty and anguish—in short, the doubleness—that mirrors the complex feelings he himself had carried to his chance encounter with her (46–47). For two days afterward, Pierre "wrestled with his own haunted spirit," and in the end he regained "the general mastery of himself," at least for a time (50). While occasionally he has stray thoughts of seeking out the owner of the phantom face to learn something more about her, he always manages to conquer such impulses. But he is not always able to exercise control over "the comings and goings of the face" in his own mind; sometimes "the old, original mystic tyranny would steal upon him" without bidding, on one occasion even compelling him to share his secret with his beloved Lucy. It is one of the novel's fundamental ambiguities, therefore, that Pierre's split is somehow both willed and fated, shaped by forces that cannot be precisely measured or defined (53–54).

Still, Pierre might have kept his division from deepening, or even possibly healed it, if he had been open and honest about his strange new feelings. An important sign of his growing division, however, is the little dishonesty he begins to practice when, as they walk home from the sewing circle, his mother questions him about his peculiar silence. "It is nothing—nothing, sister Mary; just nothing at all in the world. I believe I was dreaming—sleep-walking, or something of that sort," he says vaguely (48). In this peculiar statement of truth, which is also an evasion, Pierre hints at the awakening of a second self within him. Yet even before the two-day struggle that ends with his return to his "former self" (53), he registers annoyance at his prevarication while ad-

mitting puzzlement as to its cause. So removed does he become from the events that gave birth to his new self that he cannot understand the motive that led him not merely to hide his true feelings from his mother but, as he says, "to parry, nay, to evade, and, in effect, to return something alarmingly like a fib, to an explicit question put to him" by her (50).

Yet when Isabel's face suddenly returns to his imagination, Pierre's first thought is to grow secretive once more and go back to the Miss Pennies by himself to try to clear up the mystery. Only when he stops to realize that gossip about his visit would be sure to get back to his mother, thus putting an end to her belief in his "immaculate integrity," does he decide against such a course of action (52). Nonetheless, unable to free himself of the image of the phantom face, Pierre commits himself to finding out what he can about its owner, and in doing so he commits himself also to a life tainted with lies. When one night soon thereafter an obscure Diogenes-like figure with a lantern comes searching to deliver the letter that will call him to Isabel's aid, Pierre is not, therefore, the world's lone honest man that he once might have seemed (61).

Just as revealing of the split growing in Pierre early in the novel is the break with Lucy that occurs on the day they take the old phaeton into the hills near Saddle Meadows for a lovers' outing. There, on a day "mad with excessive joy" (35), after Pierre innocently promises her "all the immutable eternities of joyfulness, that ever woman dreamed of," Lucy confesses her premonition that Isabel's mysterious face will keep her from ever marrying him. When she asks him to explain the mystery for her by telling again the story of the face, Pierre instead makes a second grave mistake. Rather than trusting the infinite power of Love to see them through this crisis, as he had done earlier, he suddenly grows fearful and reverts to the un-Romantic assumption that Love is a finite commodity that needs to be jealously guarded. "Cursed be the hour I acted on the thought, that Love hath no reserves," he cries reproachfully. "Never should I have told thee the story of that face, Lucy. I have bared myself too much to thee. Oh, never should Love know all!" Lucy's reproving rejoinder, a speech remarkable for its Romantic faith, establishes her as the moral center of the novel, the Lucille or "light" of all truth, and reveals why Pierre should never permit himself to become alienated from her:

> *Knows not all, then loves not all,* Pierre. . . . Did I doubt thee here;—could I ever think, that thy heart hath yet one private nook or corner from me;— fatal disenchanting day for me, my Pierre, would that be. I tell thee, Pierre— and *'tis Love's own self that now speaks through me*—only in unbounded confidence and interchangings of all subtlest secrets, can Love possibly endure. Love's self is a secret, and so feeds on secrets, Pierre. Did I only

know of thee, what the whole common world may know—what then were Pierre to me?—Thou must be wholly a disclosed secret to me. . . . swear to me, dear Pierre, that thou wilt never keep a secret from me—no, never, never;—swear! (emphasis added)

Pierre's reply, which suggests that his behavior at this point is a baffling mix of fate and free will, reveals that he is already losing touch with Lucy, though it provides little explanation why: "Something seizes me. Thy inexplicable tears, falling, falling on my heart, have now turned it to a stone. I feel icy cold and hard; I will not swear!" And in response, Lucy twice cries Pierre's name, thus symbolizing that to her there are now two of him, and one of the two she does not know (37).

Returning from the hills to the plain, where he and Lucy "find peace, and love, and joy again," Pierre also returns to his former self, or so it seems (38). The two young lovers make plans for an evening of innocent pleasure together. But Pierre is not, in fact, fully restored to himself, or to her. When later that day he goes to Lucy's chamber to retrieve her blue portfolio of pencil sketches, he sees the reflection of Lucy's snow-white bed in the mirror. "For one swift instant, he seemed to see in that one glance the two separate beds— the real one and the reflected one—and an unbidden, most miserable presentiment thereupon stole into him" (39). What is captured in this frozen moment is the suggestion that Pierre has begun to develop an anxious, debilitating capacity for apperception. For in gaining the capacity to look at the world with a divided will, he has acquired the ability to see what is not there as well as what is, as in this scene where he is suddenly able to imagine the possibility of never sharing Lucy's bed, at the same time he dreams about the time when he will do so.

Soon thereafter, as Pierre leaves Lucy's cottage with the intention of returning later that evening, his split grows clearer still; "the sweet chamber scene abandoned him" and, by what appears to be an instance of unconscious transference, Isabel's "mystical face recurred to him, and kept with him" (40). Then, finding his own house empty, he is said to wander away "in reveries" down to the nearby riverbank, where the image of Isabel's face returns to him in the lone pine tree there. Here, in the novel's longest soliloquy, Pierre reveals his growing vacillation—his fear of the grief that can mature the heart and his growing pleasure at the prospect of this same grief, his wariness of the misery he knows to anticipate from Isabel's claims on him, and his unconscious desire for her to love him ("Surely, thou lovest not me?" he asks of the image disingenuously [41]).

Yet when the face disappears, Pierre feels joy again and swears that if he is ever deprived of the bliss of loving his dear Lucy, "I feel I should find cause for deadly feuds with things invisible" (41). When he has a premonition of the bitter, wintry future that fate has in store for him if he were to pursue an alliance with Isabel, he suddenly asserts himself, arguing that after all he at least has some control over the comings and goings of the face, even though clearly he does not want to abandon it entirely.

> Now, then, I'll up with my own joyful will; and with my joy's face scare away all phantoms:—so, they go: and Pierre is Joy's, and Life's again. Thou pine-tree!—henceforth I will resist thy too treacherous persuasiveness. *Thou'lt not so often woo me to thy airy tent,* to ponder on the gloomy rooted stakes that bind it. Hence now I go; and peace be with thee, pine! That blessed sereneness which lurks ever at the heart of sadness—mere sadness—and remains when all the rest has gone;—that sweet feeling is now mine, and cheaply mine. I am not sorry I was sad, I feel so blessed now. (emphasis added)

Immediately switching, however, to the opposing side in what fast becomes an ongoing debate with himself, Pierre thinks of his "dearest" Lucy once again and of the "pretty time" they will have together that evening (42). The attractions of the dark lady and the light, standard figures in the domestic novel of this period, are made to compete with one another repeatedly in *Pierre*, but in Melville's hands they do so in a way that emphasizes the hero's growing psychological rift.

Once the face vanishes from sight, Pierre is left alone "with his soul's joy"— significantly, this occurs as the sun goes down—and the prospect of formally proposing marriage to Lucy before the day is through (60–61). His feeling of happiness, invariably associated with Lucy, is the major sign that Pierre is for the moment at one with himself. However, that evening, while en route to Lucy's, he is intercepted by the messenger carrying Isabel's letter, and the whole future course of his life is changed as a consequence. Even so, it is important to note that Pierre's big transformation occurs before he knows it was Isabel who had sent the letter or even before he knows the incriminating story it contains.

Initially assuming he would continue on to Lucy's and wait to read the message afterward, Pierre suddenly feels his resolve melt away when he touches the knocker on the cottage door and discovers that its "sudden coolness caused a slight, and, at any other time, an unaccountable sympathetic sensation in his hand" that warns him to stop and go back to read the mysterious letter. With

this masterstroke of psychological realism, Melville captures his hero's change-ability and suggests that human fate sometimes hangs from the thinnest thread imaginable. "Yielding now," we are told, "half alarmed, and half bantering with himself, to these shadowy interior monitions, he half-unconsciously quitted the door; repassed the gate; and soon found himself retracing his homeward path" (62). It is a moment when Pierre reacts almost automatically, as one possessed, but the presence of some consciousness on his part makes his motives so ambiguous as to be impenetrable. However, that he has become not simply divided but *changed,* that he has turned a corner in his development, moving from one personality to another, is clear from the evidence of his own reactions, particularly the act of extinguishing the "light" (always in this book associated with Lucy) in his heart, and from the strange new look on his face.

Returning to his room and there lighting a lamp, Pierre is startled, in a scene reminiscent of Poe's "William Wilson," to see the image of his "double" in the mirror. "It bore the outline of Pierre, but now strangely filled with features transformed, and unfamiliar to him." Still, the change he has undergone is hardly complete. Even before he has so much as glanced at the superscription on the letter, Pierre contemplates destroying it—that way foreclosing the possibility of any further development of his emerging self—only to discover that he has already unconsciously torn the note in two. In still another about-face, then, which shows his self-division to be growing, Pierre feels shame for "the first time in his whole life," for the selfishness of this unconscious act that would protect his future happiness with Lucy (62–63).

Melville's description of Pierre's internal debate over whether or not to open the torn letter indicates that the dilemma for Pierre does not involve an illicit erotic interest in Isabel—at least not yet. Even before he knows the gender of the author of the letter, not to mention her identity, Pierre defines his dilemma in purely ethical terms, weighing what is selfish or narrowly self-interested on the one hand, namely, the prospect of a life of happiness with Lucy, against what is selfless or "manly" on the other, that is, the responsibility to do the noble thing regardless of the consequences to himself. In short, he defines the problem confronting him in terms of a divided self, with an Ur-self serving as arbiter in the conflict between the two sides:

> Pierre now seemed distinctly to feel two antagonistic agencies within him;
> one of which was just struggling into his consciousness, and each of which
> was striving for the mastery; and between whose respective final ascen-
> dencies, he thought he could perceive, though but shadowly, that he him-
> self was to be the only umpire. One bade him finish the selfish destruction
> of the note; for in some dark way the reading of it would irretrievably

entangle his fate. The other bade him dismiss all misgivings; not because there was no possible ground for them, but because to dismiss them was the manlier part, never mind what might betide. This good angel seemed mildly to say—Read, Pierre, though by reading thou may'st entangle thy- self, yet may'st thou thereby disentangle others. Read, and feel that best blessedness which, with the sense of all duties discharged, holds happiness indifferent. The bad angel insinuatingly breathed—Read it not, dearest Pierre; but destroy it, and be happy. Then, at the blast of his noble heart, the bad angel shrunk up into nothingness; and the good one defined itself clearer and more clear, and came nigher and more nigh to him, smiling sadly but benignantly; while forth from the infinite distances wonderful harmonies stole into his heart; so that every vein in him pulsed to some heavenly swell. (63)

Yet what Pierre defines as a conflict between selfishness and selflessness can be seen, in this passage, to be a more puzzling and treacherous conflict still— an antagonism between two kinds of selfish desires, a yearning for happiness, which Pierre always links with Lucy, and a longing for blessedness, which he comes to link always with Isabel.[8] Short of death, Melville seems to say, there is no escape from the self, not even in "selfless" acts of moral uprightness.[9]

After Pierre reads the letter in which Isabel impugns his father's reputation and claims herself to be Pierre's illegitimate half-sister, he sits motionless like a wounded man, holding the note as one who has been stabbed to the heart would hold the dagger "in the wound, to stanch the outgushing of the blood." He is now fatally divided, "hurt with a wound," as the narrator explains, "never to be completely healed but in heaven." Now that his father seems to him no more a saint, Pierre finds "the before undistrusted moral beauty of the world is forever fled." Staggering to his feet, he thus swears, like the speaker in Emerson's "Each and All," not to devote himself to deceitful Beauty but to follow only Truth—"glad Truth, or sad Truth; I will know what *is*, and do what my deepest angel dictates." Immediately contradicting this vow, however, he brashly exclaims the letter to be a forgery, only to reverse himself again when new suspicions beset him. Soon losing himself in a mental darkness, which is mirrored in the darkness of the night, Pierre moves almost inexorably from a mood of speculation to a feeling of certainty that Fate has singled him out for special disillusionment, when he begins to sense he has been personally wronged, that his sense of pride, of selfhood, has been deeply injured.

At the end of this long soliloquy, Pierre impulsively completes his reversal when he concludes that "nothing but Truth" could have moved him as he was moved by the conviction that he has been cheated, and on that slight basis he

swears his faith that the letter is *not* a forgery. "Oh! Isabel, thou art my sister; and I will love thee, and protect thee, ay, and own thee through all. Ah! forgive me, ye heavens, for my ignorant ravings, and accept this my vow.—Here I swear myself Isabel's" (65–66). Mistakenly trusting the force of his feelings as the only test of what is true, Pierre, a true example of the youthful Romantic, here willfully turns an ambiguity into a certainty, and thus *perhaps* deceives himself in assuming that the claims in Isabel's letter are genuine. It is a crucial misjudgment, for all his subsequent actions are predicated on this assumption of the truth of what is, in fact, ambiguous.

Pierre is typical of Melville's autobiographical protagonists in that he is quick to feel injury, and quick, too, to react nobly, even suicidally, as he tries to maintain his lofty image of himself. "Sweet Isabel!" he exclaims rhetorically, "would I not be baser than brass, and harder, and colder than ice, if I could be insensible to such claims as thine? . . . God demands me for thy comforter; and comfort thee, stand by thee, and fight for thee, will thy leapingly-acknowledging brother" (65–66). Pierre, however, is an unusual figure among Melville's heroes because, lacking any knowledge of the authenticity of Isabel's claims, he never knows for sure whether he has suffered an actual wound or only an imagined one. No other character in Melville's fiction is obliged to struggle with such profound ambiguity.

In this first crisis, then, Pierre is confronted with several difficult choices, and he fully appreciates their dual claims on him: to open the letter or destroy it; to believe the story it tells or reject it; to assume the duties of a brother or refuse them. Although in each instance he makes a decision that takes him along a single path, he continues to feel the lure, too, of the option he had rejected. Thus, choose though he does at each turn, the intensity of his desire to resolve the agonies of his self-division makes him like Agnello in Dante's *Inferno*, "not double now, / Nor only one!" (85). The ambiguities of his situation, of the world he inhabits, remain painfully alive to him.

The next section, Book IV, "Retrospective," serves not to validate Isabel's claim on Pierre's conscience but simply to provide "some random hints" as to why he believes her claims to be true and why, once he comes to believe those claims, the letter throws him into such a "tumultuous mood" (68). Subtly and carefully, Melville has laced with ambiguity each of the four principal pieces of evidence that Pierre dredges up from his childhood in support of his father's alleged connection with Isabel. Thus, while the material grounds, when lumped together, *seem* condemning of Pierre's father, the proof is still all purely circumstantial. Pierre's father's feverish deathbed ramblings—when little Pierre himself had heard him call "My daughter! my daughter!"—might have been the eleventh-hour confession of a guilt-wracked conscience. But they might

also have been nothing more than the delirious murmurings of a dying man, what the attending nurse calls signs of "that mysterious thing in the soul, which ... will still dream horrid dreams, and mutter unmentionable thoughts" in spite of the dreamer's innocence (70–71). So, too, the chair-portrait showing Pierre's father to be a "fine-looking, gay-hearted, youthful gentleman," an early likeness that Pierre's mother "could never abide," might contain a precise image of the man when he was said to be "secretly in love with the French young lady" recently emigrated to America. But it might also be nothing more than a "fancypiece," a willful projection of the artist, uncle Ralph Winwood, who, it is said, was "one of those who a little fancied that [Pierre's] father was courting her" (72, 76–77).

A third piece of evidence, the suspicions of Aunt Dorothea about the affair, might be well-founded; it might be true, as she believes, that Pierre's father had been wooing the beautiful young noblewoman who, falling on hard times during the French Revolution, had been forced to emigrate and then mysteriously disappeared. But it might be true instead, as at one point it is suggested, that he simply "made her acquaintance; and with many other humane gentlemen of the city, provided for the wants" of the young woman and several other poor strangers (75–76). And finally, Mrs. Glendinning's distaste for the clandestine portrait of her husband might stem from her intuition that "the glance of the face in the portrait, is not, in some nameless way, dedicated to herself, but to some other and unknown object" (82). However, it might also stem simply from unfounded jealousy, a paranoiac insecurity such as she demonstrates when Pierre leaves home to help Isabel.

Because all of these incriminating pieces of evidence are ambiguous, and for other reasons as well, Pierre's father is an ambiguous figure. It is possible that he was always an honest, integrated personality, a paragon of virtue. But the reader's lasting impression of him is of a man as divided as Pierre himself—secretive, duplicitous, perhaps even corrupt. This impression, however, is just that, an impression. Because he is dead when the story begins and never appears on stage, we can never make our own firsthand assessment of the elder Glendinning's character. Instead, he is always presented through the eyes of others, characters who are themselves typically divided or who show evidences of duplicity in their own conduct, as cousin Ralph the artist does when he is said to have "slyly picked" Pierre's father's portrait. We cannot, finally, know whether the suspicion of the elder Glendinning's dualism is merited or not, the product, possibly, of nothing more than the prejudicial coloring of other characters. We learn, for instance, in Book IV that Pierre had experienced a growing split regarding his father at "about the period of adolescence"—that is, following latency, when a young boy's rivalry with his

father typically gains momentum—when he first tried to explain to himself his mother's dislike for the chair-portrait (82).

When Pierre imagines the portrait speaking the following words to him, therefore, it could be that he is shrewdly putting together several stray pieces of evidence in such a way as to see his father's doubleness for what it is. But it could also be that he is merely projecting onto the painting his own adolescent turmoil—the deep-seated struggle to displace the father, the longing to enjoy the mother without competition, and, most insidious of all, the awakening to doubt that characterizes the late phases of youth:

> —Pierre, believe not the drawing-room painting; that is not thy father; or, at least, is not *all* of thy father. Consider in thy mind, Pierre, whether we two paintings may not make only one. . . . Look again, I am thy father as he more truly was. In mature life, the world overlays and varnishes us, Pierre; the thousand proprieties and polished finenesses and grimaces intervene, Pierre; then, we, as it were, abdicate ourselves, and take unto us another self, Pierre; in youth we *are*, Pierre, but in age we *seem*. (83)

It is clear, of course, that Pierre's father "had long stood a shrine," as Melville says, in the young boy's heart (68). But critics have failed to recognize that Pierre also has reason to hurt his father or to see him as being unworthy of *his* love. While on his deathbed, the elder Glendinning had feverishly cried out for his "daughter" but had failed to call out for little Pierre. This failure was sorely felt by the boy, who desperately tried to gain the dying man's attention. When his unresponsive father again called for his "daughter," the little boy "snatched the dying man's hand," and though "it faintly grew to his grasp," the other hand "now also emptily lifted itself, and emptily caught, as if at some other childish fingers" (70–71). In this poignant scene of the father's seeming rejection of the young boy, Melville thus provides Pierre with a powerful motive to injure, even destroy, the memory of his father. The existence of such a motive complicates the Freudian view that Pierre's decision to go to Isabel's aid is prompted simply by the youth's anima fixation or erotic attachment to her. So severely divided is Melville's young hero that in choosing to believe Isabel's story—try though he does, on the one hand, to preserve his father's immaculate reputation by keeping her alleged paternity a secret—he may, on the other hand, be acting out of a deeply repressed desire to add fuel to the fire that would consume his father's good name.

The question of unconscious motives aside, the fact remains that Pierre has deeply felt conscious motives, too, for coming to Isabel's aid, and these have nothing to do with any sexual attraction he might feel toward her. As the nar-

rator observes, once the young hero has regained his calm after reading Isabel's heart-wounding letter, the confounding question for Pierre was not "*What must I do!*" but "*How* must I do it?" Spontaneously, he knew "the direct point he must aim at"—namely, to do the thing of greatest "difficulty" for himself, the thing of greatest cost to his own interests (87–88). He is determined to do the moral thing. Even when he begins to consider the woeful impact that his momentous decision will have on Lucy, it is his fear of succumbing to purely selfish desires—"his last hopes of common happiness" with her—that is finally decisive in his effort to put all thought of Lucy out of his mind.

The question uppermost in his mind at this juncture is "how could he insure himself against the insidious inroads of self-interest, and hold intact all his unselfish magnanimities, if once he should permit the distracting thought of Lucy to dispute with Isabel's the pervading possession of his soul?" Deciding, therefore, to scorn "all personal relationship" and hold all "his heart's dearest interests for naught," Pierre would in effect attempt to transcend himself, to escape his earthly nature. Such is the paradox of the selfless self promulgated in the New Testament. It is in this context that we can best appreciate Pierre's overall effort to become "the Enthusiast to Duty," that rare exemplar in whom, as the narrator explains, "the heaven-begotten Christ is born" (106).

It is one of the book's supreme ironies, then, that on the very next page Pierre is said to feel convinced that Isabel's "womanly beauty, and not womanly ugliness, invited him to champion the right" (107). For what Pierre takes as confirmation of his choosing the right course in aiding Isabel, the narrator suggests, is in fact a sign of Pierre's "clay," though, to be precise, it should be recognized that it is a sign of *both* of these things. The young hero's eagerness regarding the added inducement of Isabel's physical charms does not negate his Christ-like motive; it simply makes his motives ambiguous or double. When the narrator says of Pierre that, "though charged with the fire of all divineness, his containing thing was made of clay," he is not arguing that Pierre is all clay and his divineness entirely an illusion. He is not even arguing, as the novel's Freudian critics do, that the forces that make up the hero's "clay" are the dominant ones. What he asserts is that Pierre is of two natures, each in conflict with the other. Part flesh and part spirit, he is deeply, irremediably divided. Struggle though he does with all his might to be "immaculate" in all his actions, Pierre is still susceptible "to the inevitable nature and lot of common men" (107–08). But the fact that he will fail at his intentions does not deny that he is engaged in the profoundly human struggle to achieve the divinity, the self-transcendence, he imagines for himself.

The ambiguities of Pierre's situation grow more complicated when he stops to consider whether to tell his mother about the allegations in Isabel's letter

and his own determination to help Isabel. For at that point, having an "electric insight" into his mother's true character, he sees her doubleness, and something of the doubleness of the world generally. He cannot confide in his mother, he suddenly realizes, because she does not love him "with the love past all understanding"—the kind of love that Lucy will show she has for him. Mrs. Glendinning's heart is divided, her love for Pierre warring with her "immense pride;—her pride of birth, her pride of affluence, her pride of purity, and all the pride of high-born, refined, and wealthy Life, and all the Semiramian pride of woman." Indeed, as he continues to think about it, he sees that even what he had always regarded as his mother's love for him shows signs of her own self-love, of her narcissism. "Me she loveth with pride's love," he observes to himself, thinking back to her early happiness with him; "in me she thinks she seeth her own curled and haughty beauty; before my glass she stands,—pride's priestess—and to her mirrored image, not to me, she offers up her offerings of kisses" (88–90).

When Pierre returns to the house at Saddle Meadows, therefore, following the Walpurgis Night of his soul, he has already decided against telling his mother the "infernal" truth about his father. She, in turn, immediately perceives in her son's haggardness the symptom of some inner turmoil and rushes to comfort him. In their embrace, however, "Pierre miserably felt that their two hearts beat not together in such unison as before" (95). Now dropping her playful role as Pierre's "sister," Mrs. Glendinning assumes the role of a genuinely protective parent, and for one brief moment she becomes a sympathetic figure.

Ironically, at the same time, Mrs. Glendinning feels her effort at motherliness to be wholly frustrated as she detects in Pierre a determination to hide from her whatever is troubling him. Thinking back to the night before when her son had shown himself to be strangely preoccupied while on their way back from the Miss Pennies', she entreats Pierre not to withhold any confidence from her. "It may prove a fatal thing. Can that be good and virtuous, Pierre, which shrinks from a mother's knowledge? Let us not loose hands so, Pierre; thy confidence from me, mine goes from thee," and with these last words she shows that, like Lucy, she, too, understands why love can suffer no secret (96).

For his part, Pierre is clearly of two minds on the matter of whether to reveal his secret to his mother—"Mother, stay!—yes, do, sister," he says confusedly, when she asks if he is ready to have her put an end to their conversation by summoning the butler (96). But ultimately he cannot bring himself to confide in her. When, then, she summons the servant, the time-serving Dates enters to announce the arrival of the Reverend Falsgrave, the fawning minister whose presence signals the new falsity in Pierre's relationship with

his mother. Once divided within their hearts toward one another, Pierre and
his mother have now become openly divided against each other as well.

The next morning at breakfast, after Pierre has heard the first part of Isabel's story, he acknowledges his mother's anxiety about his welfare but accuses her of letting her pride mask how "deeply offended" she is by his behavior (129–30). For his part, however, he will not speak openly about the dramatic change he has undergone during the previous night. Soon after Pierre's hasty exit, we learn that Mrs. Glendinning has been false to her son in still another way, hiding from him the fact that she, too, had seen something "most surprising" in Isabel's face on the night of the sewing circle. What is just as important, we learn that her self-division, like her son's, seems fated by her nature even as she wills it. And, in the end, her self-division is just as impossible to mend: "Sometimes I have feared that my pride would work me some woe incurable," she extemporizes, "by closing both my lips, and varnishing all my front, where I perhaps ought to be wholly in the melted and invoking mood. But who can get at one's own heart, to mend it? Right one's self against another, that, one may sometimes do; but *when that other is one's own self,* these ribs forbid. Then I will live my nature out. I will stand on pride. I will not budge" (131; emphasis added).

The evidence supporting Isabel's claim to the Glendinning name, as presented in her two-part story, seems to fit, as a hand a glove, the facts of Pierre's father's early lifestory, which the boy dredges up from memory in Book IV, "Retrospective." However, the fit may be purely a matter of coincidence, like the "coincidence" of Pierre's going to meet Isabel, in order to learn her story, at the Ulver farm, where a parallel case of illegitimate birth has just recently been unfolding (111). As Pierre himself recognizes after hearing the first part of the "mystery" of Isabel, the fact of her being his sister, though "intuitively certain," was "literally unproven" (139). And it remains unproven even after the second interview.

Still, it is symbolically significant that Isabel's story is divided into two parts and that she tells her tale in what is identified as "the room of the double casement" window. For like virtually everything else in this novel, it is two-sided, susceptible of conflicting interpretations. It is possible that her whole story is make-believe, an elaborate scheme or con game, like some of the apparent con games in *The Confidence-Man*, designed to gain a portion of the Glendinning wealth. To cite just one source of suspicion, Isabel's gestures often have a studied theatricality about them, such as when she asks Pierre to feel the hardness of her hand after she has explained how "poor Bell" came to work in the neighborhood of Saddle Meadows as a seamstress (154).

Yet even assuming the honesty of her intentions, it is quite possible, given her mental abstraction much of the time, that her story is simply the product of craziness, a fabrication—based on bits and pieces of information overheard here and there in the vicinity of Saddle Meadows—of a highly susceptible, associative imagination. The closest thing to a hard piece of evidence that Isabel has to offer is a handkerchief embroidered with the name of "Glendinning," or so she claims. Yet, strange to say, Pierre *never* sees it, and neither do we. As in *Othello,* so here, the handkerchief may be nothing more than the clever device of a scheming third party, concocted for the purpose of convicting an innocent person of a wholly imaginary sexual misdeed. Moreover, the name "Glendinning," which Isabel asserts to be embroidered on the corner, could just as well have been the first name of the mysterious gentleman of her story as his last, just as it is the first name of Pierre's young cousin, Glendinning Stanly.[10] Yet no critic has ever raised any questions about the matter; all seem simply to have assumed that the handkerchief existed, that it was in fact embroidered with the name of Glendinning, that Glendinning was its owner's surname, and that it belonged to Pierre's father.

It is typical of Melville's young protagonist that he would himself simply "surmise," and not seek some evidence to corroborate, the validity of Isabel's tale regarding the identity of her father, for this makes possible an extraordinary opportunity for himself to become the "heroic man." Pierre consciously decides not to pry any further into Isabel's claims by "craftily interrogating" his father's remaining relatives, for instance, because to do so "would only serve the more hopelessly to cripple him in his practical resolves" (141). He wishes to repress the cautious, introverted, Hamlet side of himself and let loose the enthusiastic, extroverted, Memnon side. Though he recognizes that his meditativeness has given him the knowledge of "Gloom and Grief . . . that an heroic man should learn," he at this point feels "all meditation is worthless, unless it prompt to action" (169).

Following his second interview with Isabel and some fitful rereading of the *Inferno* and *Hamlet,* Pierre chides himself as "a skulking coward" for failing to make public acknowledgment that Isabel is his sister and, further, for permitting his mother to "grow tall and hector over him." "Did he, or did he not vitally mean to do this thing?" he challenges himself. "Was the immense stuff to do it his, or was it not his?" Then, for the first time realizing that his resolution to acknowledge Isabel and his determination to keep her existence a secret from his mother are "impossible adjuncts," he heaps scorn on himself as a "Fool and coward! Coward and fool!"; an "unaccountable infatuate!"; a "blind grub"; and more. Desperately struggling to be a man who can love himself for his deeds of heroic charity, he turns on himself with fu-

rious self-hatred for the shortsightedness that makes him, he believes, but a common man after all. The end of Book IX rises to a fevered pitch, as we are told that "The cheeks of his soul collapsed in him: he dashed himself in blind fury and swift madness against the wall, and fell dabbling in the vomit of his loathed identity" (170–71).

Pierre's determined desire to escape his hated self—the side of him that is young and commonplace, prone to commit mistakes in understanding and judgment—is mainly what lies behind his decision, at the start of Book X, to feign marriage with Isabel as a way of hiding what he takes to be his true blood-tie with her. Though he wakes the next morning "with the foretaste of what then seemed to him a planned and perfect Future," he is not aware that, as before, the lie he would fabricate in an effort to resolve his conflicting de-sires has the consequence of deepening his division. More than anything else, what blinds him to the true consequences of his plan is what he takes to be the most "wonderful" thing about it, namely, "its unequaled renunciation of himself" (172). Like the idealist Hollingsworth in Hawthorne's *The Blithedale Romance* (1852), Pierre would attempt to stand before the world a perfectly selfless man, one dedicated absolutely to the service of others yet blind to the fact that any such effort runs the risk of being purely selfish in motive.

Melville understood that human action can have its origin not simply in one's conscious intentions or unconscious will but also in one's effort to achieve a particular kind of identity or image of one's self. Even the most self-renouncing people will behave selfishly if they believe a given action will bring the satisfaction of knowing they are living up to their identity ideal. Thus, we are told, the idea that Pierre's father's good reputation could only be preserved by the son's "free sacrifice" of all his own earthly happiness "but struck a still loftier chord in the bosom of the son, and filled him with infinite magnanimities" (177).

Determined as Pierre seems to be at this point to follow his chosen path, it soon becomes evident that the divided self, in Melville's conception, is never more than momentarily free of conflict. Struggling to set in motion his reso-lution to become Isabel's protector, Pierre shows himself to possess one of those hearts that, "during the tyranny of a usurper mood," as Melville care-fully explains, are "all eagerness to cast off the most intense beloved bond, as a hindrance to the attainment of whatever transcendental object that usurper mood so tyrannically suggests." In such moods, we deny our humanity; we think we have become "as immortal bachelors and gods." But "like the Greek gods themselves," Melville adds ominously, "prone we descend to earth; glad to be uxorious once more; glad to hide these god-like heads within the bo-soms made of too-seducing clay" (180). Thus Pierre now proves himself an

example of a vulnerable god. Hardly does he get on his feet again, confident that "all the horizon of his dark fate was commanded by him; all his resolutions clearly defined, and immovably decreed," when suddenly there "slid into his inmost heart the living and breathing form of Lucy." Then, cast down and aghast once more, Pierre felt that, "for the time, all minor things were whelmed in him; his mother, Isabel, the whole wide world; and one only thing remained to him;—this all-including query—Lucy or God?" (181) As this stark formulation of Pierre's dilemma suggests, Melville's hero comes to feel, at the major turning point of his life, that his choice is not between two women, Lucy or Isabel, but between two sides of himself, two versions of his identity—the earthly side that wants only the happiness of a life of love with Lucy and the spiritual side that wants only the blessedness of a life of godlike virtue.

Pierre's decision to choose "God" rather than "Lucy" falls exactly in the middle of the book. While the first half of *Pierre* presents a carefully detailed study of the complex motives and mental processes leading up to the young hero's resolution to simulate marriage with Isabel, the second half presents an equally detailed study of the complex motives and mental processes leading away from that resolution—the souring and final reversal of it. As a novel of psychological development, therefore, *Pierre* can be seen to have a perfectly parabolic structure that belies the many critical complaints about its formal weakness or failure.[11]

Immediately following Pierre's decision to enter into a mock marriage with Isabel (at the end of Book X), Melville introduces an important ambiguity that subverts the implication that Pierre had made a free choice in the matter. Book XI opens with the image, borrowed from Edwards's *Freedom of the Will*, of a row of billiard balls, an analogy meant to stand, Melville says, for the "long previous generations, whether of births or thoughts," through which "Fate strikes the present man" or the ball at the end. "Idly he disowns the blow's effect, because he felt no blow, and indeed, received no blow. But Pierre was not arguing Fixed Fate and Free Will, now," he explains; "Fixed Fate and Free Will were arguing him, and Fixed Fate got the better in the debate" (182). Then, in Book XII, Pierre experiences the "terrible self-revelation" of his sexual attraction to Isabel, a discovery that calls into question the purity of his motives for wanting to help her (192). Finally, in Book XIV, following a short book concerning his preparations for leaving Saddle Meadows, Pierre happens on Plinlimmon's pamphlet, which argues the foolish impracticality of the kind of self-sacrificing decision Pierre has just committed himself to. Thus, in quick succession, the young hero's resolution is undermined, or made

ambiguous, by the introduction of three issues: Was his decision free? Was his
motive pure? Was his action right?

Pierre begins his protracted fall from grace at the opening of Book XIV when, entering the coach that will take him and his companions to the city where all hearts seem to have grown hard, he "instinctively clutched" the crumpled leaves of the pamphlet that had been discarded there. As if to suggest that Pierre was already becoming disunited with himself again and unconsciously seeking some way to overturn his resolve, Melville observes that "the same *strange clutching mood of his soul which had prompted that instinctive act,* did also prevail in causing him now to retain the crumpled paper in his hand for an hour or more" of their early morning ride without even looking at it (205; emphasis added). While Pierre sits clutching it in his hand, seemingly absorbing its impious message through osmosis, his "thoughts were very dark and wild; for a space there was rebellion and horrid anarchy and infidelity in his soul." It was as if the Evil One himself, Melville suggests, had proposed to him "the possibility of the mere moonshine of all his self-renouncing Enthusiasm. The Evil One hooted at him, and called him a fool," as Pierre imagines Plinlimmon himself to do later from his window as he looks down on the young man's apartments (205). In this richly ironic scene, Melville hints that Plotinus Plinlimmon—author of the lecture on "Chronometricals and Horologicals" that pretends to explain why the moral doctrine of Christianity is "entirely impracticable"—is the Devil incarnate (215).[12] Although the point is made more than once that when Pierre came to read the pamphlet he thought he had failed to comprehend its curious central conceit, we are told also, with typical equivocation, that in the end Pierre may not be "entirely uninfluenced in his conduct by the torn pamphlet, when afterwards perhaps by other means he shall come to understand it; or, peradventure, come to know that he, in the first place, did" (209–10). In this strange world, where ambiguities are so abundant, it is possible for a person to know a thing, Melville suggests, and not know that he or she knows it.

It is significant of Melville's intention to portray Pierre as a type of the divided self within us all that, in introducing Plinlimmon's pamphlet, he places Pierre's effort at self-sacrifice in the context of nearly nineteen centuries of Christian history. Here Pierre is made an example of all "earnest-loving youths" who come, at the period of consciousness, to discover the startling contradiction that "while, as the grand condition of acceptance to God, Christianity calls upon all men to renounce this world; yet by all odds the most Mammonish part of this world—Europe and America—are owned by none but professed Christian nations, who glory in the owning, and seem to have some reason therefor" (207). It is hardly an exaggeration to say that all of Western

culture is as deeply divided as its more conscious members such as Pierre. This is as true today, according to Jung, as it was in Melville's time, for "disunity with oneself is the hall-mark of the civilized man." "Self-division," as Jung explains, "is intimately bound up with the problem of our time and really represents an unsuccessful attempt on the part of the individual to solve the general problem in his own person."[13]

When an "earnest youth" such as Pierre, argues Melville, turns from a fresh reading of the Sermon on the Mount to view the world he has been living in, he finds instantly that "an overpowering sense of the world's downright positive falsity comes over him; the world seems to lie saturated and soaking with lies." Because the routine practices of this world differ so radically from Christ's ethical teachings, such a youth necessarily finds himself divided in his desires. "Hereupon then in the soul of the enthusiast youth two armies come to the shock," Melville says, recapitulating the thesis of his novel; "and unless he prove recreant, or unless he prove gullible, or unless he can find the talismanic secret, to reconcile this world with his own soul, then there is no peace for him, no slightest truce for him in this life." He will remain divided as long as he has consciousness. For consciousness, Melville recognized, means division. The only way one can escape the grievous sense of self-division is to deny one or the other set of conflicting claims on the self—that is, to become, in an absolute sense, a worldly pragmatist (one who is "recreant") or an unworldly innocent (one who is "gullible") (208).

As for the third alternative, that of finding the "talismanic secret" that would reconcile the opposing claims of the self, Melville says emphatically that it "has never yet been found; and in the nature of human things it seems as though it never can be" (208). Plato, Spinoza, Goethe, and other worthies have tried; but according to the very sternest tests, none has succeeded. Unlike the Emerson of *Nature* or even of the more somber "Fate," Melville saw no hope at the time he wrote *Pierre* for making a monism out of a philosophical dualism, of reconciling the world with one's own soul.

Although *Pierre*'s critics have expressed little doubt about the meaning of Plinlimmon's pamphlet, they have carried on a lengthy, sometimes heated debate about Melville's own attitude toward it, and hence about its place in the novel. Judging from the narrator's preliminary remarks, however, the pamphlet did not have—indeed, could not have had—Melville's unqualified support, even though it contains enough good sense, or what passes for such, for him to have assented to certain sentiments in it. Despite the fact that Plinlimmon admits by way of preamble that all human wisdom is "provisional," he writes, and lives, as though he had in fact found the "talismanic secret" (211). Such caveats notwithstanding, he is wonderfully at peace with himself.

Though hardly a Neoplatonist, like his namesake Plotinus, Plinlimmon can be said, ironically, to belong to that very "guild of self-impostors" he condemns for pretending to have got "a Voice out of Silence" (208). For, without any proof in the matter, he claims to know the Creator's mind. He presumes to know, for example, that God occasionally sends "a heavenly chronometer" into the world for the purpose of giving "the lie to all the world's time-keepers" (212). More importantly, he professes to know that a virtuous expediency "is the only earthly excellence that their Creator intended" for most people to follow (214).

Yet despite a few limited concessions to the demands of conscience—advising, for instance, that one should give "with a certain *self-considerate* generosity to the poor"—Plinlimmon has escaped the trials of self-division by advocating a purely self-protective, purely "recreant" ethic, one that shows regard for others only insofar as it is convenient or advantageous to oneself (emphasis added). As Plinlimmon declares, man's "mere instinct for his everyday general well-being" will instruct him to make "certain minor self-renunciations" in his interactions with other people (214). That is to say, Plinlimmon is nothing more than a subtle kind of horologue, one who advocates a policy of moderate self-denial as a way of easing one's conscience about his own selfishness and not as a means of benefiting other human beings. The reason, then, that the author of the pamphlet is later seen to have a repelling look of "non-Benevolence" about him is plain: there is nothing benevolent about him (290). Such a view is entirely consistent with the narrator's earlier ironic confession that "I myself can derive no conclusion" from the Lecture "which permanently satisfies those peculiar motions in my soul, to which that Lecture seems more particularly addressed"(210).

While there are certainly temperamental dissimilarities between Pierre and Plinlimmon that help to account for the differences between their philosophies, Melville argues at some length that the differences between them are, as much as anything, simply the product of age. Each man holds the view that he does because of his particular stage in life. As a youth of nineteen, it is natural for Pierre to look at the world with the eyes of an idealist, to be all fire and rage. Similarly, as a man of "mature age," it is natural for Plinlimmon to look at the world with the eyes of a realist, to be all caution and cool detachment (290). Pierre's cousin, Glen Stanly, in turn, provides an example of the in-between stage and thus helps to fill out Melville's rather simple but psychologically shrewd developmental theory. Describing Glen Stanly's change of heart toward Pierre, after Glen returns from his foreign travels, Melville writes:

In the earlier periods of that strange transition from the generous impulsiveness of youth to the provident circumspectness of age, there generally

intervenes a brief pause of unpleasant reconsidering; when finding itself all wide of its former spontaneous self, the soul hesitates to commit itself wholly to selfishness; more than repents its wanderings;—yet all this is but transient; and again hurried on by the swift current of life, the prompt-hearted boy scarce longer is to be recognized in matured man,—very slow to feel, deliberate even in love, and statistical even in piety. During the sway of this peculiar period, the boy shall still make some strenuous efforts to retrieve his departing spontaneities; but so alloyed are all such endeavors with the incipiencies of selfishness, that they were best not made at all; since too often they seem but empty and self-deceptive sallies, or still worse, the merest hypocritical assumptions. (218)

More than anything else what accounts for the different levels of emotional development in the young men is that Glen's age cycle has been greatly accelerated by foreign travel and residence in the heartless city, while Pierre's has been correspondingly retarded by his seclusion at Saddle Meadows. It should be noted that few, if any, of Melville's male characters in *Pierre* make the transition to maturity successfully, or even live long enough to complete it. With the exception of Charlie Millthorpe's father, an "old" man who spends his adult life in poverty, the only male figures in the book who survive into mature age are the self-protective bachelors, Plotinus Plinlimmon and Reverend Falsgrave (278). Pierre's father, Lucy's father, and Glen's father all die before middle age. In portraying a world without successful fathers, men who live by principle yet at the same time are capable of succeeding on the world's terms, Melville underscores how difficult it is to avoid the pitfalls of self-division in America and how fatal its costs can be.

The second half of *Pierre* details the process of the title character's abrupt shift from adolescence to the adult stage of Melville's tripartite developmental scheme. It describes his growing misanthropy, his "Timonization" (255), and his various efforts to shed the innocent youthfulness that prevents him from "reconciling the world with his own soul." In each case his effort at renunciation, whether of his paternity, his past, or "all his foregone self," is marked by a fire, a symbolic burning, first of his father's chair-portrait, family letters, and other memorabilia; then of all his correspondence, going back to when he was a much-petted juvenile author; and finally of all his own early writings. But in each case the attempted purging fails. Following the third of these ritualistic fires, for instance, when Pierre learns of his cousin Glen's pursuit of Lucy, it is clear that his heart is still divided. He continues to live in the past. Not only does he still love Lucy, but he hates Glen for having inherited his

own "noble patrimony" and for attempting to win Lucy Tartan's heart. It is in
the nature of the male ego, Melville seems to suggest, to be possessive and
resent any attention that another man might shower on a woman he once
favored, even after he himself has cast her off. Like other men, Pierre, too, or a
part of him, would "selfishly appropriate all the hearts which have ever in any
way confessed themselves his" (287–88).

The turning point in Pierre's development at this stage, and the clearest
sign that he had not had a true change of heart earlier, occurs in response to
the news that Glen Stanly has become Lucy's suitor. "Deep, deep, and still
deep and deeper must we go," Melville says mysteriously, "if we would find
out the heart of a man; descending into which is as descending a spiral stair in
a shaft, without any end, and where that endlessness is only concealed by the
spiralness of the stair, and the blackness of the shaft." What makes the news of
cousin Glen's suit especially galling to Pierre is the recognition that his cousin
has become something of an alter-ego, living out the dream life of half his
divided self. "Indeed, situated now as he was Glen would seem all the finest
part of Pierre, without any of Pierre's shame; would almost seem Pierre himself—what Pierre had once been to Lucy." As he conjures up the image of
Glen "transformed into the seeming semblance of himself," and imagines it
paying homage to Lucy, "an infinite quenchless rage and malice possessed
him." This feeling is akin, Melville explains, to the "indefinable" wrath one
feels "for any imposter who has dared to assume one's own name and aspect
in any equivocal or dishonorable affair." Yet here the emotion is aggravated by
the fact that the imposter is "almost the personal duplicate of the man whose
identity he assumes" (288–89). In this moment Pierre experiences with full
intensity the struggle of his divided will, the clash of his dual inheritance:

All his Faith-born, enthusiastic, high-wrought, stoic, and philosophic defenses, were now beaten down by this sudden storm of nature in his soul.
For there is no faith, and no stoicism, and no philosophy, that a mortal man
can possibly evoke, which will stand the final test of a real impassioned
onset of Life and Passion upon him. Then all the fair philosophic or Faith-
phantoms that he raised from the mist, slide away and disappear as ghosts at
cock-crow. For Faith and philosophy are air, but events are brass. Amidst
his gray philosophizings, Life breaks upon a man like morning. (289)

While in this mood, Pierre sees no benefit to be gained from his chosen
course and turns in hate upon himself, cursing himself "for a heartless villain
and an idiot fool;—heartless villain, as the murderer of his mother—idiot fool,

because he had thrown away all his felicity . . . resigned his noble birthright to a cunning kinsman for a mess of pottage." The accomplishment of such a sudden transvaluation of values, whereby Pierre's and Isabel's good intentions are equated with a "mess of pottage," is testimony to the power of Pierre's jealousy and the depth of his ambivalence. Again he turns to deception to mask his split, resolving now "to hide these new, and—as it latently seemed to him—unworthy pangs, from Isabel, as also their cause." In an effort to soothe his anguished heart before Isabel sees him again, Pierre starts out for a walk, but no sooner does he leave his chamber than he comes upon Plotinus Plinlimmon, Melville's ironic example of the modern hero, whose air of well-being evidences not simply freedom from worry but a complete lack of heart. It is a symbolically important encounter, for Plinlimmon is the man whom one side of Pierre longs to be, a man without a conscience (288–89).

While later, at the Apostles, the sight of Plinlimmon's face in the window goads Pierre into having doubts about himself and his commitment to Isabel, the young hero persists in his efforts, on several fronts, to try to satisfy his higher nature. He devotes all his energies during the daylight hours to completing his book; he allows himself to be "deluded," as Melville says, into practicing the Apostles' painful "Flesh-Brush Philosophy" (300); and in general, he makes every effort to deny he is a man with two equally demanding kinds of needs, one for the body and one for the soul. Assuming that "convivial authors" are incapable of giving voice to "the sublimest wisdom," Pierre makes a virtue of his poverty by forbidding himself even the few earthly comforts within his reach—a fire, decent food, a good night's sleep. In the winter, he shuts himself away with his book in an unheated room, his body so thickly muffled against the cold that he is made a kind of "cripple" (299–301). Day after day, shut in from the changing seasons and the march of holiday celebrations, he works away silently on his book. "In the midst of the merriments of the mutations of Time," Melville observes, underscoring the perversity of his young hero's maniacal endeavor, "Pierre hath ringed himself in with the grief of Eternity" (304).

The outcome of Pierre's relentless idealism, of the suppression of his natural appetites, is predictable. He soon hardens into a misanthrope, charged to the hilt with *ressentiment,* hatred for the world and for himself.[14] He soon comes to loathe all earthly satisfactions, even food, and to seek only to mortify his flesh, by waking before dawn, taking ice-water baths, and chastising his skin with flesh-brushes. Even his mounting hatred for Glen and the fading of his devotion to Isabel can be regarded as signs of his deepening resentment. Like Vivia, the thinly disguised author-hero of his book, Pierre, too, is tortured with black thoughts and so resents the happiness of others as to dismiss all happiness as a delusion: "oh God," he has Vivia say, "that men that call them-

selves men should still insist on a laugh! I hate the world, and could trample
all lungs of mankind as grapes, and heel them out of their breath, to think of
the woe and the cant,—to think of the Truth and the Lie! Oh! blessed be the
twenty-first day of December, and cursed be the twenty-first day of June!" (302–
03). But as the sudden eruption of Pierre's forbidden desire for Isabel reveals,
the pleasure principle cannot long be repressed before it asserts itself in perverse ways that also attest to the youthful hero's mounting *ressentiment.*

Melville's criticism of Pierre at this juncture, for his eagerness in following
the "Transcendental flesh-brush philosophy," seems remarkably open and
unequivocal. In Book XXII, he condemns those of this school generally who
refuse to accept the contradictions of humanity's dual nature and try vainly
to make the body fit for heaven while still living in this world. Here he argues
that while the gods love the soul of a man, they "abominate his body; and will
forever cut it dead, both here and hereafter. So, if thou wouldst go to the gods,
leave thy dog of a body behind thee." All efforts to prepare the body as an
offering to the gods, whether by cold-water baths or rough scrubbings or weird
dietary practices, will prove futile. Instead, Melville advocates an enthusiastic
embracing of this inescapable dualism. "Feed all things with food convenient
for them," he advises, "—that is, if the food be procurable. The food of thy
soul is light and space; feed it then on light and space. But the food of thy
body is champagne and oysters; feed it then on champagne and oysters; and
so shall it merit a joyful resurrection, if there is any to be" (299).

Because Pierre refuses to accept his self-division, he becomes a reverse
image of his former self, a man of hate where earlier he had been a man of
love. More generally, the action in the concluding books of the narrative is a
mirror image of that of the opening ones, another sign of the doubling or
"ambiguity" at the heart of Melville's novel. Whereas earlier, for example,
Pierre had been reluctant to receive the letter from Isabel that eventually blocks
the consummation of his innocent love for Lucy, now he "vehemently" demands to be given the letter from Lucy that would block the consummation
of his illicit desire for Isabel (309). And whereas he had initially regarded the
first letter as "impertinent," a minor interruption in his evening's plans (62),
his mood on receiving the second—worldly wise as he has now become—is
filled with foreboding: "he could not reasonably look for any tidings but di-
sastrous," he thought, "or at least, unwelcome ones" (308).

Significantly, in this novel of psychological realism, Pierre's expectations
on both occasions are wrong. But the fact of his division, like the pattern of
reversals in the second half of the novel generally, grows more and more obvious, in the young hero's increasingly angry treatment of Isabel and in the sudden return of his love for Lucy after he reads her "angelical letter" promising

always to stand by him (311). Yet even in this last moment of seeming transcendence, Melville complicates the issue of Pierre's love for Lucy. First he suggests that it has about it an element of self-love, or pride, for Pierre's once possessing the wisdom to fall in love with a girl who would later acquit herself so majestically as Lucy does here. Second Melville suggests that Pierre's love for Lucy, "passionate" as it is, is hardly so erotically charged as his attraction for the "all-ravishingly" beautiful Isabel, whose unfathomably dark-eyed image returns unexpectedly to him even as he is thinking of Lucy (312).

Although Melville certainly recognized the extraordinary power of Eros, it was not to him, as it has been to Freud and his followers, *more* powerful than the spiritual forces with which it is often in conflict. In certain moments one may be predominant, but repeatedly Melville argued that we cannot know which one is in the ascendancy. For him, human motivation was not susceptible to scientific measurement. The human heart is unknowable, ambiguous, *because* it is capable of division. Lucy's presence at the Apostles has the double effect of soothing Pierre's soul and aggravating his relationship with Isabel, a fact not acknowledged by the Freudians who have analyzed Pierre's character. Immediately on reading the letter from Lucy that expresses her "immortal faith" in him, Pierre, having by this time become used to looking at humankind with a "suspicious disdain," suddenly feels the shock of being "brushed by some angelical plume of humanity" (310–11). "Wonders, nay, downright miracles and no less were sung about Love," thinks Pierre to himself; "but here was the absolute miracle itself—the out-acted miracle." And with this thought, not only his whole attitude, but his whole philosophical mind-set changes, at least for a time: "Now, that vague, fearful feeling stole into him, that, rail as all atheists will, there is a mysterious, inscrutable divineness in the world—a God—a Being positively present everywhere;—nay, He is now in this room; the air did part when I here sat down. I displaced the Spirit then—condensed it a little off from this spot. He looked apprehensively around him; he felt overjoyed at the sight of the humanness of Delly" (317).

As if to second this newfound conviction concerning the presence of some divineness in the world, Pierre's irrepressible friend, Charlie Millthorpe, unexpectedly enters to work a little magic of his own. After briskly proclaiming his own recent accomplishments and adroitly dispensing with the porter who has just arrived with Lucy's trunks (while Pierre moves as in a trance, dazed at the prospect of her arrival), Millthorpe reports that he has paid off one of Pierre's bill collectors for him. "I was suddenly made flush yesterday:—regular flood-tide. You can return it any day, you know," he says brightly (319–20). Here is an example of the "Voice" that had earlier been said to break the "Si-

lence" now and then (208). But like the sound of the bird that, in a still earlier scene, had been heard to "cheerfully chirp" from atop the Terror Stone, as Pierre lay waiting to be crushed beneath it, the Voice that breaks the Silence sometimes speaks strangely, in tones we fail to hear or in a language we are too stubborn, or obtuse, to understand (135).

Not long after Lucy's arrival, Isabel begins to notice a change come over Pierre, and she grows suspicious. She observes him looking at Lucy sometimes with a more than "merely cousinly" eye and at other times with an expression of "fear and awe"(337). Clearly, Pierre's love for Lucy has returned; and clearly, too, his despair at his obligation to Isabel is now growing. But to each woman he continues to live a lie. From Isabel, he hides what Lucy once was to him; from Lucy, he hides what Isabel is.[15] Sensing the falsity of Pierre's claim that Lucy is nothing more than a "nun-like cousin" of his (310), Isabel grows suspicious, then jealous, and finally devious in her ways. Indeed, like Pierre, she begins to deceive herself, lapsing into the public fiction that she is Pierre's wife and not simply his sister: "am *I* not enough for thee?" she asks jealously, when told of Lucy's intention to come and live with them (312).

Repeatedly now, Isabel tries to test Pierre's love or insinuate herself back into his affections, offering, for example, to give up the heat in her own room to warm Lucy's chamber or, later, to sell her own teeth and hair in a desperate effort to match Lucy's more practical plan to raise money by selling charcoal portraits. While such efforts do force Pierre's hand, bringing out at least a semblance of his love for her, they typically also reveal just how ambivalent and grudging his feelings for her are. At one point when, trying to break through his new state of revery, Isabel draws close to him and touches his leg, Pierre instinctively recoils from her and then tries to paper over his instinctive rejection of her by explaining, lamely, "When we would most dearly embrace, we first throw back our arms, Isabel; I but drew away, to draw so much the closer to thee" (332–33). For her part, Isabel soon takes every opportunity to drive a wedge between Pierre and her new rival, as when at one point she slyly kicks open the door to Lucy's chamber just as Pierre is embracing Isabel out of simple affection at the announcement of her promise to try to make some money for the household.

While this brief scene discloses the true nature of Pierre's allegiances toward the two women during the penultimate stage of his career—his love for Lucy and his equivocal sense of duty and sexual attraction for Isabel—it also indicates that his conflicting desires are genuinely deadlocked. In this mood of utter frustration, then, Pierre must confront the added difficulty of suffering public disgrace or humiliation at the hands of Glen and Lucy's brother, both

of whom are now bent on saving her from what they assume to be Pierre's evil clutches. Significantly, what Pierre feels is not fear but an exceptional "pride-horror, which is more terrible than any fear," a crazed defiance, such as Melville's White-Jacket had felt, at the prospect of public shaming. When "a proud and honorable man," Melville says, contemplates the likelihood of his own humiliation, "then, by tremendous imagery, the murderer's mark of Cain is felt burning on the brow, and the already acquitted knife blood-rusts in the clutch of the anticipating hand" (336). Still, the frustration of Pierre's desires for Isabel and Lucy contributes mightily to his bloodlust, as Melville describes it:

> when he thought of all the ambiguities which hemmed him in; the stony walls all round that he could not overleap; the million aggravations of his most malicious lot; the last lingering hope of happiness [with Lucy] licked up from him as by flames of fire, and his one only prospect a black, bottomless gulf of guilt, upon whose verge he immediately teetered every hour [as a result of the threat of incest with Isabel];—then the utmost hate of Glen and Frederic were jubilantly welcome to him; and murder, done in the act of warding off their ignominious public blow, seemed the one only congenial sequel to such a desperate career. (337)

Like Ahab, Pierre would become a maniacal murderer to preserve his pride, because pride is the only thing of real value that remains to him, or so he believes.

Pierre is finally a more complex psychological figure than the tragic hero of *Moby-Dick,* however; for unlike Ahab, Pierre is deeply divided against his own pride. When Glen and Frederic fail to make their anticipated appearance, Pierre continues to labor at his book; but the more he writes and the deeper he dives, the more clearly he sees "the everlasting elusiveness of Truth; the universal lurking insincerity of even the greatest and purest written thoughts." Hating the lies that every writer ends up speaking, Pierre is so profoundly split as to feel that "there was nothing he more spurned, than his own aspirations; nothing he more abhorred than the loftiest part of himself" (339). Driven, nonetheless, by his "Titanic soul" to complete his book, all the time loathing himself for the paltriness of his performance, his conflicting desires eventually become deadlocked or self-cancelling, and he has a temporary physical and emotional breakdown (341).

One night while out on his regular walk, Pierre experiences a terrible feeling of vertigo, the cessation of all "ordinary life-feeling," and then passes out in the gutter. Refusing to heed even these potent symptoms of the unnatural-

ness of his struggle, Pierre returns the next morning to his book only to be overcome by "a general and nameless torpor—some horrible foretaste of death itself" (341–42). In a trancelike state, he has his dream of Enceladus, the armless Titan who spends an eternity trying to free himself from the earth while being forced to repel, with nothing more than his mutilated trunk, the giant stones thrown down on him from the mountaintop (345). The dream of Enceladus is but another warning from Pierre's unconscious to give up his determination to "sail on," as he says, regardless of "the inevitable rocks," and make "a courageous wreck" of his life (339).

Melville's description of Pierre's interpretation of this dream is character- istically enigmatic. Without articulating what Pierre's reading in fact was (the narrative voice in the second half of the novel becomes more distant as it shifts from first to third person), he says only that his "elucidation was most repulsively fateful and foreboding," and then offers the equivocal explanation that this was so "*possibly* because Pierre did not leap the final barrier of gloom; *possibly* because Pierre did not willfully wrest some final comfort from the fable; did not flog this stubborn rock as Moses his, and force even aridity itself to quench his painful thirst" (346; emphasis added). The first of these possibilities suggests that there is a "final barrier of gloom" beyond which one can expect to find glory and light—a Carlylean "Everlasting Yea" beyond the "Everlasting No." But the second seems to suggest that any comfort one can manage to extract from the Enceladus story is illusory, the product of the reader's own wishful thinking—an hypothesis that seems entirely consistent with Melville's introduction to the Enceladus myth. There he takes the posi- tion that Nature is not so much "her own ever-sweet interpreter" as the "mere supplier of that cunning alphabet, whereby selecting and combining as he pleases, each man reads his own peculiar lesson according to his own peculiar mind and mood." And in support of this subjectivist theory he cites the inci- dent of the naming of this same Mount of Titans at Saddle Meadows by "a high-aspiring, but most moody, disappointed bard." For this name, he ar- gues, completely obliterated its former title, "The Delectable Mountains," which had been conferred on it many years earlier by an old Baptist farmer, "an hereditary admirer of Bunyan and his most marvelous book" (342).

When Melville himself plays the role of Moses, therefore, and prefaces his reading of the Enceladus story by saying, "Thus smitten, the Mount of Titans seems to yield this following stream," we should recognize that his interpreta- tion contains some comfort that is beyond Pierre's more embittered under- standing. What is more, we should realize that possibly it contains conclu- sions about the human lot that are somehow self-serving for the author, or his narrator, and are not, therefore, in any absolute sense true:

Old Titan's self was the son of incestuous Coelus and Terra, the son of incestuous Heaven and Earth. And Titan married his mother Terra, another and accumulatively incestuous match. And thereof Enceladus was one issue. So Enceladus was both the son and grandson of an incest; and even thus, there had been born from the organic blended heavenliness and earthliness of Pierre, another mixed, uncertain, heaven aspiring, but still not wholly earth-emancipated mood; which again, by its terrestrial taint held down to its terrestrial mother, generated there the present doubly incestuous Enceladus within him; so that the present mood of Pierre— that reckless sky-assaulting mood of his, was nevertheless on one side the grandson of the sky. For it is according to eternal fitness, that the precipitated Titan should still seek to regain his paternal birthright even by fierce escalade. Wherefore whoso storms the sky gives best proof he came from thither! But whatso crawls contented in the moat before that crystal fort, shows it was born within that slime, and there forever will abide. (347)

While Melville may seem here to be arguing that a person's determination to "storm the sky" proves that he has a heavenly origin, he actually says only that it constitutes the "best" proof of such an origin. It seems fair to say he recognized there could be no certain proof of such a thing on this side of the grave.

Though we know only vaguely that Pierre's interpretation of the Enceladus vision was a forbidding one, we can see evidence of his unceasing division in the way he responds to it. We are told, at least in general terms, that, after recovering a little from his trance, he concentrated all his remaining energies and resolved, by a "violent change," to overcome all his ailments—"the strange malady of his eyes, this new death-fiend of the trance, and this Inferno of his Titanic vision." Part of him, obviously, still strains against his own willful self-destruction and would make one last, heroic effort to reverse his fate. What is not clear is whether "the little design" he is said to cherish involves anything more than the proposal he makes to his companions for a little respite—namely, to get out of the freezing metropolis and take a sunny walk to the wharf, and "then for some of the steamers on the bay"—or whether it includes a secret intention finally to track down evidence that might discredit Isabel's story, a plan to free himself of his whole burdensome connection with her (347–48).

Melville seems purposely to complicate or obscure Pierre's intentions at this point by suggesting that guarded, perhaps unconscious, motives may be propelling him. Thus, just before Pierre asks Lucy and Isabel to join him for an afternoon stroll, Melville says that his young hero "rapidly conned over" in his mind "what indifferent, disguising, or light-hearted gamesome things he should

say" to them when suggesting his plan. And when he has the thought of looking in the mirror to see if he has a suitably cheerful expression on his face, Pierre suddenly resists the urge when he recalls that he had lately come to dread seeing some "dark revealments" in his own reflection—an admission that now he is trying to hide his deepest feelings even from himself (347). But when Pierre explains to Isabel that his interest in going out for a walk does not mean he has completed his book, as she had hoped, Melville introduces Pierre's poetic rejoinder with the observation that "a hectic unsummoned expression" suddenly displaced "all disguisements" on his face. Pierre thus seems to reveal all there is to know about his motives for wanting to go for an outing down by the water when he answers, in effect, that he simply needs a change in scenery:

> Not so; but ere that vile book be finished, I must get on some other element than earth. I have sat on earth's saddle till I am weary; I must now vault over to the other saddle awhile. Oh, seems to me, there should be two ceaseless steeds for a bold man to ride,—the Land and the Sea; and like circus-men we should never dismount, but only be steadied and rested by leaping from one to the other, while still, side by side, they both race round the sun. I have been on the Land steed so long, oh I am dizzy! (348–49)[16]

Despite Pierre's continuing ambivalence about Isabel, the unfolding of his unconscious desire to be free of her is clearly evidenced in the gallery scene, en route to the wharf, and again in Pierre's brief sail with his two companions across the bay. Impulsively stopping to visit a display of imported paintings in a gallery along the way, Pierre happens on the unsigned portrait of a "Stranger's Head," which bears a striking resemblance both to Isabel and to his father's chair-portrait (349, 351). Though to Isabel he dismisses the likeness as a mere coincidence, Pierre himself experiences "wild thoughts . . . hurrying and shouting in his heart" once the three of them resume their walk. "The most tremendous displacing and revolutionizing thoughts were upheaving in him, with reference to Isabel," Melville explains; "nor—though at the time he was hardly conscious of such a thing—were these thoughts wholly unwelcome to him." Struggling consciously now to reverse his fate, Pierre asks himself how he knew Isabel to be his sister. And, after running through all the facts once more in the light of this new discovery, he concludes that this "portrait of a complete stranger—a European; a portrait imported from across the seas"— could just as readily serve to argue that its original was the father of Isabel as the chair-portrait had once served to convince him that its original, his own father, was her parent (353).[17]

Only at this point, then, does Melville reveal that Pierre had "of late" been feeling, with new vividness, that the whole story of Isabel seemed "an enigma, a mystery, an imaginative delirium." As Pierre imagines the situation now, "By some strange arts Isabel's wonderful story might have been, someway, and for some cause, forged for her, in her childhood, and craftily impressed upon her youthful mind." "Tested by any thing real, practical, and reasonable, what less probable, for instance," he wonders, "than that fancied crossing of the sea in her childhood," once it came out, under questioning, that she was ignorant even of the fact that the sea was salty (352–54).

In view of this discovery, and of Pierre's growing skepticism generally regarding Isabel's story, it is thus evident that he had intended, if only unconsciously, to test her reaction to the sea water when he proposed taking a walk to the wharf and riding across the bay. For on seeing that Isabel became excited not at the brine but at the motion of the waves, his face grew "pale" and "staring," as this apparent proof of her earlier sea experience begins to sink in, and he fell into "silence and revery." "It was impossible," he now thought, "altogether to resist the force of this striking corroboration of by far the most surprising and improbable thing in the whole surprising and improbable story of Isabel." But there is a deeper irony here than the fact that Isabel's whole story seems unexpectedly confirmed. For the evidence of her excitement at the motion of the waves does not in fact refute the evidence of the strange portrait; it simply counterbalances it. The two are "mutually neutralizing," in Melville's phrase, but nothing more (355). And so, in the end, the truth of Isabel's story is ambiguous still, and Pierre's willingness to come to her aid remains divided.

Once Isabel claims to see that she stands in the way of Pierre's "felicity" with Lucy, she suddenly makes a move to plunge over the side of the ferry, but Pierre manages to stop her, and they immediately return to the Apostles (355). There, after sitting for a while silently by the stove, a symbol of the earthly happiness that has eluded Pierre since Isabel first came into his life, he was "on the point of entering his closet" for some ambiguous, unspecified reason, when Delly stops him to say that two letters had been delivered in his absence: Was he simply going back to work on his book? Or was he intending to destroy the manuscript and start a new life? With typical ambiguity, Melville fails to say. Even before reading the letters, Pierre immediately decides what they mean and the nature of his own response to them, as he had earlier when he received Isabel's letter. In a double sense, he holds his fate in his hands; in a double sense, he seems determined to be wounded. "In these hands I feel that I now hold the final poniards that shall stab me," he suddenly cries out,

lifting the letters away from himself; "and by stabbing me, make *me* too a most swift stabber in the recoil" (356).

Reading first his publishers' claim that he is a swindler, and then Glen and Fred's still more scornful accusation that he is a liar, Pierre asserts that "These are most small circumstances; but happening just now to me, become indices to all immensities." Then, trampling them underfoot, he exclaims, "For now am I hate-shod! On these I will skate to my acquittal!" Before rushing off to restore his self-pride, however, Pierre shows an equal and opposite capacity for self-contempt by hatefully condemning "this swindler's, this coiner's book" and fiercely nailing it to his desk "for a detected cheat" (357). Though earlier that day, before departing for the wharf, Pierre had looked at Lucy with a "momentary rapt glance," he now tells her, while rushing out of their apartments, that the flame of their love is "all extinguished" (348, 358). Certain that he will never otherwise be free from his own division, he prays as he takes his leave that Lucy and Isabel—the two women who have split his heart in two—"may never stir alive" from their chairs, and he vows to quit them "forever" (358). When he goes off, then, to confront Glen and Fred, Pierre goes to do battle with two characters who symbolize the two sides of himself that have been at war from the start. In Glen he will face a man who loves Lucy, the woman he has always adored; and in Lucy's brother Fred he will vie with a man who is all eagerness, as Pierre himself had been early in the narrative, "to engage in a mortal quarrel on a sweet sister's behalf" (7).

Pierre's abiding self-division—proof of his full humanity—ends only with his death. As he looks back from his prison cell over all the carnage and confusion of his last days and weeks, he proclaims, "It is ambiguous still. Had I been heartless now, disowned, and spurningly portioned off the girl at Saddle Meadows, then had I been happy through a long life on earth, and perchance through a long eternity in heaven!" Ambiguous though his situation is and remains, this last expression of regret is delusionary, for had Pierre abandoned Isabel at the start, he would have been so "heartless" as to be unfit for an eternity in heaven (360). Even the seemingly unequivocal, life-hating act of suicide in the end, "to be rid," as he says, "of this dishonored cheek," is made ambiguous, as an indication of what his final attitude might have been, by his very last act—the "one speechless clasp" of life and love that he gives to the hand of Charlie Millthorpe—as Pierre lies dying in his cell. Thus Isabel's dying words, "All's o'er, and ye know him not!"—intended, ostensibly, to refute Fred's ignorant cursing of Pierre as a "juggler," Charlie's simplistic blaming of Pierre's "too moody ways" as the cause of all his troubles, and even Lucy's fatal misunderstanding of Pierre's relationship with Isabel when the latter calls

him "my brother"—are directed in the end at everyone, including the reader, who witnesses Pierre's end. They constitute Melville's final warning not to judge what is beyond our understanding (360, 362). For, ironically, not even Isabel, who thinks his intentions have been purely benevolent, can be said to know Pierre's heart, when Pierre himself cannot say with certainty just what his motives have been at each turning point in his life. If, as Melville claimed, he himself, as Pierre's creator, had been "more frank with Pierre than the best men are with themselves," it was because he did not wish to cast praise or blame on Pierre's character or on the course of his decisions but to make a more searching inquiry than any novelist had ever attempted before to "find out the heart of a man; descending into which," as he came to see, "is as descending a spiral stair in a shaft without any end" (108, 289).

Melville's *Pierre* is a more ambiguous, intellectually challenging novel, and a less sickly, lugubrious one, than most critics would have us believe. To be sure, it is not a study in humor.[18] Melville was writing during the "sentimental years" of the novel, when women readers, who dominated the marketplace, were thought to want to experience tears of sadness, not tears of laughter.[19] However, *Pierre* is still a work of remarkable wit, as well as high seriousness, and not alone the product of "Melville's unconditional surrender to the forces of the unconscious" proclaimed by psychologists, important as his openness to such forces might have been to his writing of this novel. Such broad claims for the prominence of underlying psychological motives in the origin of *Pierre* have become quite suspect in recent years in light of the revelation that the novel was based on Melville's discovery that his own father had apparently sired an illegitimate daughter; it did not emerge whole cloth out of his troubled unconscious, as Murray and others have assumed. On the contrary, with almost Jamesian care and craft, and the kind of cunning displayed in *The Turn of the Screw,* Melville created a domestic tragedy concerning the young protagonist's allegedly wanton father and supposedly illegitimate sister that is as teasing in its ambiguities as the hero's dilemma is perplexing. Virtually every feature of Isabel's and the elder Glendinning's stories is uncertain, subject to conflicting interpretations.

Henry Murray, a trained psychiatrist, saw the majority of the ambiguities in *Pierre* as the product of Pierre's own "ambivalences," or, more clinically, of his "one nuclear conflict" resulting from the discovery of his father's sin and the repression of his own forbidden sexual urges.[20] Failing to acknowledge the existence of epistemological ambiguities stemming from extra-psychological sources—assuming that the world operates always according to ratio-

nal principles congenial to our desire to know what is true, failing to recognize the inherent ambiguity of much of the information the world supplies to us—Murray believed that the reader would necessarily share Pierre's early conviction that the elder Glendinning fathered Isabel, something we cannot know for sure and something that grows more doubtful as the narrative draws to a close.[21]

Once the ambiguity of the evidence concerning Isabel's claim to the Glendinning name is recognized, however, Pierre's story gains in richness and complexity, in realism and purpose. *Pierre* becomes a more perplexing, more penetrating novel, one consistent with Melville's preoccupation with epistemological issues elsewhere in his writings—the uncertainties of knowing the natural world in *Moby-Dick,* for instance, or the uncertainties of knowing other people in *The Confidence-Man,* for another. Indeed, epistemological ambiguity is the hallmark of the best writing of Melville's major phase; it is what gives it its characteristic depth and power, its rich irony and remarkable modernity. If Melville's only purpose were to present a psychological study focusing on his character's experience of the conflict between conscious and unconscious motives, there would be no need for him to weave the elaborate network of circumstantial evidence that he did in support of Isabel's claim. He simply could have supplied hard proof at some point—a secret diary known to be in Pierre's father's hand containing references to his illicit affair, an unequivocal deathbed confession, or some less shopworn piece of evidence—to put to rest any doubts the reader might have about the truth of her story. But by making the evidence ambiguous, Melville made Pierre's dilemma a tougher test of the youth's loftiness and a truer measure of his humanity than it would have been otherwise. For, strange to say, he thereby extended Pierre's freedom of action. If Pierre had known for sure that Isabel was his sister, he would have been simply a cad if he abandoned her or failed to help her in some way; he would have had no excuse to justify refusing her claims on him. And if he had known for a fact that she was not his sister, he would have been a cad and more if he abandoned Lucy, or done anything to jeopardize his relationship with her, to help Isabel.

Given the uncertainties of Isabel's story, however, Pierre is caught in a bona fide dilemma. He is free to believe or not believe her story; free to change his mind or to doubt the evidence; free to condemn himself for his "weakness" whenever he manages temporarily to forget about his obligation to Isabel and for his "heartlessness" whenever he fails to meet his obligation to Lucy; and in general free to behave in the vacillating manner of a flesh-and-blood human being rather than compelled to act in the unswerving fashion of a chivalric hero in a sentimental romance.

Though Pierre, in his psychological fluctuations, is a realistically portrayed character, neither he nor his world is so naturalistic, or so prosaic, as most critics would have us believe. While correcting the inflated view of Pierre as a Christ-like figure that had prevailed before 1949, Murray substituted a diminished view of him as a rather mean-spirited character whose every move is determined, finally, by unconscious drives. According to this view, Pierre is a mother-dominated youth with the soul of a "pathetic little waif" who is almost saved when Isabel, awakening the repressed forces of his unconscious, compels him to break all conventional attachments to pursue his "anima love"; but as the result of "a long series of fantastic errors of judgment" and a deficiency in "heroic substance," he suppresses his awakened sexual instinct again and puts his libido energy at the service of his ambition as a writer, only to regress in the end to a wailing, self-destructive infant when his "delusional grandeur" is frustrated.[22]

I think Melville's rendering of Pierre's character is nobler than that, less Lawrencian, and more complex. If Pierre failed as a consequence of the fact that his "strength of heart . . . was unequal to the thing that he attempted," this is true not because Melville, enamoured by Pierre's greatness, misconceived him, but because Melville adhered to a principle of literary realism. Pierre failed not because of any weakness of heart or character but because of the impossibility of the thing he attempted.[23] I believe Melville recognized that no one possesses the strength required to accomplish the high things he can imagine; there is, as he said emphatically, no "talismanic secret" according to which one can "reconcile this world with his own soul" (208). Murray and others have foundered on this rock. Unwilling to accept the view that man's relationship with the world is one of continuing, irreducible conflict, these critics have taken the position that Pierre should have made a Plinlimmonesque adjustment to reality in his expectations—to devise, in Murray's words, "a workable and unhurtful strategy based on realistic moral values." As a rule they have also shared Murray's conclusion that Melville's formulation of the human condition evidenced an unconscious desire to postpone "the dreaded curative decision" indefinitely, if not a psychological incapacity to will his way "out of discord."[24]

What is missing from such assessments is some recognition—amounting, I would say, to an axiom of belief for Melville—that such adjustments to reality can be as damaging to the spirit as the failure to make them. Moreover, if the assumption that Melville held such a belief has any basis in fact, it cannot be argued that Melville was any more divorced from reality than the psychological theorists or analysts themselves, in so far as they, too, assume to know what is true and in so far as they, too, pretend to know what is healthy for the

human spirit. I suspect that Melville would have shared Murray's own opposition, understandable for a psychiatrist, to "the Christian premise that sorrow is the divinely decreed law of life."[25] But I suspect also that, unlike Murray and others who hold fundamentally Freudian assumptions about reality, Melville would have found such a premise inescapable. More than anything else, it is Melville's refusal to abandon this premise that keeps him from being a wholly modern figure and allies him with the ancient Judeo-Christian world view.

The fundamental difference between Murray's attitude toward Pierre and what I take to be Melville's is suggested in the difference between the objectives of psychiatry and those of Christianity: where the former aims at the individual's achieving an earthly state of human happiness, the latter is committed to the individual's achieving a spiritual state of what Melville referred to as human blessedness. While I do not mean to suggest that Melville's attitude was orthodoxly Christian, I do think he shared the Christian view of the tragic irreconcilability of the life of conscience and the life of the everyday world. In its portrayal of the divided self, *Pierre* thoroughly evidences Melville's understanding of the view that Christ made explicit in the Sermon on the Mount (Matthew 6:24) when he said that "No one can serve two masters; for either he will hate the one and love the other, or he will be devoted to the one and despise the other. You cannot serve God and mammon." If *Pierre* registers Melville's own division as well as Pierre's, it registers also an unusual kind of emotional vitality, a strength of will that refused to rest in compromise or evasion—a fierce love of the life of principle, and an equally fierce love of the life of worldly pleasure.

Melville's wryly obsequious dedication "To Greylock's Most Excellent Majesty" suggests that *Pierre* was written by a man who intimately knew the mountain, a symbol of inspiration and unconquerable grandeur—knew it and continued each day to face it, not as a broken subject but as a seasoned combatant who was willing to admit that he had been at least temporarily vanquished. Like Pierre of the Enceladus dream, he seems to have made a Titanic but unsuccessful assault on this mountain, and yet, like Ishmael returning from the sinking of the *Pequod,* he has survived the ordeal and is moved to leave a record of his struggle, while he waits to recover the strength necessary to make still another offensive.[26] Melville's tone in the dedication, like that in much of the novel proper, seems mischievous in its evasiveness—quietly sardonic, as befits a man who spent himself trying every way possible to find the "talismanic secret" that would end his own division, and at the same time grudgingly respectful, as befits a man who still had the fortitude to settle in the shadow of Greylock—the highest mountain in Massachusetts—his "sovereign lord and king," refusing to accept defeat as a permanent state of affairs or

otherwise dodge the frustrations of the challenge "to reconcile this world with his own soul," silently watching, waiting, working (208).

In addition to underestimating the complexity of Pierre's character, Murray made the mistake of equating Melville with his title character when he said that the novel's "organic worth is invalidated by the sickness of despair."[27] If we can judge from his own testimony at about the time he had begun to work on *Pierre*, Melville, then thirty-two years old, had matured to the point where he was no longer susceptible to the kinds of disappointments that can lead to lasting despair, even while he continued vigorously to struggle, to work, and to write. Now he struggled for the sake of the struggle, worked for the sake of the work, wrote for the sake of the writing, and for the sense of contentment that came at the end of a day of honest labor.

Although he perhaps overstated the case, his disclaimer to the contrary notwithstanding, Melville had achieved an extraordinary acceptance of the strange workings of the world in spite of his equally extraordinary defiance of them. Responding with candor and fullness of heart to Hawthorne's private review of *Moby-Dick* sometime in the middle of November 1851, Melville revealed a serenity, and a savvy about the literary marketplace, that seems to belie the possibility of his succumbing to despair during the next four or five months—mostly uneventful months, even if one considers the appearance of several abusive reviews of *Moby-Dick* during that time—while he composed *Pierre*:

People think that if a man has undergone any hardship, he should have a reward; but for my part, if I have done the hardest possible day's work, and then come to sit down in a corner & eat my supper comfortably—why, then I don't think I deserve any reward for my hard day's work—for am I not now at peace? Is not my supper good? My peace & my supper are my reward, my dear Hawthorne. So your joy-giving and exultation-breeding letter is not my reward for my ditcher's work with that book, but is the good goddess's bonus over and above what was stipulated for—for not one man in five cycles, who is wise, will expect appreciative recognition from his fellows, or any one of them. Appreciation! Recognition! Is love appreciated? Why, ever since Adam, who has got to the meaning of this great allegory—the world? Then we pygmies must be content to have our paper allegories but ill comprehended. . . .

. . . A sense of unspeakable security is in me this moment, on account of your having understood the book. I have written a wicked book, and feel spotless as the lamb. Ineffable socialities are in me. I would sit down & dine with you & all the gods in old Rome's Pantheon. It is a strange feel-

ing—no hopefulness is in it, no despair. Content—that is it; and irrespon-
sibility; but without licentious inclination. I speak now of my profoundest
sense of being, not of an incidental feeling.[28]

While the critical reception of *Moby-Dick* was undoubtedly cause for deep
disappointment to him, it seems unlikely, given the conviction of this remarkable letter, that it was the cause of despair. To be sure, one's mood can
change from month to month, even day to day, and Melville admitted as much
in this same letter. But he had comforts to sustain him that few writers ever
enjoy. He knew he had written an uncommon book, and he knew that the
man whose opinion he most valued had understood it.[29]

Judging from the self-characterizing remarks of *Pierre*'s curious narrator,
and assuming Melville's own frame of mind to be reflected in them, we can
see further that Melville was hardly the desperate, soul-sick, mentally unstable figure he is widely thought to have been at this point in his career.
Though not so explicit a self-portrait, or so memorable, as the one provided
in the opening lines of *Moby-Dick*, the first sentences of *Pierre* are revealing of
Melville's emotional state at the time:

> There are some strange summer mornings in the country, when he who is
> but a sojourner from the city shall early walk forth into the fields, and be
> wonder-smitten with the trance-like aspect of the green and golden world.
> Not a flower stirs; the trees forget to wave; the grass itself seems to have
> ceased to grow; and all Nature, as if suddenly become conscious of her
> own profound mystery, and feeling no refuge from it but silence, sinks
> into this wonderful and indescribable repose.
>
> Such was the morning in June, when, issuing from the embowered and
> high-gabled old home of his fathers, Pierre, dewily refreshed and spiritual-
> ized by sleep, gayly entered the long, wide, elm-arched street of the village,
> and half unconsciously bent his steps toward a cottage, which peeped into
> view near the end of the vista. (3)

Melville's narrator implies here that he knows from personal experience what
it is to be a sojourner from the city (Melville himself had moved to the Berkshires from Manhattan in the fall of 1850). More importantly, he implies that,
though an older man than Pierre and wiser in the ways of the world, he himself is neither so jaded nor so alienated as to have lost the capacity for wonder.
He is still able to respond to the fullness of June's promise, to sense the mystery of Nature's ways, and even to appreciate the freshness of love's bloom.[30]

Pierre's opening pastoral love scenes have usually been criticized as being either grotesquely sentimental or abstrusely mock-Romantic—the product of too little taste or, it might be said, of too much.[31] But I believe that Melville was neither so lost to emotion nor so distrustful of it as these judgments suggest. To my mind, what is distinctive, particularly about the opening paragraphs of the book, but also of the early pastoral scenes more generally, is how close Melville came in them to pure lyricism.[32] To be sure, there is more than a hint of irony—of ominous developments, of loss and disillusionment, of a narrative *plot*—in the references to sleep and waking and in the repeated suggestions that Saddle Meadows has been lulled into careless languor by an excess of natural fecundity and emotional contentment. When Pierre comes forth, he is "spiritualized by sleep" and "half unconsciously" makes his way to Lucy's cottage; the cows in the distance are "dreamily wandering" to their pastures; the whole of Nature seems to be held in a drowsy trance.

To read these lines without irony is to forget what few modern readers can, that this is Herman Melville talking, America's great nineteenth-century worrier. But to regard irony as the dominant mood here, and thereby assume that the irony cancels the passage's genuine lyricism, is either to deny, as a general proposition, that there can ever be such summer mornings or to deny that Melville was susceptible to their charms. I believe *Pierre* was written with knowledge of the existence of such lovely mornings and such romantic love, as much as it was written with knowledge of their mutibility. It is that doubleness—the knowledge of the promise that was and of the failure that is, and not alone the knowledge of the wretched failure—that accounts for the peculiarly ambivalent tone of Melville's novel, its singular amalgam of wistfulness and knowingness, poignancy and detachment, sweet pleasure and bitter pain.

What distinguishes the Melville of *Pierre* from the domestic or sentimental novelists of his time, with whom he has sometimes been compared, is the fullness of his vision, what I have been calling his "division"—his capacity both to feel emotion deeply and to assess it critically, not to favor one at the expense of the other. It is as much a wrenching of the truth to argue that in *Pierre* he lapsed into the excesses of the popular romantic fiction of the day as it is to argue that he ridiculed the emotions on which they are based. "Love may end in grief and age, and pain and need, and all other modes of human mournfulness," Melville said emphatically in his early three-page paean to Love, the fourth section of Book II; "but love begins in joy. Love's first sigh is never breathed, till after love hath laughed. Love laughs first, and then sighs after" (33). Melville wrote *Pierre* from the point of view of one who knew Love's sighs, not of one who knew only Love's laugh. But he did not therefore value any less the experience of Love's laughter.

The cloying quality, and the caricaturing of stylistic cloyingness, thought to mark much of the language in the early chapters of *Pierre* seem to me to fade and all but disappear when the lines in question are read in context. For instance, the seemingly saccharine, or snide, conceit emphasizing the voluptuous influence of Nature—"far out at sea, no more the sailors tied their bowline-knots; their hands had lost their cunning; will they, nill they, Love tied love-knots on every spangled spar"—*can* be read straight, particularly when one realizes how severely Melville has qualified the conditions required for such an occurrence (and keeps in mind that it is intended as a trope, not as a scientifically precise observation). The paragraph in which this statement appears begins, "That morning [when Pierre and Lucy took their phaeton ride into the hills] was *the choicest drop* that Time had in his vase. Ineffable distillations of a soft delight were wafted from the fields and hills. Fatal morning that, *to all lovers unbetrothed . . .*" (32; emphasis added). Though rare, such miraculous mornings do occur—mornings so irresistible in their power as to soften all but the most hardened sailor or reluctant lover. And the fact that they occur justifies the mood of lyrical outpouring that begins in the next paragraph with one of the most evocative lines—a line drained of irony, I would say—in all of Melville's writing: "Oh, praised be the beauty of this earth, the beauty, and the bloom, and the mirthfulness thereof!" (32) Practically speaking, such lyricism serves to explain Melville's division. It stands as linguistic evidence of the idea that Melville, like his contemporary Emily Dickinson, could not bring himself to commit his whole being to the life of the soul because he was too much in love with the world to give it up.

It is because Herman Melville tried to present the whole of what he knew—the much he did *not* know, as well as the much he did—that *Pierre* is not, finally, the sentimental novel it initially seems to be, but an unexampled psychological study. And it is for this reason, too, that *Pierre* offers no moral, no solution to the problems it raises, at least not the kind of moral or solution one typically finds in novels. Melville knew, what Pierre came to see by "infallible presentiment" after the shock of his first interview with Isabel, namely that

> wedding-bells peal not ever in the last scene of life's fifth act; that while the countless tribes of common novels laboriously spin vails of mystery, only to complacently clear them up at last . . . *yet the profounder emanations of the human mind, intended to illustrate all that can be humanly known of human life;* these never unravel their own intricacies, and have no proper endings, but in imperfect, unanticipated, and disappointing sequels (as mutilated stumps), hurry to abrupt interminglings with the eternal tides of time and fate. (141; emphasis added)

I believe this is as clear a statement of his policy of literary realism as Melville ever wrote. However, it does more than explain what separated him from the popular domestic novelists of his era. It suggests also that he was a radically skeptical writer, one who stubbornly refused to provide the answers his readers expected from fiction, because he himself so longed for the real thing. A man more in love with the idea of fulfillment than most of us, Melville stubbornly refused to settle for its counterfeit.

෮

Rewriting America's Past:

Israel Potter as Historical Novel

Unlike Melville's other novels, *Israel Potter* is not an original work but a narrative based on the lifestory of an actual personality, an obscure Revolutionary War figure whose simple memoirs were ghost-written, we now know, by a hack writer named Henry Trumbull. From *Typee* on, Melville had always secretly relied on secondary sources to flesh out the autobiographical skeleton of his novels—to supply background information, historical details, even incidents and minor characters. But he had never before attempted to write anything in the mode of fictional biography or history. Clearly, in this work he was setting out on a new path—something objective, a cultural and historical study that carried Melville outside his own life experience.

Until recently, however, Melville specialists have not known how to classify this most uncharacteristic of the author's novels. In part, this is so because Melville himself was more than a little misleading about the matter. In the dedication he called the book a "biography" and claimed to have preserved Potter's story "almost as in a reprint." But we now know he greatly understated the extent to which he revised, amplified, and departed from the incidents of Potter's own story, to the point where more than half of the book concerns Potter very little or not at all and is of Melville's own making.

Several critics, recognizing the inadequacy of the term "biography" in relation to a work of the imagination, have applied the terms of various genres of the novel to *Israel Potter*. Richard Chase and others, for example, have tried to see it in the context of the picaresque tradition.[1] However, while "picaresque" has the virtue of capturing something of the comic tone and gritty realism of

the book, it fails to take into account the important historical dimension of the novel. Walter Bezanson, in his scrupulous examination of Melville's use of a wide range of historical sources for the book, is surely on the right track in emphasizing that the book is more of a historical novel than it is a biographical one.[2] But even his fine discussion fails to acknowledge that the book is thoroughly self-reflexive. Throughout the novel Melville has satirized the conventions of the form or turned them on their head, creating a revisionist version of the historical novel that almost everywhere carries the mark of the author's inventiveness and ironic humor.

In rewriting the form of the historical novel Melville was also rewriting American history. For *Israel Potter* portrays the American Revolution and its participants not in the mood of high seriousness or sentimental reverence that typifies the Revolutionary War literature written before this time, from the histories of Jared Sparks to the novels of James Fenimore Cooper, but in a fresh mood of comic realism. Iconoclastic, biting, earthy, and episodic, like certain of today's philosophical comic strips, it presents a wry, insider's view of familiar and unfamiliar people and events. In tone and intention, it is far from the popular romantic fiction contemporary with it, and it is hardly at all like Melville's previous long narratives, the epic *Moby-Dick* and the psychological novel *Pierre*. It is not moralizing in a high-minded way; it does not take a noble view of human nature or assume an idealistic theory of human conduct. The Americans in it are not portrayed as saints; and just as important, and rare for a work of American fiction, the British are not depicted as scoundrels.

Instead, the novel takes an ironic view—critical, sardonic, though hardly mean-spirited—like several works of comic realism that began to appear in the United States several decades later, including *Huckleberry Finn* (1884), *Maggie* (1893), *Babbitt* (1922), *Augie March* (1953). Like these later works of satire, or like Melville's own early "Authentic Anecdotes of Old Zack," *Israel Potter* was designed to burst the complacency of America's middle classes, to redefine their heroes, and to reconstruct their heritage and even their cultural identity. In offering the American public a "dilapidated old tombstone retouched," Melville was trying to reshape his compatriots' sense of their own past so as to take in not just the buried life of the Revolution's "anonymous privates," like Potter, or the little-known foibles of some of America's more colorful founding fathers, such as Ben Franklin and John Paul Jones, but the rugged, raucous, rudely comic muddle that our national history has often been, as events in our own time—Watergate, the Iran-Contra scandal, the PTL debacle, for example—repeatedly confirm (vii–viii). "While we revel in broadcloth," Melville's narrator quips when the young Potter decides to take up arms in the American cause, "let us not forget what we owe to linsey-woolsey" (13).

As a writer of historical fiction, Melville showed little interest in examining the causes of the War for Independence—the conflicting interests, the mounting grievances, the spiraling course of events. Instead he wanted to capture the true character or "temper" of the men of the Revolutionary War era, substituting an ironic, sometimes slightly jaundiced view of his subject for the rose-colored perspective typically found in such fiction. From the very beginning, Melville structured the novel in such a way as to make clear that the national character had degenerated, and not simply changed, since the early years of the eighteenth century. Though he may have been doing nothing more than adopting the ironist's pose, it is worth noting that, as in *Typee,* so too in *Israel Potter,* Melville saw decay, not progress, when he surveyed a culture over time.

Chapter 1, "The Birthplace of Israel," begins with the device of placing the reader in the role of a present-day, mid-nineteenth-century traveler who journeys in the leisurely old way, on horseback, into the historical territory of Israel's birthplace. Throughout this chapter Melville emphasizes the many differences between life in the past in the mountains and life in the present in the cities outside them. For the early inhabitants of the Berkshires, life was rugged, lonely, physically challenging, and so unhurried as to seem almost frozen in time. The first settlers tended to live and work near the tops of these "pastoral mountains" and to enjoy great health and hardiness (3); only in later generations, as the rocky soil became exhausted, did the people begin to move down into the rich valleys, where "unwholesome miasmas" threatened their health. What most impresses the modern mountain-traveler are the huge farmhouses—symbols of "ancient industry"—with their "immense," towerlike stone chimneys and the stone fences "of uncommon neatness and strength." "The number and length of these walls," Melville's narrator says admiringly, "is not more surprising than the size of some of the blocks comprising them. The very Titans seemed to have been at work. That so small an army as the first settlers must needs have been . . . should have accomplished such herculean undertakings with so slight prospect of reward; this is a consideration which gives us a significant hint of the temper of the men of the Revolutionary era" (4–5).[3] By contrast, mid-nineteenth-century life is comfortable, swift-paced, sociable, pleasant. Latter-day tourists are accustomed to travel by locomotive and to pay for hospitality at commercial inns; they are not used to rough roads and the hard inconveniences common to an earlier period (3).

While Israel Potter is hardly mentioned in the opening chapter, we expect that, when he does make his entrance, he will emerge as one of the giants pictured there constructing mountain farms out of massive stones. When, in the second chapter, he makes his first appearance, therefore, it is startling to discover he is of a later generation and that the process of decay from the

time of the original settlers is already well under way. Far from being one of the early Titans, Israel is just a youth when the story begins—eighteen years old, meek, earnest, cautious, and green as grass. And his first action is anything but that of a larger-than-life hero. From the mythic realm, the story passes quickly to the comic, the ironic, or what Frye calls the low mimetic, there to remain for virtually the rest of the book. Oppressed by his father, who forbids a match with the youth's chosen sweetheart, the submissive Israel can bring himself to do nothing more than "quit them both, for another home and other friends." Even his exit is performed in an unheroic fashion; when he goes, he goes secretly, under the cover of darkness, after "pretending to go to bed." On the sultry night in July when he makes his pathetic declaration of independence, it is with tears in his eyes, a bundle over his shoulder, and his tail, so to speak, between his legs (7–8).

Much later, particularly on the several occasions when his life is endangered, Potter will be seen to be capable of being very aggressive and resourceful indeed, but his conduct in this initial scene is nonetheless typical. For example, in his early wanderings through the new countries north and west of his home in search of farm jobs and cheap land, Israel is not afraid of hard work, but he is generally too pliant to gain much more than his labor for his pains. When one employer refuses to pay him his three-months' wages, Israel does not force the matter and instead simply looks around for some other way to earn a living. Noting the all-too-human passivity in Potter's conduct in this scene, while calling attention to a certain realistic complexity in his personality, the narrator sums up Potter's character by observing that, "however brave-hearted, and even much of a dare-devil upon a pinch," Israel "seems, nevertheless, to have envinced, throughout many parts of his career, a singular patience and mildness" (8).

Three years later, after further adventures, a series of other jobs, and few successes, Israel comes back home, only to find that "his love still seemed strangely coy" and his father still stubbornly opposed to their marriage. If *Israel Potter* were a Revolutionary War novel in the sentimental vein, like Cooper's *The Spy* (1821), to name one of the most familiar examples of the genre, we would at this point witness the young hero vowing, despite the formidable odds, to win the hand of his beloved. Instead, Israel "mildly yielded to what seemed his fatality," this time running away to sea in the hope of forgetting his sorrows (9–10). When he returns for the third and last time, it is only to learn that the "dear, false girl, was another's" (11). This anticlimactic development occurs at the end of the second chapter; at a stroke, the love interest has thus been just about knocked out of the book, though Potter's adventures have hardly started.

In plot and character, in theme and structure, Melville's narrative inverts the conventions of the sentimental historical novel and of the popular Revolutionary War novel in particular. The spirit of parody—of comedy, satire, slapstick, and burlesque—runs more or less throughout the rest of the book, at least until the last few naturalistic chapters. Melville was not simply of a mind to make moral judgments in pointing to Potter's failings, however, as several critics have argued; instead, he was attempting to overthrow the prevailing tradition of the Revolutionary War novel, the most common form of historical fiction written in America during the first half of the nineteenth century, according to Ernest Leisy.

This popular genre typically had a "dashing, noble rebel officer" for a hero, who was expected to conquer not only the king's red-coated military forces but the loyalist sympathies of his loved one's father.[4] Melville was clearly determined to put in its place a more lively and lifelike equivalent, a historical novel of comic realism. To accomplish this revolution, he simply did what no one had ever done before; he made art imitate life—or a version of life. He used the chronicle of an actual person—the pathetically comic record of the historical Potter's personal testimony—for the basic outline of his subject and fleshed it out with bits and pieces of local, personal, and national history. By contrast, his predecessors, in relying on the endlessly variable formulas of popular fiction, were merely making art imitate itself. Yet at the same time, in writing a parody of the popular historical novel, Melville made *Israel Potter* as self-consciously literary as the other novels of his mature period—as self-reflexive, if not so obviously so, as *Moby-Dick* or *The Confidence-Man*.

Just as Potter breaks the mold of the conventional suitor, so too does he break the mold of the conventional "rebel" officer or heroic American soldier. To be sure, he is firmly planted on the American side of the conflict with England; and he is a crack shot. In these ways he conforms to the sentimental stereotype. But he is not really high born or well bred; he is not an officer; and he does not spring full-blown on the first page into a noble-hearted, right-thinking, straight-shooting hero. Instead, Melville portrays Potter as following a circuitous, even haphazard, career while developing into a plausible "rebel" and sharpshooter. Forced to scramble to make a living, Potter becomes by turns a farmhand, a surveyor, a hunter and trapper, a land developer, a peddler to the Indians, and, at last, a sailor and whaler. "In this way," explains Melville, whose own life was hardly less checkered than his protagonist's, "was bred that fearless self-reliance and independence which conducted our forefathers to national freedom" (20).

In a similarly matter-of-fact way, Israel and the other "hunter-soldiers" who fought at Bunker Hill were "tutored" to become marksmen of men by

learning first to be hunters of deer and harpooners of whales (9). The American character, as represented by Israel Potter, is shaped chiefly by the chaotic, down-to-earth American experience, not by the ideals found in popular novels, the war rhetoric, or the political declarations of the time. Significantly, we are never provided a clear motive for Potter's joining the rebel forces. Melville says simply that, when "the difficulties long pending between the colonies and England, were arriving at their crisis," and Americans began preparing themselves, Israel "enrolled himself" in the regiment of Colonel John Patterson of Lenox. When news of the Battle of Lexington reached Berkshire county, "the next morning at sunrise, Israel swung his knapsack, shouldered his musket," and marched with Patterson's regiment toward Boston (12–13).

Throughout his adventures, Israel is portrayed as one who reacts to the circumstances of his life rather than as one who initiates action on his own. Beyond his increasingly frustrated desire to return to America after he lands in England, he has no long-term goals or objectives, no will of his own. In this respect, too, he departs from the conventional sentimental hero, who attempts to move life from a fixed ideal within himself or to shape his life and character according to a firmly held set of beliefs. To be sure, Israel is a morally upright young man; he worries, for instance, about the propriety of spending the money he finds in the pocket of the corpse of Squire Woodcock, and he refuses out of patriotic principle to honor King George's personal request to serve in the royal army. But otherwise, like the antihero of later nineteenth- and twentieth-century fiction, he simply moves with the flow of life in response to the circumstances in which he happens to find himself. Accordingly, he takes on an almost bewildering variety of roles, disguises, and occupations as his various life situations demand, from Yankee soldier and secret courier to impressed sailor, lunatic, honest Englishman, and pauper; from old ditcher and cripple to king's gardener, dead man's ghost, and scarecrow; from molder of bricks and repairer of chairs to maker of matches and trash collector.

Of course, from the reader's point of view, Potter does remain the same recognizable personality throughout the tale, despite such superficial alterations. He is not such a truly protean, ambiguous personality as Melville would later portray in *The Confidence-Man*—all glittering surface and seeming darkness at the core. But he is a sufficiently rich and contradictory character that his behavior cannot be regularly predicted or his personality easily summarized. He is, in fact, the central example of the idea, found running throughout the book, that character is largely the product of circumstance and as such is subject to change with changes in the environment. An early instance of behaviorist thinking, this idea ran counter to the notion of the sentimental novelists, who subscribed to a theory of ineluctable "types." At the same time,

it anticipated one of the fundamental assumptions that would emerge among writers of realist fiction in the next generation.

The idea that character depends, for its definition, on the press of circumstance is developed further in Melville's portrayal of the other figures, even the powerful historical personalities who appear in the course of Israel's adventures. Such an idea, it will be seen, is central to the novel's comedy, wherein characters are more pliant and complex than we imagine they will be, or even than they imagine themselves to be. Sir John Millet, for instance, once seen in the flesh, proves not to be the"domineering,""imposing,"Yankee-hating nobleman of popular imagination (24). Though nonplussed by the republican Potter's refusal to address him in the standard English fashion as "Sir," he goes out of his way to supply the down-and-out American with food and clothes, a place to rest, and a job. Strangest of all, he even pledges his honor never to betray Potter's true identity to the British authorities.

Though far from an American sympathizer, the "good knight" thus proves unaccountably to be the "benefactor" of an American rebel (25). Clearly, he does not conform to the stereotype of the imperious English aristocrat; but just as clearly, the only reason he fails to do so, here, is that for once he has to deal with a real-life democrat. In the abstract, as in his wish to be addressed formally, Sir John thinks of himself as embodying the standards of the English knight and thus as deserving all the honors customarily accorded men of his station. The comedy of the scene, in turn, results from the clash between abstract theory and concrete reality, between the expectation of Sir John's lordliness and the resisting circumstance of Israel's stubborn republicanism. But it results, too, from the good knight's unanticipated readiness to turn around and accommodate himself to the circumstance of Potter's need— to protect him and the secret of his identity as an American.[5]

When Israel, in a shadowy scheme, is engaged by Squire Woodcock and his fellow conspirators to carry secret papers to Benjamin Franklin, the new nation's envoy in Paris, Melville treats his readers to the first of three major portraits of major Revolutionary figures. In each case—Franklin, John Paul Jones, and Ethan Allen—Melville set out to capture bona fide national heroes, men whose characters had already been stereotyped by history, simplified by the popular imagination and historical memory. To some degree, therefore, Melville was obliged to remain true to the celebrated stereotype of each man; if he departed from it too far, his rendering would have been unrecognizable and run the risk of being dismissed as malicious or absurd.

Thus in our first view of Franklin, when Potter enters his secluded Paris apartments, he is seen to be the shrewd, lecturing, practical-minded know-it-all so familiar to every American schoolchild. Immediately sensing Israel to

be an American courier on special mission but failing to realize that Potter's outrageously high heels contain secret documents, Franklin admonishes Potter, needlessly, even foolishly, about the waste and danger of such youthful foppery. Sententious, sharp-eyed, and paternalistic, the Franklin of this first scene, despite the oriental conjuror's look of his dress and the necromantic furnishings of his chambers, seems little more than the "homely sage, and household Plato" of legend, a perfect, if sly, parody of the famous author of *Poor Richard's Almanac.*

In the next chapter, however, we learn that this is but a single side of a multifaceted personality, and a consciously manufactured side at that. In Franklin's own time, the narrator explains, correcting the simplified view of the man common among later generations, he "was famous not less for the pastoral simplicity of his manners than for the politic grace of his mind." While it is to be expected, the narrator says, that Franklin would be known to later Americans for his "unselfish devotion," there can be detected in him, as in the Old Testament partriarch Jacob, a "deep worldly wisdom and polished Italian tact, gleaming under an air of Arcadian unaffectedness." Like the complex Jacob, Franklin combined "the apostolic serpent and dove" (46).

Yet Franklin is not just double; he is truly multiform. Though aged seventy-two and widely known for his frugality, he managed at the same time to gain "the good opinion even of the voluptuaries of the showiest of capitals." Stranger still, Franklin was "not less a lady's man, than a man's man, a wise man, and an old man." The key to the richness of his personality is described very simply: "Having carefully weighed the world, Franklin could act any part in it. By nature turned to knowledge, his mind was often grave, but never serious." Thus in Franklin, personality is, at least on the surface, a fabrication; he can be virtually anyone or anything he wants to be. For Melville, an enabling identity, or series of identities, comes with knowledge—knowledge of a particular pursuit, or set of pursuits, and of the world at large. But even so, such a range of identities as Franklin demonstrates can be attained only if one has a deeper, prior identity, what in his case Melville calls the "philosophical levity of tranquility" at the heart of Franklin's personality, like the "insular Tahiti" that Ishmael, another polymath, claims to lie at the center of his soul.[6] "Printer, postmaster, almanac maker, essayist, chemist, orator, tinker, statesman, humorist, philosopher, parlor-man, political economist, professor of housewifery, ambassador, projector, maxim-monger, herb-doctor, wit:—Jack of all trades, master of each and mastered by none—the type and genius of his land. Franklin was everything but a poet."[7]

In a statement that has important ramifications for the study of personality in *Israel Potter,* Melville goes on to say that the Franklin on display in his

> But since a soul with many qualities, forming of itself a sort of handy index
> and pocket congress of all humanity, needs the contact of just as many
> different men, or subjects, in order to the exhibition of its totality; hence
> very little indeed of the sage's multifariousness will be portrayed in a simple
> narrative like the present. This casual private intercourse with Israel, but
> served to manifest him in his far lesser lights; thrifty, domestic, dietarian,
> and, it may be, didactically waggish. There was much benevolent irony,
> innocent mischievousness, in the wiseman. Seeking here to depict him in
> his less exalted habitudes, the narrator feels more as if he were playing with
> one of the sage's worsted hose, than reverentially handling the honored hat
> which once oracularly sat upon his brow. (48)

Surely Melville felt he was risking censure in portraying Franklin in the vein
of comic realism that typifies this novel. But surely, too, he felt genuine admiration for the man and his intelligence and for his myriad accomplishments.

The idea that personality flourishes among other personalities or requires
contact with a variety of other people to bring out the full range of one's
latent qualities constituted for Melville a theory of personality and a theory of
fictional character, even a theory of the novel. For it can be seen to operate
not only in his portrayal of the richly multifarious Franklin but in his portrayal of the rather simple Potter and of others in the book as well. One of the
things that readers of the book have faulted in Potter's behavior is its inconsistencies. Mild in some instances, for example, as he is in response to the
machinations of his father, he is belligerent in others.

But instead of regarding these disparities as flaws in Melville's presentation
of Potter's character, we should view them as expressions of the idea that personality is multifaceted, capable of taking on different forms in response to
different people or situations. Thus in his exchange with King George, Potter
is himself uncharacteristically imperious, refusing to acknowledge the British
sovereign as his king. And in his moments with the waggish Franklin, he himself grows unusually ironic in tone; nowhere is he so sly as when he is discern-
ing just how sly Franklin is with him. Indeed, what is so funny about Potter's
scenes with the American sage is that he grows as shrewd as the old genius
himself and manages to see through Franklin's smooth rhetorical posturings.
When his host makes visit after visit to strip his room of its few amenities, for
instance, all the while talking as though he had only Potter's own best interests at heart in making his pilferings, Israel observes keenly that "Every time
he comes in he robs me . . . with an air all the time, too, as if he were making

me presents" (53). Later, with John Paul Jones, Potter shows another side of himself when he becomes a "tiger" capable of heroism in battle, simply at Jones's boisterous urging (89). Such fluidity of character is not so much a matter of inconsistency as it is evidence that Melville was working from a sophisticated and realistic conception of personality.

In presenting each of the important historical figures in the book, Melville portrayed rich, complex, comic personalities in the realistic mode, characters who can change their spots according to the company they keep. However, at the same time, Melville was determined to explore the sources of their greatness. Indeed, this was one of the major responsibilities of the historical novelist, in Melville's view, or so it seems.

For as with the portrait of Franklin, so too with that of John Paul Jones: our introductory view makes him appear to be something of an enigma, a contradiction. Secreted behind a screen, Israel first catches just a glimpse of him pinching and bussing the chambermaid as he chases her up the stairs leading to Franklin's apartments. But when Jones makes his entrance into the room, he seemed "to have undergone a complete transformation." Though extravagantly dressed, with a touch of the Parisian salon about him, he is hardly the young dandy he first appeared to be. Indeed, "he did not seem to be altogether civilized." Repeatedly the words "savage" and "barbaric" are used to describe what is distinctive about him; he had an "aspect as of a disinherited Indian Chief in European clothes," we are told, and a "savage, self-possessed eye." Proud, scornful, intrepid, "he looked like one who never had been, and never would be, a subordinate," and so he insists, when, in his first speech (using didactic language that shows Franklin's sudden influence), he says he would "teach" the British that Paul Jones "is no subject of the British King" (56). Just as there is a "touch of primeval orientalness" in Franklin, buried under his eighteenth-century practical-mindedness, so there is a "pagan," "New Zealand warrior's" indominability in John Paul Jones hidden behind his stylish ruffles and ladies' jewelry (62–63).

This intriguing view of the future father of the American navy is developed further in an extraordinary scene when Potter, feigning sleep in his Paris room, watches as the restless Jones paces the floor until he glimpses his own image in the mirror. Rolling up a sleeve, he reveals "certain large intertwisted cyphers covering the whole inside of the arm . . . with mysterious tatooings." Unlike the patterns on most sailors' bodies, this one was "such as is seen only on thorough-bred savages—deep blue, elaborate, labyrinthine, cabalistic"—like those found all over Queequeg's body. Covering his arm, Jones resumes his pacing, but now "a gleam of the consciousness of possessing a character as yet unfathomed, and hidden power to back unsuspected projects, irradiated his

cold white brow." It is important that Jones thinks no one has seen him, for he believes the special power of his private character depends on its remaining concealed from others (62–63).

Melville, however, goes on to assert that such power sleeps in everyone, awakening in times of public strife, such as war or revolution, or personal crisis. Mankind cannot be divided into simple categories of good and evil, refined and ferocious, as popular historical novelists of Melville's own time tended to do. In Melville's view, we are all capable of all. "So at midnight," he observes, "the heart of the metropolis of modern civilization was secretly trod by this jaunty barbarian in broad-cloth; a sort of prophetical ghost, glimmering in anticipation upon the advent of those tragic scenes of the French Revolution which levelled the exquisite refinement of Paris with the blood-thirsty ferocity of Borneo; showing that broaches and finger-rings, not less than nose-rings and tattooing, are tokens of the primeval savageness which ever slumbers in human kind, civilised and uncivilised" (63).

Jones's "primal savageness" is an important clue to the powerful nature of his character, but it is not the key to his greatness. Only later, when he and Potter meet again on the sea, do we learn the cause of Jones's deep desire to unleash the savagery that will one day carry him to fame. A man of great pride and honor, and immense ego, Jones found that his good name had been besmirched in his own town of Whitehaven, Scotland, where the story had circulated that he had once flogged a sailor to death. Holding the story to be a lie—"I flogged him," he admits, "for he was a mutinous scamp. But he died naturally, some time afterwards, and on board another ship"—Jones vowed vengeance on his slanderers. "When last I left Whitehaven," he proclaims, with the resoluteness of a monomaniac, "I swore never again to set foot on her pier, except, like Caesar at Sandwich, as a foreign invader" (91).

The key to Jones's personality, then, is the singlemindedness of his determination to restore his good name. His savagery is the efficient cause of his rise to prominence; it supplies the energy. But the final cause of his daring achievements is the vulnerability of his ego, the intolerable pain of his wounded self-esteem. He cannot live with the image of himself as a heartless bully, and to regain the respect of his detractors, he would perform such feats of courage that they would have to submit to him as their lord and conqueror. Such is the desperate logic of an injured, if mighty, ego.

Although the mood of *Israel Potter* grows more elevated, and less comic, with the appearance of John Paul Jones, Melville continues in these chapters to undercut the conventional, sentimental view of America's War for Independence and its participants. Jones is a heroic figure, to be sure, a man of extraordinary fortitude and command. But in Melville's portrayal of the man

these personal virtues are not called out by the grand ideals of the American cause—justice, freedom from tyranny, the pursuit of happiness—nor are they provoked by the evils or injustices of the British. Jones's behavior is explained on purely personal grounds as resulting from a local spat between the Scottish town of Whitehaven and the man who was to become its most famous son. Far from being a selfless hero, fighting to free America from British oppression, John Paul Jones is, in Melville's phrase, "the Coriolanus of the sea." Like the Roman conqueror, he is moved to action by the desire for revenge against the city that had sullied his reputation and disowned him (95).

When Melville turned to the famous sea fight between the *Bon Homme Richard* and the *Serapis,* the encounter in which Jones made his name, he assumed the task of presenting what is, for the Revolutionary War novel, the obligatory big battle scene.[8] Though Melville's mood is serious, even at times solemn—in retelling the story of the horrible slaughter of the encounter he was touching on one of those distinctly Melvillean themes of profound mystery—it is clear he was determined to subvert conventional renderings of such episodes as found in popular historical novels. Not only would Melville present the true nature of this conflict, he would supply the reader a proper understanding of it as well. The dramatic confrontation of the *Serapis* and the *Bon Homme Richard* is not described as a fight between a heroic, upright power and a tyrannical, malevolent one. Instead, there is bravery to be found on both sides, and a horrifying savagery, which at moments is so senseless as to be absurd.

Contrary to the popular view, Paul Jones's American forces are so riddled with jealousy and feelings of mutiny as to be a liability to the Revolutionary cause. Noble qualities—the kind that typify the characters in popular historical novels—are hardly in abundance here. When Jones tries to stir up the interest of the captains of his fleet in engaging the English, he gets nowhere by appealing to their "gallantry." However, when he sets a sizable ransom for them instead, he meets with instant success (116). Even more condemning of the rebel participants, one of the consorts of America's lead ship inexplicably fires on her several times, right at the very height of the conflict. While Jones is unfailingly courageous in attacking the enemy—his famous exclamation, "I have not yet begun to fight," is a just indication of his heroism—he is not portrayed as an all-powerful, all-determining hero such as the popular imagination always hungers for. It was "luck," Melville says, that threw in his way the great action of his life, "the most extraordinary of all naval engagements" (119); and for once the ever-changeable wind, which earlier had frustrated Jones's plans time and again, worked to his advantage, too, in the end.

The historical novelist with a penchant for realism must do more, however, than portray real-life characters and events in all their contingency and complexity—the way they actually appeared in their own time and place. He must portray them symbolically as well, to suggest their full national significance. He must help the reader gain an appreciation of those discrete historical events, such as the famous sea battle between the *Serapis* and the *Bon Homme Richard,* that have truly national importance, not just in their immediate effects but in their more distant implications. He must, as Melville says stiffly, show of what the event in each case is "indicatory." "In itself so curious," the engagement between these two fighting vessels has still greater interest if seen as "a type, a parallel, and a prophecy" of America's national character. "Sharing the same blood with England," he concludes, "and yet her proved foe in two wars; not wholly inclined at bottom to forget an old grudge: intrepid, unprincipled, reckless, predatory, with boundless ambition, civilized in externals but a savage at heart, America is, or may yet be, the Paul Jones of nations" (120).

Insofar as the spirit behind the American Revolution is captured in the spirit of this fight, we have to conclude that Melville saw the American people as motivated most deeply, in their War for Independence, not by high ideals but by anger and hatred—anger at an old wrong and hatred for an old oppressor. Yet it is the kind of anger and hatred that one can feel only for those one once loved or with whom he or she has shared a long-standing familial bond. That the two ships become lashed side by side, bow to stern, is deeply fitting and profoundly symbolic. So closely bound were they and so relentlessly, so ragingly warring with each other that "It seemed more an intestine feud, than a fight between strangers. Or, rather, it was as if the Siamese Twins, oblivious of their fraternal bond, should rage in unnatural fight" (125). Their hatred had grown so intense as to be self-destructive, and so it proved in this unparalleled fight, when the victorious *Richard,* severely damaged by fire, the next day went down.

With the end of the fight between the *Bon Homme Richard* and the *Serapis* and the gradual disappearance of the prideful Paul Jones, the mood of *Israel Potter* returns to the low comedy of the earlier chapters. Openly signaling this shift, Melville explains that "across the otherwise blue-jean career of Israel, Paul Jones flits and re-flits like a crimson thread. One more brief intermingling of it, and to plain old homespun we return" (131). Making their way back to America some months later in another ship, Jones and Potter and the rest of the crew have a brief run-in with a British letter-of-marque that fakes surrender and then suddenly pulls away just as Potter, in his eagerness, is jumping on board. The next scene, which shows Israel desperately wandering

the large enemy fighting ship in a vain attempt to insinuate himself into one of the several quarters of the crew, is one of the most comically absurd pieces in all of Melville's writings, the equal of such moments as Pip's wisely foolish colloquies with Ahab in *Moby-Dick* or the Cosmopolitan's cunning exchanges in *The Confidence-Man.*

Unlike comparable situations in conventional historical novels, however, where the hero manages to disguise himself so well as to move freely among the enemy, this scene repeatedly insists on the failure of Potter's masquerade as a lost member of the British crew. The men of the enemy ship are not so obtuse as to be taken in by Israel's deception and think he is one of their own. The comic realism of this scene depends on the repeated frustration of Potter's efforts, on the deepening desperation of his plight as an American sailor on an enemy warship. But it depends, too, on the jaunty, Chaplinesque way he persists in his attempts to install himself among the crew and on the equally cartoonish rebuffs he meets in return. In the main-top, for example, he is threatened with being dropped to the deck "like a jewel-block" if he refuses to leave; among the sheet-anchor-men he is fetched "a terrible thump" and pushed "ignominiously off the forecastle" as a strange interloper (133–34). Wherever he goes, insult is added to injury. Trying to insinuate himself among the waisters with the cheerful reminder that their ship is homeward bound, he is told to "sit on your head"; and when he changes tactics and tries to lift up their spirits with a song, he is shouted down with the claim that he sounds worse than "a broken-nosed old bellows" (135). Such rejoinders are the very stuff of realistic comic fiction: downbeat, earthy, even nasty, they defeat the hero's desires without turning his antagonists into the stark villains of melodramatic historical fiction.

Besides providing a memorable example of Melville's comic realism, chapter 20, "The Shuttle," which details Potter's ineffectual efforts at passing himself off as a member of the British crew, offers some oblique commentary on the problems Melville thought his readers would face when encountering a realistic character like Israel Potter in a novel of the American Revolutionary War. Here Melville's remarks center, ostensibly, on the absurdity of Potter's presence on a British letter-of-marque, but by implication they comment also on the absurdity of his presence in a novel treating America's legendary past. Given conventional expectations in either context, Potter should not be where he is. The resistance to him demonstrated by the British warship's officers and crew should be read as suggestive of what Melville anticipated his audience's reaction would be toward the discovery that Israel had been given the central role in a Revolutionary War narrative. As the officer of the deck exclaims to the sailing master, it is not simply a matter of the unfathomable stranger be-

ing "out of his mind," as he says of Potter. It is the fact of his very existence
that is so baffling. "He's out of all reason; out of all men's knowledge and
memories! Why, no one knows him; no one has ever seen him before; no
imagination, in the wildest flight of a morbid nightmare, has ever so much as
dreamed of him" (137). Israel Potter could not be invented; he represents the
kind of historical truth that is stranger than fiction—at least stranger than the
conventional fiction of the early nineteenth century.

When the British warship reaches Falmouth, England, Potter catches first
one glimpse and then another of Ethan Allen, the third and last of America's
great Revolutionary War heroes limned by Melville and the one truly larger-
than-life figure in this otherwise realistic narrative. At the time a prisoner of
war, Allen is portrayed as "a martial man of Patagonian stature . . . whose
defiant head overshadowed" his captors', "as St. Paul's dome its inferior
steeples." Repeatedly he is described in epic terms as "the giant" or "the colossal stranger" or in images of powerful wild animals, such as "a great whale" or
a "tormented lion" (142ff). Melville often borrowed language from the tall
tale to describe him, as when at one point he says Allen spoke with such a
"blast" of contempt that he blew backward the British officer who had been
tormenting him, "as from before the suddenly burst head of a steam-boiler,"
forcing him to stagger away "with a snapped spine" (144).

Allen's own language, too, sometimes crackles with the colorful excesses
of the gritty heroes of America's Western frontier, whose rough-and-tumble
stories in a realistic vein had been made popular in Melville's own time in W.
T. Porter's *The Spirit of the Times* (1831–61) and elsewhere. In one particularly
notable outburst, Allen denounces the leader of the British North American
forces, General Lord Howe, as "that toad-hearted king's lick-spittle of a scarlet poltroon; the vilest wriggler in God's worm-hole below" (144). More important still are the incredible acts of derring-do that make Allen a close kin
to Mike Fink and Davy Crockett. At one point, while handcuffed, Allen manages to disarm an insulting captor without even using his hands when he
catches the young private's sword between his teeth, wrenches it from his
grasp, and then sends it flying with a toss of his head. Such actions are what
Western folktales and legends were being made of even at the time when *Israel Potter* was being published. Indeed, Allen is, Melville writes, the Western
spirit incarnate: "Though born in New England, he exhibited no trace of her
character. He was frank; bluff; companionable as a Pagan; convivial; a Roman;
hearty as a harvest. His spirit was essentially western" (149).

Even in spite of his outsized qualities, however, Allen is portrayed in an
essentially realistic way. For Melville shows that, like the tall-tale heroes, Allen
has adopted the larger-than-life Western spirit as a pose. Everything he does is

a conscious fabrication, a ruse or ploy. As is revealed in the scene where a group of admiring ladies visits the notorious American giant in prison, Allen is able to cut almost any figure the circumstances call for. Here he shows he can talk "like a beau in a parlor; this wild, mossed American from the woods," as one female observer exclaims (145). On another occasion he shows he can speak like a Christian gentleman to a clergyman, as in a brief episode when he requests a bowl of punch. Thus when he at one point says, in response to one of several questions about his past, "at present I am a conjuror by profession," he is slyly hinting at the fact that he is always acting one part or another (146). This is confirmed when Melville, assessing Allen's "scornful and ferocious" posture toward his British captors, explains it is a conscious strategy adopted in response to the "inexcusable cruelty and indignity" of his treatment as a prisoner since his defeat at Montreal. Allen has discovered, Melville surmises, "that by assuming the part of a . . . braggart barbarian, he would better sustain himself against bullying turnkeys than by submissive quietude." "When among wild beasts," he says tersely, "if they menace you, be a wild beast" (149–50).

Potter never actually meets Ethan Allen. Though he had designed "a little scheme . . . for materially befriending" him, Israel is forced to beat a hasty retreat before he can put the plan into play (152). Fearing that his identity as an American had been exposed, and that he might be impressed into service in the British navy in Falmouth harbor, Israel decides to flee to London and try to lose himself in the crowds there. With this last of his escapes from the enemy, which he seals when he stops along the way to disguise himself in the discarded rags of a "pauper suicide," the Revolutionary War portion of Potter's story comes to an unceremonious, but symbolically significant, end (153). In the concluding chapters, then, Melville is left with two major tasks: He must explain the nearly incredible fact of the more than forty-year delay in Potter's return to America, and he must render his return, when it finally occurs, in a way that will bring his story to a pointed yet realistic close.

The first thing to be noticed about Melville's narrative treatment of the period of Potter's exile is that it is even more condensed than Trumbull's treatment was. The difference is not to be attributed to any squeamishness that Melville might have felt regarding his hero's extraordinary miseries in London, however, as more than one prominent critic has argued.[9] And it is not really to be attributed to the concern Melville expresses for the squeamishness of his reading public, when at one point he says that even "the gloomiest and truthfulest dramatist seldom chooses for his theme the calamities" of paupers, rather than of kings, knowing as he does that few people will be "enticed to the shanty, where, like a pealed knuckle-bone, grins the unupholstered

corpse of the beggar" (161). Melville wanted to go on record at this juncture as a pragmatic, even hardheaded author who was forced by the predilections of his audience to draw the line of his own performance at what later writers would call "tenement fiction."

However, we should not think of him as backing away from the realist writer's resolve to face the most loathsome facts in human experience without blinking. For he does not eliminate or sidestep Potter's sufferings so much as he abbreviates them—in his own words, he "skims events to the end"— while at the same time inventing a few horrifying ones of his own, such as the hungry Potter's "wrangling with rats for prizes in the sewers" of the city (161– 62).[10] Instead, Melville seems simply to be providing a rationalization for his desire to wrap up Potter's story in a way that is consistent with the brisk plotting of the earlier episodes.

While the concluding chapters show some signs of hurry or a kind of wry impatience, they also show signs of Melville's masterly hand. In general, Melville altered the mood and method of his narrative, and even the character of Israel Potter, from what they were in the original ghost-written version. To some extent, these changes follow similar developments in Trumbull's account of Potter's life, which darkens conspicuously in the bleak London years. But in important ways Melville made changes that were wholly his own, in an effort, I would say, to show Potter's protracted exile to be believable, while at the same time trying to wrap up the tale as expeditiously as possible. Specifically, the robust, Fieldingesque sense of humor found in most of the earlier chapters of the book has been replaced by a modern mood of grim irony, as Israel, "desperate with want," stops outside the city for several weeks to work in the muddy pit of a great brickyard, where he promptly takes on "the reckless sort of half jolly despair" felt by the other "dismal desperadoes" there (154–55). Moreover, the relatively simple and direct method of comic realism that Melville followed in the earlier chapters has been all but discarded in favor of an insistent symbolism and a moody naturalism that typify the fiction of Melville's magazine period, particularly "The Tartarus of Maids," "Jimmy Rose," and "The Bell-Tower."

Except for the hint that the original Potter had once worked in a brickyard, chapter 23, "Israel in Egypt," is entirely of Melville's own making. Clearly, it is intended as a transition to the London years of hardship and exile. While he had used symbolism sporadically earlier in the narrative, Melville switched in this chapter to a sustained symbolic mode bearing the marks of the work of his middle period—the resonant ironies; the reaching for profound effects; the worldly wise, even mocking, yet sometimes reverent air of meditation. In

the brickyard episode, where bricks become types in a series of sardonic meditations on the vanity of all human effort, the symbolic mode becomes a clever method of shorthand. It conveys in a condensed, intensified way a sharp sense of the grueling work, the oppressive poverty, and the life-sapping despair that characterize Potter's late years in England, and at the same time it convincingly suggests that Potter's suffering was not the product of a special gift for ineptitude, that he was not unique but representative of a whole class of luckless wretches living in London at the start of the previous century.

Working in the pit of one of a score of "melancholy old mills" in this great brickyard, Israel is but one insignificant cog in a vast machine, which is itself but a cog in the still vaster machine centering on London, its bricks all going to supply the huge market there. For the "muddy philosophers" who work in the pits, slapping mud into rude wooden trays day after day, week after week, their lives are of no more worth than the dough that goes to make up those very bricks. To them, "men and bricks were equally of clay. What signifies who we be—dukes or ditchers? thought the moulders; all is vanity and clay." While Melville's own comment on this scene is less despairing than the ditchers', it too is naturalistic. Seeming to excuse the nihilism of these desperate figures, he explains that "their vice was like that weed which but grows on barren ground; enrich the soil, and it disappears" (155). Such a remark is as behavioristic in its implications as the philosophy behind Davis's "Life in the Iron Mills" (1861), Crane's *Maggie* (1893), or Dreiser's *An American Tragedy* (1925). But, even so, Melville's view seems to grow more deterministic still when he returns to the image of man as a brick and begins to consider the cosmology that such a trope suggests to him:

> brick is no bad name for any son of Adam; Eden was but a brick-yard; what is a mortal but a few luckless shovelfuls of clay, moulded in a mould, laid out on a sheet to dry, and ere long quickened into his queer caprices by the sun? Are not men built into communities just like bricks into a wall? Consider the great wall of China: ponder the great populace of Pekin. As man serves bricks, so God him, building him up by billions into edifices of his purposes. (156)

More distant, more detached even than in his previous remark, Melville here anticipates the hard naturalistic view of humanity presented in the grim fable in Mark Twain's *The Mysterious Stranger* (1916), wherein the God-like Satan fashions a colony of tiny people out of clay simply to demonstrate his power and their utter insignificance to him.

Despite the grimness of the brickmakers' lot, Israel somehow perseveres.
After thirteen weeks in the brickyard, he finds himself with a tolerable set of
clothes and a little money in his pocket, so he sets off once more for London,
this time "to seek his fortune" (158). "Not by constitution disposed to gloom,"
Melville observes, using a naturalistic language of his own, Israel thus continues to set himself up for the kind of defeated expectations that become the
hallmark of realist fiction later in the century (160). For London, among the
working classes, is a world of unending drudgery, disappointment, and despair.

Again turning to symbolism to suggest the powerful naturalistic forces at
work in Israel's story, Melville makes London Dante's "City of Dis." Even as he
enters the metropolis, Potter becomes a condemned soul in "that hereditary
crowd—gulf-stream of humanity—which, for continuous centuries, has never
ceased pouring, like an endless shoal of herring, over London Bridge." Grotesque and aged, with a grimly violent history, the Bridge—like London itself
and everything in it—is black, "besmoked," funereal. The Thames is so polluted as to be but "one murky sheet of sewerage"; the "black vistas of streets
were as the galleries in coal mines"; and the pale, sooty faces of the people drift
by Israel like the aspects of "uninvited ghosts in Hades." From the moment he
sets foot in the city, and witnesses the mournful faces of this mournful scene,
Potter knows that "being of this race, felicity could never be his lot" (158–60).

Throughout Melville's unrelentingly grim, three-page portrait of London,
it is evident that his main objective was to establish the dark fatality of Israel's
protracted separation from America; in making London an urban inferno,
Melville was trying to create an environment from which there would appear
to be no exit. Thus we are told that "by sickness, destitution, each busy ill of
exile, [Israel] was destined to experience a fate, uncommon even to luckless
humanity; a fate whose crowning qualities were its remoteness from relief
and its depth of obscurity; London, adversity, and the sea, three Armaged-
dons, which, at one and the same time, slay, and secrete their victims" (160).
Though Melville's characterization of London is based on a slight five-line
journal entry he made at the time of his own visit there several years earlier,
he can hardly be said to have been trying to cut corners in this late scene of
Israel Potter by recycling material he had worked up earlier.[11]

In the few remaining pages, Melville provides just enough details about
Potter's life during his forty-five-year exile in London to render an impression of its general squalor and of his eventual decline into penury and virtual
senility. We are told of "a sort of humble prosperity" that he enjoyed for a
while and of his consequent "hopes of being able to buy his homeward passage"

once the war was over. But this promising start is, almost predictably, turned on its head. As "stubborn fate would have it," Potter sustains an injury one day, falls in love with the shopgirl who nurses him back to health, and ends up spending his savings to marry her. When the peace between England and America comes, therefore, he is no longer free to travel alone, and he cannot afford to leave England with his new family. Worse still, once the end of the war swells the ranks of London's laboring classes and depresses all their wages, he suddenly finds it hard to get work. "Driven out of his previous employ" as a warehouse porter, Israel takes up a series of the lowliest jobs, including chair-bottoming, match making, scrap collecting, and at last scavenging. At the same time that he slides into brutal poverty, in accord, as Melville says, with certain inexorable laws of class economics, he is weighted down with greater responsibilities, as, "according to another well-known Malthusian enigma in human affairs, his family increased." Before he knows it, he has eleven children, though all but one die an early death (162).

In the concluding pages, we learn that the downward curve of Potter's life is finally halted, and even modestly reversed, for a period of almost twenty-five years, during the French revolutionary and Napoleonic wars, when London was relieved of a portion of its "superfluous hordes" (163). But a return to itinerant chair-bottoming is the best he ever manages; and when a second peace, that of 1817 (1815), brings its disbanded soldiers back into London, Israel is reduced to competing with them for the "chance threepenny job." Why he persists, in the face of such woeful circumstances, is a question Melville answers with a stark naturalistic simile when he likens Potter to one of "those tough old oaks of the cliffs, which, though hacked at by hail-stones of tempests, and even wantonly maimed by the passing woodman, still, however cramped by rival trees and fettered by rocks, succeed, against all odds, in keeping the vital nerve of the tap-root alive" (165).

In the end, however, Israel is more than an example of simple organic persistence. Something—the memory of his past life in "the far Canaan beyond the sea"—persists within him to feed the thin fire of his vitality. In the difficult years following the second peace, Israel seems to have given up hope of ever returning to America; when his one surviving child asks him when he will take him there, we are told that "'Some day to come, my boy'; would be the hopeful response of an unhoping heart" (166). But in the last pages, Melville goes out of his way to dramatize the tenacity of Potter's boyhood memories. Observing that sometimes, when provoked by some stray incident, "thoughts of home would . . . overpower him for a time to a sort of hallucination," Melville invents two brief but poignant scenes wherein Israel begins to relive a reminis-

cence out of his New England youth. In the first of these, while working in St. James Park, and lost in a reverie, he hears a sound that leads him "insanely" to imagine that Old Huckleberry, a favorite horse from his youth, is reminding him of feed time; and in the second, many years later, while making his way through a London fog, he hears a call for help to head off some bewildered cattle and finds himself so overtaken by "monomaniac reminiscences" that he "dreamed himself home into the mists of the Housatonic mountains; ruddy boy on the upland pastures again" (164–65). Melville says only that such imaginings constitute Israel's major form of relief from his dismal lot in England. But it is clear that they also serve a dramatic function, providing a brief but credible rationale for the fact of Israel's return to America in the final chapter. For they reveal, in ways made familiar later by such masters of psychological realism as Davis, Crane, and Dreiser, the psychological impact of the misery Israel has experienced during his London years, and they convey in a striking, subjectively felt way his deep and abiding hunger for escape.

Ironist to the end, Melville undercuts the expectation that Israel's suffering and fidelity to his dream of returning to "the Fortunate Isles of the Free" will be rewarded at last, as they would be in a conventional historical novel. Israel does return, but not through any effort of his own—no determined plotting, no pinching of hard-earned pennies—and the land he returns to is hardly the Promised Land he remembers, fondly but mistakenly, from his youth. It is his sole surviving child—the "spared Benjamin of his old age"—who perseveres "against every obstacle" and in the end secures their ocean passage from the American consul in England. Israel only sows "the seeds of his eventual return" by painting for the boy's imagination "scenes of nestling happiness and plenty, in which the lowliest shared," scenes from which he has conveniently excised every trace of his own youthful miseries (166). And when he finally arrives in America, all he encounters are disappointments—fragments of his boyhood past that are too broken and scattered to gather together again and shore against his ruins. When he lands in Boston during the Fourth of July festivities there, he finds so little of the Bunker Hill days of 1775, now almost fifty years later, that he is not only unappreciated but wholly unrecognized. When he leaves Boston for his old home in the Berkshire mountain country, he discovers that no one there recalls him or even remembers his name. And when he tries to hunt up his father's old homestead, he is informed it had burned down long before and the last surviving member of his family had gone West.

Not until Israel makes his way into a vaguely familiar old wood, where he happens upon a decaying half-cord of hemlock, does he begin to sense he may

have found his boyhood haunts. There, as he stands contemplating a "strange, mouldy pile" of firewood, the memory—or is it merely a "vision" (169)?— suddenly comes back to him that he was the one who, as a boy, had stacked this very pile, since "abandoned to oblivious decay. Type now," as Melville says, summing up the many ironies of Potter's life, "as it stood there, of for ever arrested intentions, and a long life still rotting in early mishap" (168).

Israel's own life, however, has not been entirely wasted; the son by his side is testimony to the fact that his existence has borne at least a little fruit and that his dreams will continue, even if in ways he can hardly anticipate. But the decaying woodpile aptly captures the ironic truth—the kind of truth that such realist writers of the next generation as James, Howells, and Chopin were to make their stock in trade—that the shape of Israel's life has proved to be anything but the shape he had originally planned. He does manage to find his way back to the very spot where he had grown up when he momentarily stumbles on the nearly buried hearthstone of his family's former house. He can thus exclaim, with what are almost his last words, "The ends meet" (169).

But the neatness of even this conclusion is ironic and illusory. Israel's final statement is not made in satisfaction at any fulfillment of his fifty-year quest to return to the place of his birth; it is made in despair at his discovery of the utter absence, in this region that was once his home, of any connecting link to his past. Although the beginning of his life and the end can be said to meet here, there is no redemptive meaning in their convergence. There is only the simple fact of their coming together and Israel's realization that their doing so leaves him no better off; that it leaves him with nothing.

In a brief concluding paragraph, we are told matter-of-factly of the final ironies in Israel's life: he was "repulsed in efforts, after a pension, by certain caprices of law"; the little book he dictated in his last attempt to secure fame and fortune has long since "faded out of print . . . his name out of memory"; he died on "the same day that the oldest oak on his native hills was blown down" (169). Melville's narrative is thus a work with a decidedly closed ending—more so than Potter's own could have been, for it ends with the death of its title figure. However, the irony of Israel's return home, like the irony of the book generally, keeps the conclusion from being satisfying in the way that stories of the lives of historical figures usually are. There is no final happiness here, no resolution or handsome payoff after protracted, herculean struggles. *Israel Potter* is a modest book written "on salary," as Mark Twain might have said, with a little man, who is deeply familiar with defeat, for a hero. But it is an important, if long neglected, harbinger of the realist fiction that would begin to emerge in America in the decade of the 1860s, particularly along the comic end of the spectrum represented by Twain and Crane.

Melville's novel thus stands as one of the very earliest instances of realistic writing by an American—the first by a major figure—and is contemporaneous with the great period of realist writing in France. Indeed, it predates by almost a decade Flaubert's *Salammbô* (1862), a work that George Decker has credited with having "opened the doors of the historical novel to realism."[12] That honor, I believe, should in fact go to Melville's own "Revolutionary narrative of the beggar."[13]

Chapter Nine

∾

Dialogue of Crisis:
The Confidence-Man
as Experimental Novel

The Confidence-Man: His Masquerade (1857) is Melville's most puzzling narrative, and his most modern. Though set on the American frontier in the middle of the last century and packed with caricatures of contemporary personalities and cultural symbols, it has the absurdist tone and texture, theme and structure of some of the most brilliant experimental fiction of the twentieth century.[1] Indeed, it is the clearest example of the experimental novel—not only in Melville's writings, but in the whole of the nineteenth century, in America or Europe. By nature a sui generis work, it nonetheless falls within a tradition of experimental fiction that looks back to Sterne's *Tristram Shandy* (1760–67), a book Melville first read on his 1849 trip to London,[2] and forward to the modernist works of Joyce, Kafka, and Borges; to the "new novel" of Robbe-Grillet and other French writers of the 1950s; and even to the postmodernist writings of Vonnegut, Pynchon, Coover, and Barthelme.

Like the incisive, often playful narratives of these other writers, *The Confidence-Man* deconstructs conventional notions of character, plot, and point of view (though not always in the same way they do, to be sure). Rather than focusing on the history and trials of a single character, as Melville's previous novels and the novels of virtually all of his contemporaries and predecessors had done, *The Confidence-Man* presents a series of encounters with problematic figures whose pasts are, and remain, shrouded in mystery. Instead of defining a single, linear action, his narrative inscribes a plot that repeats itself

This chapter appeared in a different version as "The Dialogue of Crisis in *The Confidence-Man:* Melville's 'New Novel'" in *Studies in the Novel* 6 (Summer 1974): 16–85. Copyright 1974 by North Texas State University. Reprinted by permission of the publisher.

285

almost endlessly yet seems to go nowhere. And rather than adopting the point of view of a self-effacing but omniscient authorial presence, it employs a narrator who frequently interrupts the story to offer brief asides that call into question the motives and intentions of the book's characters or to deliver meditations on the author's craft. Even the setting, a Mississippi riverboat traveling south from St. Louis, is unconventional—transient, public, dreamlike; certainly it is not stable or rooted in a single "place," where characters would typically be shown to grow or deepen. And although the action is confined to a single day, the day is April 1, when trickery and confusion have virtual license. Perhaps most problematic of all, instead of defining a single powerful theme or thematic conflict and bringing it to resolution, *The Confidence-Man* insinuates a rich but ambiguous melange of themes that has so puzzled readers as to leave many of them in doubt even as to what the book is about.[3]

When viewed within the context of the experimental novel, however, these many signs of unconventionality and sources of puzzlement in *The Confidence-Man* can be seen to be entirely purposeful. Though often marked by a profound iconoclasm and mischievousness, the experimental novel is not, generally speaking, opposed to tradition simply out of love of opposition or out of anger or nihilism. Woolf, Joyce, Faulkner, Ellison, and the other great experimenters of this century certainly chafed at the limits of traditional realism, but none of them wrote simply out of hostility to what is old or established. Like Melville, they were fueled by a desire to create a new kind of realism, a truer, more sophisticated, more lifelike rendering of experience than could be found in the conventional realistic novel. As Melville concluded in *Moby-Dick,* the key to an enhanced understanding of life is not to "enlarge" the mind but to "subtilize" it.[4]

The novelist's job, then, is to render experience in such a way as to show it to be as problematic or inscrutable as life itself. But to do that, the novelist has to shock us out of our conventionality and give us a renewed appreciation for just how problematic or inscrutable life can be. Stein, Woolf, Joyce, and other experimenters typically managed this objective by exposing the reader to the subjective chaos or hidden life of their characters via stream-of-consciousness or related techniques. Melville took a very different approach, closing off the interior life of his characters almost entirely while insinuating the presence of deeper motives and nefarious machinations operating below the surface, and in that way creating a subjective chaos, a feeling of relativity, within the reader. The uncertainty we feel about theme and meaning, the opacity we encounter regarding action and character, in *The Confidence-Man,* then, is designed to unsettle us and make us question our own assumptions, values, and behavior, in the way that life, in its more difficult and arresting moments, can do.[5] In the

end, it is the slipperiness and inscrutability of experience, particularly social experience, that is the subject of Melville's book. Given such a theme, virtually everything about the novel as vehicle had to be turned on its head.

Just how radical and prescient, how "modern," Melville's insight was into the social dimension of the human condition, and how radical and "modern" his artistic conception of his task, can begin to be suggested by observing that *The Confidence-Man* anticipates the "existentialist" conclusion reached by William James almost four decades after Melville's book was published, when the American pragmatist wrote of the difficulty of functioning in a post-Christian world, a world where traditional authority was thought to be "dead." Explained James, "there is really no scientific or other method by which men can steer safely between the opposite dangers of believing too little or of believing too much. To face such dangers is apparently our duty, and to hit the right channel between them is the measure of our wisdom as men."[6] Although in *The Confidence-Man* Melville seems most interested in charting the practical or material dangers of too much confidence and the spiritual or emotional risks of too much doubt, I believe he did so to evoke in his readers the same troubling problem that by the mid-1850s had become something of a crisis for him, the problem of discovering "the measure of our wisdom," of hitting the right channel between these opposing dangers. Unlike James, however, Melville focused not so much on the proper course of religious faith (though clearly that remained a vital concern of his, from the rehearsal of Pauline notions of charity in chapter 1 to the questions at the end of the novel about the status of the Apocrypha and the coming of the Apocalypse) as on the proper course of social or communal faith, of one person's faith in another and, by extension, in all others. His novel, finally, is a study of the social and psychological health of the nation at midcentury.

What is most problematic about *The Confidence-Man* is that it demonstrates (in almost every scene) that we cannot, in the existential moment, have certain knowledge of another person and thus cannot know whether that person deserves our trust or our skepticism. In spite of broad hints, suspicious coincidences, and potentially ironic insinuations to the contrary, we do not know—indeed, we cannot know—whether the confidence man in any of his guises dupes anyone on the *Fidèle,* and we cannot know because we are never permitted to witness the consequences of his several encounters. Certain knowledge about the apparent machinations of the confidence man is not so much the gift of prescience as it is the gift of the future itself, and in *The Confidence-Man* the future is always structurally hidden from our view. Like a number of French "new novels" that, in the formal sense, lack a future, Melville's, too, recreates in its readers the pressures of the time to come, pressures that we naturally seek to

escape by finding answers where none are given. In the social sphere, as in every other, presumably, all knowledge is deeply subjective. As the novel's initial scene suggests in a dramatic way (paralleling what I have quoted James as saying discursively), there are no secure choices betwixt or between the uncritical "charity" of the man in cream colors and the barber's "No Trust."

While most commentators have noted one kind of ambiguity or another in this work, it is curious that so few, most notably, Philip Drew, have argued that the title character *might* not be a "con man."[7] To be sure, the book does invite the unambiguous interpretations of the confidence man that have predominated; the subtitle alone is cause for at least some suspicion of his activities, though it hardly constitutes proof of his duplicity. But as a rule, critics seem simply to have assumed he is a swindler, and in a few notable instances they have done so despite their claims for the work's thoroughgoing ambiguity. Leon F. Seltzer, for example, who first demonstrated *The Confidence-Man's* modernity by maintaining that it embodies the philosophy of Camus's "absurd man," initially concludes that "Nowhere is there any ground for belief, for nowhere is there any concrete evidence of an inner core of truth." But he then goes on to assert that Melville "implicitly ask[s] us to trust that his confidence man is, indeed, an actual confidence man."[8]

The arguments of the prevailing school, furthermore, appear even more convincing when coupled with the knowledge that, as Hawthorne wrote in the fall of 1856 after *The Confidence-Man* had been submitted for publication, "Melville has not been well, of late; he has been affected with neuralgic complaints in his head and limbs, and no doubt has suffered from too constant literary occupation, pursued without much success, latterly; and his writings, for a long while past, have indicated a morbid state of mind."[9] But to base the argument for Melville's "cynicism" and "bitterness" in *The Confidence-Man* on his illness and the unpopularity of his works, as many critics have done, is tenuous conjecture at best and a weak critical practice.[10] Who, except perhaps Melville himself, is capable of penetrating the connection between the author's mental state and his literary imagination? It was not necessary for Melville himself to be "mad" when he wrote about Pip in *Moby-Dick* (1851); that he was evidently ill when he wrote *The Confidence-Man* is *perhaps* of no consequence to the work itself. At the risk of being too credulous about this work, or perhaps too skeptical, it seems to me remarkable that commentators generally have felt so confident of their own immunity from the ironies of a book that not only begins and ends on April Fools' Day but that Melville also apparently chose to have published on that day.[11]

Drew's argument implies that too much suspicion on the part of Melville's readers is just another form of overconfidence. And the two positions *are* quite

relative, as the cosmopolitan knows. Speaking of the "robberies and murders
alleged to have been perpetrated" at the time of the "alleged Lisbon earthquake" (while adroitly begging the question of the verity of those crimes and
of that of the earthquake itself), he observes that "The infidels of the time
were quick to credit those reports and worse. So true is it that, while religion,
contrary to the common notion, implies, in certain cases, a spirit of slow
reserve as to assent, infidelity, which claims to despise credulity, is sometimes
swift to it."[12] But an even more important point is implied by Drew's argument, and this one he all but denies: too much suspicion mistakenly dimin-
ishes the book's meticulously studied and skillfully handled ambiguities, and
hence its central meaning as well. All knowledge is subjective; there is no
certain course in this world by which we can steer safely between the Charybdis
of too much confidence and the Scylla of too much skepticism.[13]

Drew undermines his own case when he concludes that the cosmopolitan's
"encounter with Charlie Noble has shown that true charity, if vigilant, is not
necessarily duped," for this is, as Drew himself suggests, "not necessarily" true,
not even in this example.[14] It is questionable whether the cosmopolitan engages in "true charity," because it is he who tests (and finds wanting) Charlie
Noble's Pollyanna pretentions to confidence in humanity, and not Charlie who
tests his. Moreover, the motives of the cosmopolitan himself are not beyond
question; for, although he later proves to have in his possession the amount of
money requested, he might simply be scheming to acquire fifty dollars more.
However, we can only suspect him of this. And so, as in every other encounter
on the *Fidèle,* uncertainty is our lot, and the resulting sense of crisis is our fate.
In short, I am not denying that the confidence man is a "con man"; I wish only
to deny that we can know he is one. More than any of Melville's other works,
The Confidence-Man lacks the neat resolutions we tend to expect from narrative fiction and instead demands of us "cooperation, an active, conscious, *creative* assistance," which Robbe-Grillet has identified as a distinguishing characteristic of the "new novel," a characteristic represented in this book both
substantially by its ambiguous, hence lifelike, portrayals of the confidence man's
avatars as well as formally by its open-endedness concerning the future of
each incident and by the ambivalent, yet seductive, rhetoric of its narrator.[15]

For those who retain some reservations about whether the confidence man
is to be trusted, the ambiguities in this work are compounded by the absence
of a totally reliable narrator. If it was Melville's intention to leave "open" the
question of the trustworthiness of his title character, then it would be fitting
to have a narrator who is himself ambiguous in character. "If the world of the
book is without meaning," Wayne Booth has asked, "how can there be a reliable narrator? What is he to be reliable about? The very concept of reliability

presupposes that something objectively true can be said about actions and thoughts."[16]

Although the world of *The Confidence-Man* is not entirely without meaning, it does lack certain meaning, for the only thing we can say about the thoughts and actions of the confidence man that is objectively "true" is that they are ambiguous; hence, the suggestions of absurdity and meaninglessness of life on the *Fidèle* do predominate. And even though the narrator is not completely unreliable, we cannot depend on him to rectify the book's inconsistencies or to supply the kinds of information we normally find in novels. By failing to resolve, for example, the crucial issue of the two contradictory biblical aphorisms (one said to be "certain truth" and the other "apocryphal")—"There is a subtle man, and the same is deceived," and "Believe not his many words—an enemy speaketh sweetly with his lips"—he encourages us to conclude, first, that we must have confidence and, then again, that we must have none (26, 242–43). Of course each of these maxims is used in such a way as to seem an appropriate "conning" technique, the first by John Ringman to undermine the shallow skepticism of the college disciple of Tacitus and the second by the cosmopolitan to bolster the equally shallow confidence of the Simeon-faced old man, although as usual the proof we need is lacking in each case. But the more troubling fact remains that Melville's narrator, through his reticence, in effect sets the Word against the Word, leaving us to reconcile the contradictions.

Yet his responsibility for the contradictions is often more obvious, his deceptiveness more clearly designed, and so he is even more justifiably culpable than the previous example might suggest. The type of narrator found in *The Confidence-Man* is generally termed "omniscient," but this one is not consistently all-knowing. More important, when he does display omniscience he often provokes our suspicion of the character in question, though he never offers proof of ill-intent; and when he professes ignorance about a particular character, the effect is strangely the same. On the one hand, by means of the license granted him as omniscient narrator, he can enter the mind of the collegian and inform us, though with some ambiguity, that the man with the weed "fascinated" him. And in conjunction with earlier descriptions of the man with the weed "slowly sliding along the rail" and "softly sliding nearer" just prior to his request ("by way of experiment," it should be noted) for the collegian to have "confidence" in him, we are thus encouraged to view John Ringman as something of a snake (25–27).

Indeed, some readers have seen Ringman, along with the other avatars of the confidence man, as an incarnation of the arch swindler Satan.[17] The man with the weed, under suspicious circumstances, has already secured a "loan"

from the country merchant (though whether it is a bona fide loan or a fleecing by another name is never revealed), and so we quite reasonably expect that in this case, too, "confidence" to him means another "loan." But the implication is never tested; the collegian simply walks away. Of course the narrator's insinuations might be justified nonetheless, because it seems the collegian has been tempted by John Ringman at least to "Drop Tacitus," thus setting him up for the apparent scheme of the confidence man's next avatar, the transfer agent of the Black Rapids Coal Company, from whom he subsequently buys some "shares" (26). But there is no way for us to know whether this stock is bogus, and so we can be no more certain that the transfer agent is a con artist than we can be that John Ringman is one. More than anything else what is satirized here is the collegian's self-interestedness and foolish self-assurance. "No appearances can deceive me," he boasts to the agent (48).

On the other hand, the narrator at times willfully withholds the information that would satisfy our expectations and constitute the proof necessary for us to form just accusations of the confidence man's avatars. And yet in this way, too, he inspires our distrust of them. (Significantly, he almost never offers an interior view of them, only of their "victims.") After the cosmopolitan has made an agreement with the barber, for instance, the latter decides he has been duped and tears up their contract, "which he felt the more free to do," says the narrator, "from the impression that in all human probability he would never again see the person who had drawn it." Although the narrator knows many things, including what the barber is thinking at this moment, he informs us only that "Whether that impression proved well-founded or not, does not appear" (237). Of course it appears as though the barber's impression is well-founded. But, if Melville had wanted us to be sure, he could have had his narrator tell us the cosmopolitan never returned to fulfill his part of their bargain. Instead, he has the narrator test the quality of *our* confidence and of *our* skepticism by not allowing us to rest in certainty, though his narrator raises doubts aplenty in this book "bordering . . . upon the smoky" before making, as the latter says, "the best use the smoke can be turned to . . . by retiring under cover of it" (239).

In still other instances the narrator makes statements that ostensibly argue in favor of confidence in the various avatars, but because of the circumstances, as well as the whimsical tone, they easily can be read ironically, too, thus undermining the very trust he seems to encourage. Irony, however, is very unstable, particularly in this work; "irony is so unjust . . . something Satanic about irony," the cosmopolitan tells Pitch (136). It is "Satanic" because it is always implicit, thus tempting us perhaps to deceive ourselves by pridefully

reading ironies where none are intended, or, more to the point, where they are intentionally equivocal. Accordingly, irony is at least potentially "unjust" as well; if our accusations of the confidence man are founded on nothing more than ironic readings of statements or descriptions, we accuse him without proof. In fact, he himself is "no inexperienced thinker," as seen in his own doubly cautious remark on the cosmopolitan's response to Mark Winsome's question as to whether the rattlesnake is morally accountable: "If I will not affirm that it is," he returned, "*with the caution of no inexperienced thinker,* 'neither will I deny it'" (191; emphasis added).

The cosmopolitan's elusive statement quite succinctly describes the frustrating techniques of the narrator himself, techniques that belie the traditional function of a reliable narrator: if he will not affirm that the confidence man in any of his forms is in fact a "con man," neither will he deny it. But because he encourages our skepticism more than not, in net effect he is like Tacitus, who, to quote the man with the weed, "Without confidence himself . . . destroys it in all his readers" (27). Thus we should heed, though perhaps with reservation, the son of Sirach's advice whenever we meet with observations by the narrator who pilots us through this work and "Believe not his many words—an enemy speaketh sweetly with his lips." One of the finer ironies Melville presumably learned at sea is that the term for the steerage of a ship, as well as for the station of the man who directs it, is "con."

The impossibility of determining whether another person merits our trust is underlined in *The Confidence-Man* by Melville's choice of a Mississippi River setting where transients are the norm, a setting where the confidence man's avatars are necessarily strangers to their "victims." The man in cream colors, the herb doctor, the man with the violet vest, and the cosmopolitan are all referred to explicitly as "strangers." Furthermore, the PIO man is clearly a stranger to Pitch; the man with the book is a stranger to the collegian; and the man with the weed, while professing to be an old acquaintance, is thought to be a total stranger by the country merchant. Of course it is to the advantage of the true "con man" not to be known for what he is; otherwise he would soon run out of business, or be run off the boat. But the fact that so many passengers do trust these "strangers" argues not only for their own gullibility but for the ambiguity of these putative "con men" as well. If as a general rule we are tempted to conclude that strangers are not to be trusted, then we must recognize that the consequence is not simply skepticism but cynicism about the nature of humanity. As the cosmopolitan points out to the barber, whose "No Trust" is based on such a rule, "does not that imply something like saying that mankind is not to be trusted; for the mass of mankind, are they not necessarily strangers to each individual man?" (229).

It is important also to notice that other characters, such as Mark Winsome and the man with gold sleeve buttons, are introduced as "strangers." Each person is a stranger to every other in the world of the *Fidèle*, because, in the words of the narrator (and here he is reliable), "no one man's experience can be coextensive with *what is*" (70). Certain knowledge of the world, of other people, and frequently even of oneself is not possible here. Indeed, "where in this strange universe is not one a stranger?" Winsome, seemingly out of character, beseeches the cosmopolitan (196). "What are you? What am I?" he implores. "Nobody knows who anybody is. The data which life furnishes, toward forming a true estimate of any being, are as insufficient to that end as in geometry one side given would be to determine the triangle." Of course the cosmopolitan, apparently unaware of the Emersonian notion that "A foolish consistency is the hobgoblin of little minds," points out that Winsome's "doctrine of triangles" contradicts his "doctrine of labels" (193).[18] And this contradiction constitutes an unequivocal irony, for it is according to the latter doctrine that Winsome would warn the cosmopolitan against the wiles of Charlie Noble, whom he suspects to be a "Mississippi operator"—the same Charlie Noble from whom the cosmopolitan had previously solicited a fifty-dollar "loan" (196). Hence we must conclude in this case at least, though unhappily, that his "doctrine of triangles" is the more reliable of the two.

Winsome's "doctrine of labels" is more than ineffectual, however. When too blithely subscribed to, it also encourages one person to do a serious injustice to another. Charlie Noble may very well be a "Mississippi operator," but, as pointed out earlier, we have no reason to conclude that he is anything more than a smiling Janus. As the cosmopolitan suggested previously to Charlie, after the latter unjustly accused Pitch of being a "comprehensive Colonel Moredock" (Pitch proves finally to have confidence enough to try another boy, despite thirty-five prior failures), "never a sound judgment without charity. When man judges man, charity is less a bounty from our mercy than just allowance for the insensible lee-way of human fallibility" (155–56).

The "doctrine of labels" in Mark Winsome's hands (and in ours, too, insofar as we see the avatars of the confidence man as swindlers) has become more important than the humanity of the person to whom he applies it. His selfish desire for certain meaning, his need for closure, is more important than the respect for another's inscrutability that is necessary if Winsome is to maintain his own humanity. His automatic dismissal of the disheveled petitioner whom he labels a "scoundrel" in turn reveals the mystic's inhumanity in action (195). In the words of Egbert, his disciple, Winsome's "rule forbids" that he risk personal loss by showing confidence in another human being; and it is a convenient feature of his philosophy that all who ask for confidence are by definition

"scoundrels" (202). Winsome's encounters with others consequently tend to be coldly ritualistic, even to the point of substituting his practical disciple for himself when asked for an explanation of his transcendental philosophy.

Although the "doctrine of labels" has the potential for doing an injustice to others, it is relatively harmless as long as it involves nothing more than name calling and cold rebuffs. But when it is tested in the world, when one sets out to prove the validity of such a doctrine, the result can be literally dehumanizing; it can lead to a denial of life. To Colonel John Moredock, who also subscribes to a "doctrine of labels," the only good Indian is a dead Indian, and he proves the "truth" of his pernicious stereotype by killing as many as he is able to catch in his rifle sights. As several critics have pointed out, the story of the Indian hater is presented in such a way as to convince us that Moredock's monomaniacal thinking, while regrettable, is nonetheless justifiable. Indeed, John Shroeder has concluded that the "Indian-hater is the world's only remedy against the confidence-man," because "a severe disease calls for a strong purge."[19]

But there are a few hints—aside from the plain murderousness of his philosophy and the ironic suggestion that it constitutes a form of "metaphysics"—that should lead us to doubt that this is Melville's own position on the question of Indian-white relations. For one, in the midst of a long description of Moredock's painstaking preparations for ensuring revenge on those who killed his mother and siblings, we are told that "the actual transgressors" were "outlaws even among Indians" (153). Moredock, however, does not stop once "the actual transgressors" have been exterminated; "to kill Indians had become his passion," for to him all Indians are outlaws (154).

Another important clue as to Melville's sentiments on this question is slipped in with the advice it is said the backwoodsman ought to give his son: "however charitable it may be to view Indians as members of the Society of Friends, yet to affirm them such to one ignorant of Indians, whose lonely path lies a long way *through their lands,* this, in the event, might prove not only injudicious but cruel" (146; emphasis added).[20] As wryly as this point is made, it reveals Melville's discomfort with the white man's appeals to "manifest destiny," so popular at this period in America's history. And so, if crimes committed in defense of one's homeland are as pardonable for the Indian as for the white man himself, even the murder of Moredock's "pioneer" family, the original cause of his Indian-hating "metaphysics," has *some* justification (152).

Finally, although there are several suggestions that the Indians figure allegorically as devils, both in the story of the Indian hater and elsewhere, it should be pointed out that they are referred to explicitly as "human beings" and that, according to "those who best knew him," it is Moredock himself who "felt"

them to be so (155).[21] Surely this reference is ironic, but whether the irony cuts against the Indians or against Moredock is not clear. And the fact that the report of this sentiment does not come to us directly from Moredock serves to muddy the waters even more. Once again, we find only ambiguities.

The conclusions of Winsome and Moredock as well as those of the other characters in the book who lack confidence, such as Charlie Noble and the one-legged cynic, tend to gain our approval as long as we agree that the confidence man's avatars are bona fide "conmen" (or, in Moredock's case, as long as we agree that the Indians are devils). But once we admit to even the slightest ambiguity in the behavior of these avatars, or in the book's preferred explanations for their behavior, these conclusions themselves become highly suspect, for we see they are based on stereotypes and hence on a generalized cynicism. Moreover, the cynicism we are encouraged to approve in these specific cases—the cynicism many commentators have seen as reflecting Melville's own—has to be squared somehow with the icy inhumanity of Mark Winsome, the monomaniac "metaphysics" of Colonel Moredock, and the *self*-destruction that can result from cynicism, as demonstrated by the Methodist minister's striking reductio ad absurdum: "I have been in mad-houses full of tragic mopers, and seen there the end of suspicion: the cynic, in the moody madness muttering in the corner; for years a barren fixture there; head lopped over, gnawing his own lip, vulture of himself; while, by fits and starts, from the corner opposite came the grimace of the idiot at him" (16).

By making the confidence men "strangers," Melville also emphasizes the fact that true confidence is no more based on knowledge than reflex cynicism is. If we "trust" someone whom we *know* we can trust, we are not "trusting" that person at all. As the man with the book says to the old miser when the latter asks for some proof he is not being bilked: "No ifs. Downright confidence, or none. So help me heaven, I will have no half-confidences" (75). Yet we know from the example of the old man at the end that the innocent eye sees nothing; confidence without skepticism is blind and, at least potentially, sheer folly. It is true—at least it is not illogical—that in the world of the *Fidèle* "Looks are one thing, and facts are another," as the man with the wooden leg claims; but whether the two are in fact at any time contradictory is entirely another question, for the "facts" are never made known (14). We must, therefore, *risk* something when asked to demonstrate true confidence—either our money, our face, or, in the extreme case, our very life.

Most of the apparent diddlings in Melville's novel involve a simple exchange of money for confidence. The man with the weed receives a "loan" from the country merchant; the man with the book sells "shares" in the Black

Rapids Coal Company; the herb doctor peddles Omni-Balsamic Reinvigorator to a sick man; and the Widow and Orphan Asylum representative collects "contributions" from a clergyman and others. However, the claims made by each of these "con men" can be neither proved nor disproved; the question the cosmopolitan asks the barber, while a standard "conning" device, is nonetheless potentially innocent, and so it is one we must answer, too: "Is it so *certain* you are going to lose?" (237).

Even the herb doctor—by profession alone the most suspect of the lot, though he charges the least for others' confidence in him—claims to devote "to some benevolent purpose, the half of the proceeds of sales," and in one case at least he does so (90). Moreover, the argument that he dispenses nothing more than groundless hopes also has its counterargument; as the herb doctor points out to the doubting Pitch, a life without confidence is a life of "disease." "Granting that his dependence on my medicine is vain," he hypothesizes, speaking of the old miser, "is it kind to deprive him of what, in mere imagination, if nothing more, may help eke out, with hope, his disease?" (110). Yet even if the confidence man's avatars could be proved to be diddlers in any of these cases, no one stands to lose anything more than a few dollars, or perhaps his pride; while, on the other hand, should the apparent victim's trust subsequently prove to be well founded, he would gain something of value.

Of course money is not the root of all evil on the *Fidèle*, uncertain as the reality of that evil may be. "How much money did the devil make by gulling Eve?" the man with the wooden leg asks. And, significantly, he rebukes his listeners with the charge of "green-horns" for thinking money is "the sole motive to pains and hazard, deception and deviltry" (32). If the loss of lucre were the only risk, the question of "confidence" would be academic indeed. But the one-legged cynic's reproach indicates that the loss of face also is a matter of concern for both the "con man" and his "victims"; and this requires that we approach the question more directly in terms of human values. The loss of face strikes nearer to the heart of our identity, for when we are duped we are exposed for being other than we would like to think we are—shrewd judges of other people. Our pride is damaged, to be sure; but, more important, the charge of innocence is strangely more disgraceful, socially, than the charge of cynicism. The narrator himself admits his fear of playing the fool in public when he says, "never mind how convinced one may be that he is never in the wrong; yet, so precious to man is the approbation of his kind, that to rest, *though but under an imaginary censure . . .* is no easy thing" (183; emphasis added). If there is a devil lurking in *The Confidence-Man,* he plays on our fear of this "imaginary censure," tempting us to become cynics in order to avoid becoming fools.

Obviously, if we cannot prove any of the confidence man's avatars to be a swindler, neither can we prove that anyone has been duped, and so we cannot prove whether anyone has been labeled a fool justifiably. But we can evaluate the effect of the charge of "fool" on various characters by their reactions to it, and we find, none too surprisingly, that (with the exceptions of the confidence man's avatars themselves) they always make the choice of "no confidence" rather than risk seeming foolish to others whenever the accusation is invoked or suggested. Black Guinea, for example, receives alms (uncharitably as they are given) from the other passengers until the one-legged cynic enters to cry— and it is a cry that echoes throughout the book for us: "You fools! . . . you flock of fools, under this captain of fools, in this ship of fools!" (15). He offers no proof that Black Guinea is a fraud, but he does give us cause to doubt the trustworthiness of his cynicism when he claims the search for the men who might vouch for the black cripple will prove a "wild goose chase." "Don't believe there's a soul of them aboard," he says confidently (14). Yet at least five of the eight "ge'mman" listed by Black Guinea do appear, and one of them, the man in the gray coat (the only one asked), claims to know him.[22]

The fear of being made fools helps to explain the crowd's willingness to believe the cynics on the *Fidèle* rather than the advocates of confidence; and it helps to explain the thinking of those who are more or less confirmed cynics as well. Pitch, for example, who thinks the fools in this world outnumber the knaves for "the same reason . . . oats are numerically more than horses," is more troubled by what he takes to be the certainty that the PIO man has made a "ninny" of him than by the apparent loss of his money (107, 130). The fear of being made fools might even explain our own inclination to have more faith in the cynics in this work (including the narrator) than in the confidence men. If so, *The Confidence-Man* is much more than the "philosophical satire on optimism" envisioned by Elizabeth Foster; it is also a satire on the equally American doctrine of "self-interest," which A. N. Kaul has described as one of the two main drives behind "the type of American experience." The assumptions of most readers of this novel tend to substantiate the validity of Melville's attack, while at the same time they confirm his method. To prevent being labeled fools ourselves, we assume others to be knaves, thus unwittingly condemning ourselves at the same time we condemn others. Perhaps it is significant of our time, as it was of Melville's, that we have tended to underestimate his concern for the other element in the generative "type" of American experience defined by Kaul, namely, the concern for "Christian social ideals."[23]

Melville encourages the development of our suspicion of the confidence man in the beginning, to the feeling of certainty about him in the end, simply

by presenting one suspicious personality after another and by never allowing more than one avatar to appear at a time, thus implying they are all one arch deceiver playing a variety of roles. With the possible exception of the herb doctor, however, no one avatar is inherently any more suspicious than any other, and although it becomes more difficult for us to be charitable with each successive confidence man, we risk doing an injustice no less to the last than to the first when we condemn him without proof. Having read to the end of *The Confidence-Man,* we find ourselves in the same position as Pitch, who must admit to the PIO man concerning his thirtieth rascally boy: "But I could prove nothing. Expressed to him my suspicions" (118). It is important that the PIO man finally succeeds in his attempt to sell Pitch another rascal, and it is just as important that Pitch immediately suffers loss of faith. Suspicion alternates with confidence, confidence with suspicion. The process, we know, will continue indefinitely for him, because, contrary to what his name implies, he does not "stick" to what he says (117). His own humanity is ultimately more important to him than his "general law of distrust systematically applied to the race," the only law that can save him from the charge of being a fool (130).

The question of confidence becomes still more difficult, of course, when people are forced to choose between their life and their humanity. Melville offers three examples in which the loss of life either occurs or is threatened as a result of one person's confidence in another: the little colony of Wrights and Weavers, who are murdered by the Indian Mocmohoc; China Aster, who suffers ruin and death as a result of the loan he unwillingly receives from Orchis; and the old man at the end of the book who is given what seems to be a chamber pot for a life preserver by the cosmopolitan. In the first two examples there is no ambiguity about whether these deaths result, at least in large part, from misplaced confidence. Because each is an "inset" story told by one passenger to another, and not part of the main action on the *Fidèle,* the outcome is given to the reader in both cases. There are contributing factors, to be sure; but the point of each story is that the trustee of the victim's confidence is unworthy. The third example is more ambiguous, not only because we are not privy to the consequences of this commodious joke (if, indeed, it is intended as one), but because of the ambiguous nature of the cosmopolitan himself. It is of course possible to read ironically his admission of ignorance about the chamber pot/life preserver—"I don't pretend to know much about such things, never using them myself"—but there is no way we can be sure the irony is not directed at our own ignorance rather than at the old man's (251). When the cosmopolitan extinguishes the lamp at the end of this scene, which is also the end of the book, and "kindly" leads away the old man, only the reader is left in the

dark; and it is a symbolic as well as a literal darkness, symbolic of our own uncertainty. Suffice it to say, confidence is sometimes dangerous, even deadly.

Although the victims in these three instances are at the time unaware of the consequences their confidence will have, and thus for them it is not a question of choosing between trust on the one hand and their own well-being on the other, the problem remains for Melville's readers. It might seem a weakness that Melville did not approach this question more directly, but I believe he felt he had to be careful not to let the pathos of tragedy undercut the prevailing comic tone of his satire. And this explanation in turn suggests another: life on the *Fidèle* holds no possibility for tragedy. In a world where people cannot know whether others are trustworthy and where they cannot even know that their life is the price they might pay for their confidence, paradigmatic tragedy is impossible. Here, absurdity rules. Of course a life without confidence also is absurd, absurdly meaningless; there are always those madhouses where the cynic daily gnaws his own lip. We find no unequivocal satisfactions in *The Confidence-Man,* however, because Melville outlines only the alternatives. He does not prescribe. Indeed, he cannot. But he does make us aware that if in this scheming world it is hard to save one's pocketbook, one's reputation, and one's life, it is harder still to save one's more vulnerable soul.

According to several commentators, the structural weakness, even the structural failure, of *The Confidence-Man* is that it does not provide from among the passengers a model who exemplifies a satisfactory solution to the problem the book raises: How are we to make our way between the twin dangers of too much and too little faith?[24] Yet the book does invite a kind of resolution to our difficulties, though an unsatisfying and untraditional one, by the *method* it forces us to engage until—out of frustration, anxiety, or perhaps even despair—we conclude that we simply do not know whether the confidence man's avatars are to be trusted.

As feeble and disconcerting as this conclusion is, it is important to notice that in order to reach it we have had to enter into a continuous dialogue of skepticism *and* credulity, of suspicion *and* confidence, almost simultaneously, the one counteracting the other, until finally we are resigned to the fact that his character is equivocal, or until we fall into the trap of "No Trust" or that of blind confidence—and they are much the same, the trap of false certainty. Our study of the character of the confidence man must have, as Frank Kermode has said of the study of the modern situation, "a certain complexity and a sense of failure."[25] The sick man who pleads with the herb doctor, "But to doubt, to suspect, to prove—to have all this wearing work to be doing continually—how opposed to confidence," understands but half of Melville's

impossible yet necessary program. The "wearing work" of close scrutiny is opposed to confidence, but it is also opposed to cynicism. And if "It is evil!" as the sick man maintains, it is nevertheless a necessary evil (83). For in the absence of a "guardeen," the nonexistence of which is felt so deeply by the old miser and by so many others as well, this "wearing work," imperfect as it is, will have to suffice (103).

To some extent, therefore, I share the view of others who have argued that Pitch offers the best method of dealing with the confidence man, because he most fully engages in the laborious "dialogue of crisis," especially in his encounter with the PIO man.[26] As in other cases, however, there is no proof that Pitch is *not* defrauded by him. He, too, must ultimately rest his case on faith, as his sudden feeling he has been duped makes clear. But his relapse into cynicism is self-condemning, and makes him another kind of fool.

Because the character of the confidence man remains equivocal throughout the narrative, this is a novel of continuing crisis rather than one of unfolding development, and in this respect, too, it is a remarkably modern work. *The Confidence-Man* not only portrays crises, situations in which men and women must act despite their uncertainty about the outcome of their decisions; it evokes a disturbing sense of crisis in its readers, too. Like the passengers on the *Fidèle*, we cannot project ourselves beyond the situations that demand our attention to discover whether our expectations will be fulfilled, because we are never offered the sort of information necessary to satisfy those expectations. We, too, must judge on the basis of limited and equivocal evidence, on the appearances within our immediate field of perception. For, unlike the traditional novel, *The Confidence-Man* offers neither a higher (at least not a reliable) conscience to control our reactions to the characters who act out their ambiguous parts before our eyes nor a final resolution of our difficulties, a traditional ending giving form and meaning to all that has gone before. Thus *The Confidence-Man* lacks a traditional structure for the same reason the avatars of the title character remain ambiguous: the future is hidden from the reader.

As certain knowledge of the confidence man is dependent on knowledge of the future consequences of one's confidence, so narrative structure in the traditional sense is dependent on an ending that makes known the unknown. This book is strikingly modern because, to borrow from Kermode's assessment of the "new novel" of Robbe-Grillet and others, it is "always *not* doing things which we unreasonably assume novels ought to do: connect, diversify, explain, make concords, facilitate extrapolations."[27] The narrator's apology in chapter 14 for portraying inconsistent characters—the first of three chapters in which Melville interrupts the story to present his unorthodox theory of

realism in fiction—is simply the most explicit evidence of Melville's interest in undermining such assumptions.[28]

Rather than finally fulfilling our expectations in an unexpected way, *The Confidence-Man* defeats them at every turn. It does not provide the traditional novel's single, instructive peripeteia, which normally brings us to a surprising and satisfying discovery or recognition. Instead it provides a series of half-reversals that in each case undermine on the one hand the short-lived certainty that the book encourages on the other.[29] These half-reversals are instructive, but not in the customary way. They inform us of the truth of the confidence man's ambiguity, not of the more desirable truth of his real character. Just when we begin to feel sure each avatar is a "con man," we are given some bit of information, some gratuitous act of kindness, or some explicable though suspicious coincidence that partially negates our suspicion and fully negates our certainty. Qualification is piled on qualification, contradiction on contradiction; in this respect, too, *The Confidence-Man* is like the "new novel," which, according to Robbe-Grillet, "repeats itself, bisects itself, modifies itself, contradicts itself, without even accumulating enough bulk to constitute a past—and thus a 'story,' in the traditional sense of the word." And in the end we find no resolution, only a thoroughly defined problem. In *The Confidence-Man,* as in the "new novel," "Rival versions of the same set of facts . . . co-exist without final reconciliation."[30] Life doesn't reconcile the contradictions we encounter in our everyday experience; the novel shouldn't try to do so either.

By defeating the reader's expectations, Melville managed to achieve a new form of realism in fiction—a "new realism" for him to be sure, and, it would seem, for his time as well. According to Kermode, the "story that proceeded very simply to its obviously predestined end would be nearer myth than novel or drama. Peripeteia, which has been called the equivalent, in narrative, of irony in rhetoric, is present in every story of the least structural sophistication."[31] In *The Confidence-Man* Melville's use of peripeteia, like his use of irony, is highly muted and extra-paradigmatic; he has sophisticated and complicated the peripeteia, rather than eliminated it altogether, and this, too, argues for the work's modernity. The book does *not* proceed "very simply to its obviously predestined end." Like the "new novel," it is quite distant from myth and "story," because it encompasses large chunks of human experience without clear narrative development, without enlightening commentary, and without an illuminating ending. It represents the contingency of reality unmediated, to a remarkable extent; and so, like our quotidian world, *The Confidence-Man* is subject to contradictory interpretations and a great deal of puzzlement.

In his explanation of the way modern literature of the absurd grew out of

tragedy, itself a form of Apocalypse, Kermode argues that "a strict concordance between beginning, middle, and end . . . remains a deeply desired object, but it is hard to achieve when the beginning is lost in the dark backward and abysm of time, and the end is known to be unpredictable." He is speaking of changing conceptions of Apocalypse, of the continuity of extraliterary versions of the end of the world, and specifically of the emergence of the philosophy of existentialism and the cult of the absurd. The absurd is a product of the modern view that the world lacks the form that an end implies. But, Kermode concludes, "This changes our views of the patterns of time, and in so far as our plots honour the increased complexity of these ways of making sense, it complicates them also."[32]

Early commentators frequently remarked that Melville never completed *The Confidence-Man,* and although there has been a growing tendency in recent years to accept it as "finished," readers still ponder its inconclusiveness.[33] This *is* a novel without an ending in the traditional sense. The concluding statement, "Something further may follow of this Masquerade," begs completion and is itself equivocal; something further *may* follow, and then again it may not. Actually, of course, "something" *will* follow, but the point is that we are not permitted to see what ensues. Melville purposely hides the future from our view, and so the sense of crisis is perpetuated and ensured.

This is the problem defined by the book: the uncertainty of the future, the absence of certain knowledge of consequences, of ends. The man in the sleeping quarters who, in the last chapter, mistakes the word "apocrypha" for "Apocalypse"—"What's that about the Apocalypse?" he implores from the darkness of his berth—clearly indicates the profound anxiety about the future that is felt by those who ride into the night on this ship named *Fidèle* (243). They need news about the future, certain knowledge of their destinies; they need forms and endings to redeem the endlessly meaningless and critically uncertain present. Theirs is a world in which people literally cry out in the dark for Apocalypse. But all they find is, to quote Yeats, the poet of crisis, "antithetical multiform influx" without end. Life on the *Fidèle* is a perpetual state of crisis, an endless series of anxiety-producing yet absurdly comic confrontations that the mind must continue to relive in its ceaseless attempt to overcome its ignorance.

The sense of crisis, which is such a significant feature of the modern literature of the absurd, results from a lack of confidence in endings; it results from our awareness of the uncertainty and remoteness of the future, and in *The Confidence-Man* the uncertain future is intimately connected with our awareness of the remoteness of those people in whom we contemplate investing our confidence. Kermode asserts that "the End itself, in modern literary plotting,

loses its downbeat, tonic-and-dominant finality, and we think of it, as the theologians think of Apocalypse, as immanent rather than imminent."[34] As in modern literature, the "end" of each incident in *The Confidence-Man,* because it is postponed indefinitely, becomes incorporated into our experience of the immediate moment; and so, contrary to traditional expectations, it is not possible for us to regard it as that portion of the future that will make sense of the meaningless present. In a moment of crisis the future is split into antithetical possibilities—favorable and unfavorable—and both are felt simultaneously. It is because we can foresee the possibilities and yet cannot know which one the future holds for us as a result of the decision we must make in the present that readers of this book, like people of the modern world more generally, suffer this feeling of crisis, what Henri Focillon has called "intemporal agony."[35]

The Confidence-Man was, for Melville, a literary experiment, and I think it was a successful one. Our bafflement at the book probably does have its extraliterary meaning; the light extinguished at the end of the novel—the last work of prose fiction Melville is known to have written for over three decades—is apparently a covert admission that his confidence in narrative fiction, or, perhaps, in his audience, had run out. But our bafflement has its literary meaning as well. April 1 is, after all, a day of trickery and confusion. I believe Melville intended us to remain puzzled by the ambiguities in this work, and to the extent that our puzzlement at the book inspires a sense of puzzlement at our own life situation the book succeeds. It is when we begin to think we can see through the title character with any certainty that the book fails, or, rather, that we have failed the book. In a world where ethical and biblical admonitions have become contradictory, their authority uncertain and "apocryphal," one person cannot know the truth about another. People no longer act in prescribed ways, if indeed they ever did. What is more, it is foolish and inhuman for anyone to try to act in such ways. But if in the present we cannot know the truth about others, by confronting slippery personalities who solicit our confidence we can come to know something about ourselves.[36] The test of our confidence, and our humanity, must be met in the present. The proof we need can only follow the agony of that test.

This work reveals neither a loss of Melville's creative power and control, nor his mental instability at the time of its composition—unless the modern sense of crisis is considered a form of "insanity," and indeed it has been called such. On the contrary, the sense of "new realism" seen in *The Confidence-Man* betrays an acute awareness of the immanence rather than the imminence of the End on Melville's part, an awareness that temporal ends, though highly desirable, were becoming more difficult to imagine and that the "intemporal agony" of crisis was becoming a permanent state of affairs for him. Melville's

views of the "patterns of time" were growing more and more complicated. And, not by coincidence, they were growing more and more modern, more lifelike. For the sense of "new realism" seen in this book shows Melville's understanding of his own frustration at being unable to capture the truth, and it shows, too, his consequent recognition of the distressing meaning of faith. As his friend Nathaniel Hawthorne said of him upon seeing Melville in England in the fall of 1856, a little more than a month after *The Confidence-Man* had been deposited with its American publisher, "He can neither believe, nor be comfortable in his unbelief; and he is too honest and courageous not to try to do one or the other."[37]

∾

The Dilemma

of Nature & Culture:

Billy Budd as Problem Novel

Since the 1962 appearance of the Hayford-Sealts edition of *Billy Budd, Sailor,* there has been no break in the critical inquest (initiated by Joseph Schiffman's ironist reading in 1950) into Melville's view of Vere's decision to execute Billy.[1] Edward H. Rosenberry and Paul Brodtkorb, Jr., each attempted to settle the dispute in the mid-1960s, but the publication of conflicting assessments by Bernard Rosenthal and B. L. Reid shortly thereafter made it clear the debate was likely to rage as long as Melville's novel is read.[2] The very difficulty critics have had in resolving the controversy may, however, indicate that Melville intended neither to endorse nor to condemn Vere's judgment. Indeed, Hayford and Sealts have concluded that the effect of Melville's "noncommittal 'alienation,'" achieved by his late dramatizations of what earlier had stood as partisan statements, was "often—perhaps usually—deliberately sought."[3]

Still, perhaps some progress in this celebrated case can be made, first by examining closely the necessity for Vere's decision and then by suggesting what might have been Melville's purpose in creating that necessity. In my reading, *Billy Budd* is a prime example of the "problem novel," the narrative equivalent of the more famous "problem play."[4] It poses a fundamental human question that the author makes little attempt to resolve but instead leaves his readers to answer for themselves: Does the end—civilization—justify the inevitable sacrifice of the natural man?[5]

This chapter appeared in a different version as "Vere's Use of the 'Forms': Means and Ends in *Billy Budd*" in *American Literature* 47 (March 1975): 37–51; reprinted in *On Melville: The Best from "American Literature,"* ed. Louis J. Budd and Edwin H. Cady, Duke University Press, 1988. Reprinted by permission of the publisher.

Captain Vere's reasoning, while it may seem to have had Melville's reluctant sympathy, cannot be said to have had his full support. For in his presentation of Vere's handling of the case, Melville merely brings into focus the means-and-ends dilemma. Rather than an autocratically held end in itself, every one of Vere's applications of the "forms, measured forms" of standard naval practice, like each of his deviations from them, is a deliberately chosen means to the end of insuring the security of England and the salvation of "the Old World" (128, 54). Billy, like Christ, is sacrificed not by a "martinet" but by a benevolent despot who uses inhuman means to effect ends that are at once tragic and potentially redeeming, even "divine": the death of a blameless man and the "peace of the world and the true welfare of mankind" (128, 63).[6]

Although the Christian parallel cannot be said necessarily to signal Melville's endorsement of Vere's decision, it can be said to signal his larger intent. By focusing on the means-and-ends dilemma through this secularized version of the Crucifixion story, Melville makes us sensible of the price of civilization, and he reminds us that the responsibilities of the survivors, like the "agony" of authority and the passion of the victim, are features of our everyday lives, not antique curiosities (115). Civilized people bear a responsibility to the sacrificial victim who, as an "upright barbarian," symbolizes the natural in every one; thus they bear a responsibility to themselves, or a portion of themselves, to make their civilized lives worthy of the ideal in whose name the sacrifice is made (52).[7] First Adamic, then Christ-like, this "child-man" whose life was taken in his twenty-first year is finally a type of us all (86). His fate is the universal human fate. It is because Melville sought to awaken us to the common fate and its attendant responsibility that he could go no further in his defense of Vere. He had to stop where he did in order to prevent this work of imaginative literature from becoming the political treatise it is often taken to be.

Despite the many indictments, it is remarkable that those who condemn Vere's decision seldom offer more than ad hominem arguments based on ironic readings of the text. Vere is viewed as a tyrant who blindly or weakly or insanely follows, rather than manfully defies, the "forms" of the Mutiny Act that demand death as the penalty for striking an officer. Thus he is supposed to have violated those "primitive instincts," forming the basis of natural law, that demand mercy for one who is not only innocent of intent but, as even Vere felt sure, has also rid the world of an "Ananias" (109, 100). To condemn Vere on such grounds, however, is in itself to violate the principles of natural law. It is to look but to the "frontage," as war and the Mutiny Act are said to do, and to judge Vere by the consequence of his decision rather than by his intent, as Vere said the court must judge Billy (112).

Yet Vere's decision invites condemnation, as surely as it was meant to. Melville knew it would, because he knew from the experience of his cousin, Guert Gansevoort, that the comparable conduct of the *Somers* affair had been condemned.[8] Moreover, the *Bellipotent*'s surgeon, the court, and later "some officers" criticized Vere's handling of the case (103). While Melville was concerned to demonstrate the need for compassion, for Vere no less than for Billy, he was equally concerned to demonstrate that compassion alone will not suffice for either of these tragic figures. The power of compassion cannot exceed the power of historical circumstance to create the tragic necessity for inhuman action, and in this Melville could rely on the authority of the Father of the crucified Christ. Sympathetic understanding of Vere's rationale is warrantable, but so is indignation at the necessity of Billy's death. One must feel both pity and fear in response to this tragedy.

Melville's intention to portray the grim necessity of Billy's execution is revealed by the fact that the narrative cards could hardly have been stacked more expertly to force Vere's hand. Indeed, that "the unhappy event" of Claggart's death at the hand of Billy "could not have happened at a worse juncture was but too true." If Melville's intention, as the ironists argue, was in fact to strike out at arbitrary authority, it seems reasonable to ask why he bothered to place the event at a juncture that included among its critical factors not only the recently "suppressed insurrections" at Spithead and the Nore but a tightly interlocked and painstakingly detailed arrangement of other circumstances: that there were some on board who had participated in those insurrections; that England's defense rested on her navy; that the enemy had been sighted just before Claggart speaks his accusation; that the *Bellipotent* stood at the moment "almost at her furthest remove from the fleet"; and that the incident occurred "in the latter part of an afternoon watch," when the cover of night, so conducive to the kind of intrigue earlier refused by Billy, was soon approaching (102, 90). Important as it is, the argument from the author's need for dramatic tension seems inadequate; for what on one level is dramatic tension becomes on another the source of the problem and of the debate.

From the outset Vere is portrayed not as a man imprisoned by forms or conventions but as one who is independent in mind and nonconformist in manner. In conversation, for example, the narrator remarks that the "honesty" of "natures constituted like Captain Vere's . . . prescribed to them directness, sometimes far-reaching like that of a migratory fowl that in its flight never heeds when it crosses a frontier" (63). This simile, coming as it does at the end, emphasizes Vere's characterization throughout chapters 6 and 7 as a man who does not fear to transgress the world's boundaries—its customs, its forms—in

pursuit of a distant goal. More pertinently, neither is the Captain portrayed as a mechanical formalist in his attitude toward the crew or toward Billy. We are told that, "though a conscientious disciplinarian, he was no lover of authority for mere authority's sake," and in his speech to the court ("I feel as you do for this unfortunate boy") and in his closeted interview with the foretopman we witness Vere's heartfelt desire to do Billy justice (104, 113). But Billy is the "man trap" Claggart claims him to be, one Vere knows he must avoid (94). Unlike Ahab, Vere knows the cruel injustice of the fact that "whatever devotes itself to justice at the expense of reality," in the memorable words of Frank Kermode, "is finally self-destructive."[9] But Vere knows, too, as his own subsequent death shows, that there is no cause more worthy of devotion. In the fight against the *Atheist*, he dies for the same cause for which he sacrifices Billy—the defense of his nation and his view of what constitutes justice to mankind.

Unconcerned about self-destruction, Vere is unswervingly concerned about the destruction of the British community for which he speaks and acts. He is "prompted by duty and the law," he says in formulating the case against Billy, and duty to that community demands that he prevent a mutiny on his ship (113). In this time of war, a mutiny would have endangered not simply the lives of those on board; as the spread of insurrection in the Great Mutiny had shown, it would have endangered also the very life of a fleet that was "the right arm of a Power then all but the sole free conservative one of the Old World." Hence mutiny had the potential for becoming to "the British empire . . . what a strike in the fire brigade would be to London threatened by general arson" (54). Vere has to choose, therefore, either individual justice or communal justice, for in the fate of Billy Budd possibly rests the fate of an entire nation, perhaps even of "the Old World."

Given this context, only two issues could have made Vere's decision debatable: the question whether the possibility of mutiny on the *Bellipotent* was real and present; and the danger of encountering the enemy before the case could be referred to the admiral. That Vere's fear of mutiny was not paranoiac is suggested by the narrator's assertion that "Discontent foreran the Two Mutinies, and more or less it lurkingly survived them. Hence it was not unreasonable to apprehend some return of trouble sporadic or general" (59). What is even more pertinent, Vere knew that the *Bellipotent* was at the time "mustering some who . . . had taken a guilty part in the late serious troubles" and "others also" who had been impressed into her duty (92). The impressed men, too, were not trustworthy: "sometimes," particularly before twilight, they were "apt to fall into a saddish mood which in some partook of sullenness" at the thought of their families at home (49–50). While "very little in the manner of the

men . . . would have suggested to an ordinary observer that the Great Mutiny was a recent event," some grounds arise to substantiate Vere's sense of the potential mood of his men (59–60). At least they are not docilely responsive to his every word, as seen on three occasions—the announcement of Billy's execution, the execution itself, and Billy's sea interment—when order has to be restored by a "strategic command" for an uncustomary use of the forms. On the first occasion there went up from the crew a "confused," on the second an "inarticulate," and on the third a "strange human" murmur, the last followed by an "uncertain movement . . . in which some encroachment was made" (117, 126–27). That Vere's judgment against Billy provokes these disturbances is beyond question. But it is also true that the potential for mutiny is shown to exist in these incidents, both before and after the judgment is announced.

According to Ralph W. Willett, Vere's "fear of mutiny serves to rationalize" his "hasty" judgment that Billy must hang; for, Willett hedgingly asserts, Melville "points out" that the possibility of mutiny "is in no way suggested by the behavior of the *Bellipotent*'s crew." Attributing Vere's prejudgment to the temporary impairment of his "powers of cerebration," Willett argues that "The most clearly ironic example" of his "rashness" "begins with Vere's attempt to forestall mutiny by making an example of Billy Budd; this only serves to stimulate discontent among the crew and to make Billy a martyr."[10] There is irony here, to be sure, but "the *might-have-been*," as the narrator observes, "is but boggy ground to build on" (57). There is simply no way for Vere, as there is none for us, to be sure how the crew would have acted had Budd not been executed. Though there is no certainty that Billy's hanging prevented a mutiny, Willett begs the question when he concludes that its "only" effect is the ironic one.

Furthermore, that Vere's fear of mutiny is not a rationalization but a serious, continuing concern can be seen as early as midway in Claggart's accusations, even before Billy has been named. Vere is said to have concluded that even "if in view of recent events prompt action should be taken at the first palpable sign of recurring insubordination . . . not judicious would it be . . . to keep the idea of lingering disaffection alive by undue forwardness in crediting an informer, even if his own subordinate and charged . . . with police surveillance of the crew" (93). Thus, too, by reserving judgment about his master-at-arms's report, the Captain early reveals his willingness to deviate from the forms when his crew's steadiness is at issue.

Once again, Vere's fear of mutiny is not self-contained; it is related to his more comprehensive determination to maintain full strength in the event of a confrontation with the enemy, which in turn is related to his larger concerns for the defense of England and "the peace of the world and the true welfare of

mankind." Such a confrontation almost occurred just before Claggart accused Billy, when an enemy frigate was sighted and the *Bellipotent* gave chase. The fact that this was a frigate is important, because it implies the proximity of a French squadron or fleet, frigates being sent out alone primarily as scouts; as Hayford and Sealts point out, they "formed no part of the line of battle."[11] Then, too, it was while on "a somewhat distant" expedition, the *Bellipotent* being "almost at her furthest remove from the fleet," that she unexpectedly sighted the frigate; consequently, there was time in which to encounter enemy battleships before Billy's case could be brought to Vere's superior (90). Neither fanciful nor fanatical, Vere's desire to insure full strength for an enemy engagement is vindicated by the subsequent clash with the *Atheist*. Indeed, Melville seems to have been doubly willing to vindicate the Captain in this matter by contriving the French line-of-battle ship's defeat. Though Vere loses his life in the fight, like Lord Nelson he fulfills his duty to maintain England's security.

Although the possibilities of a mutiny and of a meeting with the enemy are the two critical factors in Vere's decision, his detractors have tended to focus only on the first of these and on subsidiary questions relating to his conduct of the trial. Besides his failure to place the case in the admiral's hands, these include Vere's demands for secrecy in the proceedings against Billy; his determination of the irregular makeup of the court; his demand for dispatch in reaching a verdict; his briefs to the court and virtual usurpation of its role; and, running through each of the others, the question of his mental stability at the time. It is here that examination of Vere's use of the forms most clearly reveals his deliberateness; for in each of these matters except the last—and this turns on his thinking in the others—Vere clandestinely deviates from or manipulates them to his advantage. And he does so for the same reasons he espouses in adhering to the forms of the Mutiny Act in the final verdict; he has to insure the stability of his men and the safety of his nation.

Vere's demands for secrecy, like his other contrivances for assuring his command, commence immediately after Claggart accuses Billy, when the Captain shows "perplexity" chiefly about "how best to act in regard to the informer." Although at first "he was naturally for summoning that substantiation of his allegations which Claggart said was at hand," Vere realizes that "such a proceeding would result in the matter at once getting abroad, which in the present stage of it, he thought, might undesirably affect the ship's company." Thus deserting the customary course, which he feels free to do because his crew has as yet no precise expectations, Vere "would first practically test the accuser" by shifting the scene from the "broad quarter-deck" to his cabin and their scrutinizing "the mutually confronting visages" on the reiteration of Claggart's charge. His fear of publicity even at this early stage seems appropriate, be-

cause "the interview's continuance already had attracted observation" from some of the sailors (96–98).

Vere's desire for secrecy following Claggart's death is consistent with that before it, and from then on he is even more cautious. "Here he may or may not have erred," the narrator says equivocally. But still it is suggested that this and every subsequent decision has been thoroughly considered: "Until he could decide upon his course, and in each detail; and not only so, but until the concluding measure was upon the point of being enacted, he deemed it advisable, in view of all the circumstances, to guard as much as possible against publicity" (103). Thus, having earlier used Albert, in whose "discretion and fidelity" he had "much confidence," to retrieve Billy, Vere is so careful as to hide Claggart's body from the hammock-boy's view when he is summoned again to send for the surgeon (97). Though Vere's wariness is called into question by the surgeon, it is later seen to have been warranted by the crew's continued curiosity in the affair. For, while "less than an hour and a half had elapsed" between Claggart's disappearance and the announcement of Billy's execution, it "was an interval long enough . . . to awaken speculations among no few of the ship's company as to what it was that could be detaining in the cabin the master-at-arms and the sailor" (116). Though Vere, also in the cabin during this period, did not witness their curiosity, he was a commander "long versed in everything pertaining to the complicated gun-deck life, which like every other form of life has its secret mines and dubious side, the side popularly disclaimed" (93). While it can be said that there would have been no cause for rumors had Vere proceeded aboveboard throughout, as was customary in capital cases, it cannot be known whether in that event there might not have been cause for mutiny.[12]

Why Vere hastens to call a drumhead court, like the question of why he demands dispatch in its reaching a verdict, is answered by his remark near the end of the trial: "while thus strangely we prolong proceedings that should be summary—the enemy may be sighted and an engagement result" (112). Thus keeping his eye on larger responsibilities, Vere deviates from usage; for the surgeon and the court agree that it would be best to confine Billy, "and in a way dictated by usage," and wait until the matter can be referred to the admiral (101). In fact, the "case indeed was such that fain would the *Bellipotent's* captain have deferred taking any [final] action whatever respecting it." But with the "self-abnegation" of a monk, he chose to keep "his vows of allegiance to martial duty." This statement, suspect in isolation, is translated to mean not that Vere weakly subordinated the claims of his conscience but that he steadfastly attempted to maintain his crew's stability: "Feeling that unless quick action was taken on it, the deed of the foretopman, so soon as it should be

known on the gun decks, would tend to awaken any slumbering embers of the Nore among the crew, a sense of the urgency of the case overruled in Captain Vere every other consideration" (104).

There has been less dispute among critics about Vere's determination of the court's irregular makeup, although in selecting the officer of marines to sit with the sea lieutenant and the sailing master he again "perhaps deviated from general custom." He did so because "he took that soldier to be a judicious person, thoughtful, and not altogether incapable of grappling with a difficult case unprecedented in his prior experience." Yet even as to him Vere had "some latent misgiving" about the reliability of his "extremely good-natured" character in "a moral dilemma involving aught of the tragic." Nonetheless, the marine captain seemed to be more suitable as a judge than the other two "honest natures," for "their intelligence was mostly confined to the matter of active seamanship and the fighting demands of their profession" (104–05). While they are hardly ideal jurists (Vere regards them as "well-meaning men not intellectually mature"), in light of their demurrers during the trial—particularly those voiced by the soldier, "the most reluctant to condemn of the members"—it cannot be claimed that Vere has unfairly stacked the court in this departure from custom (109, 129).

Once the court has been convened, Captain Vere interferes in its role and deliberations in at least four ways. First, though "temporarily sinking his rank" because he is the only witness in the case, he is cautious enough to maintain it "in a matter apparently trivial" by testifying from the ship's elevated side (105). Second, he instructs the court to confine its attention to the blow's consequence, not its provocation or intent. Third, he assumes the role of "coadjutor," arguing against allegiance to Nature and in behalf of allegiance to the King (110). And, last, he warns against mitigating the sentence. While each interference entails a violation of due process or a departure from custom, Vere's rationale in each instance, as seen in his reply to the marine captain's inquiry about leniency, returns to his persistent fear of mutiny: "consider the consequences of such clemency," he explains. "'The people' (meaning the ship's company) 'have native sense; most of them are familiar with our naval usage and tradition. . . . [To] the people the foretopman's deed . . . will be plain homicide committed in a flagrant act of mutiny.'" If the well-known penalty does not follow, "Will they not revert to the recent outbreak at the Nore?" (112).

These interferences, together with the concluding warning against clemency, make it obvious that Vere's primary interest is to bring the secret court's verdict into line with public expectations. That this verdict was demanded by "the law of the Mutiny Act" (or so Melville thought) is important to Vere because the law corresponded with and defined his crew's expectations (111).

If, having already decided against Billy, the Captain then railroads his judgment through the court, why does he bother to convene it? One implicit explanation is that, because Vere could not know beforehand how the court would decide, its concurrence was at least an even wager—a good bet for someone trying to insure the stability of his crew. More importantly, Vere is "very far" from wishing to monopolize "the perils of moral responsibility." Hence his motivation for not varying from "usage" in turning "the matter over to a summary court of his own officers" is not self-serving.[13] Rather, it stems from his awareness of the limited "moral" capacity of one man to decide such an issue. Vere knows he is not God. Yet he also knows that he has sole responsibility for any of the crew's actions that might result from a lenient verdict by the court. Thus he reserves "to himself, as the one on whom the ultimate accountability would rest, the right of maintaining a supervision of it, or formally or informally interposing at need" (104).

Even Vere's subsequent interference, then, has been anticipated. He is a deliberate, even prescient man. While his calculations, like his justifications, might still be judged "insane," it cannot be argued that he has lost self-control (102). It is as true of Vere as of Nelson that "in foresight as to the larger issue of an encounter, and anxious preparations for it . . . few commanders have been so painstakingly circumspect as this same reckless declarer of his person in fight" (57–58).

Because all proceedings after the announcement of Billy's hanging are necessarily public, Vere feels an even greater need to be circumspect at that point. Accordingly, once Billy was transferred from the Captain's quarters "without unusual precautions—at least no visible ones," then "certain unobtrusive measures were taken absolutely to insure" that no one but the chaplain had communication with him. Contrary to the narrator's assertion, however, Vere does not observe "strict adherence to usage" in every public proceeding "growing out of the tragedy," despite the fact that in no point could there be a deviation from usage "without begetting undesirable speculations in the ship's company" (117–18). When Vere orders the drummer to beat to quarters "at an hour prior to the customary one" in response to the crew's "encroachment" following Billy's burial, the narrator explains: "That such variance from usage was authorized by an officer like Captain Vere . . . was evidence of the necessity for unusual action implied in what he deemed to be temporarily the mood of his men" (127–28).

Though Vere risks the consequence of manipulating the forms in public only under the most pressing circumstances, this stratagem shows the power of the forms to be such that their use is imperative in all dealings with the crew. "'With mankind,'" Vere would say, "'forms, measured forms, are everything;

and that is the import couched in the story of Orpheus with his lyre spellbinding the wild denizens of the wood.' And this he once applied to the disruption of forms going on across the Channel and the consequence thereof" (128).[14] It is a mechanically inhuman, unredeemed society that Vere sees, but it is the reality he could not ignore despite his desire to do Billy justice. Vere's statement is an insight of tragic dimension and a lament for the inexorable state of things as they are, not a declaration of personal philosophy. It was not with Vere but with "mankind," and in particular these men-of-war's men who are "of all men the greatest sticklers for usage," that the forms are sacrosanct (117). Almost at the moment Claggart falls, Vere, who is "in general a man of rapid decision," speaks his full comprehension of the paradoxical situation before him: "Struck dead by an angel of God! Yet the angel must hang!" (103, 101).

Vere knows, therefore, that the lyre's forms do indeed "lie." But he knows, too, that only the forms can "spell-bind" his crew. Unlike Billy and the *Bellipotent*'s other prelapsarian sailors, Vere has partaken of the "questionable apple of knowledge" (52). It is not with him that the forms are "everything." With him, there are also the otherwise "wild denizens" of the man-of-war world and the inhuman "consequences" of the "disruption of forms going on across the Channel"—the "wars which like a flight of harpies rose shrieking from the din and dust of the fallen Bastille" and the attendant chaos responsible for both the abrogation of the Rights of Man in Billy's impressment and the destruction of Starry Vere (66).

Yet Vere's tragedy is not that he dies in service to mankind. His tragedy is that he has to use the inhuman forms of the Mutiny Act to attempt to secure more human forms, and not merely to conserve the stability of the larger community. A "bachelor," without wife and child at home to protect, Vere "disinterestedly opposed" the theories of the revolutionary innovators "not alone because they seemed to him insusceptible of embodiment in lasting institutions, but at war with the peace of the world and the true welfare of mankind" (60, 62–63). Certainly the objective of "world peace" has been invoked to embolden the schemes of tyrant and madman; but, for that very reason, it is not an objective we can afford to live without. Everyone with an objective—whether Claggart, Billy, or Vere; whether Satan, Christ, or God—must use the imperfect means of the world to achieve his or her end. And this is, I think, the legacy of Melville's tragic, anti-Transcendentalist vision. His portrayal of Vere's dilemma presents the means-and-ends riddle with a vengeance, and our recognition of the riddle in *Billy Budd* makes it impossible to read this work as Melville's "testament of acceptance."[15] The arbitrary fate of Captain Vere makes us feel the human need for the forms, but the unjust fate

of Billy Budd makes us, like Vere, feel the need to change the state of things as
they are and so to make more human forms possible.

Following Billy's early-morning sea burial, "the circumambient air in the clearness of its serenity was like smooth white marble in the polished block not yet removed from the marble-dealer's yard." These are the last words of Melville's narrative, save the "three brief chapters" of its "sequel," and they suggest not an end but the possiblity of a new beginning. The day is pure potentiality for those who witness the common fate; the world has begun anew, as it had for the survivors of an earlier Gethsemane. But it can truly begin anew only if the sacrifice of the natural "child-man" awakens us to the recognition that our potential salvation has its price—our debt to the victim and our responsibility to create a world worthy of his sacrifice. The world as it stands, like the book that mirrors it, lacks the "symmetry of form attainable in pure fiction"; it, too, is "less finished than an architectural finial" (128). Most important, it has not been, nor is it meant to be, "accepted" as it is. The marble still lies in waiting; civilized, human form has yet to be realized.

In his travels, Melville had seen people in all corners cutting themselves off from Nature or ruthlessly being cut off from it by representatives of civilization. And what he found in civilization was not sufficiently redeeming to justify the loss without perturbation. This was especially true because civilized people had blithely forgotten the loss in their pursuit of "that manufacturable thing known as respectability." The "doctrine of man's Fall," according to the narrator, is "a doctrine now popularly ignored," even though it implies the death of the Budd in every civilized person. For he observes that "where certain virtues pristine and unadulterate peculiarly characterize anybody in the external uniform of civilization, they will upon scrutiny seem not to be derived from custom or convention, but rather to be out of keeping with these, as if indeed exceptionally transmitted from a period prior to Cain's city and citified man" (52–53). Still, Melville seems not to be proposing a Rousseauist rejection of civilization. Having made the discovery more than forty years earlier when he wrote *Typee*, Melville still knew that once a person had bitten of "the questionable apple of knowledge" he or she could not return to Nature and the time before Cain. *Billy Budd* suggests that the Fall is a rite of passage as irreversible as it is perilous.

The inadequacy of the chaplain's Christian "consolation," which he extends to the still prelapsarian Billy awaiting death, seems to imply that in his last years Melville himself could not find consolation in institutionalized Christianity (120). But in a work in which he more than once voiced the expectation that his readers would find the novel's "savor of Holy Writ" disagreeable,

it is fitting that Melville's retelling of the Crucifixion story on the historical plane should reveal his support of the essential truth of the complexly tragic and triumphant Christian story as human drama (76). Like Christ, Billy is forced to play his role by the necessities of time and by his awful responsibility to a community that fails to understand, yet unknowingly benefits from, his sacrifice. Melville's "inside narrative" strikes that uneven balance and recalls to us what we were and are, though it foretells nothing about what we shall become. To be sure, prophecy is not the function of tragedy. But, having gained the burdensome knowledge of duty, we thus are free to change ourselves and our world. Like all deeply problematic writing, *Billy Budd* ends not so much with an answer and an ideological stand as with a question and a challenge to remake the world in a more benevolent image. Unless Billy's sacrifice "vitalizes into acts" the heroic potential of those in whose name the sacrifice is made, as it vitalizes Vere's in his fight against the *Atheist*, then such sacrifice is indeed "vainglory," as the Benthamites claimed of the death of Nelson; then, too, "affectation and fustian is each more heroic line" of *Billy Budd*, and our investigations into its meaning are little more than antiquarianism (57–58).

~

Notes

1. Cather 304.

2. Three book-length studies of the subject are Bowen, *The Long Encounter: Self and Experience in the Writings of Herman Melville;* Dillingham, *Melville's Later Novels;* and Bellis, *No Mysteries Out of Ourselves: Identity and Textual Form in the Novels of Herman Melville.* Bowen examines "the part played by the concept of selfhood" in Melville's writings generally (2); Dillingham argues that the central subject of Melville's later fiction is "survival through self-knowledge" (xi); and Bullis focuses on three distinct versions of identity—bodily, genealogical, and textual. Though all of these are relevant to my study, none explores the subject in the context of the tradition of the novel.

3. Matthiessen; Blackmur 124–44; Charvat 223; Brodhead, *Hawthorne, Melville, and the Novel;* and Baym.

4. See Anderson 179–95.

5. Leyda 1:274–75. Even at this point, however, in the same letter, dated March 25, 1848, months after *Typee* and *Omoo* had appeared in print, Melville refused, despite repeated requests, to provide Murray with any "documentary evidence" of his ever having been in the South Seas, "wherewithall to convince the unbeleivers [sic]," though in a still later letter (June 19, 1848) he claimed to have acquired such evidence but then "mislaid" it. See Ibid. 1:278.

6. Ibid. 1:413.

7. See Porte; and Bell, *The Development of American Romance.*

8. Brodhead, *Hawthorne, Melville, and the Novel* 3.

9. See Todorov, *The Poetics of Prose* and *Genres in Discourse;* Hirsch; Hernadi; Jauss; Culler, *Structuralist Poetics* and *The Pursuit of Signs;* Scholes; Fowler; and Rosmarin. Other critics whose discussions of genre have aided my own understanding of this complex subject include Heather Dubrow, Thomas Kent, and Joseph P. Strelka.

10. Fowler 38, 27.

11. Culler's "Foreword" to Todorov, *Poetics of Prose* 11.

12. Rosmarin 46–47.

13. Jauss 79–80.

14. Fowler 18.

15. Scholes 51.

16. Todorov, *Genres in Discourse* 15.

17. Gombrich 25, 323.

18. Fowler 32.

19. Hirsch 74–76.

20. Beaver 28.

21. Higgins and Parker, "Flawed Grandeur" 162–96, *Critical Essays* 1–27, and "Reading *Pierre*" 211–40.

22. See David Reynolds 159–61, 292–94.

23. See the "Preface," "Editors' Introduction," and "Notes & Commentary" in the Hayford and Sealts edition of *Billy Budd, Sailor.* This is the so-called "Reading Text" of *Billy Budd;* there is also a cloth edition, called the "Genetic Text," that contains an analysis and transcription of the manuscript.

24. Metcalf, *Cycle and Epicycle* 284.

25. See especially Erikson, *Identity: Youth and Crisis* and *Childhood and Society.*

26. *Omoo* 27; *The Confidence-Man* 12.

27. *White-Jacket* 346.

28. See Kring and Carey 11–15.

29. Letter dated June 1 (?), 1851, in Davis and Gilman, eds., 130.

30. Davis and Gilman, eds., 143.

CHAPTER 1
The Flesh Made Word, the Word Made Flesh: *Typee* as Romance

1. Leyda 1:225; see also 275.

2. Ibid. 210, 211, 216.

3. Ibid. 225–26; see also 200–201, 205.

4. Anderson 168, 193, 69–70, 113, 199; *Typee* xiv. Subsequent references to *Typee* are to the Hayford, Parker, and Tanselle edition.

5. Leyda 1:226; see also 278. It might be noted here also that, during the months when Melville was complaining most bitterly about the incredulity of his readers, he wrote—without acknowledging in any way the irony of his duplicity—and submitted to Gansevoort's friend Alexander Bradford, for publication in the *Morning Courier and New-York Enquirer,* an anonymous response to skeptical reviews of *Typee,* pretending to attest to the authenticity of the author's portrayal of his Polynesian experience. See Leyda 1:214.

6. Ibid. 199.

7. A relatively recent study that sees *Typee* and Melville's other early works as examples of travel writing is Giltrow, "Speaking Out: Travel and Structure in Herman Melville's Early Narratives." A related assessment is Roripaugh, "Melville's *Typee* and Frontier Travel Literature of the 1830s and 1840s," which places the work in a still narrower subgenre. While many critics have called *Typee* a "novel" or pointed out the presence of fictional scenes or other elements, the only one to give it extensive treatment as a novel is Paul Witherington, who emphasizes its experimental qualities. No one previously has attempted to show how Melville's narrative is structured according to the basic conventions of the popular romance.

8. Howard 95. See also Merrell R. Davis 8.

9. Leyda 1:196.

10. Ibid. 188.

11. Elsewhere Melville said that he "had long supposed him to be dead" (ibid. 222). See also ibid. 220 and *Typee* 271.

12. Leyda 1:200.

13. Ibid. 201.

14. Ibid. 274.

15. Emerson 44.

16. Hawthorne, "Preface," *The House of the Seven Gables* 1.

17. Frye, *The Secular Scripture* 4, 15.

18. See Anderson 72–74.

19. Leyda 1:210.

20. *Omoo* 3.

21. Anderson 106–07.

22. Freud, *Totem and Taboo* 137.

23. Leyda 1:413.

24. Frye, *Secular Scripture* 81.

25. An earlier nonfiction form popular in America, the "Indian captivity," also on occasion combined themes of captivity and the threat of rape (of women), but instances of this linkage in historical narratives written before the 1790s are in fact quite rare. For the most part, it was fiction writers of the nineteenth century who brought together these themes and sensationalized them. For an overview of scholarship on the "Indian captivity" genre, see Kolodny. An illuminating comprehensive study is Namias, *White Captives: Gender and Ethnicity on the American Frontier* (see esp. 21–48, 49–83, 84–112).

26. Frye, *Secular Scripture* 86. Though this may seem an extravagant claim, the idea finds much support in the psychoanalytic studies of Erik Erikson; see especially *Identity: Youth and Crisis.*

27. Cf. Hawthorne's famous description of romance, in "The Custom House," the introduction to *The Scarlet Letter,* as combining a geographical place and a mental landscape—a "neutral territory, somewhere between the real world and fairy-land, where the Actual and the Imaginary may meet, and each imbue itself with the nature of the other" (36).

28. Frye, *Secular Scripture* 91.

29. See Anderson 114–15.

30. Frye, *Secular Scripture* 104, 110, 118.

31. Though I do find Tommo's identity to be somewhat malleable under the pressures of Typee culture, I think Robert E. Abrams, in his stimulating "*Typee* and *Omoo:* Herman Melville and the Ungraspable Phantom of Identity," goes too far in arguing that it becomes so plastic as to be lost altogether. A view much closer to my own is Wenke, "Melville's *Typee:* A Tale of Two Worlds." An intriguing deconstructionist interpretation of the book that sees Melville as trying to unite the Western and Polynesian cultures "in harmonious felicity," rather than playing the one against the other, is Grenberg, "*Typee* and *Omoo:* Green Thoughts in a Green Shade."

32. This is Joseph Campbell's term, found in *The Flight of the Wild Gander.* Campbell argues that, to its young, every society operates as "a kind of exterior 'second womb'" (53).

33. Montaigne 105–19.

34. Thomas H. Johnson, ed., 473–74. Dickinson's statement is recorded in the letter Thomas Wentworth Higginson sent his wife following his first visit with the Amherst poet, August 16, 1870.

35. Frye, *Secular Scripture* 124–25.

36. In a related vein, Bryan C. Short argues that the narrative of Tommo's experience among the Typees simulates the buried tale of Melville's "self-discovery as a writer" (386). That self-discovery, in turn, "carries the force of a conversion experience, an inconceivable but undeniable election" to the vocation of writer (403).

37. *Moby-Dick* 47–48.

CHAPTER 2

"On the Move" in Polynesia: *Omoo* as Picaresque Novel

1. A good many critics over the years have commented on the lack of unity, or artistic deliberation more generally, in *Omoo.* These include Mason 32–34; Berthoff 23; Hayford and Blair, eds.,

Omoo xix, xliv; Rosenberry, *Melville* 39–42; and de Paul, "The Documentary Fiction of Melville's *Omoo*" 51–72. Even Edwin M. Eigner, who argues for the unity of *Omoo* in the matter of character, emphasizes the digressive quality of the book's action or plot. More recently, John Samson has asserted that "the digression, the light tone, the humor," which many critics have regarded as detracting from Melville's achievement, are in fact "vital indicators" of a process of profanation that pervades the entire narrative. This includes profanation of virtually everything the missionaries hold to be sacred, to be sure, but it also includes profanation of "the proprieties and rituals of narrative form" (509). None of these critics entertains the possibility that Melville patterned his narrative after the picaresque novel, and none recognizes the digressiveness of the picaresque as a legitimate narrative model in its own right.

2. Letter dated "July 15th 1846," in Davis and Gilman, eds., 41. In a later letter to Murray, dated September 2, 1846, Melville spoke more forcefully about the distinctiveness of his second book: "you must not Dear Sir expect another Typee [sic]—The fates must send me adrift again ere I write another adventure like that exactly" (ibid. 45; see also 50).

3. While picaresque fiction is generally thought to date from 1554, with publication of the anonymous *Lazarillo de Tormes,* the term "picaresque" was apparently only beginning to be used in English during Melville's own time; the *OED* lists three entries before 1847, but none earlier than 1810. By contrast, it lists three entries for "picaro" from the early seventeenth century.

4. Lawrence 140. At least a dozen later critics—too many to list here—have used the term in discussions of *Omoo.*

5. Dillingham, in "Melville's Long Ghost and Smollett's Count Fathom," discusses parallels between Omoo's companion and Smollett's title character, but he otherwise makes no attempt to place *Omoo* in the context of the picaresque tradition.

6. See Sealts, *Melville's Reading* 3–28.

7. *Omoo* 247, 310, 12, 292. Subsequent references to *Omoo* are to the Hayford, Parker, and Tanselle edition. Melville owned two editions of *Hudibras,* one of which he purchased in London in 1849 but gave to Evert Duyckinck after returning to New York; the acquisition date of the other is unknown. See Sealts, *Melville's Reading* 45. Sealts provides two entries on *Don Quixote* and one on a work of Smollett's, namely *Roderick Random,* all with dates after 1847, when *Omoo* was published. Melville, of course, may have made his first acquaintance with these works at an earlier date.

8. The second and third of these figures, of course, are the title characters of Smollett's *Peregrine Pickle* (1751) and *The Adventures of Ferdinand Count Fathom* (1753). "Amelia," according to Hayford and Blair, may be Emelia Gauntlet, Peregrine's beloved (426); but given that he speaks of "three volumes," Melville may have been thinking of the title character of Fielding's last novel (1751) instead.

9. *Redburn* 139; *White-Jacket* 34, 46. On Melville's borrowings, see Sealts, *Melville's Reading* 95, 74.

10. *White-Jacket* 46. Regarding Melville's purchase of *Guzman,* see Metcalf, ed., *Journal* 75, 153. Smollett translated *Gil Blas* in 1749.

11. Assuming that, with respect to this all-important economic factor, *Omoo* is in fact autobiographical, it should be noted that, although Melville himself was born into an aspiring, upper-middle-class family with patrician roots in America and aristocratic roots in Europe, his father's financial collapse and death in 1832 forced his family to retrench so severely that they were on the verge of slipping into poverty by the time Melville was in his late teens and looking around for something to do with his life. Furthermore, because a national depression had frustrated Melville's initial efforts to start in one of the professions—first as a schoolteacher and then as a surveyor for the Erie Canal—he turned to that last resort of the dispossessed and unemployed, the sea, thus beginning the extraordinary, five-year period of picaresque wandering that was to form the basis of each of his first six books.

12. Melville never suggests that his title character reaches the point of becoming a "beachcomber," a type mentioned in *Omoo* whose homelessness is more the product of deliberate choice than that of the picaro: "reckless and rollicking," ship-hopping sailors, these "roving characters," he says, are "wedded to the Pacific, and never dreaming of ever doubling Cape Horn again on a

homeward-bound passage" (81). Whatever his motive for returning home, Melville's own drift back—first on the whaler *Charles and Henry* and then, after a sojourn in Hawaii, on the frigate *United States*—appears in retrospect to have been intentional and sure, if dilatory. While he probably did not hear that his mother's financial situation had in fact improved during his absence, he is likely to have learned, while in Honolulu, that the nation's economy was recovering, news that might have prompted his curiously abrupt departure. See Howard 89.

13. For the contrary view, namely that Omoo "is almost constantly concerned with the idea of work" and feels something like the "horror" of Conrad's Marlow at "the pleasant, leisurely way of life in Tahiti," see Dillingham 83–84, 88–102. I think such a view overlooks the mischievous, devil-may-care quality of Omoo's character. While it is true that Omoo is a diligent sailor, when he gets on the islands he is hardly more enamored with the idea of performing any kind of physical labor than Long Ghost is.

14. Lawrence 140.

15. See Stuart Miller 78–85.

16. By giving Omoo the role of engineering the petition of grievances for the purpose of stabilizing the crew, it is clear Melville was trying to make him a more judicious and forceful figure than he himself had been, for, according to Hayford and Blair, the Round Robin episode is "evidently fictitious" (366). Several intriguing parallels with several features of Melville's portrayal of the conflict between Captain Guy and the crew of the *Julia* can be found in Smollett's *Roderick Random,* wherein the title character writes a personal petition to the tyrannical Captain Oakum requesting permission to move to healthier quarters on the plague-ridden *Thunder.* The captain, with the nasty sycophant Doctor Mackshane to support him, had recently announced that there would be no sick men on his ship while he commanded her. See Smollett 190, 157*n*.16.

17. For a brief discussion of the typical picaro's relationship with legal authorities, see Monteser 19.

18. Stuart Miller 72–73.

19. See Bjornson 207–13.

20. Lawrence 140.

21. See Blackburn 20–22.

22. Interestingly, the word "bashaw," an unusual variant of "pasha," meaning an important or self-important person, appears twice in *Roderick Random* (157, 208).

23. Robert E. Abrams offers a very different view, arguing that Omoo "sloughs his inherited identity" and develops into a "fluid, pliable character impossible to pin down" (45–50). In Abrams's provocative reading, Omoo is essentially without identity by the end and, in this respect, modern. The similarities between Abrams's conception of Omoo and Blackburn's conception of the traditional alienated picaro are striking, but coincidental. More recently, de Paul, in "Documentary Fiction," has argued that the narrator's ability to break out of a strictly Western perspective and to achieve a sympathetic understanding of Polynesian culture is symptomatic of a fluid paradigm of the self, one which was to influence Melville's outlook and artistry from this point on in his career. But de Paul, too, sees no connection with the picaresque, and concludes only that *Omoo* is such a "loose and open" text as to resist "generic classification" altogether (51).

24. While the precise etymology of "picaro" is uncertain, there is some agreement among literary historians that the word was used early to refer to one who engages in "evil living." See, to cite one source, Alexander A. Parker 4.

25. Whitman 32, l. 79.

26. Quoted in Leyda 1:260–61. Note, however, that according to Anderson, "nine-tenths of the contemporary reviews of *Omoo*" and most of the authorities on Tahiti "during the period just prior to and contemporary with Melville's residence" agreed with his unfavorable assessment of the impact of Christian civilization there (272–73). See also Hayford and Blair, eds., xlv–xlix.

27. Concerning the *Lucy Ann* and the view that "Melville may have dramatized the deplorable plight of the ship" in *Omoo,* see Anderson 200–203.

28. See Roper 321. Melville, of course, needed no literary precedent for this episode, but it

might be noted nonetheless that there is a parallel in *Roderick Random,* where many sailors die as the result of Captain Oakum's ruthless order to clear the sick bay (158-59).

29. Frye, *Secular Scripture* 97–126, esp. 115–17.

30. See Anderson 206, 274.

31. For a catalog of variations of these common picaresque motifs, see Stuart Miller 97.

32. On Melville's exaggerations of the population and depopulation figures, see Anderson 278–81.

33. In Marx's view, it is typically the best, not the worst, of the wild and the civilized that come together to form the pastoral "middle ground." See Marx 21–24.

34. See Bjornson 239.

35. See Stuart Miller 132.

36. See Frye's discussion of "themes of ascent" in *Secular Scripture* 129–57.

37. See Howard 89–104.

38. See *Omoo* 159, 245–48, 284–86.

39. See Davis and Gilman, eds., 41.

CHAPTER 3
Breaking Away: *Mardi* as Imaginary Voyage

1. Branch 317–36; Beaver 28–40; Anderson 342; Dillingham, *An Artist in the Rigging* 112; Chase 2; Arvin 90; Julie M. Johnson 229; Howard 122; Berthoff 12; Mason 49; Howard 114–17; Rosenberry, *Melville and the Comic Spirit* 65.

2. See Berthoff 28.

3. Brodhead, "*Mardi:* Creating the Creative" 30. Wenke, in his valuable "Melville's *Mardi:* Narrative Self-Fashioning and the Play of Possibility," is one critic who sees the book as improvisational, but he also regards it as an "eclectic hybrid" in form, and in the end he concludes that Melville was "trying to invent his own form" (412). A conspicuous example of a critic who skirts the issue is Merrell R. Davis, though he does call the central portion of the book, that is, the voyage through Mardi, a "travelogue-satire" (142).

4. Baker 36. For a more recent discussion of the imaginary voyage form, see Adams 112–47. Adams, who in his brief survey of this "huge body of literature" mentions works by Gabriel de Foigny, William Sympson, Chetwood, Defoe, Swift, Johnson, and Voltaire from the seventeenth and eighteenth centuries and Lucian, Apuleius, the author of *Mandeville,* Sir Thomas More, and Rabelais, among others, from earlier times still, refers to *Mardi* but once, and then only in passing (146).

5. Melville's letters to John Murray contain much evidence of his literary ambition in writing *Mardi.* See also his letters to Richard Bentley, dated June 5 and July 20, 1849, in Davis and Gilman, eds., 85–89.

6. Davis and Gilman, eds., 65–67.

7. Ibid. 67–68.

8. Ibid. 70.

9. Mason 64.

10. Recorded in Leyda 1:291.

11. Davis and Gilman, eds., 75–76; Leyda 2:917.

12. *Mardi* 595. Subsequent references to *Mardi* are to the Hayford, Parker, and Tanselle edition.

13. Gove 3.

14. Tieje 90–91.

15. Eddy 10.

16. These definitions of fantasy and the fantastic derive chiefly from Eric S. Rabkin. While I am much indebted to Rabkin for his precise definitions and illuminating discussions, I tend to agree with Brian Attebery's view that Rabkin's definitions are too narrow.

17. Nuita 12–13. Pascal's famous statement, number 139 of *Pensées* (1670), is a pertinent Western version of Nuita's idea, and one that was familiar to Melville: "I have discovered that all human evil comes from this, man's being unable to sit still in a room."

18. Rabkin 42.

19. Twain 404.

20. Hawthorne, *The House of the Seven Gables* 1. Significantly, no other reader of Melville's time appreciated *Mardi* so much as Hawthorne, who called it "a rich book, with depths here and there that compel a man to swim for his life." See Leyda 1:391.

21. Within this dream, moreover, other dreams are to be found. Yillah is said to be "rapt in a dream" while being carried to her fate on Tedaidee (140); and she has "imaginings" and "celestial visions" of an earlier state of existence that are heightened by the "dreamy seclusion" of her life on Amma (153). While it is true that almost all she knows of her past has been conveyed to her by Aleema, he claims that her early history had been revealed to him "in a dream" (137). When Aleema comes to convey her to Tedaidee, he reports that in a dream of his she had been recalled to Oroolia, her home (138), itself a "fairy tale" (145). Furthermore, Taji thinks that, like other victims of the arts of the island priesthood, Yillah indulges in "rapt fancies" and "seraphic imaginings" (139). Yet whenever she looks at him, he feels himself to be in "a spell" (152). Yillah's "dreams seemed mine," Taji says at one point (159). Ultimately, it is said, even she "verily believed herself a being of the lands of dreams" (158). While dream imagery is especially apparent in chapters 38–51, it is so deeply embedded in the poetic language of the book generally as to dull the reader's awareness that the novel is cast as an extended dream vision, like Bunyan's *Pilgrim's Progress* or such medieval dream allegories as Langland's *The Vision Concerning Piers Plowman* or Chaucer's *The Hous of Fame, The Boke of the Duchesse,* or *The Romaunt of the Rose.*

22. See "Hawthorne and His Moses," Melville's anonymous review originally published in the *Literary World* in two parts, on August 17 and 24, 1850.

23. So overpowering, in fact, is the satire of kingly pretention in the remaining pages that it swamps and all but sinks the dark romantic interest of Taji's quest for Yillah. The comic satire overwhelms the tragedy. The result is a bit like watching outtakes from Zeffirelli's *Romeo and Juliet* mixed in with long stretches of the Marx Brothers' *A Night in Casablanca.* Later, in *Moby-Dick* and *The Confidence-Man,* Melville would fuse his tragic and comic sensibilities more artfully than he managed to do in *Mardi,* where the mixture is likely to leave even the most devoted reader a little dizzy.

24. This is the common-sense definition of the term provided by Plath in his introduction to *Aware of Utopia* (7).

25. "Varieties of Literary Utopias," in Frye, *Stubborn Structure* 109–10.

26. Ibid. 121.

27. Several years later, Melville noted on the manuscript of his poem "A Reasonable Constitution" that "Observable in Sir Thomas More's 'Utopia' are First Its almost entire reasonableness. Second Its almost entire impracticability[.] The remark applies to the Utopia's prototype 'Plato's Republic.'" See Melville, *Collected Poems* 487.

28. Many readers have been puzzled by the fact that, while Taji evidently commits suicide in the end, a narrator who is assumed to be the very same figure somehow survives to tell the whole tale of *Mardi* from beginning to end. See, for example, Stern, who argues that "the disintegration of structure at times makes it impossible to know just who is narrating the story" (69–70). A few critics have offered rather complicated explanations for this apparent inconsistency; two of the most intriguing ones can be found in Dryden 49–56 and Dillingham, *An Artist in the Rigging* 110–13. While Dryden's view is, in some significant respects, similar to my own—"the narrative method of *Mardi*," he says, "is based on the recollecting of past fantasies"—it is fundamentally

different, too, and more complex. Where I have tried to show *Mardi* to be an example of the imaginary voyage cast in the form of an extended dream vision, Dryden argues that "Taji's journey into the world of dreams" is subordinated to "the drama of the narrator's self-conscious creation of it." For Dryden, "*Mardi* becomes not only an account of past dreaming but an account of present dreaming as well."

29. Eliot, "The Love Song of J. Alfred Prufrock" 7.

30. For another view of what *Mardi* reveals about Melville's marriage and his feelings for Elizabeth Shaw, see Haberstroh, "Melville, Marriage, and *Mardi*."

31. Evidence of Mrs. Melville's intention to leave her husband, uncovered several years ago, consists of two letters from May 1867 written to Henry Whitney Bellows, minister of the Melville family's Unitarian church in New York City, the first by Elizabeth's half-brother, Samuel S. Shaw, and the second by Elizabeth herself. Originally published by Walter D. Kring and Jonathan S. Carey under the title "Two Discoveries Concerning Herman Melville," in *Proceedings of the Massachusetts Historical Society* 87 (1975): 137–41, the letters have been reprinted, with assessments by a dozen scholars, in *The Endless, Winding Way in Melville*.

32. According to Howard, Elizabeth was quite familiar with *Mardi* even as it was being written (114–15, 122–23). Melville typically read each day's output to her, and she is known to have helped in making the fair copy for the publisher. However, even a more suspicious reader than she is thought to have been would not necessarily have drawn any personal conclusions from Yillah's death or sensed any parallels between Yillah's relationship with Taji and her own marriage to Melville. My point is not that *Mardi* is about the author's disillusionment with his young wife once the honeymoon was over; that was the catalyst for the book, but not its subject. *Mardi*, in my reading, is about the mind's making and unmaking of illusions or dreams more generally.

33. Stevens 174.

CHAPTER 4

"Gentleman Forger": *Redburn* as Bildungsroman

1. Schroeter; Arvin 103.

2. Franklin, "Redburn's Wicked End." See also Gross 599; Lish; Dryden 66–67; Seelye 52; Bell, "Melville's *Redburn*" 558–72; McCarthy, "Opposites Meet" 40–54; Edwin Haviland Miller 160-61; Pry 181–88; Duban 46–52; and Martin 41–58.

3. See Leyda 1:347, 412.

4. See Erikson, "The Life Cycle: Epigenesis of Identity" 91–141, in *Identity: Youth and Crisis,* for a discussion of developmental stages on which my study is based.

5. Ibid. 22–23.

6. *Redburn* 71. Subsequent references to *Redburn* are to the Hayford, Parker, and Tanselle edition.

7. Erikson, *Identity: Youth and Crisis* 23.

8. Quoted in ibid. 19. See James, *Letters* 1:199.

9. Bercovich provides a pertinent discussion of Redburn's relationship with his father.

10. Erikson, *Childhood and Society* 263.

11. Whether he holds back "his whole soul" also because of a growing awareness of (and indisposition toward) what some readers have taken to be Harry's homosexuality is perhaps more problematic, but I don't think so. In my reading, Redburn registers little recognition of any homosexuality in Harry, though he is aware of much that is mysterious about him. Indeed, the question of Harry's sexuality is itself problematic. To be sure, the youth whom Redburn several times calls "my Bury blade" is repeatedly described in the "effeminate" terms of a common stereotype of the homosexual (257); and the pleasure dome known as Aladdin's Palace, with its mirrors, marble "serpents of vice" (234), and "knots of gentlemanly men" (228), does bear a strong resemblance to what

Rogin and others have called a "male brothel" (70)—a place, it needs to be noted, that fills Redburn
with a vague but "terrible revulsion" (233). But if we are to take these as evidences of Harry's
homosexuality, it remains difficult to account for Harry's repeated references to an earlier romantic relationship with one Lady Georgiana (and possibly a second relationship also), unless we assume he is bisexual. Two partially conflicting but quite searching recent discussions of Harry's
homosexuality are Justice, "*Redburn* and *White-Jacket*: Society and Sexuality in the Narrators of
1849," and Martin, *Hero, Captain, and Stranger* 41–58. To me, what seems noteworthy about Melville's
treatment of the issue is his (or his autobiographical hero's) seemingly matter-of-fact acceptance
of Harry's sexual ambiguity, though Melville's attitude in this regard is in keeping with his large-
minded treatment of other marginalized figures and groups throughout his career.

12. Franklin, "Redburn's Wicked End" 193–94.

13. For a discussion of the Melville family's financial troubles during this period, see Gilman
146–47.

14. Letter dated April 5, 1849, in Davis and Gilman, eds., 83.

15. My conception of the bildungsroman derives primarily from my reading of numerous instances of this popular form, but in recent years my earlier views have been aided and enlarged by
the following critical studies: Hardin's "Introduction," Martini's "Bildungsroman—Term and
Theory," and Sammons's "The Bildungsroman for Nonspecialists: An Attempt at a Clarification,"
all in Hardin, *Reflection and Action: Essays on the Bildungsroman;* Franco Moretti's penetrating
study, *The Way of the World: The Bildungsroman in European Culture;* and Patricia Alden's *Social
Mobility in the English Bildungsroman: Gissing, Hardy, Bennett, and Lawrence.*

16. Buckley 23–24. On the autobiographical elements of *Redburn,* see Gilman. The confessional
writers, with whose work Melville was familiar at this time, included Augustine, Sir Thomas Browne,
and probably also Rousseau. See Sealts, *Melville's Reading* 40, 159, 209.

17. For a less sanguine account of Redburn's development, one that sees him as maturing as a
social being but unable to "move beyond [his] loss of innocence," see Haberstroh, *Melville and
Male Identity* 73–84.

CHAPTER 5
Power and Dignity in a Man-of-War World: *White-Jacket* as Political Novel

1. One of the various types of the political novel defined by Blotner is "The Novel as Political
Instrument," the distinguishing feature of which is that it is "meant to have definite political consequences" (8). Systematic discussion of the political novel dates from Speare's *The Political Novel:
Its Development in England and in America;* two more recent studies are Irving Howe's *Politics and
the Novel* and Gordon Milne's *The American Political Novel.* For a provocative discussion of flogging
in *White-Jacket* as a "politically significant personal obsession" of Melville's, one having profound
cultural and psychological connections with chattel slavery, see Rogin 90–101.

2. Some critics have difficulty even recognizing the book as a novel. Wilson Heflin, for example,
asserts that "*White-Jacket* defies conventional classification as to literary genre." Though he acknowledges, as do Anderson and others, that it "contains fiction of a special kind," he asserts that it
"does not qualify [as a novel] as to complexity of plot or depth of characterization." Instead, he sees
it as "a complex of diverse parts"—a "hybrid" of autobiography, fiction, documentary, and polemical tract (153). Other critics consider it a mistake to regard *White-Jacket* as a novel at all. For instance, Warner Berthoff, who shows a keen appreciation for Melville's technical strengths as a novelist, argues that the main reason the book has been hard to place critically is that contemporary
standards of the novel have been misapplied. "For *White-Jacket*," he asserts, "is not a novel. . . . Its
motives are chiefly documentary and polemical" (34–35). I would argue, instead, that it is possible
for a narrative to be both a novel and a polemical tract; in fact, in most instances this combination
is what distinguishes the political novel.

3. "La politique dans une oeuvre litteraire, c'est un coup de pistolet au milieu d'un concert, quelque chose de grossier et auquel pourtant il n'est pas possible de refuser son attention" (Stendhal 2:236–37; translated by the author).

4. Letter to Richard Henry Dana, Jr., May 1, 1850, in Leyda 1:374.

5. *White-Jacket* 282. Subsequent references to *White-Jacket* are to the Hayford, Parker, and Tanselle edition.

6. Leyda 1:412.

7. *Moby-Dick* 145.

8. See Anderson 429–31, 487–88. Melville, it has often been noted, had changed his mind about the practice of flogging sometime after writing *Omoo* (1847). There, just three years earlier, he had said that "I do not wish to be understood as applauding the flogging system practiced in men-of-war. As long, however, as navies are needed, there is no substitute for it. War being the greatest of evils, all its accessories necessarily partake of the same character; and this is about all that can be said in defense of flogging" (108n). Speaking of the "legitimate" toughening that young boys at sea receive as the result of flogging, Melville nonetheless treated the practice only incidentally in *Omoo*, whereas in *White-Jacket* he elevated it to a position of central importance.

9. Erikson, *Identity: Youth and Crisis* 133.

10. For a view quite different from my own, one that sees White-Jacket's identity as at best ambiguous or even hollow at the center and defined only "negatively by external pressures" (278), see de Paul, "Melville's *White-Jacket.*" Though de Paul offers an unusually illuminating discussion of America's cultural "ambivalence about the limits of modern political sovereignty" (271), I would say he fails to recognize that White-Jacket has both a private self, which was reasonably well formed at the start of the experience described in this novel and remains recognizable throughout, and a public self, which is both a playful fabrication and a cultural construction defined by his shipboard experience as "White-Jacket." De Paul seems, furthermore, to have a Platonic or "Hobbesian" conception of the self as something fixed and "innate," or else as entirely a social construction, rather than as a fluid mix of the two, as in the Eriksonian model, according to which the self evolves over time through the whole life of the adult, both in relation to and in opposition to the changing culture(s) of which that individual is a part.

11. Letter dated October 6, 1849, in Leyda 1:316–17. To be sure, Melville had read Dana's account at this point; see Hart. He had even borrowed rather liberally from it in the composition of *White-Jacket;* but the fact he had done so can be taken as another sign of his fictionalizing of his own account. See Lucid.

12. Larry J. Reynolds esp. 27. For a more recent assessment of the narrator's "antidemocratic" attitude that views it as evidence of just one of "several Melvilles" in the book, see Dimock, "*White-Jacket:* Authors and Audiences" esp. 302–03.

13. Although my reading of *White-Jacket* sometimes verges on being a Marxist interpretation, I think the book fails to provide all of the ingredients of a classic case study. Particularly, it was not capitalism but draconian legislation—especially the Articles of War—that was the root of all evil in an American man-of-war, in Melville's view. As I have tried to show, the man-of-war world traded more on raw power and a bogus kind of dignity than on the trappings of materialism. To be sure, that world, in its full historical context, might be seen as lending itself to a Marxist interpretation— the main business of a frigate at midcentury was to defend the trade routes and the coastlines of a sprawling capitalist nation increasingly interested in foreign resources and markets—but not in Melville's presentation of it. It needs to be added, perhaps, that although his heart was on the side of the working classes, at least when it had to take sides, and although he cried out in *White-Jacket* and elsewhere against their exploitation by the powerful, Melville was not in any precise sense of the term a "Marxist." It is possible, moreover, that he had not, in 1849, even heard of Marx's name, let alone read even portions of his writings. *Communist Manifesto,* the first of Marx's works to receive wide attention, was published the previous year, but it was not translated into English until 1850, and Melville apparently never understood enough German to read such a text in the original.

14. Cf. Larry J. Reynolds 18.

15. See Zirker.

16. An unusually explicit, later instance of Melville's quarrel with Transcendentalist ethics is his marginal comment on his copy of Emerson's "The Poet," which he acquired on March 22, 1862: "Another species of Mr Emerson's errors, or rather, blindness, proceeds from a defect in the region of the heart." See Leyda 2:648–49, 714–15, 720.

17. Despite calling himself a "hermit" on the *Neversink,* White-Jacket makes several acquaintances among "the people" in addition to his friends Nord, Lemsford, Williams, Chase, and his "comrades of the main-top." Among his messmates there are Bob, to whom he tries to trade his jacket, and Shenly, who succumbs to a pulmonary illness while White-Jacket attends him in the sick bay. From Rose-Water and Broadbit, the former an assistant to the ship's cook and the latter a sheet-anchor-man, he borrows various books. And, on separate occasions, three others—Shakings, the "holder" (241); Candy, a foretopman (223); and a youth referred to as "Frank" (243)—choose to confide their troubles to him.

18. See Anderson 418; Vincent, "'White-Jacket': An Essay in Interpretation" and *The Tailoring of Melville's White-Jacket* 221–33; James E. Miller, Jr.; McCarthy, "Symbolic Elements in *White-Jacket*"; Browne, *Melville's Drive to Humanism* 30–37; and Albrecht.

19. Curiously, Melville's previous commentators seem not to have found this ludicrous garment to be funny—an indication, I think, of a failure to appreciate the tone of Melville's writing in this book more generally. Whether, moreover, there *ever* really was such a jacket, or whether Melville himself ever demonstrated the kind of insouciance while on the *United States* that his protagonist does on the *Neversink* is open to question. Melville claimed, in the letter of May 1, 1850, to Dana, that "it was a veritable garment," but whether it was so outlandish as he portrays it in his book is doubtful. Still, it is tempting to think that sheer anger at having to wear an insulting jacket like his protagonist's was behind Melville's final disposal of the garment which, he said, "I suppose is now somewhere at the bottom of Charles river." Seeming to confirm such an idea, he confessed further to Dana that "I was a great fool, or I should have brought such a remarkable fabric (as it really was, to behold) home with me." See Leyda 1:185. See also Anderson 417–18 for information supporting his assertion that "it would have been possible at any time for Melville to have drawn a pea jacket" from the ship's purser.

20. *Moby-Dick* 507. As Ishmael's discussion of "The Whiteness of the Whale" (chapter 42) makes clear, white was, in Melville's mind, the color of "dignity," of "noble things," of "divine spotlessness and power," of "whatever is sweet, and honorable, and sublime" or "grand or gracious"; it was "the imperial hue," the color of "such power" as Moby Dick possesses and, of course, of much else besides.

CHAPTER 6

Sounding the Self: *Moby-Dick* as Epic Novel

1. While I feel obliged to follow Melville's public testimony here, I suspect Harrison Hayford's theory is right: "Melville wrote the essay not before but after he met Hawthorne." See Hayford's dissertation, "Melville and Hawthorne: A Biographical and Critical Study" 69.

2. Melville, "Hawthorne and His Mosses" 253.

3. Still, the number who have featured the subject of the epic are surprisingly small. In addition to Arvin's "The Whale" (in *Herman Melville*) and Pommer's "Poetic and Epic Influences of *Paradise Lost*" (in *Milton and Melville*), these include just two essays, both from the previous decade: Lord's "The Ivory *Pequod* and the Epic of Illusion" and McWilliams's "Till a Better Epic Comes Along." Two essays from the 1970s that would seem especially pertinent, Slotkin's "*Moby-Dick:* The

American National Epic" (in *Regeneration through Violence*) and Rosenberry's "Epic Romance: *Moby-Dick*" (in *Melville*), in fact offer little discussion of Melville's novel as an epic per se.

4. See Hutson and McCoy 9ff.

5. See Franklin, *The Wake of the Gods*.

6. As seen in his letter of June 1[?], 1851, to Hawthorne, written while finishing *Moby-Dick*, Melville doubted that his effort would be appreciated, but his mistrust masks his intention: "What's the use of elaborating what, in its very essence, is so short-lived as a modern book? Tho I wrote the Gospels in this century, I should die in the gutter." See Leyda 1:411. In a recent study that indirectly supports my own view, Lawrence Buell has argued that Melville's novel can be read as an instance of scripture; see his "*Moby-Dick* as Sacred Text."

7. See Abercrombie; Cook; and Newman.

8. Campbell, *The Hero with a Thousand Faces* 30.

9. Eliade, "Initiation and the Modern World" esp. 115. Eliade here distinguishes among three types of initiation: puberty rites, initiation into secret societies, and shamanic initiations. These last two both involve the "deepening of the religious experience and knowledge," even to the point of a "death" and "resurrection" wherein the initiate emerges in a new form, namely, as a spiritual being. Shamanic initiations are reserved for teachers or medicine men and "consist in ecstatic experiences (e.g., dreams, visions, trances) and in an instruction imparted by the spirits or the old master shamans (e.g., shamanic techniques, names and functions of the spirits, mythology and genealogy of the clan, secret language)." I see Ishmael's initiation as combining these last two types—initiation into the whaling fraternity and into the ways and knowledge of the shaman or "consecrated individual" (114–16).

10. See Campbell, *Hero with a Thousand Faces* 15.

11. Merchant, in his survey of the form, argues that, while *The Waste Land* lacks the "discursive variety of epic," it has "many features in common" with it and with modern poetic versions of the genre such as Ezra Pound's *Cantos* (92). Because it lacks the amplitude of the true epic, however, Eliot's poem qualifies technically only as a "mini-epic."

12. Abercrombie 16.

13. Eliot, *The Waste Land* 67, l. 431.

14. For an illuminating study of Ishmael as a survivor of an apocalyptic catastrophe, like the survivors of the Holocaust, see the work of my former student, Janet Reno.

15. *Moby-Dick* 3. Subsequent references to *Moby-Dick* are to the Hayford, Parker, and Tanselle edition.

16. Campbell, *Hero with a Thousand Faces* 29.

17. Ibid. 69–73.

18. Note that Mapple's description of Jonah's escape route calls attention to the fact that the Mediterranean is shaped like a whale, thus symbolically conveying the idea that Jonah can be said to be already in the "belly of the whale" even at the moment when he is trying to flee God (43).

19. Cf. "The Lamp," chapter 97, one of many instances of this image that appear throughout *Moby-Dick*.

20. Cf. Melville's remark in his June 1[?], 1851, letter to Hawthorne, written while completing *Moby-Dick:* "The reason the mass of men fear God, and *at bottom dislike* Him, is because they rather distrust His heart, and fancy Him all brain like a watch." See Davis and Gilman, eds., 128–29.

21. This is an early example of the displacement of roles and multiplication of characters typically found in epics, where themes are built up through variation and duplication to create the effects of richness and resonance, of plenitude and depth, and where indirection is necessarily the overriding method. Virtually everything in *Moby-Dick* is presented indirectly, rather than directly, as if seen in a mirror: Jonah's story is seen through Mapple's eyes; Mapple's story through Ishmael's; even Ishmael's story is presented not as it happens but after the fact, namely, "now that I recall all the circumstances," as he says (7), or after he has had time to reflect on it. It is, of course, in the nature of all literature to work by indirection. But in an epic it is among the chief techniques the

poet has at his disposal for generating the sense of heft or weight so characteristic of the genre. In effect, it creates a "double" sense of the subject and thus gives it "double" weight. Thus, the hundreds of instances of "doubling" in the opening chapters of *Moby-Dick* that Harrison Hayford has brought together in his illuminating essay, "Unnecessary Duplicates: A Key to the Writing of *Moby-Dick*," are not evidences of Melville's failure to edit out the early version of his book from the final one, as Hayford argues. Instead, I believe they are evidences of Melville's epic intentions, some of them, such as the famous tiller that turns into a wheel, presumably playful or ironic in intent.

22. Cf. "The Pipe," chapter 30, where Ahab, finding that his pipe "no longer soothes," tosses it into the sea (129).

23. Tillyard 15–16. As illuminating as I find Tillyard's theoretical statements about the epic, I do not agree with his view that *Moby-Dick* fails to qualify as an example of the form. Tillyard argues that Melville's narrative is a "great book" but that it is not "choric." However, if we take Ishmael to be the central hero, rather than Ahab, and define the group Ishmael is speaking for not simply as rude whalemen but as "modern democratic man [and woman]," or "the American at midcentury," I believe the book qualifies even on this count, as well as on many others.

24. Abercrombie 16–17.

25. See Winnifrith; and Newman 20–21.

26. Abercrombie 68–69.

27. Merchant 27.

28. Campbell, *Hero with a Thousand Faces* 15.

29. See ibid. 59–60.

30. See ibid. 101.

31. Ibid. 25, 40ff.

32. Campbell appropriates the term from Nicholas of Cusa, in *De visione Dei*, as cited by Anada K. Coomaraswamy, "On the One and Only Transmigrant," in *Supplement to the Journal of the American Oriental Society* (April-June, 1944): 25.

33. Campbell, *Hero with a Thousand Faces* 109–11.

34. The *Pequod*'s first whale sighting is described at the end of "The Mat-Maker," but in response to Tashtego's cry of "There she blows!" Ishmael "gaz[es] up at the clouds whence that voice dropped like a wing" (215). Even while standing watch, he confesses, he "kept but sorry guard" (158). And, as we are told here, he has his back to the whale, even when he is in close proximity and in hot pursuit. Until the very end, he is never in a position to see a live whale close up and out of the water; and, as he explains elsewhere, seeing a dead whale out of the water is a very different matter.

35. See Davis and Gilman, eds., 78. Quotations from Emerson 35.

36. Campbell, *Hero with a Thousand Faces* 118.

37. In substituting the whale's head for its "belly" in the mythical journey of the hero, Melville might be said to have subscribed to the view of one Bishop Jebb, who had once defended the truth of Jonah's story on the grounds that "it is not necessary . . . that we consider Jonah as entombed in the whale's belly, but as temporarily lodged in some part of his mouth." The distinction, of course, does not much matter, finally, given the metaphoric character of Melville's writing generally in this narrative. In this same chapter, "Jonah Historically Regarded," Melville even suggests that the "whale" in the biblical story might have been nothing more than a ship of that name or, more outrageously, a "life-preserver—an inflated bag of wind—which the endangered prophet swam to, and so was saved from a watery doom" (364–65).

38. "A Squeeze of the Hand" is thus also an instance of the bath motif, found especially in oral epics and discussed recently by Foley at some length, along with the greeting and feast motifs, in connection with the *Odyssey* (248–57). As both Foley and Arend point out, this theme includes "washing, annointing, and donning new clothes," a combination of activities that makes Melville's juxtaposition of "A Squeeze of the Hand" and "The Cassock," chapters 94 and 95, especially significant.

39. Campbell, *Hero with a Thousand Faces* 145.

40. See M. H. Abrams.

41. See Campbell, *Hero with a Thousand Faces* 40–41; see also Eliade, *The Sacred and the Profane* 42–47.

42. See Greene 15–18.

43. The only previous discussion of the *Pequod*'s captain as an exemplar of the Fisher King is Dow, "Ahab: The Fisher King."

44. Weston 13, 24.

45. Freud, *Three Essays* 21.

46. As Newman has pointed out, tragedy has always been closely associated with epic, Homer being credited with the invention of both forms (15). See also Ker 16; and Greene 16.

47. Weston 13.

48. In this respect, I have to disagree with McWilliams's conclusion, in "Till A Better Epic Comes Along," that *Moby-Dick* departs from the paradigm of Campbell's "monomyth" by failing to develop the third stage, or "return," and neglecting to define a community "to which the tale may be recounted" (203, 209). Though in general I find McWilliams's discussion to be both apt and illuminating, I would argue instead that the "return" stage is defined mainly by the period of Ishmael's composition of *Moby-Dick* and that his tale is intended for the whole community of Americans he left on land in the beginning of his narrative. More generally, however, all of the book's landlocked readers the world over could be said to constitute the "community" to which the story is directed.

49. Campbell, *Hero with a Thousand Faces* 177.

CHAPTER 7

The Divided Self: *Pierre* as Psychological Novel

1. All of the known contemporary reviews of *Pierre* as well as a generous sampling of early and more recent commentaries on the book are reprinted in Higgins and Parker, eds., *Critical Essays on Herman Melville's* Pierre: or, The Ambiguities. Of the many discussions of the formal defects or inconsistencies of *Pierre,* two of the more extensive are Leon Howard's portion of the "Historical Note" in the Northwestern-Newberry edition (365–79) and Higgins and Parker's "The Flawed Grandeur of Melville's *Pierre.*" For a carefully considered rejoinder to Howard's reading of the novel, see Milder, though even he refers to the novel at one point as a "debacle." Two of the more interesting attempts to explain the supposed failure of the novel are Brodhead's "The Fate of Candor: *Pierre: or, The Ambiguities*" and Wald's "Hearing Narrative Voices in Melville's *Pierre.*"

2. Evert and George Duyckinck's *The Literary World* reviewed *Pierre* on August 21, 1852; quoted in Leyda 1:457–58.

3. *Pierre* 356. Subsequent references to *Pierre* are to the Hayford, Parker, and Tanselle edition.

4. Leyda 1:449–50. Richard Bentley, Melville's English publisher at the time, had earlier brought out *Mardi, Redburn, White-Jacket,* and *Moby-Dick.*

5. Emmers presents evidence of a dark autobiographical parallel to the precipitating event in *Pierre,* namely, that Melville's own father had once had a mistress with whom he conceived an illegitimate daughter. For additional information about the identities of the alleged mistress and her daughter, see Murray, Myerson, and Taylor.

6. Murray, ed., lviii–lix.

7. For the argument that romantic lovers habitually embrace whatever will block or frustrate the culmination of their love, and in that way prevent it from dying, see de Rougement. Cf. Melville's allusion in *Pierre* to "that climax which is so fatal to ordinary love" (16).

8. Characteristically, when they meet for the first time in the red farmhouse, Isabel "blesses" Pierre and promises "blessings" to him if he will protect her; what is just as telling, she admits never to have known "happiness" (112–14, 119).

9. I think it is most apparent here that Melville did *not* believe, with the deconstructionists, that the self was an empty illusion, "vacant" because "unknowable," as Dimock has argued in her

stimulating essay "*Pierre:* Domestic Confidence Game and the Drama of Knowledge." Dimock seems to assume (with Pierre!) that, to be "knowable," the self must be one, or of a single purpose, rather than divided or ambiguous in its desires and intentions. What Melville shows instead, I believe, is that the self is typically multilayered and often deeply at war with itself. The fact of its division *is* its identity.

10. The character of Othello is mentioned on page 217 of *Pierre.* Also to be noted here is the fact that, within Melville's own family, "Gansevoort" provided a parallel case of a last name (i.e., the maiden name of Melville's mother) that also served as a given name (i.e., for one of Melville's brothers).

11. Several critics in recent years have emphasized the importance of psychological themes in *Pierre;* among the most provocative are Lewis and Shepherd. Some, including Brodhead (181) and Higgins and Parker ("Flawed Grandeur" 193), have even commented on the book as an example of the psychological novel, though in very different terms from the ones I present here, Brodhead emphasizing the unfolding conflict between "Pierre's conscious idealizings and his unconscious sexuality" (178) and Higgins and Parker emphasizing Isabel's role as Pierre's unconscious (171). Even these critics, however, see disunity in the first and second halves of the novel and fail to recognize the psychological *principle,* namely, the hero's growing self-division, that informs the overall structure, and intention, of the narrative. For a discussion of a very different formulation of the novel's basic structure, one that nonetheless complements my own, see Canaday's "Pierre in the Domestic Circle." Canaday describes two major domestic circles in *Pierre,* the one rural, centered at Saddle Meadows and defined in conventional, sentimental, female terms; the other urban, centered in New York City and defined in subversive, heterogeneous, male terms—terms that severely undercut or problematize the first domestic circle.

12. Cf. Matthew 5:22, where Christ, in the Sermon on the Mount, states that "whoever says, 'you fool!' shall be liable to the hell of fire." Cf. also I Corinthians 2:14, which would seem to apply to Plinlimmon: "The unspiritual man does not receive the gifts of the Spirit of God, for they are folly to him, and he is not able to understand them because they are spiritually discerned."

13. Jung 19–20.

14. See Scheler.

15. Still, it is at least confusing, if not a sign of Melville's nodding, that Isabel fails to take note of Mrs. Tartan's revelation that Lucy is "her own husband's paramour" (329).

16. It is easy to imagine how fervently Melville himself must have subscribed to these sentiments at the time he was attributing them to Pierre. Then in the final stages of his seventh novel in as many years, Melville had been to sea just once since the fall of 1844—a brief voyage in 1849 to London to promote the *White-Jacket* manuscript to publishers there. Still, clearly Pierre has nothing more in mind than an afternoon's trip across the bay and back—a little breather, hardly the extensive rehabilitative effort at "driving off the spleen, and regulating the circulation" that Ishmael imagines when he speaks of his sailing "the watery part of the world" (3). Significantly, perhaps, though Ishmael's story was written first, it begins where Pierre's story ends—with a desire to go to sea to escape a suicidal depression. Pierre's mood at the end (without the overlay of Ishmael's humor and controlled calm, to be sure) is strangely captured by Ishmael's description of his own feelings in his opening lines, beginning "Whenever I find myself growing grim about the mouth...."

17. Of course, given the many other coincidences in this novel, there is no reason to dismiss the possibility that the stranger's head is "a pure fancy piece," as Pierre briefly speculates. Even in this minor instance it is clear that Melville carefully crafted the world Pierre inhabits so it would be without any epistemological resting place. For this reason, too, it seems, Melville decided that the stranger's portrait would be one by an "Unknown Hand" and, further, that it would be placed in a show filled with apparent fakes. Such ambiguities are perfectly consistent with the dictates of "realism"; without them, professional sleuths such as Bernard Berenson would be out of business.

18. Even so, mention could be made of the early bantering between Pierre and Lucy and Pierre and his mother; portions of the scenes with Reverend Falsgrave; much of Melville's treatment of the commercial New York literary establishment and of the Apostles, the irrepressible Charlie in

particular; and some of the incidental figures, such as the greatly put-upon Dates and the mercenary policeman who helps Pierre on his first night in the city. Though much of the book's humor is of the gallows sort, much of it also depends on the exaggerated poses, actions, and expressions characteristic of opera or comic strips, as when Pierre returns to the precinct house to discover a riot in progress and Isabel in the clutches of a "half-clad reeling whiskerando" of a prisoner. "With an immense blow of his mailed fist," exclaims the narrator, pulling out all the stops, "he sent the wretch humming, and seizing Isabel, cried out to two officers near, to clear a path for him to the door" (241). Surely this scene—decried by critics as an instance of Melville's faltering prose—is intended as a sly commentary on the innocent melodrama that is one feature of Pierre's heroic mindset.

19. For evidence that in *Pierre* Melville was writing for a decidedly more female market than in his earlier works, see his January 8, 1852, letter to Sophia Hawthorne (Leyda 1:443–44). However, for a cautionary reading of this letter, see Milder 187.

20. Murray, ed., xcvii, xv–xvi, xlvii.

21. Ibid. xlvii. Indeed, Melville himself may not have felt sure about the paternity claims lodged against his own father. Insofar as we can make it out today, the case is far from certain.

22. Ibid. lii–lv, cii, xcii.

23. Ibid. ci–cii.

24. Ibid. xvii, c.

25. Ibid. lxxxvii.

26. One more or less contemporaneous indication of Melville's appetite for the most strenuous kind of metaphysical debate is recorded in Hawthorne's journal entry for August 1, 1851, on the occasion of an impromptu visit from his Pittsfield neighbor: "Melville and I had a talk about time and eternity, things of this world and of the next, and books, and publishers, and all possible and impossible matters, that lasted pretty deep into the night" (quoted in Leyda 1:418–19).

27. Murray, ed., xciii.

28. Leyda 1:434–35.

29. The view that Melville became exhausted by the ordeal of writing *Moby-Dick* and then grew dejected by its failure to generate an enthusiastic following is a critical commonplace that has recently been contradicted; see, most notably, Higgins and Parker's introduction to *Critical Essays on Herman Melville's* Pierre: or, The Ambiguities (esp. 1–4).

30. In late May or early June of 1851, not long after he had become settled in the Berkshires and just before he began writing *Pierre*, Melville wrote a long letter to Hawthorne and, in closing, mentioned the transcendental philosophy of Goethe. At first dismissing Goethe's advice to "Live in the all" as useless to a man with a "raging tooth-ache," Melville went on to say, in a postscript, that "This 'all' feeling, though, there is some truth in. You must often have felt it, lying on the grass on a warm summer's day. Your legs seem to send out shoots into the earth. Your hair feels like leaves upon your head. This is the *all* feeling. But what plays the mischief with the truth is that men will insist upon the universal application of a temporary feeling or opinion." Melville's postscript might be read as a gloss on his attitude toward the young would-be Transcendentalist Pierre. See Davis and Gilman, eds., 130–31.

31. From the time of Mumford's *Herman Melville*, most commentators on the subject of *Pierre*'s style have deplored its sentimentality as patently excessive, especially in the early books. But since Braswell's essays on the topic appeared—first "The Satirical Temper of Melville's *Pierre*" and then "The Early Love Scenes in Melville's *Pierre*"—at least a few critics have taken the countervailing, ironic view of the matter.

32. In this respect, as in a good many others, Melville seems in *Pierre* to have reversed the pattern of Warner's *Wide, Wide World*, where life in New York City is portrayed in the early chapters as rich and comfortable, while life in the upstate New York village is depicted as impoverished, even barren.

1. Chase 176. One of the most recent critics to use the term is Obuchowski. For the view that in *Israel Potter* Melville moved through a succession of genres, from dedication to epitaph and including picturesque travel sketch, biography, narrative of adventure, gothic tale cum ghost story cum grotesque farce, patriotic tribute, and tall tale, see Cohen. All of these genres, I believe, can be said to co-exist within what I would call Melville's master-genre of the historical novel.

2. See "Historical Note" in *Israel Potter* vii. Subsequent references to *Israel Potter* are to the Hayford, Parker, and Tanselle edition. Two recent critics who have focused on the historical dimension of Melville's narrative are Rosenberg and Bellis. Rosenberg argues that Melville is parodying the conservatism of specifically *British* historical literature, as represented in Scott, Carlyle, Ruskin, and Dickens; and Bellis argues that Melville is exploring the unbridgable gap between "individual self-consciousness (autobiography) and the wider perspective of history as a whole" (607).

3. Obviously Melville did not mean "the Revolutionary era" in the exact sense of the term, or else he made a slip, for the sentence begins by speaking of the "first settlers," who were a very different bunch from the "men of the Revolutionary era," such as Potter.

4. See Leisy 10, 14.

5. King George's stutter is the sort of realistic detail—like Joanna Wilks's harelip in *Huckleberry Finn* or the webbed fingers of Marek Shimerda in *My Ántonia*—that seems designed to expose the reader's sentimentality; realist writers often seem to take pleasure in reminding their readers of genetic flaws and other imperfections in the natural order.

6. *Moby-Dick* 274.

7. This last statement is not the condemnation of Franklin's whole character that it is sometimes taken to be. Melville still recognized Franklin to be one of the consummate stylists in the history of English prose. "He dressed his person as his periods," he remarked of Franklin earlier in *Israel Potter;* "neat, trim, nothing superfluous, nothing deficient. In some of his works his style is only surpassed by the unimprovable Hobbes of Malmsbury, the paragon of perspecuity" (59).

8. Melville chose to depart from historical truth when he made Potter a participant in this famous sea fight rather than portray him in the equally famous battle of Bunker Hill, in which he did take part. Perhaps he decided to make this change because sea battles can be dramatized more sharply or economically than land battles, and possibly, too, because he himself was so well versed in the movements of ships at sea.

9. See especially Kriegel viii.

10. Melville invented a few of the other incidents mentioned in *Israel Potter,* too, as McCutcheon has pointed out (167).

11. Melville's entry, dated "Nov 9th," 1849, reads in part: "While on one of the Bridges, the thought struck me again that a fine thing might be written about a Blue Monday in November London—a city of Dis (Dante's) clouds of smoke—the damned &c—coal barges—coaly waters, cast-iron Duke &c—its marks are left upon you, &c &c &c" (*Journals* 14).

12. See Decker, ed., 90.

13. Melville, *Journals* 43.

CHAPTER 9

Dialogue of Crisis: *The Confidence-Man* as Experimental Novel

1. In addition to the work of Robbe-Grillet, the following critical discussions have been especially helpful in forming my understanding of the experimental novel: Ryf's "Character and

Imagination in the Experimental Novel"; Glicksberg's "Experimental Fiction: Innovation Versus Form"; Raymond Federman's "Surfiction—Four Propositions in Form of an Introduction"; Butler's "Scepticism and Experimental Fiction"; Fletcher and Calder's introduction to *The Nouveau Roman Reader;* Caserio's "The Novel as a Novel Experiment in Statement: The Anticanonical Example of H. G. Wells."

2. See Leyda 1:348. Rosenberry discusses several parallels between Melville's novel and Sterne's (*Melville and the Comic Spirit* 146–48). However, he does so not as evidence of Melville's experimentation with fictional conventions, as I do here, but to demonstrate the whimsical strain in Melville's "comic ambiguity."

3. The effort in Melville criticism to pin down a central theme or unified interpretation of *The Confidence-Man,* as Hershel Parker ("Foreword") was the first to point out, goes back to Shroeder and Foster and lasted until the early 1970s. Since then, there has been an opposite tendency to problematize the text by emphasizing its ambiguities or multiplicity of meanings. Interpretations that fall into this latter category are too numerous to mention, but a representative sampling would include those by Blair, Gaudino, Lee, and Bellis.

4. *Moby-Dick* 331.

5. Butler, especially, emphasizes the importance of skepticism, and of skeptical epistemology, in experimental fiction and argues that writers of postmodern fiction in particular tend to share Richard Rorty's view that we must learn to "eschew totalisation" and become comfortable with "discontinuity and openendedness and contingency" (49–51). Rorty examines the idea, which he dates to the late eighteenth century, that truth is not something out there in the world but something made by the human imagination (esp. chap. 1).

6. James, *The Will to Believe* xi.

7. Even Drew, however, contradicts his own findings, but he does so in an unusual way. After arguing that the title character *might* not be a "con man," he goes on to maintain that the confidence man's "actions and sentiments carry the weight of Melville's *sympathy*" and, therefore, that the work offers "an *unequivocal* lesson in *charity*" (424, 429; emphasis added). Like Drew, Buell also has argued that the true identity of the confidence man is uncertain. For him, Melville maintains "a sly balance between possibilities suggested and the secret withheld" ("Last Word" 26). But instead of exploring this idea or drawing meaning from it, Buell uses it to form the basis of his argument regarding the book's comic tone.

8. Seltzer 15, 21–22. For similar general conclusions and the authors' own exceptions to them, see also Winters 224, 227; and Cawelti 279–80, 283.

9. Entry dated November 20, 1856, in Hawthorne, *The English Notebooks* 432; see also 437.

10. See, for example, Howard 237; and Foster xx–xxxiii, where a full account of Melville's health is presented.

11. Significantly, this is the American edition. See Foster xxxi.

12. *The Confidence-Man* 157. Subsequent references to *The Confidence-Man* are to the Hayford, Parker, and Tanselle edition.

13. Glicksberg is especially illuminating on the importance of subjectivity (or the relativity of knowledge) and the absence of reliable authorial commentary in the experimental novel.

14. Drew 433.

15. Robbe-Grillet 156. As Glicksberg, among others, has pointed out, furthermore, openendedness or "open form" has been a feature of experimental fiction since *Tristram Shandy* (132).

16. Booth 299. Critics who have noted the untrustworthiness of Melville's narrator, without demonstrating the case in detail, include Dryden (152–54, 171–74, 195), Bowen ("Tactics" 402–03), Seelye (124–25), and Buell ("Last Word" 17). For a more comprehensive summary of the scholarship on the narrator, see Bryant 337–39.

17. See Shroeder 369–71; and Foster xlix–l.

18. For Melville's caricature of Emerson as Winsome, see Parker, "Melville's Satire."

19. Shroeder 379. See also Sedgwick 192–93. For dissenting views, see Pearce; Fussell 318–25; and Adler 424. For a reading that sees the whole issue as irresolvable, see Ramsey.

20. Cf. Foster's assertion that in Melville's adaptation of James Hall's *Sketches of History, Life, and Manners, in the West* (1835) he "carefully omits all of Hall's references to the initial aggressions of the whites; he deletes Hall's extenuating explanations of Indian rapine as revenge for white injustice; and he makes Indian-hating a simple and inevitable consequence of the original and unexplained wickedness of the Indians" (lxvii).

21. For a discussion of this episode as a "satiric allegory in which the Indians are Devils and the Indian-haters are dedicated Christians, and in which the satiric target is the nominal practice of Christianity," see Parker, "The Metaphysics of Indian-Hating."

22. The five who appear are the "ge'mman wid a weed" (John Ringman), the "ge'mann in a gray coat and white tie" (the representative of the Widow and Orphan Asylum), the "ge'mann wid a big book" (the president and transfer agent of the Black Rapids Coal Company), the "yarb-doctor," and the "ge'mann wid a brass plate" (the PIO man). The remaining three mentioned by Black Guinea—"a ge'mann in a yaller west," "a ge'mman in a wiolet robe," and "a ge'mman as is a sodjer"— do not seem to materialize, at least not as avatars of the confidence man, although the man with gold sleeve buttons is dressed in white (he could be the "ge'mann in a yaller west"), Charlie Noble has a violet vest (not a violet robe), and the "soldier of fortune" could be the "ge'mann as is a sodjer," but he is not generally regarded as an avatar (13). For possible candidates for the latter three, see Franklin, *The Wake of the Gods* 162–63 and passim. Though apparently not included in Black Guinea's list, the cosmopolitan is usually considered as yet another avatar.

23. Foster xiv; Kaul 11.

24. For the view that the book is an artistic failure, see Mason 201; Hoffman 310; and Pearce 942n. Those who see the book as lacking a formal resolution include Cawelti (288) and Seelye (130). Dubler argues that the "principle of the golden mean" is "implied" (313), whereas Seltzer finds a "highly unified" structure (14–15), and Mitchell concludes that the structural difficulties can be resolved by defining confidence as "activity," not as "essence."

25. Kermode 164. I am much indebted to Kermode's study, which was formative in my understanding of the "new novel" and of the modern sensibility.

26. See Shroeder 371–73; Fussell 315–16; Bowen, "Tactics" 411–13; Seelye 127–28; and McCarthy, "Affirmative Elements" 59–60.

27. Kermode 21.

28. See Ryf 322–27. Ryf argues that such "digressions," where the author explains his or her own work, are but one evidence of the fact that the central subject of the experimental novel is not the ostensible material per se but the play of the shaping power of the writer's (and reader's) imagination on the material.

29. Cawelti uses the comparable term, "incomplete reversals" (282–83).

30. Kermode 19.

31. Ibid. 18.

32. Ibid. 30–31.

33. For example, Matthiessen wrote, "Melville was so far from having imagined a conclusion for *The Confidence Man* that he could only break it off as a distended fragment" (412). Horsford finds "some evidence," largely external, for its incompleteness.

34. Kermode 30. He is referring to modern, "existentialist" theologians, such as Bultmann, who says, "in every moment slumbers the possibility of being the eschatological moment" (25). It is the traditionalists who regard the End as imminent.

35. Ibid. 101.

36. In an unusually fresh and intriguing reading, Dillingham argues that the confidence man is Melville's attempt at imagining what a man of the highest possible degree of self-knowledge would look like (*Melville's Later Novels* 297–337).

37. Entry dated November 20, 1856, in Hawthorne, *English Notebooks* 433.

CHAPTER 10
The Dilemma of Nature and Culture: *Billy Budd* as Problem Novel

1. Subsequent references to *Billy Budd* are to the Hayford and Sealts edition. Besides Schiffman, see Hayford and Sealts 26–27, 203–12 for a listing of the other pre-1962 ironist critics. See also Kilbourne; Browne, "*Billy Budd:* Gospel of Democracy"; Willett; and Rosenthal.

2. In "The Problem of *Billy Budd*" Rosenberry, a nonironist, examines the novel's tone and "ethical logic," while Brodtkorb argues that virtually "everything is demonstrable," because the novel is "unfinished." In fact, in the years since 1975, when my own essay was first published in *American Literature,* the vast majority of commentators—too numerous to mention here—have fallen into the ironist camp, though a few, like myself, have tried to get beyond the point of taking sides in the debate and instead understand why Melville would have presented a dilemma for which he offered no solution. See, for example, Barbara Johnson, Hurtgen, R. Even Davis, and Grenberg. Regardless of these critical developments, the controversy continues with remarkable energy.

3. *Billy Budd* 38.

4. There is little scholarship available on the "problem novel," though the term has fairly wide currency, thanks in part to its close parallels with the "problem play." See, for instance, Holman and Harmon 396–97. (Arnold B. Fox uses the term in a more limited way, to refer to Trollope's characteristic refusal to push a thesis in the first of his Palliser novels.) It is significant, I believe, that Melville was writing *Billy Budd* just at the time when the problem play was beginning to be formulated in England, by John Galsworthy, Henry Arthur Jones, J. M. Barrie, George Bernard Shaw, and others. As Simon points out, the problem play was a revolutionary form that served as a transition between the melodrama of the earlier nineteenth century and our own modern theater. Designed to shake audiences out of their complacency and introduce them to a world of uncertainty and doubt, it was supposed also to challenge them to become actively involved in a theatrical experience that called into question the audience's own values while forcing them to seek personal answers to contemporary human problems (vi–vii). Like readers of *Billy Budd,* they could no longer expect their faith in the morality of "virtue triumphant" to be confirmed (26). In the new era, they would come to see life as a series of conflicts, as Shaw said, between "Man's will and his environment," or social institutions, and they would have to try to resolve them on their own (49–50). Salerno's is a much briefer but still very useful discussion.

5. Other critics, of course, are likely to define the "problem" of *Billy Budd* in different terms. Still, one indication of the problematic quality of Melville's text is the fact that it has attracted much attention in recent years from new historicist "law and literature" specialists, such as Brook Thomas, as well as from legal scholars, such as Richard H. Weisberg and Richard A. Posner. Melville's novel is even used as a case study in law school classes and has served as the subject of a good many "law and literature" courses, seminars, and conferences. Some of the prominent studies in this category include the special inaugural issue of *Cardoza Studies in Law and Literature* (Spring 1989), devoted exclusively to *Billy Budd* and containing an exchange between Weisberg and Posner; McWilliams's "Innocent Criminal or Criminal Innocence"; Thomas's *Cross-Examinations of Law and Literature;* and Weiner's "Law, Literature, and the Space Between." A recent example of a very different kind of new historicist reading is Mizruchi's "Cataloging the Creatures of the Deep," which problematizes Melville's story by placing it in the context of such prominent late-nineteenth-century issues as subjectivity and indeterminacy, social "sight" and invisibility, while examining whether Melville (or his narrator) managed to escape the limited social values and point of view he attempted to critique in his narrative.

6. For an earlier treatment of the means-and-ends problem, see Glick.

7. Significantly, such a reading seems confirmed by the motto Melville is known to have pasted to his writing desk in his late years, including, presumably, the years when he wrote *Billy Budd:* "Keep true to the dreams of thy youth." See Metcalf, *Cycle and Epicycle* 284.

8. See *Billy Budd* 26–30, 181–83.

9. Kermode 105.

10. Willett 370–71.

11. *Billy Budd* 144.

12. See Ives 36.

13. In fact, Vere's argument from "usage" in this regard is tenuous. See *Billy Budd* 175–76; and Ives 32–36. Apparently this was Melville's error, as he made a related mistake earlier, when it is said that Vere had been a member of "a court-martial ashore . . . when a lieutenant" (94). "According to statute," the editors say, "regular naval courts-martial consisted of commanders and captains" (178; see also 181–82). Sealts has provided an updated evaluation of this matter in "Innocence and Infamy," esp. 417–20.

14. A more precise parallel between Vere and Orpheus is suggested by the fact that the mythical poet is known for resolving "a quarrel among the Argonauts (on whose voyage he sailed) that enabled them to reach Colchis strand and the Golden Fleece," though, unlike Vere, Orpheus achieved control over the ship's company by the eloquence of his poetry. See Cain 25. Note also that, according to one of Spenser's sources, civilization originated with Orpheus (27).

15. Watson coined this controversial term. See also Braswell, "Melville's *Billy Budd*"; Fogle; Brodtkorb; and Reid.

~

Bibliography

Abercrombie, Lascelles. *The Epic.* 1914. Freeport, NY: Books for Libraries Press, 1969.

Abrams, M. H. *The Mirror and the Lamp: Romantic Theory and the Critical Tradition.* 1953. New York: Norton, 1958.

Abrams, Robert E. "*Typee* and *Omoo:* Herman Melville and the Ungraspable Phantom of Identity." *Arizona Quarterly* 31 (Spring 1975): 33–50.

Adams, Percy G. *Travel Literature and the Evolution of the Novel.* Lexington: U of Kentucky P, 1983.

Adler, Joyce Sparer. "Melville on the White Man's War against the American Indian." *Science and Society* 36 (Winter 1972): 417–42.

Albrecht, Robert C. "White Jacket's Intentional Fall." *Studies in the Novel* 4 (Spring 1972): 17–26.

Alden, Patricia. *Social Mobility in the English Bildungsroman: Gissing, Hardy, Bennett, and Lawrence.* Ann Arbor: UMI Research Press, 1986

Anderson, Charles Roberts. *Melville in the South Seas.* 1939. New York: Dover, 1966.

Arend, Walter. *Die typischen Scenen bei Homer.* Berlin: Weidmann, 1933.

Arvin, Newton. *Herman Melville.* New York: William Sloan, 1950.

Attebery, Brian. *The Fantasy Tradition in American Literature: From Irving to Le Guin.* Bloomington: Indiana UP, 1980.

Baker, Ernest A. *The History of the English Novel.* Vol. 1: *The Age of Romance: From the Beginnings to the Renaissance.* London: Witherby, 1924.

Baym, Nina. "Melville's Quarrel with Fiction." *PMLA* 94 (October 1979): 909–23.

Beaver, Harold. "*Mardi:* A Sum of Inconsistencies." *Herman Melville: Reassessments.* Ed. A. Robert Lee. Totowa, NJ: Barnes and Noble, 1984. 28–40.

Bell, Michael Davitt. *The Development of American Romance: The Sacrifice of Relation.* Chicago: U of Chicago P, 1980.

———. "Melville's *Redburn:* Initiation and Authority." *New England Quarterly* 46 (December 1973): 558–72.

Bellis, Peter J. "*Israel Potter:* Autobiography as History as Fiction." *American Literary History* 2 (Winter 1990): 607–26.

——. *No Mysteries Out of Ourselves: Identity and Textual Form in the Novels of Herman Melville*. Philadelphia: U of Pennsylvania P, 1990.

——. "Melville's *Confidence-Man*: An Uncharitable Interpretation." *American Literature* 59 (December 1987): 548–69.

Bercovich, Sacvan. "Melville's Search for National Identity: Son and Father in *Redburn, Pierre* and *Billy Budd.*" *College Language Association Journal* 10 (March 1967): 217–28.

Berthoff, Warner. *The Example of Melville*. Princeton: Princeton UP, 1962.

Bezanson, Walter. "Historical Note." *Israel Potter: His Fifty Years of Exile*. Ed. Harrison Hayford, Hershel Parker, and G. Thomas Tanselle. Evanston, IL: Northwestern UP/Newberry Library, 1982. 173–235.

Bjornson, Richard. *The Picaresque Hero in European Fiction*. Madison: U of Wisconsin P, 1977.

Blackburn, Alexander. *The Myth of the Picaro: Continuity and Transformation of the Picaresque Novel, 1554–1954*. Chapel Hill: U of North Carolina P, 1979.

Blackmur, R. P. "The Craft of Herman Melville: A Putative Statement." *The Lion and the Honeycomb: Essays in Solicitude and Criticism*. New York: Harcourt, 1955. 124–44.

Blair, John G. "Herman Melville and God as Confidence Man." *The Confidence Man in Modern Fiction: A Rogue's Gallery with Six Portraits*. New York: Barnes and Noble, 1979. 33–52.

Blotner, Joseph L. *The Political Novel*. Garden City, NY: Doubleday, 1955.

Booth, Wayne C. *The Rhetoric of Fiction*. Chicago: U of Chicago P, 1961.

Bowen, Merlin. *The Long Encounter: Self and Experience in the Writings of Herman Melville*. Chicago: U of Chicago P, 1960.

——. "Tactics of Indirection in Melville's *The Confidence-Man.*" *Studies in the Novel* 1 (Winter 1969): 401–20.

Branch, Watson. "The Etiology of *Mardi.*" *Philological Quarterly* 64 (Summer 1985): 317–36.

Braswell, William. "The Early Love Scenes in Melville's *Pierre.*" *American Literature* 22 (November 1950): 283–89.

——. "Melville's *Billy Budd* as 'An Inside Narrative.'" *American Literature* 29 (May 1957): 133–46.

——. "The Satirical Temper of Melville's *Pierre.*" *American Literature* 7 (January 1936): 424–38.

Brodhead, Richard H. *Hawthorne, Melville, and the Novel*. Chicago: U of Chicago P, 1973.

——. "*Mardi:* Creating the Creative." *New Perspectives on Melville*. Ed. Faith Pullin. Kent, OH: Kent State UP, 1978. 29–53.

Brodtkorb, Paul, Jr. "The Definitive *Billy Budd:* 'But aren't it it all sham?'" *PMLA* 82 (December 1967): 602–12.

Browne, Ray B. "*Billy Budd:* Gospel of Democracy." *Nineteenth-Century Fiction* 17 (March 1963): 321–37.

——. *Melville's Drive to Humanism*. Lafayette, IN: Purdue University Studies, 1971.

Bryant, John. "*The Confidence-Man:* Melville's Problem Novel." *A Companion to Melville Studies*. Ed. John Bryant. Westport, CT: Greenwood Press, 1986. 315–50.

Buckley, Jerome Hamilton. *Season of Youth: The Bildungsroman from Dickens to Golding*. Cambridge: Harvard UP, 1974.

Buell, Lawrence. "The Last Word on 'The Confidence-Man'?" *Illinois Quarterly* 35 (November 1972): 15–29.

————. "*Moby-Dick* as Sacred Text." *New Essays on Moby-Dick*. Ed. Richard H. Brodhead. Cambridge: Cambridge UP, 1986. 53–72.

Butler, Christopher. "Scepticism and Experimental Fiction." *Essays in Criticism* 36 (January 1986): 47–67.

Cain, Thomas H. "Spenser and the Renaissance Orpheus." *University of Toronto Quarterly* 41 (Autumn 1971): 24–47.

Campbell, Joseph. *The Flight of the Wild Gander*. 1951. South Bend, IN: Regney/Gateway, 1979.

————. *The Hero with a Thousand Faces*. 1949. Princeton: Princeton UP, 1968.

Canaday, Nicholas. "Pierre in the Domestic Circle." *Studies in the Novel* 18 (Winter 1986): 395–402.

Caserio, Robert L. "The Novel as a Novel Experiment in Statement: The Anticanonical Example of H. G. Wells." *Decolonizing Tradition: New Views of Twentieth-Century "British" Literary Canons*. Ed. Karen R. Lawrence. Urbana: U of Illinois P, 1992. 88–109.

Cather, Willa. *The Song of the Lark*. 1915. Lincoln: U of Nebraska P, 1978.

Cawelti, John G. "Some Notes on the Structure of *The Confidence-Man*." *American Literature* 29 (November 1957): 278–88.

Charvat, William. *The Profession of Authorship in America, 1800–1870*. Ed. Matthew J. Bruccoli. Columbus: Ohio State UP, 1968.

Chase, Richard. *Herman Melville: A Critical Study*. New York: Macmillan, 1949.

Cohen, Hennig. "*Israel Potter*: Common Man as Hero." *A Companion to Melville Studies*. Ed. John Bryant. Westport, CT: Greenwood Press, 1986. 279–313.

Cook, Albert. *The Classic Line: A Study of Epic Poetry*. Bloomington: Indiana UP, 1966.

Culler, Jonathan. *The Pursuit of Signs: Semiotics, Literature, Deconstruction*. Ithaca: Cornell UP, 1981.

————. *Structuralist Poetics*. Ithaca: Cornell UP, 1975.

Davis, Merrell R. *Melville's Mardi: A Chartless Voyage*. New Haven: Yale UP, 1952.

Davis, Merrell R., and William H. Gilman, eds. *The Letters of Herman Melville*. New Haven: Yale UP, 1960.

Davis, R. Even. "An Allegory of America in Melville's *Billy Budd*." *The Journal of Narrative Technique* 14 (Fall 1984): 172–81.

de Paul, Stephen. "The Documentary Fiction of Melville's *Omoo*: The Crossed Grammars of Acculturation." *Criticism* 28 (Winter 1986): 51–72.

————. "Melville's *White-Jacket*: Sovereignty in the American Polity of Displacement." *Canadian Review of American Studies* 17 (Fall 1986): 267–83.

de Rougement, Denis. *Love in the Western World*. Trans. Montgomery Belgion. 1940. New York: Harper, 1956.

Decker, George, ed. *Documents of Modern Literary Realism*. Princeton: Princeton UP, 1963.

Dillingham, William B. *An Artist in the Rigging: The Early Work of Herman Melville*. Athens: U of Georgia P, 1972.

————. *Melville's Later Novels*. Athens: U of Georgia P, 1986.

————. "Melville's Long Ghost and Smollett's Count Fathom." *American Literature* 42 (May 1970): 232–35.

Dimock, Wai-chee S. "*Pierre*: Domestic Confidence Game and the Drama of Knowledge." *Studies in the Novel* 16 (Winter 1984): 396–409.

———. "*White-Jacket:* Authors and Audiences." *Nineteenth-Century Fiction* 36 (December 1981): 296–317.

Dow, Janet. "Ahab: The Fisher King." *Connecticut Review* 2 (April 1969): 42–49.

Drew, Philip. "Appearance and Reality in Melville's *The Confidence-Man*." *ELH* 31 (December 1964): 418–42.

Dryden, Edgar A. *Melville's Thematics of Form: The Great Art of Telling the Truth.* Baltimore: Johns Hopkins UP, 1968.

Duban, James. *Melville's Major Fiction: Politics, Theology, and Imagination.* Dekalb: Northern Illinois UP, 1983.

Dubler, Walter. "Theme and Structure in Melville's *The Confidence Man*." *American Literature* 33 (November 1961): 307–319.

Dubrow, Heather. *Genre.* New York: Methuen, 1982.

Eddy, William A. *Gulliver's Travels: A Critical Study.* Princeton: Princeton UP, 1923.

Eigner, Edwin M. "The Romantic Unity of Melville's *Omoo*." *Philological Quarterly* 46 (January 1967): 95–108.

Eliade, Mircea. "Initiation and the Modern World." *The Quest: History and Meaning in Religion.* Chicago: U of Chicago P, 1969. 112–26.

———. *The Sacred and the Profane: The Nature of Religion.* Trans. Willard R. Trask. New York: Harcourt, 1959.

Eliot, T. S. *The Complete Poems and Plays, 1909–1950.* New York: Harcourt, 1952.

———. *The Waste Land.* 1922. In *T. S. Eliot: Selected Poems.* New York: Harcourt, 1964.

Emerson, Ralph Waldo. "Nature." *Selections from Ralph Waldo Emerson.* Ed. Stephen E. Whicher. Boston: Houghton Mifflin, 1957. 21–56.

Emmers, Amy Puett. "Melville's Closet Skeleton: A New Letter about the Illegitimacy Incident in *Pierre*." *Studies in the American Renaissance* 1 (1977): 339–43.

Erikson, Erik H. *Childhood and Society.* 1950. New York: Norton, 1963.

———. *Identity: Youth and Crisis.* New York: Norton, 1968.

Federman, Raymond. "Surfiction—Four Propositions in Form of an Introduction." *Surfiction: Fiction Now . . . and Tomorrow.* Ed. Raymond Federman. 1975. Chicago: Swallow Press, 1981. 5–15.

Fletcher, John, and John Calder, eds. "Introduction." *The Nouveau Roman Reader.* New York: Riverrun, 1986. 7–37.

Fogle, Richard Harter. "*Billy Budd:* The Order of the Fall." *Nineteenth-Century Fiction* 15 (December 1960): 189–205.

Foley, John Miles. *Traditional Oral Epic: The Odyssey, Beowulf, and the Serbo-Croatian Return Song.* Berkeley: U of California P, 1990.

Foster, Elizabeth S. "Introduction." *The Confidence-Man.* New York: Hendricks House, 1954. xiii–xcv.

Fowler, Alistair. *Kinds of Literature: An Introduction to the Theory of Genres and Modes.* Cambridge: Harvard UP, 1982.

Fox, Arnold B. "Aesthetics of the Problem Novel in Trollope's *Phineas Finn*." *The Journal of Narrative Technique* 8 (Fall 1978): 211–19.

Franklin, H. Bruce. "Redburn's Wicked End." *Nineteenth-Century Fiction* 20 (September 1965): 190–94.

———. *The Wake of the Gods: Melville's Mythology.* Stanford: Stanford UP, 1963.

Freud, Sigmund. *Three Essays on the Theory of Sexuality.* Trans. James Strachey. New York: Basic Books, 1962.

————. *Totem and Taboo.* Trans. A. A. Brill. 1913. New York: Vintage, 1946.

Frye, Northrop. *The Secular Scripture: A Study in the Structure of Romance.* Cambridge: Harvard UP, 1976.

————. *Stubborn Structure: Essays on Criticism and Society.* London: Methuen, 1970.

Fussell, Edwin. *Frontier: American Literature and the American West.* Princeton: Princeton UP, 1965.

Gaudino, Rebecca J. Kruger. "The Riddle of *The Confidence-Man.*" *Journal of Narrative Technique* 14 (Spring 1984): 124–41.

Gilman, William H. *Melville's Early Life and "Redburn."* New York: New York UP, 1951.

Giltrow, Janet. "Speaking Out: Travel and Structure in Herman Melville's Early Narratives." *American Literature* 52 (March 1980): 18–32.

Glick, Wendell. "Expediency and Absolute Morality in *Billy Budd.*" *PMLA* 68 (March 1953): 103–10.

Glicksberg, Charles I. "Experimental Fiction: Innovation Versus Form." *The Centennial Review* 18 (Spring 1974): 127–50.

Gombrich, E. H. *Art and Illusion: A Study in the Psychology of Pictorial Representation.* New York: Pantheon, 1960.

Gove, Philip Babcock. *The Imaginary Voyage in Prose Fiction.* 1941. New York: Arno, 1974.

Greene, Thomas. *The Descent from Heaven: A Study in Epic Continuity.* New Haven: Yale UP, 1963.

Grenberg, Bruce L. "*Clarel* and *Billy Budd:* No Other Worlds but This." *Some Other World to Find: Quest and Negation in the Works of Herman Melville.* Urbana: U of Illinois P, 1989. 190–211.

————. "*Typee* and *Omoo:* Green Thoughts in a Green Shade." *Some Other World to Find.* 7–16.

Gross, John J. "The Rehearsal of Ishmael: Melville's 'Redburn.'" *Virginia Quarterly Review* 27 (Autumn 1951): 581–600.

Haberstroh, Charles, Jr. *Melville and Male Identity.* Rutherford, NJ: Fairleigh Dickinson UP, 1980.

————. "Melville, Marriage, and *Mardi.*" *Studies in the Novel* 9 (Fall 1977): 247–60.

Hardin, James, ed. *Reflection and Action: Essays on the Bildungsroman.* Columbia: U of South Carolina P, 1991.

Hart, James D. "Melville and Dana." *American Literature* 9 (March 1937): 49–55.

Hawthorne, Nathaniel. *The English Notebooks.* Ed. Randall Stewart. New York: MLA, 1941.

————. "The Custom-House." *The Scarlet Letter.* Centenary Edition. Columbus: Ohio State UP, 1962.

————. "Preface." *The House of the Seven Gables: A Romance.* Ed. Seymour L. Gross. New York: Norton, 1967.

Hayford, Harrison. "Melville and Hawthorne: A Biographical and Critical Study." Ph.D. diss. Yale University, 1945.

————. "Unnecessary Duplicates: A Key to the Writing of *Moby-Dick.*" *New Perspectives on Melville.* Ed. Faith Pullin. Kent, OH: Kent State UP, 1978. 128–61.

Hayford, Harrison, and Walter Blair, eds. "Editors' Introduction." *Omoo: A Narrative of Adventures in the South Seas.* New York: Hendricks House, 1969. xvii–lii.

Heflin, Wilson. "*Redburn* and *White-Jacket.*" *A Companion to Melville Studies.* Ed. John Bryant. Westport, CT: Greenwood Press, 1986. 145–67.

Hernadi, Paul. *Beyond Genre*. Ithaca: Cornell UP, 1972.

Higgins, Brian, and Hershel Parker, eds. *Critical Essays on Herman Melville's* Pierre: or, The Ambiguities. Boston: Hall, 1983.

————. "The Flawed Grandeur of Melville's *Pierre*." *New Perspectives on Melville*. Ed. Faith Pullin. Kent, OH: Kent State UP, 1978. 162–96.

————. "Reading *Pierre*." *A Companion to Melville Studies*. Ed. John Bryant. New York: Greenwood Press, 1986. 211–40.

Hirsch, E. D., Jr. *Validity in Interpretation*. New Haven: Yale UP, 1967.

Hoffman, Daniel G. *Form and Fable in American Fiction*. New York: Oxford UP, 1961.

Holman, C. Hugh, and William Harmon. *A Handbook to Literature*. 5th ed. New York: Macmillan, 1986.

Horsford, Howard C. "Evidence of Melville's Plans for a Sequel to *The Confidence-Man*." *American Literature* 24 (March 1952): 85–89.

Howard, Leon. *Herman Melville: A Biography*. Berkeley: U of California P, 1951.

Howe, Irving. *Politics and the Novel*. Greenwich, CT: Fawcett, 1957.

Hurtgen, James R. "Melville: Billy Budd and the Context of Political Rule." *The Artist and Political Vision*. Ed. Benjamin R. Barber and Michael J. Gargas McGrath. New Brunswick: Transaction Books, 1982. 245–65.

Hutson, Arthur E., and Patricia McCoy. "General Introduction." *Epics of the Western World*. Philadelphia: Lippincott, 1954. 7–15.

Ives, C. B. "*Billy Budd* and the Articles of War." *American Literature* 34 (March 1962): 31–39.

James, William. *The Letters of William James*. Ed. Henry James [his son]. 2 vols. Boston: Atlantic Monthly, 1920.

————. "Preface." *The Will to Believe and Other Essays in Popular Philosophy*. 1897. New York: Dover, 1956.

Jauss, Hans Robert. *Toward an Aesthetic of Reception*. Trans. Timothy Bahti. Minneapolis: U of Minnesota P, 1982.

Johnson, Barbara. "Melville's Fist: The Execution of *Billy Budd*." *Studies in Romanticism* 18 (Winter 1979): 567–99.

Johnson, Julie M. "Taji's Quest in Melville's *Mardi*: A Psychological Allegory in the Mythic Mode." *Colby Library Quarterly* 18 (December 1982): 220–30.

Johnson, Thomas H., ed. *The Letters of Emily Dickinson*. Cambridge, MA: Belknap, 1958.

Jung, Carl Gustav. "On the Psychology of the Unconscious." *Two Essays on Analytic Psychology*. Trans. R. F. C. Hull. 1953. Princeton: Princeton UP, 1966.

Justice, James H. "*Redburn* and *White-Jacket*: Society and Sexuality in the Narrators of 1849." *Herman Melville: Reassessments*. Ed. A. Robert Lee. Totowa, NJ: Barnes and Noble, 1984. 41–67.

Kaul, A. N. *The American Vision: Actual and Ideal Society in Nineteenth-Century Fiction*. New Haven: Yale UP, 1963.

Kent, Thomas. *Interpretation and Genre: The Role of Generic Perception in the Study of Narrative Texts*. Lewisburg, PA: Bucknell UP, 1986.

Ker, W. P. *Epic and Romance: Essays on Medieval Literature*. 1896. London: Macmillan, 1926.

Kermode, Frank. *The Sense of an Ending: Studies in the Theory of Fiction*. New York: Oxford UP, 1967.

Kilbourne, W. G., Jr. "Montaigne and Captain Vere." *American Literature* 33 (January

1962): 514–17.

Kolodny, Annette. "Among the Indians: The Uses of Captivity." *The New York Times Book Review* 98 (January 31, 1993). 1ff.

Kriegel, Leonard. "Introduction." *Life and Remarkable Adventures of Israel R. Potter.* New York: Corinth Books, 1962.

Kring, Walter D., and Jonathan S. Carey. "Two Discoveries Concerning Herman Melville." 1975. Rpt. in *The Endless, Winding Way in Melville: New Charts by Kring and Carey.* Ed. Donald Yannella and Hershel Parker. Glassboro, NJ: Melville Society, 1981: 11–15.

Lawrence, D. H. *Studies in Classic American Literature.* 1923. New York: Viking, 1961.

Lee, A. Robert. "Voices Off, On and Without: Ventriloquy in *The Confidence-Man.*" *Herman Melville: Reassessments.* Ed. A. Robert Lee. Totowa, NJ: Barnes and Noble, 1984. 157–75.

Leisy, Ernest E. *The American Historical Novel.* Norman: U of Oklahoma P, 1950.

Lewis, Paul. "Melville's *Pierre* and the Psychology of Incongruity." *Studies in the Novel* 15 (Fall 1983): 183–201.

Leyda, Jay. *The Melville Log: A Documentary Life of Herman Melville, 1819–1891.* 2 vols. 1951. Rpt. with a new supplement. New York: Gordian Press, 1969.

Lish, T. G. "Melville's *Redburn:* A Study in Dualism." *English Language Notes* 5 (December 1967): 113–20.

Lord, George de Forest. "The Ivory *Pequod* and the Epic of Illusion." *Trials of the Self: Heroic Ordeals in the Epic Tradition.* Hamden, CT: Archon Books, 1983. 157–91.

Lucid, Robert F. "The Influence of *Two Years Before the Mast* on Herman Melville." *American Literature* 31 (November 1959): 243–56.

McCarthy, Paul. "Affirmative Elements in *The Confidence-Man.*" *American Transcendental Quarterly* No. 7 (Summer 1970): 56–61.

———. "Opposites Meet: Melville, Hemingway, and Heroes." *Kansas Quarterly* 7 (Winter 1975): 40–54.

———. "Symbolic Elements in *White-Jacket.*" *Midwest Quarterly* 7 (July 1966): 309–25.

McCutcheon, Roger P. "The Technique of Melville's *Israel Potter.*" *South Atlantic Quarterly* 27 (April 1928): 167.

McWilliams, John P., Jr. "Innocent Criminal or Criminal Innocence: The Trial in American Fiction." *Law and American Literature.* Ed. Carl S. Smith, John P. McWilliams, Jr., and Maxwell Bloomfield. New York: Knopf, 1983. 45–124.

———. "Till a Better Epic Comes Along." *The American Epic: Transforming a Genre, 1770–1860.* Cambridge: Cambridge UP, 1989. 187–216.

Martin, Robert K. *Hero, Captain, and Stranger.* Chapel Hill: U of North Carolina P, 1986.

Marx, Leo. *The Machine in the Garden: Technology and the Pastoral Ideal in America.* New York: Oxford UP, 1964.

Mason, Ronald. *The Spirit Above the Dust: A Study of Herman Melville.* London: John Lehmann, 1951.

Matthiessen, F. O. *American Renaissance: Art and Expression in the Age of Emerson and Whitman.* New York: Oxford UP, 1941.

Melville, Herman. *Billy Budd, Sailor (An Inside Narrative).* Ed. Harrison Hayford and Merton M. Sealts, Jr. Chicago: U of Chicago P, 1962.

———. *The Collected Poems of Herman Melville*. Ed. Howard P. Vincent. Chicago: Hendricks House, 1947.

———. *The Confidence-Man: His Masquerade*. Ed. Harrison Hayford, Hershel Parker, and G. Thomas Tanselle. Evanston, IL: Northwestern UP/Newberry Library, 1984.

———. "Hawthorne and His Mosses." 1850. Rpt. in *The Piazza Tales and Other Prose Pieces, 1839–1860*. Ed. Harrison Hayford, Alma A. MacDougall, and G. Thomas Tanselle. Evanston, IL: Northwestern UP/Newberry Library, 1987.

———. *Israel Potter: His Fifty Years of Exile*. Ed. Harrison Hayford, Hershel Parker, and G. Thomas Tanselle. Evanston, IL: Northwestern UP/Newberry Library, 1982.

———. *Journals*. Ed. Howard C. Horsford, with Lynn Horth. Evanston, IL: Northwestern UP/Newberry Library, 1989.

———. *Mardi: And a Voyage Thither*. Ed. Harrison Hayford, Hershel Parker, G. Thomas Tanselle. Evanston, IL: Northwestern UP/Newberry Library, 1970.

———. *Moby-Dick: or The Whale*. Ed. Harrison Hayford, Hershel Parker, and G. Thomas Tanselle. Evanston, IL: Northwestern UP/Newberry Library, 1988.

———. *Omoo: A Narrative of Adventures in the South Seas*. Ed. Harrison Hayford, Hershel Parker, and G. Thomas Tanselle. Evanston, IL: Northwestern UP/Newberry Library, 1968.

———. *Pierre: or The Ambiguities*. Ed. Harrison Hayford, Hershel Parker, and G. Thomas Tanselle. Evanston, IL: Northwestern UP/Newberry Library, 1971.

———. *Redburn: His First Voyage*. Ed. Harrison Hayford, Hershel Parker, and G. Thomas Tanselle. Evanston, IL: Northwestern UP/Newberry Library, 1969.

———. *Typee: A Peep at Polynesian Life*. Ed. Harrison Hayford, Hershel Parker, and G. Thomas Tanselle. Evanston, IL: Northwestern UP/Newberry Library, 1969.

———. *White-Jacket: or The World in a Man-of-War*. Ed. Harrison Hayford, Hershel Parker, and G. Thomas Tanselle. Evanston, IL: Northwestern UP/Newberry Library, 1970.

Merchant, Paul. *The Epic*. London: Methuen, 1971.

Metcalf, Eleanor Melville. *Herman Melville: Cycle and Epicycle*. Cambridge: Harvard UP, 1953.

———, ed. *Journal of a Visit to London and the Continent*. Cambridge: Harvard UP, 1948.

Milder, Robert. "Melville's 'Intentions' in *Pierre*." *Studies in the Novel* 6 (Summer 1974): 186–99.

Miller, Edwin Haviland. *Melville*. New York: Persea, 1975.

Miller, James E., Jr. "*Redburn* and *White-Jacket:* Initiation and Baptism." *Nineteenth-Century Fiction* 13 (March 1959): 273–93.

Miller, Stuart. *The Picaresque Novel*. Cleveland: Case Western Reserve University, 1967.

Milne, Gordon. *The American Political Novel*. Norman: U of Oklahoma P, 1966.

Mitchell, Edward. "From Action to Essence: Some Notes on the Structure of Melville's *The Confidence-Man*." *American Literature* 40 (March 1968): 27–37.

Mizruchi, Susan. "Cataloguing the Creatures of the Deep: 'Billy Budd, Sailor' and the Rise of Sociology." *Boundary 2* 17 (Spring 1990): 272–304.

Montaigne, Michel de. Book I, Chap. 31., *Essays*. Trans. J. M. Cohen. 1958. Harmondsworth, Middlesex: Penguin, 1981. 105–19.

Monteser, Frederick. *The Picaresque Element in Western Literature*. University: U of Alabama P, 1975.

Moretti, Franco. *The Way of the World: The Bildungsroman in European Culture*. London: Verso, 1987.

Mumford, Lewis. *Herman Melville*. New York: Harcourt, 1929.

Murray, Henry A., ed. "Introduction." *Pierre: or, The Ambiguities*. New York: Hendricks House, 1949. xiii–ciii.

Murray, Henry A., Harvey Myerson, and Eugene Taylor. "Allan Melville's By-Blow." *Melville Society Extracts* 61 (February 1985): 1–6.

Namias, June. *White Captives: Gender and Ethnicity on the American Frontier*. Chapel Hill: U of North Carolina P, 1993.

Newman, John Kevin. *The Classical Epic Tradition*. Madison: U of Wisconsin P, 1986.

Nuita, Seiji. "Traditional Utopias in Japan and the West: A Study in Contrasts." *Aware of Utopia*. Ed. David W. Plath. Urbana: U of Illinois P, 1971. 11–32.

Obuchowski, Peter A. "Technique and Meaning in Melville's *Israel Potter*." *College Language Association Journal* 31 (June 1988): 455–71.

Parker, Alexander A. *Literature and the Delinquent: The Picaresque Novel in Spain and Europe, 1599–1753*. Edinburgh: Edinburgh UP, 1957.

Parker, Hershel, ed. "Foreword." *The Confidence-Man: His Masquerade*. New York: Norton, 1971.

———. "Melville's Satire of Emerson and Thoreau: An Evaluation of the Evidence." *American Transcendental Quarterly* No. 7 (Summer 1970): 61–67.

———. "The Metaphysics of Indian-Hating." *Nineteenth-Century Fiction* 18 (September 1963): 165–73.

Pearce, Roy Harvey. "Melville's Indian-Hater: A Note on a Meaning of *The Confidence-Man*." *PMLA* 67 (December 1952): 942–48.

Plath, David W., ed. "Introduction." *Aware of Utopia*. Urbana: U of Illinois P, 1971. 3–11.

Pommer, Henry F. *Milton and Melville*. Pittsburgh: U of Pittsburgh P, 1950.

Porte, Joel. *Romance in America: Studies in Cooper, Poe, Hawthorne, Melville, and James*. Middletown, CT: Wesleyan UP, 1969.

Pry, Elmer R. "*Redburn* and the 'Confession.'" *American Transcendental Quarterly* No. 43 (1979): 181–88.

Rabkin, Eric S. *The Fantastic in Literature*. Princeton: Princeton UP, 1976.

Ramsey, William M. "The Moot Points of Melville's Indian-Hating." *American Literature* 52 (May 1980): 224–35.

Reid, B. L. "Old Melville's Fable." *Massachusetts Review* 9 (Summer 1968): 529–46.

Reno, Janet. *Ishmael Alone Survived*. Lewisburg, PA: Bucknell UP, 1990.

Reynolds, David S. *Beneath the American Renaissance: The Subversive Imagination in the Age of Emerson and Melville*. New York: Knopf, 1988.

Reynolds, Larry J. "Antidemocratic Emphasis in *White-Jacket*." *American Literature* 48 (March 1976): 13–28.

Robbe-Grillet, Alain. *For a New Novel: Essays on Fiction*. Trans. Richard Howard. New York: Grove, 1965.

Rogin, Michael Paul. *Subversive Genealogy: The Politics and Art of Herman Melville*. New York: Knopf, 1983.

Roper, Gordon. "Historical Note." *Omoo: A Narrative of Adventures in the South Seas*. Ed. Harrison Hayford, Hershel Parker, and G. Thomas Tanselle. Evanston, IL: Northwestern UP/Newberry Library, 1968. 319–44.

Roripaugh, Robert. "Melville's *Typee* and Frontier Travel Literature of the 1830s and 1840s." *South Dakota Review* 19 (Winter 1982): 46–64.

Rorty, Richard. *Contingency, Irony, and Solidarity.* New York: Cambridge UP, 1983.

Rosenberg, Brian. "*Israel Potter:* Melville's Anti-History." *Studies in American Fiction* 15 (Autumn 1987): 175–86.

Rosenberry, Edward H. *Melville.* Boston: Routledge and Kegan Paul, 1979.

————. *Melville and the Comic Spirit.* Cambridge: Harvard UP, 1955.

————. "The Problem of *Billy Budd.*" *PMLA* 80 (December 1965): 489–98.

Rosenthal, Bernard. "Elegy for Jack Chase." *Studies in Romanticism* 10 (Summer 1971): 213–29.

Rosmarin, Adena. *The Power of Genre.* Minneapolis: U of Minnesota P, 1985.

Ryf, Robert S. "Character and Imagination in the Experimental Novel." *Modern Fiction Studies* 20 (Autumn 1974): 317–27.

Salerno, Henry F. "The Problem Play: Some Aesthetic Considerations." *English Literature in Transition (1880–1920)* 11 (1968): 195–205.

Samson, John. "Profaning the Sacred: Melville's *Omoo* and Missionary Narratives." *American Literature* 56 (December 1984): 496–509.

Scheler, Max. *Ressentiment.* Ed. Lewis A. Coser. 1912. New York: Schocken Books, 1972.

Schiffman, Joseph. "Melville's Final State, Irony: A Re-examination of *Billy Budd* Criticism." *American Literature* 22 (May 1950): 128–36.

Scholes, Robert. "An Approach through Genre." *Towards a Poetics of Fiction.* Ed. Mark Spilka. Bloomington: Indiana UP, 1977.

Schroeter, James. "*Redburn* and the Failure of Mythic Criticism." *American Literature* 39 (November 1967): 279–97.

Sealts, Merton M., Jr. "Innocence and Infamy: *Billy Budd, Sailor.*" *A Companion to Melville Studies.* Ed. John Bryant. Westport, CT: Greenwood Press, 1986. 407–30.

————. *Melville's Reading.* 1966. Columbia: U of South Carolina P, 1988.

Sedgwick, William Ellery. *Herman Melville: The Tragedy of Mind.* Cambridge: Harvard UP, 1944.

Seelye, John D. *Melville: The Ironic Diagram.* Evanston, IL: Northwestern UP, 1970.

Seltzer, Leon F. "Camus's Absurd and the World of Melville's *Confidence-Man.*" *PMLA* 82 (March 1967): 14–27.

Shepherd, Gerard W. "Pierre's Psyche and Melville's Art." *ESQ* 30.2 (1984): 83–98.

Short, Bryan C. "'The Author at the Time': Tommo and Melville's Self-Discovery in *Typee.*" *Texas Studies in Literature and Language* 31 (Fall 1989): 386–405.

Shroeder, John W. "Sources and Symbols for Melville's *Confidence-Man.*" *PMLA* 66 (June 1951): 363–80.

Simon, Elliott M. *The Problem Play in British Drama, 1890–1914.* Salzburg: University of Salzburg, 1978.

Slotkin, Richard. "*Moby-Dick:* The American National Epic." *Regeneration through Violence: The Mythology of the American Frontier, 1600–1860.* Middletown, CT: Wesleyan UP, 1973. 538–50.

Smollett, Tobias. *The Adventures of Roderick Random.* Ed. Paul-Gabriel Bouce. 1748. New York: Oxford UP, 1979.

Speare, Morris Edmund. *The Political Novel: Its Development in England and in America.* 1924. New York: Russell and Russell, 1966.

Stendhal [Marie-Henri Beyle]. *La Chartreuse de Parme.* Ed. Ernest Abravanel. Levallois-Perret: Cercle du Bibliophile, 1969.

Stern, Milton R. *The Fine-Hammered Steel of Herman Melville.* Urbana: U of Illinois P, 1957.

Stevens, Wallace. "Adagia." *Opus Posthumous.* 1957. New York: Vintage, 1982. 157–80.

Strelka, Joseph P., ed. *Theories of Literary Genre.* University Park: Penn State UP, 1978.

Thomas, Brook. *Cross-Examinations of Law and Literature: Cooper, Hawthorne, Stowe, and Melville.* Cambridge: Cambridge UP, 1987.

Tieje, Ralph E. "The Prose Voyage Imaginaire before 1800." Ph.D. diss. University of Illinois, 1917.

Tillyard, E. M. W. *The Epic Strain in the English Novel.* London: Chatto and Windus, 1958.

Todorov, Tzvetan. *Genres in Discourse.* New York: Cambridge UP, 1990.

———. *The Poetics of Prose.* Trans. Richard Howard. Oxford: Basil Blackwell, 1977.

Twain, Mark. *The Mysterious Stranger.* Ed. William M. Gibson. Berkeley: U of California P, 1970.

Vincent, Howard P. *The Tailoring of Melville's White-Jacket.* Evanston, IL: Northwestern UP, 1970.

———. "'White-Jacket': An Essay in Interpretation." *New England Quarterly* 22 (September 1949): 304–15.

Wald, Priscilla. "Hearing Narrative Voices in Melville's *Pierre.*" *Boundary 2* 17 (Spring 1990): 100–132.

Watson, E. L. Grant. "Melville's Testament of Acceptance." *New England Quarterly* 6 (June 1933): 319–27.

Weiner, Susan. "Law, Literature, and the Space Between: The Case of *Billy Budd.*" *Law and Art: Melville's Major Fiction and Nineteenth-Century American Law.* New York: Peter Lang, 1992. 139–66.

Wenke, John. "Melville's *Mardi:* Narrative Self-Fashioning and the Play of Possibility." *Texas Studies in Literature and Language* 31 (Fall 1989): 406–25.

———. "Melville's *Typee:* A Tale of Two Worlds." *Critical Essays on Herman Melville's Typee.* Ed. Milton R. Stern. Boston: Hall, 1982. 250–58.

Weston, Jessie L. *From Ritual to Romance.* 1920. New York: Peter Smith, 1941.

Whitman, Walt. *Leaves of Grass.* Ed. Sculley Bradley and Harold W. Blodgett. New York: Norton, 1973.

Willett, Ralph W. "Nelson and Vere: Hero and Victim in *Billy Budd, Sailor.*" *PMLA* 82 (October 1967): 370–76.

Winnifrith, Tom. "Postscript." *Aspects of the Epic.* Ed. Tom Winnifrith, Penelope Murray, and K. W. Grandsden. London: Macmillan, 1983. 109–18.

Winters, Yvor. "Herman Melville and the Problems of Moral Navigation." *Maule's Curse.* 1938. Rpt. in *In Defense of Reason.* New York: Swallow Press, 1947. 200–233.

Witherington, Paul. "The Art of Melville's *Typee.*" *Arizona Quarterly* 26 (Summer 1970): 136–50.

Zirker, Priscilla Allen. "Evidence of the Slavery Dilemma in *White-Jacket.*" *American Quarterly* 18 (Fall 1966): 477–92.

~

Index

The Weaver-God, He Weaves

∽

was composed in 10/13 Minion
on a Gateway 2000 PC using PageMaker for Windows
at The Kent State University Press;
printed by sheet-fed offset
on 50-pound Glatfelter Supple Opaque Natural stock
(an acid-free recycled paper),
notch case bound over binder's boards
in Kingston natural cloth,
and wrapped with dust jackets printed in three colors
on 100-pound enamel stock finished with film lamination
by Thomson-Shore, Inc.;
designed by Will Underwood;
and published by

∽

The Kent State University Press
Kent, Ohio 44242